0

6294

D0721059

The Paradise of Women

The Paradise of Women
Writings by Englishwomen of the Renaissance

edited by BETTY TRAVITSKY

Columbia University Press • New York

Columbia University Press Morningside Edition 1989

Columbia University Press   New York   Oxford
The Paradise of Women: Writings by Englishwomen of the Renaissance
Betty Travitsky, editor.
Originally published in 1981 as Contributions in Women's Studies, Number 22
by Greenwood Press, Inc., Westport, Conn.
Copyright © 1981 by Betty Travitsky.
Preface to the Morningside Edition copyright © 1989
Columbia University Press

Library of Congress Cataloging-in-Publication Data
The Paradise of women

Bibliography: p. Includes index.
1. English literature—Women authors.
2. English literature—Early modern, 1500–1700.
I. Travitsky, Betty.
PR1110.W6P3 1989 820.9′9287 89-1006
ISBN 0-231-06885-9

In memory of
A. E.

England in generall is said to be the
Hell of Horses, the Purgatory of Servants
and the Paradice of Weomen.

Fynes Moryson, *Itinerary* (1617)

CONTENTS

Part II. Writings by Exceptional Figures

ABBREVIATIONS

Ambiguous   Carole Levin and Jeanie Watson, eds. *Ambiguous Realities: Women in the Middle Ages and the Renaissance.* Detroit: Wayne State University Press, 1987.

Ascham   Roger Ascham. *The Scholemaster* . . . . London: John Daye, 1570.

Bainton   Roland H. Bainton. *Women of the Reformation in France and England.* Minneapolis: Augsburg Publishing House, 1973.

Ballard   George Ballard. *Memoirs of Several Ladies of Great Britain* . . . . Oxford, 1752. Rpt., Detroit, 1985.

Batty   Bartholomaeus Batty. *The Christian mans closet* . . . . London: T. Dawson and G. Seton, 1581.

Becon NC   Becon, Thomas. *A newe catechisme, sette forth dialoge wise* . . . . In *Worckes of Thomas Becon* . . . . London: John Daye, 1564.

Beilin CB   Elaine V. Beilin. "Current Bibliography of English Women Writers, 1500-1640." In *REP.*

Beilin RE   —— *Redeeming Eve Women Writers of the English Renaissance.* Princeton: Princeton University Press, 1987.

Bentley   Thomas Bentley, ed. *Monument of Matrones* . . . .

Bradner   Leicester Bradner, ed. *Poems of Queen Elizabeth I.* Providence: Brown University Press, 1964.

Burckhardt   Jacob Burckhardt. *The Civilization of the Renaissance in Italy, An Essay.* S. G. C. Middlemore, trans. (1860). Irene Gordon, trans., rev. and ed. New York: Mentor Books, 1960.

Cahn   Susan Cahn. *Industry of Devotion: The Transformation of Women's Work in England, 1500-1660.* New York: Columbia University Press, 1987.

Clark   Alice Clark. *The Working Life of Women in the Seventeenth Century.* London, 1919; Rpt., 1968.

Cope   Esther Cope. "Dame Eleanor Douglas: Never So Mad a
                  Ladie?" *HLQ* 50 (1987): 133-44.
Crawford   Patricia Crawford. "Women's Published Writings, 1600-
                  1700." In *Prior,* pp. 211-82.
Cressy   David Cressy. *Literacy and the Social Order: Reading and
                  Writing in Tudor and Stuart England.* Cambridge: Cam-
                  bridge University Press, 1980.
Davies   Kathleen M. Davies. "Continuity and Change in Literary
                  Advice on Marriage." In *Marriage and Society: Studies in
                  the History of Marriage.* R. B. Outhwaite, ed. New York:
                  St. Martin's Press, 1981, pp. 58-80.
Davis   Natalie Zemon Davis. "City Women and Religious Change."
                  In *Society and Culture in Early Modern France.* Stanford:
                  Stanford University Press, 1975, pp. 65-95.
DNB   *Dictionary of National Biography.* Sir Leslie Stephen and
                  Sir Sidney Lee, eds. Oxford University Press, since 1917.
Dusinberre   Juliet Dusinberre. *Shakespeare and the Nature of Women.*
                  New York: Harper and Row, 1975.
Elyot   Sir Thomas Elyot. *The Defence of Good Women.* London,
                  1540.
Erasmus CE   Desiderius Erasmus. *Colloquies of Erasmus.* Craig Thomp-
                  son, trans. Chicago: University of Chicago Press, 1965.
Foxe   John Foxe. *Actes and monuments . . . .*
Gairdner   James H. Gairdner, ed. *Paston Letters, 1422-1509.* 6 vols.
                  London: Chatto & Windus, 1904. Rpt., N. Y.: AMS Press,
                  1965.
Gardiner   Dorothy Gardiner. *English Girlhood at School: A History of
                  Women's Education Through Twelve Centuries.* London:
                  Oxford University Press, 1929.
Gouge   William Gouge, *Of Domesticall Duties, Eight Treatises.* Lon-
                  don: John Haviland, 1622.
H & H   Ruth Hughey and Philip Hereford. "Elizabeth Grymeston
                  and her *Miscelanea." Library.* 4th Series. 15.1 (1934-35):
                  61-91.
Hageman 16 c   Elizabeth H. Hageman. "Recent Studies in Women Writers
                  of Tudor England. Part I: Women Writers, 1485-1603 Ex-
                  cluding Mary Sidney, Countess of Pembroke." *ELR* 14.3
                  (1984): 409-25.
Hageman 17 c   Elizabeth H. Hageman. "Recent Studies in Women Writers
                  of the English Seventeenth Century (1604-1674)." *ELR* 18.1
                  (1988): 138-67.
Hallers   William and Malleville Haller. "The Puritan Art of Love."
                  HLQ 5 (1941-42): 235-72.

Hannay   Margaret P. Hannay, ed. *Silent But for the Word: Tudor Women as Patrons, Translators, and Writers of Religious Works*. Kent: Kent State University Press, 1985.

Hogrefe LR   Pearl Hogrefe. "Legal Rights of Tudor Women and the Circumvention by Men and Women." *SCJ* 3 (1972): 97-105.

Hogrefe TW   —— *Tudor Women, Commoners and Queens*. Ames: Iowa State University Press, 1975.

Hogrefe WA   —— *Women of Action in Tudor England, Nine Biographical Sketches*. Ames: Iowa State University Press, 1977.

Hughey   Ruth Willard Hughey. "Cultural Interests of Women in England, 1524-1640, Indicated in the Writings of the Women." Ph.D. dissertation, Cornell University, 1932.

Hull   Suzanne W. Hull. *Chaste Silent & Obedient: English Books for Women 1475-1640*. San Marino: Huntington Library, 1982.

Humankind   Katherine Usher Henderson and Barbara F. McManus, eds. *Half Humankind: Contexts and Texts of the Controversy about Women in England, 1540-1640*. Chicago: University of Illinois Press, 1985.

Hyrde   Richard Hyrde. "Dedicatory Letter." *A devout treatise . . . .* Margaret Roper, trans.

Jackson   Dorothy Judd Jackson. *Esther Inglis: Calligrapher 1571-1624*. New York: Privately printed at the Spiral Club, 1937.

Jones   Ann R. Jones. "Counter-attacks on 'the Bayter of Women': Three Pamphleteers of the Early Seventeenth Century." In *REP*.

Jordan FH   Constance Jordan. "Feminism and the Humanists: The Case of Sir Thomas Elyot's *Defence of Good Women*." *RQ* 36.2 (1983): 181-201.

Jordan SP   —— "More on the Siena Portrait of Queen Elizabeth I." In *REP*.

Kahin   Helen Andrews Kahin. "Jane Anger and John Lyly." *MLQ* 8 (1949): 31-35.

Kelly-Gadol   Joan Kelly-Gadol. "Did Women Have a Renaissance?" In *Visible*, pp. 137-64.

Kelso   Ruth Kelso. *Doctrine for the Lady of the Renaissance*. Urbana: University of Illinois Press, 1956.

King   John N. King. "Patronage and Piety: The Influence of Catherine Parr." In *Hannay*, 43-60.

Kohler   Charlotte Kohler. "Elizabethan Woman of Letters, the extent of her literary activities." Ph.D. dissertation, University of Virginia, 1936.

Krontiris   Tina Krontiris. "Style and Gender in Elizabeth Cary's *Edward II.*" In *REP.*

Lamb   Mary Ellen Lamb. "The Cooke Sisters: Attitudes toward Learned Women in the Renaissance." In *Hannay,* pp. 107-25.

Levin LJG   Carole Levin. "Lady Jane Grey: Protestant Queen and Martyr." In *Hannay,* pp. 92-107.

Levin QC   —— ."Queens and Claimants: Political Insecurity in Sixteenth-Century England." In *Gender Ideology and Action: Historical Perspectives on Women's Lives.* Janet Sharistanian, ed. Westport, Conn.: Greenwood Press, 1986, pp. 41-66.

Luce   Alice Luce, ed. "The Countess of Pembroke's *Antonie.*"

McConica   James K. McConica. *English Humanists and Reformation Politics under Henry VIII and Edward VI.* Oxford: Clarendon Press, 1965.

McCutcheon   Elizabeth McCutcheon. "Margaret More Roper: The Learned Woman in Tudor England." In Wilson *WWRR,* pp. 449-80.

McLaughlin   Eleanor Commo McLaughlin. "Equality of Souls, Inequality of Sexes: Woman in Medieval Theology." In *Ruether,* pp. 213-66.

Mendelson   Sara Heller Mendelson. "Stuart Women's Diaries and Occasional Memoirs." In *Prior,* pp. 181-210.

Moers   Ellen Moers. *Literary Women, the Great Writers.* New York: Doubleday, 1976.

More   Sir Thomas More. *Utopia.* Ed. J. Churton Collins. Oxford: Clarendon Press, 1963.

Mulcaster   Richard Mulcaster. *Positions . . . for the training up of children . . . .* London: Thomas Vautrollier for Thomas Clare, 1581.

Powell   Chilton Powell. *English Domestic Relations, 1485–1653.* New York: Columbia University Press, 1917.

Power MW   Eileen Power. *Medieval Women.* M. M. Postan, ed. New York: Cambridge University Press, 1975.

Prior   Mary Prior, ed. *Women in English Society, 1500-1800.* London: Methuen, 1985.

REP   *Renaissance Englishwomen in Print: Counterbalancing the Canon.* Anne M. Haselkorn and Betty S. Travitsky, eds. Amherst: University of Massachusetts Press, 1989.

Rewriting   *Rewriting the Renaissance: The Discourses of Sexual Difference in Early Modern Europe.* Margaret W. Ferguson, Maureen Quilligan, and Nancy J. Vickers, eds. Chicago: University of Chicago Press, 1986.

Reynolds   Myra Reynolds. *The Learned Lady in England 1650-1760.* Boston: Houghton Mifflin Co., 1920.

Roberts MS   Josephine A. Roberts. "Mary Sidney, Countess of Pembroke." *ELR* 14.3 (1984): 426-39.

Roberts MW   Josephine A. Roberts, ed. *The Poems of Lady Mary Wroth.* Baton Rouge: Louisiana State University Press, 1983.

Rose   Mary Beth Rose, ed. *Women in the Middle Ages and the Renaissance Literary and Historical Perspectives.* Syracuse: Syracuse University Press, 1986.

Rowse   A. L. Rowse, ed. *The Poems of Shakespeare's Dark Lady.* New York: Clarkson N. Potter, 1979.

Ruether   Rosemary Radford Ruether, ed. *Religion and Sexism: Images of Women in the Jewish and Christian Traditions.* New York: Simon and Schuster, 1974.

Shahar   Shulamith Shahar. *The Fourth Estate: A History of Women in the Middle Ages.* Chaya Galai, trans. London: Methuen, 1983.

Sharman   Julian Sharman, ed. *Poems of Mary Queen of Scots.*

Shepherd   Simon Shepherd, ed. *The Women's Sharp Revenge: Being a collection of five pamphlets from 1580 to 1640* . . . . London: Fourth Estate, 1985.

Spufford   Margaret Spufford. "First steps in literacy . . . ." *Social History* 4 (1979): 407-35.

Stenton   Doris May Stenton. *The English Woman in History.* London: George Allen and Unwin, 1957.

Stock   Phyllis Stock. *Better Than Rubies: A History of Women's Education.* New York: Capricorn Books, 1978.

Todd   Margo Todd. "Humanists, Puritans and the Spiritualized Household." *Church History* 49 (1980): 18-34.

Travitsky NM Betty S. Travitsky. "The New Mother of the English Renaissance (1489-1659): A Descriptive Catalogue." *BRH* 82.1 (1979): 63-89.

Travitsky PIW ——— "Placing Women in the English Renaissance: Some Introductory Comments." In *REP.*

Udall   Nicholas Udall. "Dedicatory Letter." In *The first tome or volume of the paraphrase of Erasmus upon the newe testamente.* London: Edward Whitechurche, last daie of January, 1548.

Visible   Renate Bridenthal and Claudia Koonz, eds. *Becoming Visible: Women in European History.* Boston: Houghton Mifflin, 1977.

Vives ICW   Juan Luis Vives. *Instruction of a Christen Woman.* 1521. Richard Hyrde, trans. London: Thomas Berthelet, 1529.

Vives OD   Juan Luis Vives. *Office and duetie of an husband*. 1529.
              Thomas Paynell, trans. London: I. Cawood, 1553.
Warnicke   Retha M. Warnicke. *Women of the English Renaissance and
              Reformation*. Westport, Conn.: Greenwood, 1983.
Watson   Foster Watson. *Vives and the Renaissance Instruction of
              Women*. London: Edward Arnold, 1912.
Wayne   Valerie Wayne. "Some Sad Sentence: Vives' *Instruction of
              a Christian Woman*." In *Hannay*, pp. 15-29.
Williams   Robert Williams. "A Moon to their Sun: Writing Mistresses
              of the Sixteenth and Seventeenth Centuries." *Fine Print*
              (1985): 88-98.
Wilson MWW   Katharina M. Wilson, ed. *Medieval Woman Writers*. Athens:
              University of Georgia Press, 1984.
Wilson WWRR   —— *Women Writers of the Renaissance and Reformation*.
              Athens: University of Georgia Press, 1987.
Woodbridge   Linda Woodbridge. *Women and the English Renaissance:
              Literature and the Nature of Womankind, 1540-1620*. Chi-
              cago: University of Illinois Press, 1984.
Wright   Louis B. Wright. *Middle-class Culture in Elizabethan En-
              gland*. Chapel Hill: University of North Carolina Press, 1935.
Writings   *Writings of Ed. VI, William Hugh, Queen Catherine Parr,
              Anne Askew, Lady Jane Grey, Hamilton and Balnaves*.
              Philadelphia: Presbyterian Board of Publication, 1862.
Wyntjes   Sherrin Marshall Wyntjes. "Women in the Reformation Era."
              In *Visible*, pp. 165-91.

PREFACE TO THE MORNINGSIDE EDITION

RENAISSANCE women's studies offers genuine excitement to all Renaissance scholars because the "doubled vision" it affords often generates new understanding both of the global picture of the Renaissance and of marginalized aspects of Renaissance life.[1] Moreover, as recent scholarship indicates, the pioneering work of the last fifteen years has by now led us "beyond women and the family [and] towards . . . gender analysis" as a legitimate category of historical analysis.[2] For the literary scholar, the examination of previously unnoticed, and sometimes misrepresented writings by Renaissance women (often written in unconventional genres) has raised important questions about the nature of literature and the empowerment of the literary canon; perhaps most excitingly, it has raised the prospect of altering the contours of the traditional Renaissance literary canon.[3]

The vernacular literary canons which evolved during the Renaissance are particularly appropriate fields for the application of gendered insights into literature. For one thing, there is the very nature of the Renaissance literary enterprise, the fact, as Rosalie Colie states, that "as far as *writers* were concerned, rules were there to take or leave" and that the literature of the period was characterized by "inclusionism: uncanonical forms, mixed kinds, and nova reperta."[4] These qualities legitimatize the serious investigation of women's writings which have in modern times been excluded from the traditional Renaissance canon by the (invisible) power of what Barbara Herrnstein Smith has termed a "complex evaluative feedback loop."[5] Unusual forms—particularly such "private forms" as diaries, memoirs, occasional journals, spiritual autobiographies, personal letters, and books of maternal advice—cannot legitimately be barred from the canon because they are untraditional.[6] In addition, the casual neglect for centuries of what *now* seem uncanonical forms of writing by women has made the recovery of Renaissance women's texts into a sometimes taxing scholarly activity requiring ingenuity and perseverance. Therefore the development and use of research methodology for this task is clearly important for work on Renaissance women's writings, and Renaissance literature can be viewed as an appropriate field for the application of such techniques.

If we take England as a test case and the contents of *Paradise of Women* as a model-at-hand, we find that many writings included in this anthology fall within the category of private forms which has become the focus of much scholarly interest in canon formation. To shift ground a bit, we find that these materials have not been studied as literature until very recently, and that texts of most of these materials are still not widely available. Since manuscript materials have often been inaccurately catalogued in the past, and since trenchant archival research into women's writings is but beginning, the very number of surviving private writings by Renaissance Englishwomen, the content of these writings, and their characteristics, both individually and as a body of writings, are largely ungaugeable at this time.

Even the known writings by women which fall within traditional literary genres were often written for private use and first published posthumously or through the efforts of others, or in the case of short pieces by famous women, sometimes anthologized by others. While it is true that we can usually discount many of the claims by male writers of the Renaissance that they did not intend to write for publication, such claims by women were undoubtedly closer to the truth. For writing by women was seen as a form of public instruction and as a public speaking out, two types of activity disapproved in women by even the most liberal of their advocates. Women were effectively muzzled by the stricture that "women keep silence in the churches: for it is not permitted unto them to speak; but *they are commanded* to be under obedience, as also saith the law. And if they will learn any thing, let them ask their husbands at home: for it is a shame for women to speak in the church" (1 Cor. 14: 34-35).

In light of this repressive atmosphere, as well as of many other factors which disadvantaged Renaissance Englishwomen vis-à-vis Renaissance Englishmen, we should not be surprised that the number of known writings by Renaissance Englishwomen is not large in absolute terms.[7] But we should, I believe, approach these writings with the awareness that they are large in number in comparison to the writings of Englishwomen of earlier times. The writings of Renaissance Englishwomen constitute a major early expression of the woman's voice in the English-speaking world. To me, this fact suggests a degree of change during the Renaissance which encouraged some women to break the written silence of earlier times. I think that it suggests that at least some Englishwomen did experience a Renaissance that fostered their creativity.[8]

I would not comfortably undertake a unilateral literary evaluation of these writings when accessible texts of even major works from the corpus are not yet widely available. But it is perhaps appropriate to summarize some of the more patent characteristics of these writers and writings. (The introductions to each section of this book, and the notes, provide some further information.)

When we attempt to classify Englishwomen writers and their works, we cannot equate them with most of the types which Katharina Wilson has identified on the continent—such as nuns, courtesans, scholars who composed original treatises, grandes dames who published secular works, and religious and political activists from among the urban poor.[9] What is most commonly true, and commonly recognized, is that Renaissance Englishwomen writers tended to be part of the more privileged classes of Renaissance society. And this fact is not surprising when we remember that the education of women, which was often advocated strongly during the English Renaissance, moved slowly down the social ladder during the period till it finally reached the less privileged groups in society.[10]

Perhaps the variously privileged status of most Renaissance Englishwomen writers, as well as their training in obedience and piety, accounts for what could be called a relative complacency in expressing the larger received wisdoms of their time. But if Renaissance Englishwomen seldom expressed a strong sense of resentment at the restrictions under which they lived and composed, even their compositions in traditional genres do—perhaps inadvertently—render many twists on the male point of view. Perhaps one of the most exciting facts about these writings is their (inevitably) different—shall we say "other"?—view of the world. Fixed within respectable familial and Christian orientations and tending not to question the orthodoxies of those orientations, they nevertheless often poignantly express the position of the marginalized. They provide us with the moving experiences of Wroth's Pamphilia, of Cary's Mariam, of Whitney's woman poet who will have to stop writing when she assumes family responsibilities. Where in the writings of Renaissance Englishmen do we find an equivalent to such awareness of female "interiority"?[11] How fortunate we will be when we integrate this segment of the human experience into the corpus we call English Renaissance literature!

Let us briefly describe the writings themselves. For one thing, as Ruth Hughey stated long ago, the safest type of writing for women, and the one, not surprisingly, most often attempted, was translation of an approved religious work.[12] In addition, religious sentiment impelled some women to compose original religious work for publication: Rachel Speght, for example, her *Mortalities Memorandum;* Elizabeth Colville, *Ane Godlie Dreame.* And religious considerations were a major impetus to the composition of a more private form of writing, the mother's advice book (see chapter 2), which often was printed posthumously. The authors of these tracts frequently coupled uneasiness over the very fact of their composition with a concern for a child's physical and spiritual well-being that moved the author to write, a juxtaposition that charms the reader today, although it probably was taken much more literally by the reader(s) for whom these tracts were intended.

The commonly unhappy fate of even private works written by women in recognized literary genres could not have been very encouraging to other aspiring women writers. Mary Stuart's love sonnet-letters to Bothwell, produced as evidence of her infatuation for that outlaw noble, were used against her as a means of character assassination. Printed works (especially secular ones) often led to trouble. Elizabeth Cary's closet drama *Mariam* was recalled because of family pressures; protests against male mistreatment of women were sometimes written under pseudonyms, and are sometimes attributed, for that reason, to male writers; Mary Wroth's *Urania* was withdrawn by Wroth because of public protests, and her sequel remains in manuscript; the prophetic writings of Eleanor Douglas, which led to more than one imprisonment of that noblewoman, were publicly banned.[13]

Few of those compositions by women writers which did reach print during the Renaissance were issued more than once. If, during the intervening centuries some Renaissance women's writings, such as the poems of Mary Stuart, or the devotional writings of Catherine Parr and Jane Grey, have been considered "curious" or "valid" enough to warrant reprinting, this has not been done on literary grounds until very recently. In the last few years, the picture has changed somewhat, and some writings by Renaissance Englishwomen are now available in reliable editions, while others are in preparation.[14] But there is still a dearth of available texts by Renaissance women writers for classroom, and even for scholarly use.

When the hardcover edition of *Paradise of Women* was published, just seven years ago, one could accurately note that Renaissance Englishwomen's writings had "been largely neglected by scholars," and could summarize a good deal of the existing scholarship on these writings in one fairly comprehensive footnote. Today, as this paperback edition demonstrates, and as its updated notes illustrate, interest in Renaissance women's studies is burgeoning. Scholarship about the writings of Renaissance Englishwomen has warranted the publication of several lengthy and extremely useful bibliographies of secondary studies,[15] as well as some excellent bibliographies of relevant primary materials (which often continue to be difficult to identify and locate).[16]

Eventually, projects like the computer data base of women's writings directed by Susanne Woods will make complete texts available to advanced students of early modern Englishwomen.[17] And, as archival work continues, manuscript materials will also be made available for scholarly investigation and evaluation. When that happens, we will be in a better position to refine our thinking about the Renaissance canon, to make considered decisions about the merits of materials which are still treated separately, and therefore unequally, and to revise our notion of canonicity to incorporate materials which widen our appreciation of the entire human experience.

I hope that the range of the selections in this volume, coupled with the scholarly apparatus provided for retrieval of further information, will continue their usefulness for Renaissance women's studies, and particularly for the study of Renaissance women's writings in the context of the period. It is my hope, too, that the Morningside edition will provide a useful basis for courses in European women's history, women's writing, and Renaissance women's studies.

For this edition, I have updated the notes substantially and have added references to recent bibliographies of secondary studies that direct the interested reader to much of the fine recent work which has appeared in this field. Since new work is appearing continually, I have not attempted total comprehensiveness in the notes, but I have acknowledged some of the more important and some of the more controversial material that has appeared since 1981. Some changes have been made in the text of the introduction to indicate current scholarly points of contention, and the notes to that section of the book have been thoroughly overhauled. In addition to this preface, a list of abbreviations for repeated references has been included in the front matter; but essentially the text of the book is the same.[18]

The compiling of any anthology involves some difficult decisions which by their nature are compromises and therefore arguable. One difficult decision I made in compiling this work was to assemble the contents so that they illuminated patterns in the behavior and thinking of the often unknown women writers of the English Renaissance. This arrangement does have a real disadvantage for students of literature, dividing particular women writers into parts, for example, but it has the advantage of fitting the authors and their writings as directly as possible into the general picture of the period. It was, and remains, my conviction that the present arrangement enhances our understanding of a period that has traditionally been known to us in a distorted manner, that is, largely through the viewpoint of male writers. It allows us to view the period more completely, with the aid of gendered analysis, and develops our sense of the thinking on given topics of Renaissance Englishwomen.

A second difficult decision had to be made about the inclusion of translated works. It is certainly true that translation was an important and creative Renaissance literary activity for men.[19] Moreover, translations bulked large among literary efforts by women. But, as Elaine Beilin states, translation "was both an opportunity and a limitation for women. While they contributed the fruits of their learning, especially in Scripture and religious doctrine, translation did not seem to be a training ground or preparation for further literary development."[20] Rather than include translated work by

Renaissance Englishwomen, therefore, I have chosen to print original writings in order to view these women writers on their own terms.

Finally, while I agree with several reviewers in wishing that I could have included longer selections in *Paradise of Women,* I originally decided for range and against concentration, and I could not change the contents of the book itself for this edition. I hope that the interest in this book, which has led to its reprinting, justifies my sense that these extracts have whetted the appetite of many readers for access to the writings of Renaissance Englishwomen.

PREFACE

AT THE beginning of his monumental study of the Italian Renaissance, Jacob Burckhardt states: "It is the most serious difficulty of the history of civilization that a great intellectual process must be broken up into single, and often into what seem arbitrary categories, in order to be in any way intelligible."[1]

In its much smaller way, *The Paradise of Women* has been subject to the paradoxical type of distortion to which Burckhardt alludes. Different aspects of Renaissance life have been described in different sections. Women who wrote on more than one area of life have been dissected and considered in portions in different sections of the anthology. The writings considered, albeit a large proportion of those which are extant, are the work of only certain groups among Renaissance Englishwomen. In the earlier part of the Renaissance they were the exclusive products of noblewomen and royalty; later in the period they also were the work of middle-class women. Since these writings exist in isolation, I have taken them as representative, but the fact is that there is little if any written material other than by women of the upper classes, virtually nothing from the large number of Renaissance Englishwomen from the lower classes. In addition, reputable women have been considered in this text for the most part, although other types certainly existed in the Renaissance, as in any other age.[2] Finally, even the consideration of women as a historical grouping is a distortion, since women did not exist apart from the larger bisexual society.

These limitations should be recognized by any critical reader, and it should be noted that the reflections in *The Paradise of Women* are not intended or offered as definitive. Rather they are meant to suggest possible implications, as well as open-ended questions, concerning the way of life and status of Renaissance Englishwomen, whose ambiguous development is, in my opinion, the root of the ambivalence of Western women today.

ACKNOWLEDGMENTS

WHILE compiling the first edition of this anthology, I incurred many debts for kindnesses that I take pleasure in acknowledging here.

Marcelle Thiebaux, chairperson of the English Department at St. John's University, first suggested that I attempt this task and offered helpful suggestions at various times. The late William Brickman of the Graduate School of Education of the University of Pennsylvania took a great deal of interest in the efforts of this junior faculty member at Touro College when he served as dean of the faculties there. His encouragement and suggestions were sustaining and helpful. Leonora Brodwin of St. John's University, William Helmreich and the late Edward Sagarin of City College (CUNY), and Anne Haselkorn of Fordham University were helpful at many times. Lea Hamaoui of the CUNY Graduate Center and the late Akiva Kaminsky, managing editor of *Centerpoint: A Journal of Interdisciplinary Studies,* took the time to read the introduction and to make useful suggestions about it. Anna Donnelly and Julia Cunningham of the Reference Department of the St. John's University Library (Jamaica) offered generous and skillful assistance. Finally, Marcy Epstein worked uncomplainingly with often unclear copy and with accumulations of annoying revisions.

In the years between the appearance of the first edition and this paperback reprint, I have benefited greatly from conversations with a great number of scholars presently engaged in the new scholarship on women, particularly the members of the Folger Colloquium on Women in the Renaissance and of the New York Society for the Study of Women in the Renaissance. Margaret Mikesell's brilliant work on Vives has sharpened my own thinking concerning Renaissance theories about women.

Patrick Cullen of the Graduate Center (CUNY) and Elizabeth H. Hageman of the University of New Hampshire have been lavish with suggestions for this paperback edition. And Jennifer Crewe and Susan Pensak of the Columbia University Press have been very patient about a series of revisions.

The following individuals and firms have been kind enough to grant me permission to print selections from the following works:

Bulletin of Research in the Humanities, for the essay, "The New Mother of the English Renaissance (1489-1659): A Descriptive Catalogue," vol. 82, no. 1., 1979. Used by permission of the *Bulletin.*

The Diary of the Lady Anne Clifford, ed. V. Sackville-West, William Heinnemann, Ltd., London, 1923, for pages 26-27, 28-29, 32, 51, 62, 64, 65, 66. Reprinted by permission of the publisher.

The Diary of Lady Hoby, ed. Dorothy M. Meads, Routledge, Kegan Paul Ltd., Publishers, London, 1930, for pages 62, 63, 68, 161, 195, 206, 207. Reprinted by permission of the publisher.

English Literary Renaissance, for the essay, "The Wyll and Testament of Isabella Whitney (fl. 1567-1573)," vol. 10, no. 1, Winter, 1980. Used with permission.

The History of the Most Unfortunate Prince, King Edward The Second . . . , Elizabeth Cary, from *Harleian Miscellany,* John Murray (Publishers) Ltd., London, 1808. Reprinted by permission of the publisher.

The Letters and Poems of Mary, Queen of Scots, Supposed Author, ed. Clifford Bax, Philosophical Library, New York, 1947, for Sonnets I to XII, pages 48-58. Reprinted by permission of the publisher.

The Lost Tradition: Mothers and Daughters in Literature, ed. Cathy N. Davidson and E. M. Broner, © 1980 by Frederick Ungar Publishing Co., New York, for the author's article, "Writings on Motherhood." Used by permission of the publisher.

Octonaries upon the Vanitie and Inconstancie of the World . . . [Edinburgh, January 1, 1609], Ester Inglis Kello, for the "Dedicatory Epistle" and "Octonaries III, XV, XXI." Reprinted by permission of the Spencer Collection, The New York Public Library, Astor, Lenox and Tilden Foundations.

The Poems of Mary Queen of Scots to the Earl of Bothwell, Joh. Enschede en Zonen, Haarlem, the Netherlands, 1932.

The Poems of Queen Elizabeth I, ed. Leicester Bradner, Brown University Press, Providence, R.I., 1964 for "Written on a Wall at Woodstock," "The Doubt of Future Foes," "On Monsieur's Departure," and "When I Was Fair and Young and Favour Graced Me." © 1964 Brown University. Reprinted by permission of the publisher.

Quarterly Review No. 215, for "An Elizabethan Gentlewoman," Rachel Wiegall, John Murray (Publishers) Ltd., London. Reprinted by permission of the publisher.

Queen Mary's Book, A Collection of Poems and Essays by Mary Queen of Scots, ed. Mrs. P. Stewart-Mackenzie-Arbuthnot, George Bell & Sons, London, 1907, for "Verses on the Death of Francis II" (1560), "Sonnet to Elizabeth" (1568), "Meditation in Verse" (1573), "Poem on Sacrifice" (1573), "Essay on Adversity" (1580), "Poem on Resignation" (1583), "Poem on Life (1586?), "Poem Composed on the Morning of Her Execution" (1587). Reprinted by permission of the publisher.

Saint Thomas More: Selected Letters, ed. Elizabeth F. Rogers, Yale University Press, New Haven, Connecticut, 1961, for Letters 20 and 35, pages 103-4, 105, 155. Reprinted by permission of the publisher.

The Works of William Fowler, ed. Henry W. Meikle, Council of the Scottish Text Society, for the first sonnet on page 19, vol. 1, second series, no. 6. Reprinted by permission of the Council.

The Paradise of Women

INTRODUCTION

DURING the English Renaissance, from approximately 1500 to 1640, Englishwomen composed or translated well over one hundred works. As noted above, in the preface to the Morningside edition, these writings have been largely neglected by scholars until recently.[1] In large measure, the women authors of these works were stimulated to write by the thinking and writings concerning women of Renaissance humanists and reformers. This introductory essay will review some major writings by these theorists and relate them to the writings of Renaissance Englishwomen.

Before beginning this review, it may be useful to trace briefly the place and role of women in the West through the Renaissance, as perceived by twentieth-century scholars.

In the civilizations of the ancient Greeks, Jews, and Romans, the subordinated position of the respectable woman ranged from one of almost complete seclusion, as among the Athenians of the fifth century B.C., to one conferring prestige on certain female roles within the family, as among the Jews of the Old Testament, to one of growing independence, as among the Romans of the late Republic.[2] Therefore, the development of the concept of spiritual equivalency between man and woman in the theology of Paul and the preeminence of many pious women in the early Christian era held the promise of a new status for women. The social changes which Paul's writings recognized, however, were undermined by reactions in the developing churches and in society at large.[3] During the centuries following Paul's apostolate, women lost their earlier prominence as they came to be identified more and more with the body and with temptation, in opposition to man, who was identified with spirituality and seen to be threatened in his spiritual quest by women.[4]

The position of women varied considerably during the often turbulent Middle Ages.[5] The church gave precedence to the state of celibacy over the state of matrimony, thus enhancing the position of those women who adopted the celibate life and doffed their femininity. These women found varying scope for self-development and activity ranging from an important role in the establishment of Christianity in the former Western provinces and rule by some abbesses over extensive areas, to cloistered activity under the control of male bishops. Within the family, the position of the wife was enhanced by the church insistence on monogamous marriage and the indissolubility of marriage and by its disapproval of extramarital sex. At times when family ties were important elements in the political structure, and after women had won the right to inherit property, some women played powerful political roles, as in tenth-century Italy. Aristocratic women were celebrated in the twelfth century in the literature of courtly love, which they were instrumental in fostering, although the legal position of women was not affected by this literature.[6]

However, distrust for women remained an undercurrent of medieval thought. The Gregorian revolution and the centralization of secular society in the eleventh and twelfth centuries led to a diminishment of such influence and power as had accrued to medieval women. At the close of the Middle Ages, European women were consigned to a legal status subordinate to that of men and also were widely considered to be inferior by their very nature to men.[7]

The undercurrent of distrust for women during the Middle Ages found expression in a widespread medieval genre of works of advice to women that advocated such virtues as humility, submissiveness, obedience, and chastity. The attitude of medieval thinkers is well represented by Phillipe de Navarre (d. 1270), who stated that,

> Women have a great advantage in one thing; they can easily preserve their honour, if they wish to be held virtuous, by one thing only. But for a man, many are needful, if he wish to be esteemed virtuous, brave and wise. And for a woman, if she be a worthy woman of her body, all her other faults are covered, and she can go with a high head, wheresoever she will; and therefore it is no way needful to teach as many things to girls as to boys.[8]

If we confine ourselves to England, we find that only seven works of formal instruction for women were written in English or by English writers in the whole of the Middle Ages.[9] Therefore, it is not surprising that most medieval laywomen demonstrated little consciousness of or confidence in their own intellectual abilities, if the infrequency with which they attempted to express themselves in print is taken as a basis for this assessment.[10] Only three works, for example, are believed to have been written by English-women before 1500.[11]

Although ideas like de Navarre's did not pass wholly out of currency with the waning of the middle ages,[12] the great increase in the writing activities of Englishwomen that took place during the Renaissance suggests the development of a new type of Renaissance Englishwoman. This development is corroborated by William Wotton's remark that, "[T]here are no Accounts in History of so many very great Women in any one Age, as are to be found between the years 15[00] and 1600." [13] The change is not related to legal advances, for the legal position of Englishwomen was not improved appreciably during the Renaissance. [14] But Renaissance theories did recognize the religious and intellectual potential of women and accorded them significant opportunities for personal growth. [15]

The English Renaissance began at a time when religious questions were occupying the minds of English intellectuals. The chronological joining of England's Renaissance and Reformation gave a sober, otherworldly cast to the erudite, self-aware new women created by these upheavals. In 1548, when he described the new type of Englishwomen, Nicholas Udall could write that,

It was now a common thing to see young virgins so trained in the study of good letters, that they willingly set all other vain pastimes at naught, for learning sake. It was now no news at all, to see Queens and ladies of most high estate and progeny, instead of courtly dalliance, to embrace virtuous exercises of reading and writing, and with most earnest study both early and late, to apply themselves to the acquiring of knowledge, . . . most especially of God and his most holy word. [16]

It must be emphasized that the world of affairs was not opened to most Renaissance Englishwomen. Instead, Englishwomen were educated for the sake of fulfilling specific private functions and responsibilities, in accordance with the ideas of two related but distinct groups of English Renaissance thinkers who showed significant interest in women. Christian humanists and Protestant reformers enjoined Englishwomen to exercise their newly developed understanding in private roles within the confines of their homes. [17]

The orientations of both the humanists and the reformers were in many ways similar; both groups regulated life with a degree of "measure" that seems rigorous today. [18] However, the intellectual influences on each group were somewhat dissimilar. The humanists were engaged in an examination of Christian writings and teachings and in a rediscovery of classical writings. They attempted to reconcile ideas culled from Greek and Roman materials with the teachings of the early church fathers. The reformers were interested principally in a reappraisal of biblical materials. Primarily, they used injunction and example from the ancient Hebrew culture, as reflected both in the Old and the New Testaments, to illustrate and reinforce their ideals. When they dealt with the question of women, they cited figures of model women from both testaments as models for contemporary women. And, while the goal of both groups was to produce sober, virtuous women, the humanists had an appreciation of intellectual pursuit that was generally lacking among the later reformers. This difference in attitude on the part of the two groups is reflected in the slightly dissimilar types of women they actually produced. [19]

The earlier of the two groups of theorists was composed of the predominantly Catholic early humanist scholars of the circle of Sir Thomas More, Desiderius Erasmus, Richard Hyrde, Juan Luis Vives, and Sir Thomas Elyot. Their thinking concerning women was largely inspired and often sponsored by the erudite and pious Catherine of Aragon (1485-1536), the first queen of Henry VIII, and was promulgated especially by Juan Luis Vives (1492-1540), the Spanish humanist whom Catherine brought to England to educate the Princess Mary. Catherine had been carefully educated by her own mother, Isabella of Castille (1451-1504), who was imbued with an intense love of the new learning and instilled her enthusiasm in her daughters by personally teaching them when they were young and employing tutors for them when they grew older.[20]

It can be said that the Renaissance tendency toward change regarding woman and her educational program begun in Italy came indirectly to England from Spain in the persons of Catherine of Aragon and Juan Luis Vives.[21] As queen of England, Catherine served as a catalyst for More's circle of humanists because of her own learning, piety, and intense interest in the education of her daughter, the Princess Mary. Between 1523 and 1538, seven works were written by English theorists on the education of women, largely at Catherine's behest and often with fulsome praise of the queen's sponsorship, piety, and learning.[22] An example is Vives's *Instruction* (1529), a work on the education of women prepared for and dedicated to Catherine. In the dedication, Vives states that he has, "ben moved partly by the holynes and goodnes of your lyving, partly by the favour and love that your grace beareth towarde holy study and lernying, to write some thing . . . of thynformacion & bryngyng up of a Christen woman: A matter never yet entreated of any man . . ."[23]

While they did not propose a curriculum for women identical to that offered to men,[24] the humanists modified woman's previous training, which had consisted chiefly of rudiments of religious instruction, to include newly rediscovered classical writings. These were developed into a rigorous program of private study including the reading of such classical authors as Plato, Cicero, Seneca, and Plutarch; daily readings of the New Testament; and readings in the church fathers, Christian poets, useful sciences like the preparation of medicines, and more lofty sciences like astronomy. The Christian humanist ideology of these theorists, however, directed this esoteric program of study to a perhaps inadequate end. For example, Vives states that a woman should "study . . . if nat for her own sake, at the least wyse for her chyldren, that she maye teache them and make them good."[25]

The thinking of the early English humanists concerning women proved most helpful to women of the privileged classes, some of whom became highly educated through private tutelage; for, while the humanists did not intend to restrict their ideas to the privileged, they developed no program of schooling for the common people. Toward the end of the sixteenth century, however, humanist educators were advocating programs of schooling for women. In 1581, Richard Mulcaster writes that he supports the education of girls "toothe and naile." He asks, "Is it either nothing or but some small thing, to have our childrens mothers well furnished in minde, well strengthened in bodie? . . . [I]s it likely that her children shalbe a whit the worse brought up, if she be a Laelia, an Hortensia, or a Cornelia, which were so endued and noted for so doing?"[26]

Before the advent of humanist educators like Mulcaster, and slightly later than the "Age of Catherine of Aragon," a second group of conscious innovators showed significant interest in women. This group was composed principally of Protestant religious reformers (and tended to become predominantly Puritan over the period). Prominent among them were Thomas Becon (1512-1567) and Miles Coverdale (1488–1568). These writers were concerned with clarifying the nature of marriage from a theological standpoint and defining the functioning of the family on the basis of this clarification. The domestic conduct book,[27] a subgenre that bulks large in the writings of the reformers, demonstrates their interest in the reform of the family, the redefinition of the roles of its members, and the training of children of both sexes.

Protestant thought affected women in several ways. Through the elevation of marriage to an equal rank with celibacy, and the development of the home as a school of faith, the Protestants enhanced the status of the married woman. Through the espousal of the doctrine of the priesthood of all believers, the Protestants increased the urgency of providing women, like men, with the ability to read the Bible. And through their emphasis on the importance of the inculcation of proper beliefs in children to secure their salvation, the Protestants elevated the function of the mother.[28] From the outset, the Protestants advocated a program of studies for women of all classes to prepare them for these functions. This program was less intellectually rigorous than that of the humanists and stressed knowledge of the Bible and training in practical skills. As early as 1564, Thomas Becon asks, "Is not the woman the creature of God, so well as the man? . . . Can that woman govern her house godly, which knoweth not one point of godlynes? . . . Who seeth not now then howe necessarye the vertuous education and bringinge up of the womankinde is? whiche thinge canne not be conveniently brought to passe except scholes for that purpose be appoynted?"[29]

The humanists and the reformers joined religious enthusiasm and educational impulses into ideologies aimed at producing pious, learned women.

The Christian humanists of the circle of Sir Thomas More were deeply influenced by the Platonic vision of the moral efficacy of learning. Erasmus compared the school More instituted in his home for the instruction of his son and daughters, as well as for several other pupils, not merely "to Plato's

Academy . . . [but to] a School, of University, or Christian religion."[30] More
states his educational purposes clearly in a letter he wrote to William Gonell,
one of the tutors in his household:

. . . I prefer learning joined with virtue to all the treasures of kings, yet renown for
learning, if you take away moral probity, brings nothing else but notorious and noteworthy infamy, especially in a woman. Since erudition in women is a new thing and a
reproach to the sloth of men, many will gladly assail it, and impute to learning what is
really the fault of nature, thinking from the vices of the learned to get their own
ignorance esteemed as virtue. . . . [L]earning will be a glory to her . . . because the
reward of wisdom . . . depends on the inner knowledge of what is right, not on the talk
of men, than which nothing is more foolish or mischievous.[31]

Similarly, in Richard Hyrde's "Dedicatory Letter," a manifesto for the education of women prefixed to a translation by Margaret More, Hyrde advocates
learning for women, "whiche Plato the wyse philosopher calleth a bridell for
yonge people against vice."[32]

The humanists believed in the intellectual and religious potential
of women. Vives states, "The woman is even as man is a reasonable creature,
and hath a flexible witte both to good and evill, the whiche with use and
counsell maybe be altered and turned."[33] This statement is a reflection of
Plato's discussion of women in his *Republic*. It is also a corollary to the
theology of Paul (Gal. 3:28) and to the intellectual and spiritual intercourse of
church fathers and early Christian women. More continues in the letter cited
above,

Nor do I think that the harvest is much affected whether it is a man or a woman who
does the sowing. They both have the name of human being whose nature reason
differentiates from that of beasts; both, I say, are equally suited for the knowledge of
learning by which reason is cultivated.
    . . . This was the opinion of the ancients, both the wisest and the most saintly. Not to
speak of the rest, Jerome and Augustine not only exhorted excellent matrons and
honorable virgins to study, but also, in order to assist them, diligently explained the
abstruse meanings of the Scriptures, and wrote for tender girls letters replete with so
much erudition that nowadays old men who call themselves doctors of sacred literature can scarcely read them correctly, much less understand them.

Like the humanists, the reformers advocated the education of women as a
foundation for piety. However, they emphasized biblical models and developed a less intensive educational program. For example, Thomas Bentley
devoted an entire section of his *Monument of Matrones* (1582 and 1583) to
*"the acts and histories, lives and deaths of all maner of women, good and
bad, mentioned in holie Scripture. . . . with the signification and interpretation of most of their names; and in some part paraphrastically explained and*

enlarged for the better understanding of the story, and benefite of the simple reader. . . . A treatise very necessarie, pleasant, and profitable for sundrie good uses and purposes, especially to the true imitation of vertue, and shunning of vice, by example in all women kinde."[34] The formative domestic conduct book by Heinrich Bullinger was translated into English by Miles Coverdale in 1541. In it Bullinger advocated a less intensive program of learning for women to include reading, especially of the Bible (in translation), writing, arithmetic, some history, and household skills.[35]

Englishwomen expressed their own religious fervor in translations of earlier religious works and in original compositions. In these works they gave voice to the enlightened piety inculcated in them. Renaissance women writers on religion include titled women like Lady Jane Dudley and Lady Elizabeth Colville as well as less exalted women like Bessie Clerksone and Katherine Stubbes.[36] Certainly a reader today will be impressed by the humility of Queen Catherine Parr, whose zeal to publish was motivated, she states, "by the hate I owe to sinne, who hathe reygned in me, partely by the love I owe to all Christians, whom I am contente to edifye, even with thexample of mine owne shame, . . . to confesse and declare to the world, howe ingrate, negligent, unkynde, and stubberne, I have bene to god my Creatour."[37]

The humanists and reformers recognized the spiritual value of the home. They channeled the instructed piety of Renaissance women into domestic activity, focusing especially on responsible child nurture. Even here, in a sphere that might today be considered restrictive, the new Renaissance ideals constituted a revolutionary advance over earlier medieval norms.[38] Indeed, from a historical perspective, the evolution of the woman in English Renaissance society became centered in the woman as mother, since only this facet of the woman underwent an approved rise in autonomy at this time, and there was no interest in changing the subordinate legal status of women or in allowing them to engage in a public life.

Both humanists and reformers praised the state of marriage. The humanists, who mainly were within the Catholic fold, retained great respect for the celibate ideal. Thus, Erasmus speaks approvingly of celibacy when it is honorably maintained. Yet, at the same time, he develops a strong and moving case for the sanctity of marriage, citing such biblical proofs as Christ's presence at the marriage in Cana.[39] On the other hand, the reformers denounced the advocacy of celibacy as a superior state by the Roman church and emphasized the companionate value of marriage. Becon, for example, writes, "[A]monge all these adversaries and enemies of Matrimonye, the Romanische Bishoppe . . . maybe not be passed over with silence: . . . the moste holy state of Matrimony hathe he moste viley and moste wickedly enbased, caste downe, and made almost of no reputation."[40] And Becon describes the "hie, holye and blessed" state of marriage, "wherein one man and one woman are coupled and knot togther . . . by the free, lovinge, harty, and good consente of them both, to the entente, that they two may dwel together, as one fleshe and body of one wyl and mind. . . ."[41]

Both groups of thinkers extended their approval of marriage to an investment of the role of the mother with a hitherto denied distinction. Vives states, "[O]f the woman who accustometh her children unto vertue, the maister of the pagannes Saynct Paule, speketh in this maner: the woman hath gone out of the waye by transgression, howe be it she shall be saved by bryngynge forthe of chyldren, if she contynewe in faythe, charitie, and holynes with chastitie."[42] William Gouge, a Protestant reformer, states, "[M]others should teach their children; especially when they are young, which duty so belongeth to a mother as Solomon layeth the blame and shame of the neglect thereof upon her: on the other side, the honour of well-nurturing children redoundeth especially to the mother."[43]

Thus, in addition to the new woman described above, Renaissance theorists also developed a woman who might be termed a new mother. These women's writings on motherhood constitute a distillation of the theories of the humanists and reformers. For example, Elizabeth Grymeston writes to her only son, "[T]here is nothing so strong as the force of love; there is no love so forcible as the love of an affectionate mother to hir naturall childe: there is no mother can either more affectionately shew hir nature, or more naturally manifest hir affection, than in advisinig hir children out of hir owne experience, to eschue evill, and encline them to do that which is good."[44] Writers on motherhood among Renaissance Englishwomen include such titled and middling class women as the' countess of Lincoln, Dorothy Leigh, and Elizabeth Joceline.[45]

However, the new theories concerning women constituted only a limited advance over earlier thinking, for the new Renaissance woman remained subordinated to men in practice. Vives refers to the following stirring list of models for Renaissance women: "Sara, Rebecca, Penelope, Andromacha, Lucretia, Colebolina [sic], Hipparchia, Portia, Sulpitia, Cornelia, and of our sayntes, as Agnes, Catherine, Margaret, Barbara, Monica & Apolonia . . . by whose examples thei may be styrred and provoked."[46] He expects woman to "be styrred and provoked" by her husband, or "head," and declares, "If the husbande be the womans head, the mind, the father, & Christ, he ought to execute the office to suche a man belongyng, & to teache the woman."[47] Sir Thomas More, whose narrator, Hythloday, reports that women function as soldiers and as priests and attend early morning lectures with men in Utopia, still retains a patriarchal family structure there.[48] A similar point of view undoubtedly accounts for the English translation by Gentian Hervet of Xenophon's *Oeconomicus,* a work in which a young bride is coached by her husband in the important duties of the home.[49] The Protestants advocated similar ideas. Gouge cites biblical models of correct behavior; in his encyclopedic domestic conduct book, he notes that "[t]he man . . . is the highest in the family and hath both authority over all and the charge of all is committed to his charge . . . the wife also ought to be an helpe to him therein."[50]

The new theories concerning women were often characterized by condescension. In a letter written to his beloved daughter, Margaret, during her first pregnancy, Sir Thomas More wrote, "May God and our Blessed Lady grant you happily and safely to increase your family by a little one like to his mother in everything except sex. Yet let it by all means be a girl, if only she will make up for the inferiority of her sex by her zeal to imitate her mother's virtue and learning. Such a girl I should prefer to three boys (p. 155)." Most early Renaissance Englishwomen, like Margaret More, left no signs of dissatisfaction with the thinking of Renaissance theorists like Sir Thomas More. Without any complaint, Margaret More forebore to publish her own translation from Greek to Latin of Eusebius, when she learned that Bishop Christopherson was engaged in the identical task.[51] Queen Catherine Parr almost fell victim to the suspicions of Henry VIII that she was trying to usurp authority over him, but saved her life by assuring her husband (whom she termed a "Moses" in her *Lamentacion*) of her reverence for his opinions.[52]

Even women rulers were distrusted. In 1558, in his grossly mistimed *First Blast of the Trumpet against the monstrous Regiment of Women,* John Knox vehemently attacked the rule of women, offending the new Protestant woman ruler, Elizabeth Tudor, who was the hope of his coreligionists. Knox thereby gave vent to a deep and commonly held view of the unnaturalness of female rule over men.[53] Elizabeth manipulated her public image brilliantly, as scholars have shown us in recent years, to project both a sense of her masculine, princely privilege, and to appeal to a sense of her frailty as a woman.[54] Amazingly attuned to the pulse of her subjects, she avoided the appearance of violating the norms for women. Over time, her successful reign served to elevate public opinion about women, and the new thinking about women, begun under Henry VIII, continued while she ruled.[55] Still, Elizabeth maintained her own independence by remaining single and escaping the subordination that was the lot of even a royal matron.[56] Therefore, her very success underlines the limits of the ambiguous enfranchisement of women characterizing the English Renaissance.

Not all Renaissance women were satisfied, as was Margaret More, with their anomalous position; once women were allowed and even encouraged to develop their minds, it was inevitable that some would be moved at least to ponder the larger inequities of their lives. This is not to say that these women defied or denied the major standards of their society, but merely to say that they did question them; the spark of freedom had been ignited. Thus Margaret Tyler, an obscure translator of a secular romance, protested in her letter "to the Reader" against restrictions imposed on the literary efforts of women, saying, "[M]any have dedicated their labours, some stories, some of warre, some phisick, . . . unto divers ladies & gentlewomen. And if man may & do bestow such of their travailes upon gentlewomen, then may we women read such of their works as they dedicate unto us, and if we may read them, why not farther wade in them to the serch of a truth . . . my perswasion hath bene thus, that it is all one for a woman to pen a story, as for a man to addresse his story to a woman."[57]

A small number of Renaissance Englishwomen wrote "feminist" tracts to protest the writings or behavior of particular men, but they did not suggest that women not continue to be submissive to men, their heads. Even these women were relatively submissive and conventional: they merely surpassed the women discussed above in independence by expressing independent thoughts on issues other than religion and child-rearing.[58] The societal and secular writings by Renaissance Englishwomen like Lady Mary Wroth, Isabella Whitney, Jane Anger [pseud.], and Rachel Speght[59] provide a transition to the compositions of women who defied the norms of Renaissance English society.

Of the women writers who were unable to conform to the Renaissance pattern, it can be said that they suffered cruelly for their determination and individualism.

The first, Anne Askew (1521-1546), the Protestant martyr, was unable to accept the strictures of the Catholic husband who had been selected for her (and who was the father of her two children) and tried to interpret Scripture according to her own light. She was examined, tortured, and burned at the stake, very possibly at her husband's instigation. Her two examinations and her ballad reveal her tenderness and strength, as well as her gift for expressing her ideals.[60]

The second of these writers, Mary Stuart (1542-1587), was imprisoned, dethroned, and eventually executed because she had aspired to self-realization through both power and sexuality. Mary's strong claim to the English throne as great-granddaughter of Henry VII, her actual presence for nineteen years on English soil as a major irritant and potential threat to the political and religious status quo, and her significance for Elizabethans as the out-of-bounds woman "on top," combine, I believe, to make Mary Stuart a legitimate object of concern to students of Renaissance Englishwomen's writings. But Mary's writings, often works of true literary worth, have been neglected for centuries because students of her character have been concerned with partisan questions; these compositions are considered as literature here for the first time.[61]

The third of these writers, Elizabeth Cary, Lady Falkland (1585-1639), suffered separation from her husband and children as well as grinding poverty because her idealism, brilliance, and independent mind would not allow her to rest until she had converted to the Roman faith. Lady Falkland's sensitive probing of the position of the dependent woman is recorded in her drama (the first original drama by an Englishwoman) and in the few extracts of her other writings which have survived.[62]

The writings presented in this anthology include prose narratives, verses, prayers, essays, confessions, diaries, letters, and prefaces, i.e., materials within and outside the genres which are traditionally studied as literature. They were included because they provide a broad and representative selection of the writings of Renaissance Englishwomen, and show their range of interests and accomplishments in relation to the position of and limitations on women in Renaissance English society. The materials have been included not only for literary worth—although many deserve the literary recognition they have not previously secured—but also as important social documents illuminating the position of women during the English Renaissance. Sometimes these Renaissance Englishwomen are seen to exert a real, if unobtrusive, influence on their times; most often, they are shown to be without power or security. Sometimes they effected important developments in the traditional ways open to women; if these methods are not surprising, the documentation of their use is important for a study of the position of women in Renaissance society. As I argue in the preface to the Morningside edition, they are also important for a balancing of our understanding of the period as a whole.

Translations by these women have been excluded on the grounds, discussed above in the preface to the Morningside edition, that they are essentially derivative. In the case of one work—Mary Herbert's translation of the Psalms—the exclusion was painful, since Mary Herbert made a new song of the Psalms. However, it is hoped that other works by the countess of Pembroke (which are included) will compensate for this omission. In this case, as in the case of other translations that are named but not included, bibliographical information has been included for the reader's convenience. There has been an effort throughout to provide scrupulous and abundant bibliographical information so that readers who wish to follow further lines of investigation about these undeservedly obscure women and writings will find their work expedited. References to works cited in the bibliography and in the list of abbreviations appear in shortened form in the notes.

The texts appearing in this anthology were taken from the first editions of the works, when these have been available to me. The original spelling, punctuation, and capitalization have been preserved exactly, except for the customary u/v and i/j modernizations and for the silent expansion of occasional conventional abbreviations. In the case of some of the letters, of one diary, and of the poetry of Elizabeth Tudor, a reliable and modernized text was available. It seemed "a foolish consistency" to ignore these editions; the modernized version has been included here. A translation of the original has been provided in the case of material composed in a language other than English.

Part I Writings Conforming to the Renaissance Standard

1 RELIGIOUS COMPOSITIONS

IN 1529, an unusual work called the *Instruction of a Christen Woman* issued from the press of Thomas Berthelet with a dedication by its author, Juan Luis Vives, to Catherine of Aragon, the Queen of England. Vives, a humanist brought to England by Queen Catherine, Henry VIII's first wife, to educate the Princess Mary, began his dedication with the following words:

I have ben moved partly by the holynes and goodnes of your lyvyng, partly by the favour and love that your grace beareth towarde holy study and lernyng, to write some thing unto your grace, of thynformacion & bryngyng up of a Christen woman: A matter never yet entreated of any man, amonge so great plenty and variete of wyttes and writers. For . . . [earlier writers] rather . . . exhorte and counsayle them unto some kynde of lyvyng than . . . instructe and teache them. They spende all theyr speche in the laudes and prayses of chastitie, whiche is a goodly thynge, and fyttynge for those gret wytted and holy men: How be it, they write but fewe preceptes and rules howe to lyve: supposyng it to be better, to exhorte them unto the best, and helpe them up to the hyghest: than to enforme and teache the lower thynges. But I wyll let passe all suche exhortations . . . and I wyl compyle rules of lyvyng.[1]

Vives was an intimate of Sir Thomas More's circle, that is to say, the group of early humanists who addressed themselves to a recognition and enhancement of the humanity of women. These Renaissance theorists advocated the education of women so that they could practice a Christian way of life. Accordingly, Vives stated that,

[T]he mynde, set upon lernynge and wysedome, shall not only abhorre from foule luste, that is to saye the most whyte thinge froom sout, and the most pure from spottes. But also they shall leave all suche lyght and triflynge pleasures, wherein the lyght fantasies of maydes have delite, as songes, daunces and suche other wanton and pyvyshe plaies. A woman, saythe Plutarche, given unto lerning will never delyte in daunsynge. . . . [A]nd what shall she study: . . . [T]he study of wysedom, the which doth enstruct their maners, and enfourme their lyving, & teacheth them the waye of good and holy lyfe.   [p. 9]

Frivolous learning, to varying degrees, was censured by the theorists. When Vives discussed the schooling of the girl in his *Instruction*, he stated, "[l]et not her example be voyd verses, nor wanton or triflynge songes" (p. 9). He forbade the reading of "foule rebaudy songes" (p. 11) and of "ungratious bokes" (p. 11). He stated that "a woman shuld beware of all these bokes, lyke wyse as of serpentes or snakes" (p. 12). That efforts like Vives's bore fruit in the form of a deep and informed commitment to religion by Renaissance Englishwomen is a fact attested to by both the translated and the original works by these women relating to theology and religious practices.

The strong commitment of Englishwomen to the new ideals is characteristic of the intensity of religious interest in the period. The English were more fortunate than most Europeans during their Renaissance. They experienced no civil war until the mid-seventeenth century. But religious controversy was a central controversy in Renaissance England. Succeeding English rulers changed the official religion, and the English people seesawed back and forth and debated religious questions acrimoniously (even after the Anglican compromise) until the debate deteriorated to violence with the eruption of civil war. Women, newly recognized as the spiritual equals of men, were encouraged to speak out in support of their faith. For support was needed in these stressful times, and women were not backward in seizing this opportunity for greater participation in religious life.

Some of the most celebrated of Renaissance Englishwomen are noted for translations of religious materials rather than for original compositions. Their translations included tracts and sermons,[2] as well as poetry[3] (particularly psalms, which were frequently rendered into English by pious and literary people in the period). The translators were often remarkably erudite,[4] and their skill in translation is clearly and sometimes avowedly underlined by deep religious commitment.

Nevertheless, those Renaissance women who wrote original religious works, who set down their own thoughts and feelings on religion and rendered theology a personal, intimate experience, are of even greater interest historically. Selections from their original writings are presented in the following pages.

RELIGIOUS POETRY AND POETRY OF MOURNING

The moral tone of the religious poetry and the poetry of mourning by Renaissance Englishwomen is generally consistent with that of the prose writings on religion that inspired them (such as Vives's *Instruction*) and the prose materials written by the women themselves (see the next section of this chapter). The only discernible difference is that in place of the unaffected dignity of the prose, sometimes there is a more conscious striving for artistic effect—particularly in the poetry of mourning, which, at least sometimes, draws on classical materials in addition to religious ones. One is reminded of Dorothy Gardiner's notice of "the special uses to which . . . Renaissance Englishwomen put their facility in Greek and Latin"[5] in her pioneering and still standard work on the history of women's education. The religious poetry of these women demonstrates one such use.

Indeed, the classical erudition of some of these women is apparent in poetry that is both effective and technically impressive, such as the sprightly verses of Rachel Speght and the elegant verses of Anne Dacre, Mary Herbert, and Elizabeth Russell. The later poems of Mary Stuart (see Part II) are probably the most talented specimens of this sophistication. These works were obviously inspired in part by secular love of language and classical learning.

Other women wrote less stylized or more informal poetry, which is unmistakably sincere and intensely moving despite its less artful form. Probably the most important women writers demonstrating this tendency are Anne Askew, the Protestant martyr, whose original ballad is included in Part II of this study, and Elizabeth Colville, part of whose dream vision of the afterworld is contained in this chapter. The women wrote from the Catholic and Protestant points of view, and the intensity of conviction in the verses of both factions reflects the religious fervor of the time, for most of the poetry is intensely partisan.

In fact, the most unusual of the poems by women are those lacking the typical parochialism of the period; these poems have a sophisticated flavor that makes them far more appealing to a contemporary reader than more polemical verses. The moving and excellent verses of Anne Askew and the later poetry of Mary Stuart surmount religious sectarianism and express a type of thought now considered deeper, greater, and more truly visionary and religious.

But all the verses by Renaissance Englishwomen presented in this section reflect the serious ideals of Vives and his fellow theorists. They are written by women of serious purpose who benefited from the new opportunities for personal development while remaining within conventional limits.

ELIZABETH TUDOR, QUEEN OF ENGLAND (1533-1603)

As a young woman, Elizabeth Tudor seemed to be the ill-starred daughter of an unfortunate mother, Queen Anne Boleyn (1507-1536), the second wife of Henry VIII (see chapter 2). With her half-sister, Mary Tudor, and her half-brother, Edward VI, Elizabeth was shunted from place to place and subjected to alternately harsh and pleasant treatment by her mercurial father. Ironically, Elizabeth, who outlived Henry's other children, was considered by him an insufficient guarantee of a secure succession and reign and was, because of her sex, an inadvertent element in her mother's downfall. However, as Elizabeth I of England, she proved to be a singularly long-lived Tudor. Her actual success and stature as Queen of England was a significant factor in the elevation of the position of women during the English Renaissance, although Elizabeth herself showed little interest in promoting the rights of other females. There is general agreement among the writers on Renaissance women that, in an era of limited legal enfranchisement for women, Elizabeth maintained her authority and autonomy by remaining single; the lack of confidence shown by Henry VIII in the viability of the rule of a female was not unusual in an era that distrusted women; the Virgin Queen's success presents an interesting contrast to the ill-fated career of her cousin, Mary Stuart (see Part II), who was unable either to fulfill her personal needs or to retain control of her kingdom as a married woman.

The relatively pedestrian verses by Elizabeth included in this chapter present only one facet of her personality and interests. For other aspects of her many-sided personality, see chapters 2 and 3. The following poems are taken from Leicester Bradner, ed., *The Poems of Queen Elizabeth I* (Providence, R.I.: Brown University Press, 1964).

WRITTEN ON A WALL AT WOODSTOCK

Oh fortune, thy wresting wavering state
Hath fraught with cares my troubled wit,
Whose witness this present prison late
Could bear, where once was joy's loan quit.
Thou causedst the guilty to be loosed   [5]
From bands where innocents were inclosed,
And caused the guiltless to be reserved,
And freed those that death had well deserved.
But all herein can be nothing wrought,
So God send to my foes all they have thought.[6]   [10]

ON MONSIEUR'S DEPARTURE (Date ?)

I grieve and dare not show my discontent,
I love and yet am forced to seem to hate,
I do, yet dare not say I ever meant,
I seem stark mute but inwardly do prate.
     I am and not, I freeze and yet am burned,   [5]
     Since from myself another self I turned.

My care is like my shadow in the sun,
Follows me flying, flies when I pursue it,
Stands and lies by me, doth what I have done.
His too familiar care doth make me rue it.   [10]
     No means I find to rid him from my breast,
     Till by the end of things it be supprest.

Some gentler passion slide into my mind,
For I am soft and made of melting snow;
Or be more cruel, love, and so be kind.   [15]
Let me or float or sink, be high or low.
  Or let me live with some more sweet content,
  Or die and so forget what love ere meant.[7]

MARY (SIDNEY) HERBERT, COUNTESS OF PEMBROKE (1561-1621)

The Countess, sister of Sir Philip Sidney, is characterized by Myra Reynolds as the "one lady of Elizabethan days whose fame justly exceeds that of any of her predecessors."[8] Mary Sidney was educated with her brother in Latin, Greek, and Hebrew. She married Henry Herbert, earl of Pembroke, in 1575 and lived with him at Wilton House for twenty-four years. It was there that her three children were born and her own creative activities and her activities in support of many of the artists of her time took place. She inspired the writing of her brother's *Arcadia*, called the *Countess of Pembroke's Arcadia*, and arranged for the publication of an emended edition of his poems after his early death. The Countess was a sympathetic patron of such poets as Meres, Spenser, Donne, Breton, Nashe, Harvey, and Daniel. She was also the subject of a famous epitaph, probably written by William Browne, though long attributed to Ben Jonson:

Underneath this sable hearse,
Lyes the subject of all verse
Sydney's sister, Pembroke's mother;
Death, ere thou hast kill'd another
Fair and learned and good as she,
Time shall throw a dart at thee.[9]

The Countess (discussed further in chapter 3) has importance as both a translator and composer of religious poetry; her skill in versification is universally acknowledged. She and her brother collaborated on a translation of the first forty-three of the Psalms; the Countess alone translated numbers forty-four through one hundred and fifty. The Sidneian Psalms have been termed a "school of English versification," and the contribution of the Countess is generally considered of higher quality than that of her brother. Also noteworthy is the Countess's translation of Petrarch's *Trionfo della Morte*; her skill in versification is underlined in this work by her use of the terza rima of the original.

"The Dolefull Lay of Clorinda," a pastoral elegy on Sir Philip Sidney's death, usually attributed to his sister, first appeared in Spenser's *Colin Clout comes home againe* (London: T. C. for William Ponsonbie, 1595). STC 23077. Reel no. 354.

from *THE DOLEFULL LAY OF CLORINDA*

Ay me! to whom shall I my case complaine,
That may compassion my impatient griefe?
Or where shall I unfold my inward paine,
That my enriven heart may finde reliefe?
   Shall I unto the heavenly powres it show?   [5]
   Or unto earthly men that dwell below?

. . . .

Woods, hills, and rivers now are desolate,   [25]
Sith he is gone the which them all did grace:
And all the fields do waile their widow state,
Sith death their fairest flowre did late deface.
   The fairest flowre in field that ever grew,
   Was *Astrophel*; that was, we all may rew.   [30]

. . . .

Death, the devourer of all worlds delight,
Hath robbed you, and reft fro me my joy: [50]
Both you and me, and all the world he quight
Hath robd of joyance, and left sad annoy.
   Joy of the world and shepheards pride was hee,
   Shepheards hope never like againe to see.

. . . .

But that immortall spirit, which was deckt
With all the dowries of celestial grace:
By soveraine choyce from th'hevenly quires select,
And lineally deriv'd from Angels race,
   O what is now of it become aread.   [65]
   Ay me, can so divine a thing be dead?

Ah no: it is not dead, ne can it die,
But lives for aie, in blisfull Paradise:
Where like a new-borne babe, it soft doth lie
In bed of lillies wrapt in tender wise.   [70]
   And compast all about with roses sweet,
   And daintie violets from head to feet.

. . . .

There liveth he in everlasting blis,   [85]
Sweet spirit never fearing more to die:
Ne dreading harme from any foes of his
Ne fearing salvage beasts more crueltie.
   Whilest we here wretches waile his private lack,
   And with vaine vowes do often call him back.   [90]

> But live thou there still happie, happie spirit,
> And give us leave thee here thus to lament:
> Not thee that doest thy heavens joy inherit,
> But our owneselves that here in old are drent.
> > Thus do we weep and waile, and wear our eies,   [95]
> > Mourning in others, our owne miseries.   [sigs. G-G3]

LADY ELIZABETH (COOKE) RUSSELL (1529-1609)

Lady Russell, one of the celebrated daughters of Sir Anthony Cooke, is remembered chiefly as the translator of a religious tract (see chapter 3). In 1558, she married Sir Thomas Hoby (1530-1566), translator of Castiglione's *Courtier* and a man whose interests were indeed close to her own. She corresponded with her brother-in-law, Sir William Cecil, and her "letters . . . testify to her remarkable force of character," according to the *Dictionary of National Biography* (hereafter indicated as *DNB*).[10] Among the factors leading to that evaluation was undoubtedly her priding "herself," in Doris Stenton's words, "on not allowing her second husband to have the wardship of her sons."[11] Elizabeth's second marriage, in 1574, was to John, Lòrd Russell; a verse memorial to this relationship is presented here. The poem is a moderately personalized dirge recounting the virtues of the deceased and is noteworthy for its deliberate artfulness and its formal elegaic tone.

The elegy was transcribed by Paul Hentzner, a sixteenth-century traveler who visited and described Westminster, and who copied the verses composed by Lady Russell and inscribed on Lord Russell's tomb there. They appeared in his *Journey into England in the Year MDXCVIII* (Strawberry Hill, 1757; Rpt. at the Private Press of T. E. Williams, Reading, 1807).

ELEGY

> How was I startled at the cruel feast,
> By Death's rude hands in horrid manner drest;
> Such grief as sure no hapless woman knew,
> When thy pale image lay before my view.
> Thy father's heir, in beauteous form array'd,   [5]
> Like flowers in spring, and fair, like them to fade;
> Leaving behind unhappy, wretched me,
> And all thy little Orphan-progeny:
> Alike the beauteous face, the comely air,
> The tonge perswasive and the actions fair,   [10]
> Decay: So learning too in time shall waste;
>
> But faith, chaste lovely faith, shall ever last.
> The once bright glory of his house, the pride

Of all his country, dusty ruins hide:
Mourn, hapless Orphans, mourn, once happy Wife   [15]
For when he dy'd, dy'd all the joys of life.
Pious and just, amidst a large estate,
He got at once the name of good and great,
He made no flatt'ring parasite his guest,
But ask'd the good companions to the feast.   [p. 14]   [20]

ESTHER (INGLIS) KELLO (1571-1624)

Esther Kello, a celebrated calligrapher and miniaturist, was the daughter of religious refugee parents from France; her father, Nicholas Langlois, became the master of a school in Edinburgh in 1578, in the pattern of so many refugees. Her mother, Marie Prisott, herself an accomplished penner, taught Esther calligraphy, since it was then considered a fashionable art for women. In this sense, Mrs. Kello's work is probably representative of that of many cultivated women of her time; however, the *DNB* notes that "extant manuscripts written and illuminated by Mrs. Kello are of exquisite workmanship."[12] Dorothy Judd Jackson, Kello's biographer, makes a somewhat less enthusiastic appraisal of Mrs. Kello's work and notes her lack of originality. It is more important, perhaps, to note that Jackson has located thirty-five extant manuscripts by Mrs. Kello,[13] who, unlike most of the other women discussed in this chapter and almost all the women in the period, wrote professionally, i.e., for profit, presenting her hand-illuminated works to wealthy patrons. Mrs. Kello's works are proficient; most of them are religious in theme.

The following selections are taken from a small, unpaginated volume containing fifty illuminated, eight-line verses that follow one another in the order in which they are numbered. *Octonaries upon the vanitie and Inconstancie of the World* . . . (Edinburgh: January 1, 1609).

OCTONARIE III

The fyre, aire, water, earth, the world with changes fill
They tourne and tourne again, each in the other still.
So God was pleas'd to mak what this Lowe worlde presents
Of well-agreeing warrs of contraire Elements
To teach us that we ought for our cheef good enquyre   [5]
Else-where than in the earth, the water, aire, or fyre:
That the true reste of man, rests in an hyer place
Then earth, aire, water, fyre; or they all can embrace.

OCTONARIE XV

If heav'ns a cercle be, and earth the midle point·
As great philosophers would have us to conceave

Why do yee all the frame of heav'n and earth disjoint
Worldlings, with endless warrs, who most of earth may have?
Why, (Worldlings) do yee still perplex your selves with paine   [5]
Guld with a foolish hope of an Ambition vaine?
O errour admirable!* What follie to confide   [*to be wondered at]
That any labour can, a parteles point divyde.

OCTONARIE XXI

The beautie of the world goes
As soudain as the wind that bloes:
As soudain as yee sie the floure
To wither from his first colloure:
As soudaine as the flood is gone   [5]
Which chaste by others one by one:
What is the world then I pray?
A wind, a floure, a flood alway.

LADY ELIZABETH (MELVILLE) COLVILLE OF CULROS (fl. 1603)

Elizabeth Colville was the daughter of James Melville and the wife of John
Colville. Alexander Hume dedicated his *Hymns or Sacred Songs* (1598) to
her. Her own composition is a poem in ottava rima which, in the words of
Ruth Hughey, contains "a fantastical description of Purgatory and Hell, inter-
spersed with slanders against Catholics."[14] It is probably a misjudgment to
say, with Charlotte Kohler, that this work is the "most complete and con-
sciously well-rounded poem written by a woman which is to be found in this
period."[15] Still, it is an effort in the tradition of the medieval dream vision of
the afterworld, including even the convention of an angelic guide. So long
and deliberate an effort deserves the attention of any student of Renaissance
women.

The following selection is taken from *Ane Godlie Dream . . .* (Edinburgh:
Robert Charteris, 1606).

from *ANE GODLIE DREAME*

Upon a day as I did mourne full sore,
With sindry things where in my soule was greeuch:
My greefe increased, and grew more and more,
I comfort fled, and could not be releeved.
With heavinesse my hart was so mischeeved,   [5]
I loathed my life, I could not eate nor drinke:
I micht not speake, nor looke to none that lived,
But mused alone, and divers things did thinke.

This wreched world did sore molest my minde,
I thoght upon this false and yron age;   [10]
And how our harts were so to vice inclinde,
That Satan seemde most fearefullie to rage.
Nothing in earth my sorrow could asswage,
I felt my sinne most stronglie to increase:
I greeved my Spirit, that wont to be my pledge,   [15]
My soule was plunged into most deepe distresse.

      .   .   .   .

[The narrator falls into a sorrowful dreame]

With sighs and sobs as I did so lament,
Into my dreame I thoght there did appeare   [90]
A sight most sweete which did me wel content,
An Angell bright with visage schyning cleare.
With loving lookes, and with a smyling cheare,
He asked me, why art thou thus so sad?
Why gronest thou so? what doest thou dwyning heere?   [95]
With carefull cryes in this thy bailfull bed?

      .   .   .   .

[The "Angell" identifies himself]

I am the way, I am the trueth and life,
I am thy spouse that brings thee store of grace;   [130]
I am thy Lord that soone shall end thy strife,
I am thy love whom thou wouldst faine unbrace,
I am thy joy, I am thy rest and peace,
Rise up anone, and follow after me:
I shall thee leade unto thy dwelling place,   [135]
The Land of rest, thou longest so sore to see.

      .   .   .   .

[The narrator dreams of a long journey to the afterworld.]

Sometyme we clamine on craigie Mountaines hie,
And sometimes staid on uglie brayes of sand: [170]
They were so stay that wonder was to see,
But when I feared, he held me by the hand.
Throgh thick and thin, throgh sea and eke throgh land,
Throgh great deserts we wandred on our way.
When I was weake and had no strength to stand,   [175]
Yet with a looke he did refresh me ay.

      .   .   .   .

Wearie I was, and thought to sit at rest,
But he said, no, thou may not sit nor stand:

Hold on thy course, and thou shal finde it best,
If thou desirest to see that pleasant land.
Though I was weake, I rose at his command, [205]
And held him fast, at length he leit me see
That plesant place, that seemde to be at hand,
Tak curage now, for thou art neare, said he.

. . . .

Though thou be near, the way is wondrous hard,
Said he againe, therefore thou must be stout:
Fainte not for feare, for cowards are debarde,
That have no heart to goe their voyage out. [220]
Pluck up thy hart and grip me fast about.
Out through this trance together we must goe:
The way is low, remember for to lout,
If this were past we have not many moe.

. . . .

[The travelers pass a fearsome sight.]

I looked down, and saw a Pit most black,
Most full of smooke and flaming fyre most fell;
That uglie sight made me to flee aback,
I feared to heare so many shout and yell. [260]
I him besought that he the trueth would tell,
Is this, said I, the Papists purging place?
Where they affirme that selie soules doe dwell,
To purge their sin, before they rest in peace

. . . .

[The traveler is told that she sees Hell itself.]

The fyre was great, the heat did pearse me sore,
My faith grew weak, my grip was wondrous small:
I trembled fast, my feare grew more and more, [275]
My hands did shake, that I him held withall,
At length thay loused, then I begouth to fall:
And cride aloud, and caught him fast againe;
Lord Jesus come and rid me out of thrall,
Courage, said he, now thou art past the paine. [280]

With this great feare I started and awoke,
Crying aloud, Lord Jesus come againe.
But after this no kinde of rest I tooke,
I pressed to sleepe, but it was all in vaine.
I would have dreamde of pleasure after paine, [285]
Because I know, I shall it finde at last:

God grant my guide may still with me remaine,
It is to come that I beleaved was past.

This is a dreame, and yet I thought it best
To wryte the same, and keepe it still in minde;   [290]
Because I knew, there was no earthlie rest
Preparde for us, that hath our harts inclinde
To seeke the Lord, wee must be purgde and finde:
Our drosse is great, the fyre must try us sore:
But yet our God is mercifull and kinde,   [295]
He shall remaine and helpe us ever more.

The way to Heaven I see is wondrous hard,
My Dreame declares that we have far to goe:
We must be stout, for cowards are debarde,
Our flesh of force must suffer paine and woe.
These dririe waits and many dangers moe   [300]
Awaits for us, we can not live in rest:
But let us learne, since we are warned so,
To cleave to Christ, for he can helpe us best.

.   .   .   .

Rejoice in God, let not your courage faill,   [385]
Ye chosen saints that are afflictit heare:
Though Satan rage, he never shall prevaile,
Fight to the end, and stoutlie persevere.
Your God is true, your bloode is to him deare,
Feare not the way, since Christ is your convoy,   [390]
When clouds are past the weather will grow cleare,
Ye sow in teares, bot ye shall reape in joy.

.   .   .   .

Now to the King that create all of nought,
The Lord of Lordes, that rules both land and sea:
That saved our soules, and with his blood us bought,   [435]
And vanquisht death, triumphing on the tree.
Unto the great and glorious Trinitie,
That saves the poore, and doth his owne defend:
Be laud and glore, honour and majestie,
Power and praise, Amen, world without end.   [440]

FINIS. [sigs. B2-C1]

AEMILIA (BASSANO) LANYER (1570?-1640?)

The dates of Aemilia Lanyer's birth and death are uncertain. She was the
wife of a court musician, Capt. Alphonso Lanyer (d. 1613), and in her youth

she had been connected with the family of the countess of Cumberland, to whom chiefly she addresses both her major work and a shorter appended piece, the "Description of Cookeham," one of the residences of the countess. As totalities, these poems are societal rather than religious in purpose. Kohler deprecates Lanyer's work as primarily sycophantic, "art for lucre's sake."[16] She thinks that disproportionate space is given to descriptions of the countess and of other women, but she is less than just to Mrs. Lanyer, probably because she does not recognize the underlying feminist focus of the poem (see chapter 3).[17] However, large sections of this work describe the sacrifice of Christ in lines which are smooth and moving and often resonant with echoes of Scripture.

The following verses are from *Salve Deux Rex Judaeorum* . . . (London: Valentine Simmes for Richard Bonian, 1611).

from *SALVE DEUX REX JUDAEORUM* . . .

O glorious miracle without compare! [1185]
Last, but not least which was by him effected;
Uniting death, life, misery, joy and care,
By his sharpe passion in his deere elected:
Who doth the Badges of like Liveries weare,
Shall find how deere they are of him respected. [1190]
No joy, griefe, paine, life, death, was like to his,
Whose infinite dolours wrought eternall blisse.

What creature on the earth did then remaine,
On whom the horror of this shamefull deed
Did not inflict some violent touch, or straine, [1195]
To see the Lord of all the world to bleed?
His dying breath did rend huge rockes in twaine,
The heavens betooke them to their mourning weed:
The sunne grew darke, and scorn'd to give them light,
Who durst ecclipse a glory farre more bright. [1200]

The Moone and Starres did hide themselves for shame,
The earth did tremble in her loyall feare,
The Temple vaile did rent to spread his fame,
The Monuments did open every where;
Dead Saints did rise forth of their graves, and came [1205]
To divers people that remained there
Within that holy City: whose offence,
Did put their Maker to this large expence.

Things reasonable, and reasonlesse possest
The terrible impression of this fact; [1210]

For his oppression made them all opprest,
When with his blood he seal'd so faire an act,
In restlesse miserie to procure our rest;
His glorious deedes that dreadfull prison sackt:
When Death, Hell, Divells, using all their powre,   [1215]
Were overcome in that most blessed houre.

Being dead, he killed Death, and did survive
That prowd insulting Tyrant: in whose place
He sends bright Immortalitie to revive
Those whom his yron armes did long embrace;   [1220]
Who from their loathsome graves brings them alive
In glory to behold their Saviours face:
Who tooke the keys of all Deaths powre away,
Opening to those that would his name obay.

O wonder, more than man can comprehend,   [1225]
Our joy and Griefe both at one instant fram'd
Compounded: Contrarieties contend
Each to exceed, yet neither to be blam'd.
Our Griefe to see our Saviours wretched end,
Our Joy to know both Death and Hell he tam'd: [1230]
That we may say, O Death, where is thy sting?
Hell, yeeld thy victory to thy conq'ring King.

           .   .   .   .

Loe here was glorie, miserie, life and death,   [1265]
An union of contraries did accord:
Gladnesse and sadnesse here had one berth,
This wonder wrought the Passion of our Lord,
He suffring for all the sinnes of all th'earth,
No satisfaction could the world afford: [1270]
But this rich Jewell, which from God was sent,
To call all those that would in time repent.   [sigs. E4-E6]

RACHEL SPEGHT (fl. 1617-1621)

Rachel Speght probably was the daughter of Thomas Speght, an editor of
and commentator on Chaucer. That she moved in good circles is shown by
the fact that Mrs. Mary Moundeford, the woman she names as her godmother in the dedication to her religious poetry, was the wife of an extremely
successful physician of the early seventeenth century. Though a young
woman, Speght apparently felt none of the diffidence about writing and
expressing her opinions which was common among women of her time, and
her attitude is even more marked in the works included in chapter 3. Clearly
she was familiar with classical materials as well as with biblical ones.

The following selection is taken from *Mortalities Memorandum* . . . (London: Edward Griffin for Jacob Bloome, 1621).

from *MORTALITIES MEMORANDUM* . . .

When *Elohim* had given time beginning,
In the beginning, God began to make
The heavens, and earth, with all that they containe,
Which were created for *his Glories sake:*
And to be Lord of part of work or'past,   [5]
He *Adam* made, and *Eve* of him at last.

In Eden Garden God did place them both,
To whom Commaund of all the trees he gave,
The fruit of one tree onely to forbeare,
On paine of *Death*, (his owne he did but crave,)   [10]
And Sathan thinking this their good too great,
Suggests the woman, shee the man, they eate.

Thus eating both, they both did joyntly sinne,
And *Elohim* dishonoured by their act;
Doth ratifie, what he had earst decreed,   [15]
That *Death* must be the wages of their fact;
Thus on them, and their of-spring thenceforth seazed
Mortalitie, because they God displeas'd.

In Adam all men die, not one that's free,
From that condition we from him derive,   [20]
By sinne Death entred, and began to raigne,
But yet in *Christ shall all be made alive.*
Who did triumph o're sinne, o're *Death*, and hell,
That all his chosen may in glorie dwell.

                . . . .

Death was at first inflicted as a curse,
But Womans seede hath brooke the Serpents head,
His bitter *Death* for us hath gained life,
His agonie hath freed his owne from dread.
Death is that guest the godly wish to see;   [95]
For when it comes, their troubles ended be.

If man were fettred in a loathsome goale,
Without one sparke of hope to come from thence,
Till Prison walls were levell with the ground,
He would be glad to see their fall Commence,   [100]

Thy bodies ruine then rejoyce to see,
That out of Goale thy soule may loosed be.

        .   .   .   .

The Mariner, which doth assay to passe
The raging seas into some forraine land,
Desireth much to have his voyage ended,
And to arrive upon the solid sand.   [190]
All creatures with desire doe seeke for rest,
After they have with labour beene opprest.

The Pilgrim, which a journey undertakes,
Feeding his fancie with exoticke sights,
Deemes not his way much irksome to his foot: [195]
Because his paine is mixed with delights.
For tis his joy to thinke upon that day,
When he shall see the period of his way.

Men are as Saylors in this irksome life,
Who at the haven alwayes cast their eye,   [200]
As Pilgrims wandring in a uncouth land.
Then who is he, that will not wish to dye?
And he whom God by *Death* dost soonest call,
Is in my minde the happiest wight of all.

        .   .   .   .

For though the seeming pleasures of this life
Doe cause us love it, yet the paines may move   [320]
Us to condemne the bait, which hides the hooke,
And rather loath, then either like or love,
A path of Ice, where footing is unsure,
Or bitter pills, though guilded to allure.

        .   .   .   .

Unto the faithful, *Death* doth tydings bring   [385]
Of life, of favour, and eternall rest,
How they from out the prison of this world,
In which with griefes they have beene sore opprest,
Shall be receiv'd through Christs eternall love
To live for ever with their God above.   [390]

For though that *Death* considered in it selfe
Be fearefull, and doth many terrors bring,
Yet unto them there is no cause of dread;
For by Christs *Death* grim *Mors* hath lost its sting,

That as a toothlesse Snake no hurt can doe,   [395]
No more can Death procure the godly woe.

   . . . .

From earth man came, to dust he *must* returne,
This is the descant of *Deaths* fatall dittie,
All men are mortall, therefore *must* they die   [465]
And *Paul* sayth, *Here is no abiding Cittie.*
Mans dayes consume like wax against the Sunne,
And as a Weavers shittle swiftly runne.

   . . . .

Unto that place prepar'd for Gods elect
Afore the world, the Lord conduct us still,
And grant that we the measure of our dayes,
To his good pleasure may on earth fulfill;
That when wee to our period doe attaine,   [755]
We may with Christ in glory ever raigne.
Amen. [pp. 13-38]

ANNE (DACRE) HOWARD, COUNTESS OF ARUNDEL (1558-1630)

The *DNB* characterizes Anne (Dacre) Howard, countess of Arundel, "as a woman of strong character, and of a religious disposition . . . whose influence soon made itself felt upon her husband. . . . The increasing seriousness of his thoughts led him in the direction of Romanism which his wife openly professed in 1582."[18] After he professed Catholicism in 1584, Arundel was imprisoned in the Tower and executed in 1595, while, the above account continues, "his wife lived in comparative poverty. His only son Thomas was born, but he was not allowed to see his wife or child." It should be noted that the countess was the friend of another Catholic woman who suffered similarly —Elizabeth, Lady Falkland, who is discussed at length in Part II. She was also a correspondent of and sympathizer with Mary Stuart; a letter from the Queen to the Countess appears in Part II.

A few stanzas of verse written by Anne Howard on the death of her husband have survived; apparently they were part of a longer poem. They express her sorrow and "submission" to her husband, whom she calls "my sonne"; her attitude is typical for the period (see Catherine Parr's *Lamentacion* in the next section). Kohler notes that these verses "are well-turned and show a greater flair for literary expression than those of many of her sister rhymers."[19]

Apparently Edmund Lodge was the first to put Anne Howard's "Elegy" in print. *Illustrations of British History, Biography, and Manners . . .*, 3 vols. (London: G. Nicol, 1791). He gives the Howard Papers as his source and describes the verses as inscribed on an envelope in the handwriting of Anne Howard.

from ELEGY

I

In sad, and ashie weeds I sigh,
   I grone, I pine, I mourne:
My often yellow reeds
   I all to jeat and ebon turne.
My watrie eyes, like winter's skyes,   [5]
   My furrowed cheekes o'reflowe.
All heavens knowe why, men mourne as I,
   And who can blame my woe?

II

In sable robes of night my dayes
   Of joye consumed be,   [10]
My sorrowe sees no light;
   My lights through sorrowe nothing see:
For now my sonne his course hath ronne,
   And from his sphere doth goe
To endless bed of foulded lead,   [15]
   And who can blame my woe?

.   .   .   .

IV

Not I, poor I alone — (alone
   How can this sorrowe be?)   [25]
Not onely men make mone, but
   More than men make mone with me:
The gods of greenes, the mountain queenes,
   The fairy circled rowe,   [30]
The muses nine, and power devine,
   Do all condole my woe.   [III, 357-59]

PROSE PRAYERS, MEDITATIONS, CONFESSIONS AND PROFESSIONS OF FAITH

The introduction of the printing press to England in 1476 led to the availability to ordinary laypeople of a mass of earnest materials by scholars and divines who established or refuted religious distinctions and exhorted conformity to one or another pattern of behavior through translations, discussions, and debates. An example of this type of exhortation, found in a preface by Richard Hyrde, is labeled "the first Renaissance document in English on the education of women."[20] In this preface, probably addressed to More's niece, Frances Staverton, Hyrde stated:

[Learning] sheweth the ymage and wayes of good lyvynge evyn right as a myrrour sheweth the symylitude and proporcion of the body. . . . I never herde tell, nor reed of any woman well lerned that ever was . . . spotted or infamed as vicious. But on the otherside, many by their lernyng taken, such encrease of goodnesse, that many may beare them wytnesse of their vertue. . . . Therfore, good Fraunces, . . . take no hede unto the leud wordes of those that dispreyse it [learning] . . . whiche Plato the wyse philosopher calleth a bridell for yonge people against vice. . . . Wherfore . . . applye all your myght, wyll & dilygence, to optayne that especiall treasure, whiche is delectable in youthe, comfortable in age, and profytable at all seasons: Of whom, without doute, cometh moche goodnesse and vertue.[21]

That some women accepted theories and standards such as these is proved irrefutably by their own lay writings on the same subjects, which clearly accept and echo the new ideals being preached to them. Indeed, the religious writings of Englishwomen swelled from a trickle during the Middle Ages to a large stream between the years 1500 and 1640.[22]

Although translated works by Renaissance Englishwomen are not considered in this chapter, a few words should be devoted to two remarkable women whose known works were limited to translations of religious materials.[23] These are a mother and daughter, Margaret Roper (1501-1544), the most famous of the daughters of Sir Thomas More, and her daughter, Mary Bassett (fl. 1553-1558). Mrs. Roper was educated with her brother, sisters, and some other young people in an experimental academy in the More home. She and her sisters were celebrated as children for their prodigious learning, which was coupled with religious humility. Margaret seems to have been the source of special pride to her father. Their correspondence and visits during the time of his imprisonment, and the legend that she preserved his severed head and had it buried with her, indicate their close relationship. Among the products of her pen was a translation of Erasmus' Latin *Pater Noster* into English; the excellence of this work inspired the famous preface by Hyrde (quoted above) on women's education. In the same preface, Hyrde notes,

that with her [Mrs. Roper's] vertuous, worshipfull, wyse, and well lerned husbande, she hath by the occasyon of her lernynge and his delyte therin, suche especiall comforte, pleasure and pastyme, as were nat well possyble for one unlerned couple, eyther to take togyther, or to conceyve in their myndes, what pleasure is therin.[24]

William Roper never remarried after his wife's death at forty-three years of age. Within her home, Margaret lived a model life: her closeness to her husband has already been noted, and she was known by her contemporaries for the careful nurture of her children. Sir Thomas More, while eager to provide his daughters with a fine education, was unconcerned with providing any outlet outside the home for the abilities he helped them to develop. And there were no complaints by Margaret on this score. Indeed, she set aside a prodigious translation from Greek to Latin of Eusebius' ecclesiastical history, although she had intended to publish it, when she learned that Bishop Christopherson was attempting the same feat.[25]

The youngest of her daughters, Mary Bassett, carried the family tradition of learning, piety, and closeness one generation further by translating her grandfather's unfinished exposition of the Passion from Latin to English; her translation was included in the 1557 edition of More's works.[26] That she maintained her grandfather's ideals of modesty is indicated by the following comment by the printer:

Somewhat I had to doo, ere that I could come by thys boke. For the gentlewoman which translated it seemed nothing willing to have it goe abrode, for that (she sayth) it was firste turned into englishe, but for her own pastyme and exercyse, and so reputeth it farre to symple to come into many handes.[27]

The original prose works on religion by Renaissance Englishwomen can be divided into two categories—learned tracts and creative works. The tracts are not included here because they are more appropriately the province of the theologian.[28] However, the prefatory letters to many of these works are included in chapter 3 as undistorted expressions of the conscious thinking of these women. The writings presented here were composed by writers attempting to articulate their personal relationship with God; they are usually addressed to the Deity, and they pulsate with the fervor of the writer. These writings are in the tradition of two of the earliest English literary works by women which are extant: the mystical *Revelations of Divine Love*, by the Anchoress Juliana of Norwich,[29] and the *Boke of Margary Kempe*, by the religious enthusiast Margary Kempe,[30] who visited and conferred with the anchoress at the beginning of her own career. Juliana's *Revelations* is a work of great intrinsic merit; Margary Kempe's *Boke*, which was written by an amanuensis at Margary Kempe's dictation, has historical importance as the earliest known autobiography in English. For possibly the most significant writings on religion by a Renaissance Englishwoman, the reader is directed to chapter 4 on Anne Askew.

ELIZABETH TUDOR, QUEEN OF ENGLAND (1533-1603)

The prayers composed by this astute and pragmatic ruler demonstrate the pervasiveness of religious sentiments among Renaissance women. They were preserved by Bentley in his *Monument of Matrones* (London: Thomas Dawson, 1582), Lampe 2, pp. 35-36.

Another praier made by hir Majestie, when she was in great feare . . .

Grant, O God, that the wicked may have no power to hurt or betraie me; neither suffer anie such treason and wickednesse to proceed against me. For thou, O God, canst mollifie all such tyrannous harts, and disappoint all such cruell purposes. And I beseech thee to heare me thy creature which am thy servant, and at thy commandement, trusting by thy grace ever so to remaine, Amen.   [p. 36]

Another praier and thankesgiving made by hir grace . . .

O Lord almightie, and everlasting God, I give thee most hartie thanks, that thou hast beene so mercifull unto me, as to spare mee, to behold this joiful daie. And I acknowledge, that thou hast dealt as woonderfully with me, as thou didst with thy true and faithfull servant Daniel the Prophet, whom thou deliveredst out of the den from the crueltie of the greedie, raging lions [Dan. 6:16 - 23]: even so was I overwhelmed, and onelie by thee delivered. To thee therfore be onlie thanks, honour and praise for ever and ever,

Amen.   [p. 36]

MISTRESS BRADFORD (fl. 1555)

Even the Christian name of the mother of John Bradford, the martyr, is unknown. The *DNB* states only that Bradford (d. 1555) came of "gentle parents in the parish of Manchester."[31]

The piety of Bradford's mother is poignantly attested to by the following prayer, preserved by Bentley in the *Monument of Matrones . . .* (1582), Lampe 2, p. 215.

The praier that maister Bradfords mother said and offered unto God in his behalfe, a little before his martyrdome

Ah good father, which dooest vouchsafe that my sonne John Bradford, being a greevous sinner in thy sight, should find this favour with thee, to be one of thy sonne Christ his captaines and men of war, to fight and suffer for his Gospels sake, I thanke thee: and praie thee in the same thy deere sonne Christs name, that thou wouldest forgive him his sinnes and unthankfulnesse; and make perfect in him that good which thou hast begun in him. Yea Lord, I praie thee make him worthie to suffer, not only imprisonment, but even verie death for thy truth, religion, and Gospell sake. As Hanna did applie, dedicate, and give hir first child and sonne Samuel unto thee [1 Sam. 1:11-2:11]: even so doo I deere father; beseeching thee, for Christs' sake, to accept this my gift; and give my sonne John Bradford grace alwaies trulie to serve thee, and thy people, as Samuel did; Amen: Amen.   [p. 215]

CATHERINE PARR, QUEEN OF ENGLAND (1512-1548)

Catherine Parr was the last of the successors to Catherine of Aragon as queen to Henry VIII. She was the daughter of Sir Thomas Parr of Westmoreland and was already widowed twice before attracting Henry's eye. After their marriage in 1543, she restored the spirit of sobriety and learning of the first Catherine to the by then dissolute court. Catherine's own mother "had devoted herself to the education of her children," the *DNB* notes, after being left a young widow, and Catherine had become an accomplished scholar as a young girl, a fact indicated both by her own writings and by the interest taken by her and the encouragement given by her "to the studies and education of her step-children."[32] Even more fundamental were the queen's efforts to improve the position and treatment of her stepdaughters, who had been harshly treated by their father for several years.

Catherine was so zealous in behalf of religious reform and became so influential with the king that she antagonized some powerful courtiers and clerics who schemed to bring about her downfall by convincing the king that she was dominating him. Because she was secretly informed about the plot, however, she was able to thwart it in a diplomatic conversation with Henry.[33]

Catherine wrote several works herself, and she published them under her own name to edify her fellow Christians. She was the first woman to publish her work in English with the intention of influencing the public. Her advice to the Princess Mary, which she did not heed, to publish her work under her own name (see chapter 2) therefore was consistent with her own behavior. The Princess Elizabeth engaged in a translation of Catherine's first work into Latin, French, and Italian, an effort indicating again the extent of Catherine's influence over her stepdaughters.

The following selections are taken from *Prayers or Meditacions . . .* (London: T. Berthelet, 1545), and from *Lamentacion or complaynt of a sinner . . .* (London: E. Whitchurche, 1547).

from *Prayers or Meditacions . . .*

Moste beninge lorde Jesu, graunt me thy grace, that it mai alway work in me, and persever with me unto the ende.

Graunt me, that I maie ever desyre and wille that whiche is most pleasaunte, and most acceptable to the.

Thy will be my will and my will be to folowe alway thy will.

Let there be alwaye in me oone wille, and one desire with the, and that I have no desire to wille or not will, but as thou wilte.

Lorde, thou knowest what thynge is moste profytable and moste expedient for me.

Gyve therfore what thou wilte, as muche as thou wilte, and whan thou wilt.

Dooe with me what thou wilte, as it shall please the, and as shal be moste to thyne honour.

Put me where thou wylte, and freely do with me in all thynges after thy wylle.

. . . .

O what thankes ought I to gyve unto the, whiche hast suffered the grevouse deathe of the crosse, to deliver me frome my synnes, and to obteyn everlastyng life for me.

Thou gavest us moste perfect example of pacience, fulfilling and obeying the will of thy father even unto the deathe.

Make me wretched sinner, obediently to use my selfe after thy wyll in all thynges, and paciently to beare the bourden of this corruptible lyfe. For though this life be tedious, & as an hevy burdein to my soule; yet nevertheles throughe thy grace, and by example of the, it is nowe made muche more easye and comfortable then it was before thy incarnacion and passyon.

Thy holy life is oure waye to the, and by folowynge of the, we walke to the, that arte our head and saviour: And yet excepte thou haddest gone before, and shewed us the waye to everlasting lyfe, who would endevoure hym selfe to folowe the? seynge we be yet so slowe and dull, havyng the light of thy blessed example & holy doctrine, to leade and directe us.

.   .   .   .

Lorde, I will knowlage unto the, all mine uprightuousnesse, and I wyll confesse to the all the unstablenesse of my herte.

Oftentymes a veraie litle thyng troubleth me sore, and maketh me dull and slow to serve the.

And sometyme I purpose to stande strongly, but whan a lytle truble cometh, it is to me great anguishe & grief, and of a right little thyng riseth a grevous temptacion to me.

Yea when I thinke my self to be sure and stronge, and that (as it semeth) I have the upper hand: sodenly I feele my selfe ready to fall with a littel blaste of temptacion.

Beholde therfore good lorde, my weakenesse, and consyder me [sic] frailenesse, best knowen to the.

.   .   .   .

[W]herfore lorde Jesu, I praye the, geve me the grace to rest in the above all thynges, and to quiete me in the above all creatures: above all glory and honoure, above all dignitie & power, above all cunnyng and policie, above al healthe and beautie, above all rychesse and treasure, above all joye and pleasure, above al fame & praise: above all myrthe and consolacion that mans hert maie take or feele besides the.

[sigs. A1-B3]

from *Lamentacion . . . of a sinner . . .*

When I considre, in the bethinking of myne evill, & wretched former life, myne obstynate, stony, and untractable herte, to have so much exceded in evilnes, that it hath not only neglected, yea contemned, & dispised goddes holy preceptes & commaundmentes: But also embrased, receyved, and estemed vayne, folish, and feyned tryfles: I am, partely ʰy the hate I owe to sinne, who hathe reygned in me, partely by the love I owe to all Christians, whom I am contente to edifye, even with thexample of mine owne shame, forced and constrayned with my harte and wordes, to confesse and declare to the world, howe ingrate, negligent, unkynde, and stubberne, I have bene to god my Creatour: and howe beneficiall, mercyfull, and gentill, he hath ben alwayes to me his creature, beyng suche a miserable, wreatched sinner. Truly I have taken no lytle small thing upon me, first to set furth my whole stubbernes, and contempt in wordes, the whiche is incomprehensible in thought (as it is in the Psalme) who understandeth his faultes? next this to declare the excellente beneficience, mercy & goodness of god. . . . Who is he that is not forced to confesse the same, if he consyder what he hath receyved of God, and dothe dayly receyve? Yea if men woulde not acknowledge, & confesse the same, the stones would crie it out . . . I counte my selfe

one of the moste wicked & myserable synners, bycause I have ben so much contrary to
Christ my saviour.

.   .   .   .

Beholde lorde howe I come to the, a sinner, sycke, & grevously wounded: I aske
not breade, but the crummes that fal from the childrens table. Cast me not oute of thy
sight, although I have deserved to be cast in to hell fier.

If I should looke upon my sinnes, and not upon thy mercy, I shoulde dispayre: for in
my selfe I fynde nothing to save me, but a donghill of wyckednes, to condemne me: . .
[T] he more I seke meanes & wayes to wind my selfe out, the more I am wrapped &
tangled therin. . . . It is the hand of the lord, that can & wyll bring me, out of this endles
mase of death. . . .

I know, O my lorde, thy eyes looke upon my fayth: Saynct Paule sayeth, we be justified by the fayth in Christe, & not by the deades of the lawe.

.   .   .   .

[T]hankes be geven unto the lorde, that hath now sent us suche a godly & learned
kynge in these latter dayes, to reygne over us, that with the vertue & force of goddes
wordes, hath taken awaye the vayles & mistes of errours, and brought us to the
knowledge of the truthe, by the lyghte of Goddes worde, whiche was so long hydden
and kepte under, that the people wer nigh famished & hungred for lacke of spiritual
foode: suche was the charitie of the spiritual curates & shepherdes. But our Moyses, &
moste godlye, wise governour, and king hath delyvered us oute of the captivitie and
bondage of Pharao. I meane by this Moyses, king Henry the eight, my most sovraigne
favourable lorde & husband. . . . And I mene by this Pharao the bishop of Rome, who
hathe bene, and is a greater persecutor of al true christians, then ever was Pharao, of
the children of Israel.

.   .   .   .

The true followers of Christes doctryne, hath alwayes a respecte, and an eye to theyr
vocacion. If they be called to the ministerie of Goddes word, they preache & teache it
sincerely, to the edifying of others, & shewe thym selfes in their living, folowers of the
same. If they be maried menne, havyng children and familie, they norish & bring them
up, without all bytternes, and fiercenes, in the doctryne of the lorde in al godlynes and
vertue. . . . If they be children, they honour theyr father & mother, knowyng it to be
goddes commaundement, and that he hath therto annexed a promise of long life. If
they be servauntes, they obey and serve theyr masters with al feare and reverence,
even for the lordes sake. . . . If they be husbandes, they love their wifes, as theyr owne
bodies, after the example as Christ loved the congregacion, and gave hym selfe for it,
to make it to hym a spouse, without spot or wrinkle. . . . Yf they be women maryed,
they lerne of Saynt Paule, to be obedient to theyr husbandes, and to keepe silence in
the congregacion, & to learne of theyr housbandes, at home. Also they weare suche
apparel as becummeth holines, and comly usage, with sobernes: . . . [T]hey teache
honest thinges, to make the yong women sobre minded, to love theyr husbandes, to
love theyr children, to be discrete, chast, huswiflie, good, obedient unto theyr husbandes: that the worde of god be not evil spoken of. Verely yf all sortes of people
would loke to theyr owne vocacion, and ordeyne the same accordyng to Christes
doctrine we should not have so many eyes & eares to other mennes fautes as we
have. . . .

God knoweth of what intent and minde I have lamented mine owne sinnes, & fautes, to the worlde. I trust no bodye will judge I have doon it for prayse, or thanke of any creature, since rather I might be ashamed then rejoyce in rehersall therof. For yf they knowe howe litle I esteme, and wey the prayse of the worlde, that opinion were soone removed & taken awaye: I seeke not the prayses of the same, neither to satisfie it, none other wise, then I am taught by Christ to dooe, according to Christen charitie. . . . I beseche god we may . . . be founde suche faythfull servauntes, and loving children, that wee maye heare the happy, comfortable & most joyfull sentence, ordeyned for the children of God, whiche is: Come hither ye blessed of my father, and receyve the kingdom of heaven, prepared for you before the beginning of the world [Luke 18:16]: Unto the Father, the Sonne, and the Holy goste, be all honour & glory worlde without ende. Amen.

Finis. [sigs. A1-H3]

LADY JANE (GREY) DUDLEY (1538-1554)

The pathetic history of Lady Jane Grey, England's "nine days' queen," is widely known and needs only brief recapitulation here. Both young Lady Jane and her husband, Lord Guilford Dudley, were sacrificed to the ambition of the duke of Northumberland, his father, who had Lady Jane (the great-granddaughter of Henry VII) proclaimed queen of England on July 10, 1553, following the death of Edward VI. On July 19, Mary Tudor entered London and was proclaimed queen; Lady Jane and her husband were imprisoned in the Tower and beheaded six months later. Lady Jane's acquiescence in her father-in-law's plot is easily understood in the context of the obedience and subservience expected of women of the time. And through an anecdote related by the famous educator Roger Ascham, we know that Lady Jane's upbringing was extremely rigid and severe and was relieved chiefly by the pleasure she took in study with a gentle tutor. Ascham tells that he came upon Lady Jane reading Plato in her study while her family was out hunting, and that she stated that, "[A]ll their Sporte in the Parke is but a shadow to that pleasure that I find in Plato . . . [for her parents] so sharply taunted, so cruelly threatened yea presently sometimes with pinches, Nips, and Bobs, and other ways . . . that I thinke myself in Hell till time come that I must go to Mr. Elmer; who teacheth me so gently . . . that I thinke all the Time nothing, while I am with him."[34] Lady Jane was celebrated for her skill in languages and literature; she was also a correspondent of such leading theologians as Heinrich Bullinger and was herself a devout Protestant. Her piety is attested to in the famous letters presented in chapter 2 and in the following touching verses. These lines, composed in Latin, were written by the Lady Jane on her cell wall with a pin and were preserved by John Foxe:

Do never think it straunge,
Though now I have misfortune,
For if that fortune chaunge,
The same to thee may happen.
Jane Dudley

If God do helpe thee,
Hate shall not hurte thee.
If God do fayle thee,
Then shall not labor prevayle thee.[35]

Three compositions follow, dating from the Lady Jane's imprisonment, and also taken from John Foxe, *Actes and monuments of these latter and perillous dayes* (London: John Daye, 1563).

A certaine prayer made of the Lady Jane in the time of her trouble

O Lorde, thou god and father of my lyfe, here me a pore and desolate woman, which fleeth unto the only in all troubles and miseries. Thou, o Lorde, art the only defendor and deliverer of those that put their trust in the: and therfore, I being defiled with sinne, encombered with affliction, unqueeted with troubles, wrapped in cares, overwhelmed with miseries, vexed with temptations, and grevousllye tormented with the long imprisonment of thys vile masse of clay my body and bloude, do com unto thee, o merciful saviour, craving thy mercy and helpe: without the which so littel hope of deliverance is left, that I maye utterly despayre of any liberty. Albeit it is expedient, that seing our lyfe standeth upon trying, we shuld be visited sometime with som adversity, whereby we might both be tried whether we be of thy flock or no, & also know the & ourselves the better: yet thou that saidst thou wouldest not suffer us to be tempted above our power, be mercyful unto me now a miserable wretche, I besech thee; which, with Solomon, do cry unto the, humbly desiring the, that I maye neither be to much puffed up with prosperity, neither to much pressed down with adversitie [1 Kings 3:6-9]; leaste I, beeing too full, should denye thee, my God, or, being to low brought, should despayre, and blaspheme thee, my Lorde and Saviour. O mercyfull God consider my misery best knowen unto the, and be thou nowe unto me a strong tower of defence. I humbly require thee, suffer me not to be tempted above my power, but eyther be thou a deliverer unto me out of thys great miserye, either els geve me grace paciently to beare thy heavy hand and sharpe correction. It was thy ryght hand, that delyvered the people of Israel out of the hands of Pharao, which for the space of iiii. C. yeares did oppresse them, and kepe them in bondage. Let it therfore likewise seame good to thy fatherly goodnes, to deliver me, sorrowfull wretch, (for whome thy sonne Christe shed his most precious bloud on the crosse,) out of thys miserable captivitie and bondage, wherin I am now. Howe long wylt thou be absent? for ever? O Lord, hast thou forgotten to be gracious, and hast thou shut up thy loving kindnes in displeasure? wilt thou be no more entreated? Is thy mercy clean gone for ever, and thy promise come utterly to an end for ever more? Why dost thou make so longe taring? Shall I despaire of thy mercy O god? Farre be that from me. I am thy workemanship, created in Christ Jesus: geve me grace, therfore, to tary thy leasure, and paciently to beare thy workes, assuredly knowing, that as thou canst, so thou wylte, delyver me, when it shall please the, nothing doubting or mistrusting thy goodnes towardes me; for thou wottest better what is good for me then I do: Therfore, doe with me in all thinges what thou wylt, & plage me what way thou wylt: Onley in the meane time arme me, I besech thee, with thy armour, that I maye stand fast, my loynes being gyrded about with veritie, having on the brestplate of ryghteousnes, & shod with the shoes prepared by the Gospel of peace; above all thynges takyng to me the shylde of fayth, where-with I may be able to quenche all the fiery dartes of the wicked, and takyng the helmet of salvation, and the swerde of the spirite, which is thy moste holy worde: praying alwayes with all maner of prayer and supplication, that I maye alwayes referre my selfe to thy wyll, abidyng thy pleasure, and comforting my selfe in those troubles that it shall please thee to sende me; seyng suche troubles be profitable for me, and seyng I am assuredly perswaded, that it cannot be but well, all that thou doest. Heare me, O mercifull father, for his sake, whom thou woldest should be a sacrifice for my synnes to whom with thee and the holy ghoste, be all honour and glory. Amen. [pp. 919-20]

from *The Communication had betwene the Lady Jane and Fecknam*

Feck: What is then required in a Christian?
Jane: That he should beleeve in god the father, the sonne, and the holye ghost, three persons and one god.
Feck: What? is there nothing els to bee required or looked for in a Christian, but to beleve in God?
Jane: yes, we muste beleve in him, we muste love him with all our heart, al our soule, and with all our minde, and our neighbour as our selfe.
Feck: Why? then fayth justifieth not, nor saveth not?
Jane: Yes verely, fayth (as Saint Paule sayeth) onely justifieth.

. . . .

Feck: Why? then it is necessarie unto salvacion to doe good workes also, and it is not sufficient onely to beleve?
Jane: I deny that and I affirme that fayth only saveth; but it is mete for a Christian, in token that he dothe followe his maister Christ, to doe good workes: yet may we not say, that they profit to salvation. For when we have done all, yet we be unprofitable servauntes, and the faith onely in Christes bloud saveth.
Feck: How many sacramentes are there?
Jane: Two. The one the sacrament of baptisme, and thother the sacrament of the lordes supper. . . . By the sacramente of Baptisme, I am washed with water, and regenerated in the spirite, and that washyng is a token to me that I am the chyld of God: The Sacramente of the Lordes Supper offered unto me, is a sure seale and testimonye that I am, by the bloud of Christe, whiche he shedde for me on the crosse, made partaker of the everlastyng Kyngdome.
Feck.: Why? what doe you receive in that sacrament? Do you not receyve the very body & bloude of Christ?
Jane: No surely, I doe not so beleve. I thynke that at the supper, I neyther receyve fleshe nor bloude, but onely breade and wyne. [pp. 917-18]

These are the words that the Lady Jane spake upon the Skaffolde at the houre of her death

First when she mounted upon the skaffolde she said to the people standing there about, I am come hether to dye, and by a law I am condempned to the same. The fact

agaynst the Quenes highnes was unlawfull and the consenting therunto by me: but
touching the procurement and desire therof by me or on my behalfe, I do washe my
handes there of in innocency before god, and the face of you (good Christian people)
this daye: and therewith she wrong her handes, wherin she had her boke. Then sayd
she, I praye you all, good Christian people, to beare me witnes that I dye a true christian
woman, and that I do loke to be saved by no other meane, but only by the mercye of
God in the bloude of hys only sonne Jesus Christe: and I confesse that when I dyd
know the word of God, I neglected the same, loved my selfe, and the world, and
therfore this plage and ponyshment is happely and worthely happened unto me for my
synnes: and yet I thanke god of hys goodnes that he hath thus gyven me a time and
respect to repent, and now (good people) while I am alyve I pray you assiste me with
your prayers. And then kneling down she turned her to Fecknam sayng: shall I saye
this psalme? and he sayd, yea, Then sayd she the psalme of miserere mei deus in
Englysh, in most devoute manour through out to thende, and then she stode up and
gave her mayden Mistres Ellyn her gloves and handkerchef, and her boke to Maister
Bruges, wherewith she untied her gowne, and the hangman pressed upon her to help
her of with it, but she desyring hym to lette her alone, turned towardes her two gentlewomen who helped her of therwith, and also with her frowes paste and neckerchefe,
giving to her a fayre handkerchefe to knyt about her eyes. Then the hangman kneled
down, and asked her forgyvenes, whome she forgave most willingly. Then he willed
her to stand upon the strawe, which doing she sawe the block. Then she sayd, I pray
you dispatch me quickly. Then she kneeled downe, saying: will you take it of before I
laye me downe? and the hangman sayd, no Madam. Then tyed she the kerchefe about
her eyes, and feling for the blocke she sayd, what shal I do, where is it? wher is it? one
of the standers by guiding her therunto, she layd her head downe upon the blocke,
and then stretched forth her body and sayd, Lord into thy handes I commend my
spirit. And so fynished her lyfe, in the yeare of our Lorde God 1553 the 12. daye of
February.   [p. 919]

KATHERINE (EMMES) STUBBES (1571?-1590)

   Katherine Emmes, the daughter of a cordwainer, married Philip Stubbes, a
zealous Puritan, in 1586 at the age of fifteen. At nineteen, she fell victim to
some complication of child-birth, a few weeks after the delivery of her first
child. In a work written a few years later, Stubbes eulogized his young wife as
a model matron. She had been notably pious throughout the four and a half
years of her marriage; he wrote, "[w]hen she was not reading, she was
conferring, talking, and reasoning with her husband of the word of God, and
of religion." She had been a "Myrrour of womanhood" by the standards of
her time in following the exhortations which "biddeth us to search the Scriptures, . . . biddeth women to bee silent, and to learne of their husbandes, . . .
[and to] suffer no disorder or abuse in her house, . . . [to be] curteous of
nature, . . . [She was] never heard to give any the lie . . . never knowne to fall
out with any of her neighbours, . . . seldome or never . . . except her husband
were in companie goe abroad with any . . ."   [sig. A2]

   During her last sickness, Mrs. Stubbes requested that her neighbors be
brought into her home so that she might confess publicly. Portions of her

supposed verbatim confession, with an appended report of her vanquishing of Satan, follow. These appeared in the memorial tract by her husband, *A Christal Glas for Christian Women . . .* (1592).

from *A most heavenly confession of the Christian faith*

Although the Majestie of God, bee both infinite and unspeakable, and therefore according to his excellent dignitie, can neither bee conceived in heart, nor expressed in words: yet to the end you may knowe what that God is, in whome I beleeve, as farre as he hath revealed himselfe unto us in his holy word, I will define him unto you, as the spirit of God shal illuminate my heart. I beleeve therfore with my heart, and freely confesse with my mouth, here before you all, that this God in whom I beleeve, is a most glorious spirite, or spirituall substance, a divine essence, or essential being, without beginning or ending, of infinite glorie, power, might and Majestie, invisible, inaccessible, incomprehensible, and altogether unspeakable . . . divided into a trinitie of persons the father, the sonne, and the holy spirit, distant onely in names and offices, but all one, and the same, in nature, in essence, substance, deitie, majestie, glory, power, might and eternitie. . . . I beleeve and confesse that this God ordereth and disposeth al things according to his good pleasure and will, and that he also foreseeth all things by his providence and prescience. . . . I constantly beleeve and confesse, that God the Father in the multitude of his mercies, when the fulnesse of tyme was come, sent his owne Sonne, Christ Jesus, foorth of his owne bosome into this miserable world, to take our nature upon him, and that in the wombe of a Virgine, without spot or blemish of sinne, and without the helpe of man by the wonderfull operation and overshadowing of the holy ghost.

And as I constantly beleeve that Jesus Christ is come in the flesh . . . so I unfaignedly beleeve, that he hath offered up his blessed bodie upon the aulter of the Crosse, as a sacrifice propiciatorie, satisfactorie, and expiatorie, for the sinnes of the whole world, and for me the chiefest of all sinners: . . . I trust and beleeve to be saved, and . . . to be set free, & pardoned of all my sinnes whatsoever . . . if the Lord should wey my very righteousnes in the ballance of his justice, rewarding mee according to the same, I should receive nothing but just damnation for my deserts.

. . . .

Further, I beleeve and confesse, that my soule, and the soules of al the elect children of God, immediately after their departure out of their bodyes, doe goe into the kingdome of heaven, into the hands of God, . . . thither are all the soules of the children of God, that die in the true fayth of Jesus Christ, received immediately after their departure hence. . . . I beleeve also and confesse, that man is justified . . . by the true and lively faith in the bloud of Christ onely, and not by his workes, merits, righteousnesse, or deserts. . . .

. . . .

I beleeve and confesse, that Jesus Christ hath left, not onely the holy Scriptures to instruct and teach his Church, but also Sacraments, in number two: to wit, Baptisme, and the Lords Supper. . . .

. . . This is my faith, this is my hope & this is my trust, this hath the spirite of God taught me, and this have I learned out of the booke of God. And (good Lord) that hast begun this good worke in me, finish it, I beseech thee: and strengthen me that I may persevere therin to the ende, and in the end, through Jesus Christ my onely Lord and Saviour.   [sigs. B-C3]

[After confessing, Katherine Stubbes repulsed an assault by Satan.]

from *A most wonderfull, conflict betwixt Sathan and her soule*

How Now Satan? what makest thou here? Art thou come to tempt the Lords servant? I tell thee, thou hell-hound, thou hast no part nor portion in me: nor by the grace of God never shalt have. I was, now am, and shall be the Lords for ever. . . . [T]herefore thou maist get thee packing, thou damned Dog, and goe shake thine eares, for in me thou hast nought. But what doest thou lay to my charge, thou foul fiend? Oh that I am a sinner, and therefore shall be damned: I confesse in deed that I am a sinner, and a grievous sinner, both by originall sinne, and actuall sinne, and that I may thanke thee for. And therefore Satan I bequeath my sin to thee, from whom it first came, and I appeale to the mercy of God in Christ Jesus.

                              .   .   .   .

But what sayest thou more, Satan? Doest thou aske me how I dare come to him for mercy, hee being a righteous God, and I a miserable sinner: I tell thee Satan, I am bold through Christ, to come unto him, being assured and certaine of pardon and remission of all my sinnes for his names sake. . . . What more, Satan? Doest thou say, it is written, that God will rewarde every one according to his workes, or according to his desertes? But it is written againe (thou deceiptfull devill) that Christes righteousnesse, is my righteousnesse, . . . and his precious bloud a full satisfaction for al my sins. . . . And therefore avoid Satan, . . . tempt me no more, for he that is with me, is mightier then thou. . . . Now am I happy & blessed for ever, for I have fought the good fight, and by the might of Christ have won the victory. Now from henceforth shal I never tast neither of hunger nor cold, paine nor wo: misery nor affliction: vexation or trouble: feare nor dread: nor of any other calamity, or adversity whatsoever. From henceforth is layd up for me a crowne of life, which Christ shall give to those that love him. And as I am nowe in possession thereof by hope, so shall I be anon in ful fruition therof by presence of my soule, and hereafter of my body also, when the Lorde shall please. . . . After which words, very suddenly she seemed as it were greatly to rejoice . . . and lifting up her whole bodie, and stretching forth both her armes, as though she would embrace some glorious and pleasant thing, said: I thanke my God, through Jesus Christ, he is come, hee is come, my good Jayler is come to let my soule out of prison. Oh sweete death thou art welcome, welcome sweet death, never was there any guest so welcome to me as thou art. Welcome, the messenger of everlasting life; welcome the doore and entrance into everlasting glorie: Welcome, I say, and thrise welcome, my good Jayler, do thy office quickly, and set my soule at libertie. Strike (sweet death) strike my heart, I feare not thy stroke. Now it is done. Father into thy blessed hands I commit my spirit. Sweet Jesus into thy blessed hands I commend my spirite. Blessed spirite of God, I commit my soule into thy handes. Oh most holy, blessed, and glorious Trinitie, three persons and one true and everlasting God, into thy blessed hands I commit both my soule and my bodie, at which words her breath stayed, and so neither mooving hand nor foote, she slept sweetly in the Lord.   [sigs. C3-C4]

BESSIE CLERKSONE (d. 1625)

Like the *Boke of Margary Kempe*, and the *Confession* of Katherine Stubbes, the *Conflict in Conscience . . . of Bessie Clerksone* was transcribed by another's hand. In a prefatory letter, "To the Christian Reader," Bessie's amanuensis, her minister, William Livingstone, explains that the conversations he recorded took place over the last years of Bessie's life. He states, too, that he is setting this account in print to correct an earlier, unauthorized version, in which, "my wordes are made hers at sometimes, and hers mine" [sig. A2]. Therefore, the reader is assured that this account of Bessie's words and thoughts is genuine. Bessie's *Conflict* presents a striking contrast to the more learned and more polished—but no less heartfelt—*Lamentacion* of Catherine Parr. Its existence shows the pervasiveness of the new thinking on religion in the different classes of Renaissance society.

The following excerpts from Clerksone's conversations are taken from William Livingstone, *The Conflict in Conscience of a deare Christian named Bessie Clerksone* (Edinburgh: J. Wreitton, 1631).

from *The Conflict in Conscience of . . . Bessie Clerksone*

Minister: Bessie how are you?
Bessie: I finde the wrath of an angry GOD, of a crabbed GOD, and all the wrath that you preached, which comes on mee now. . . .

I am not a devill to contemne God, and I cannot get faith to believe in GOD.

.   .   .   .

Min.: It is a degree of faith to finde the want of faith, it is a step to a greater growth.
Bessie: Will yee speake to mee as yee should, and say, thou wretched sinfull, and wicked woman, and not tell mee sweete words.
[Min:] I answered her, No Bessie, I must not measure you as yee doe your self by your owne sense, but to teach you to hope above hope;

[Bessie] Cease, said shee, I am but a dog, and worse nor a dog; Gods wrath is on me, for my invisible sinnes, and if I were away, there would be none but Christians on the earth: I know Christ would goe betwixt mee and all my sinnes, but one . . . despaire.

.   .   .   .

Bes: Is it God that doth this to mee. Can God spoyle himselfe? I had faith and prayer, now they are reft, couped [i.e., exchanged] and spoyled: can God doe it? will God rob himselfe? will hee take away the matter of his owne glorie? I am ashamed to looke any man in the face: I have lost the favour of God & man. *O for a drop of grace! O for as much faith as a graine of mustard seede* [Matt. 17:20]!

.   .   .   .

[Min.] When I told her of GODS dealing with his owne by diverse sorts of trouble in minde, body, and estate. Shee answereth, No trouble to the trouble in minde. I care not, said shee, for legges, armes, eyes and all the rest, if I could get comfort in the blood of Jesus. . . .

Bes: I have no pleasure in any thing, neither in husband nor childe: I can doe nothing but sinne, by life is all sinne. . . . [W]hy live I then? I can not die, said shee, I cannot live, they will burie a carcase, will they burie mee, a carcase of sinne: yea sinne it selfe.

. . . .

O that I could get that fountaine of faith, a sterne of it! O as grace wold grow! O for a blessed blinck of the favourable face of the Father of the faithfull! O to winne to that holy fountaine! I know hee is readie to give, if I were readie to receave and seeke. . . .

I want faith, said shee, I know the sinne of man is not so great, but GODS mercie is greater to forgive it, where they can repent and believe. But I have not this grace of my selfe, and God gives mee it not: Pray that ye may be preserved from the perill and plague that is come on mee.

. . . .

Bes: Happie (said shee) are they who suffer for Christs sake, for righteousnesse sake, they will be comforted now and then: but they that suffer for sinne, without sense of his favour, comfortlesse is their condition. Will one goe through the earth, up and down, to & fro, where will they find a wearied wight till they come to mee. And you that heare mee, with the pith of prayer that I can, I aske of God that yee never knowe the waye that I am in: It is lacke of faith that is my losse, want of faith is my wracke, I ly under fearefull weights, and wanteth faith to get the remission of them. I am fallen without a resurrection: . . . I find not a sparke of light, and I find no fruit of your prayers, albeit I heare them: No Christian should come neere mee.

. . . .

Now as for the end of this conflict, and death of this deare daughter of Abraham in Apryle 1625. . . . [D]eath on a suddaintie delt with her heart, that her words and speach failed her: but in presence of diverse witnesse, her hands and eyes were heaved to the heavens, and so giving that signe of victorie, shee randered her spirit: . . . I am sure there is none that is illuminate from above, & taught to discerne spiritually, that will any way dout of her blessed deliverance, albeit no outward signe had bene seene. . . . [pp. 1-4]

2 FAMILIAL AND PERSONAL WRITINGS

DURING the English Renaissance, the humanists and the Protestant reformers expressed an appreciation of the state of marriage and the value of domestic life. Interest in problematic aspects of marriage was generated and increased by the well-publicized marital problems of Henry VIII, and by differences between the Catholics and the Protestants concerning these problems. Protestants, particularly, developed the concept of the home as a "school of faith" in which the parents should teach proper Christian values to their children. Among the results of these developments over the years of the Renaissance were an increased respect for the married woman and particular appreciation of her importance in child nurture.[1] In short, there was the development of a "new mother" who was a learned, pious, and responsible woman with increased and clear-cut responsibilities for the raising of her children as well as a clearly recognized right to self-development for her own sake.

The recognition, in the Renaissance, of the importance of the mother's influence, which today seems obvious and even restrictive, must be appreciated as an advance over medieval thinking, which charged the father with the responsibility for the education of the children.[2] There were few medieval tracts on women's instruction in English, and most of those written were intended for women entering the religious life.[3] However, one tract, entitled *The Northern Mothers Blessing* (1420), confirms and illustrates that the training and aspirations of medieval laywomen were limited to narrow and unlettered goals.[4]

Conversely, the historical existence of illustrious sixteenth- and seventeenth-century Englishwomen, who were noted for the careful raising of their children, is a fact that can be explained in the light of the development of the new theories of the humanists and reformers concerning mothers.[5] Among extant writings by Renaissance Englishwomen are some illuminating writings on motherhood by Renaissance mothers.

These writings demonstrate not only the solicitude of the mothers for the spiritual well-being of their children, but the humility and submissiveness of the writers, who did not consider themselves the equals of men and did not consider themselves entirely free to write books offering advice.

As literature, the quality of these materials varies. There are sections within these tracts that detail minutiae of religious observance and fine theological distinctions tedious to the modern reader of literature. There are also portions that are eloquent, fervent, and touching. Indeed, these sections raise the tracts above the literary level of those by the men who inspired them, perhaps by virtue of the fact that the writings of the mothers are more intimate creations addressed directly and warmly to a reader, with whom the mother felt a special closeness.

Like the tracts on motherhood, the diaries and personal letters presented in the second part of this chapter demonstrate a compliance, on the part of the writers, with the religious and educational ideals of the humanists and reformers. They also constitute evidence of the subordinated position of women in Renaissance English society.

MOTHERS WRITING ON MOTHERHOOD

The theories of the Renaissance humanists concerning the mother found their main expression in the writings of Juan Luis Vives. In his *Instruction of a Christen Woman*, dedicated to Queen Catherine, Vives, attempting to fit his newly learned woman into the private sphere, stated that a mother should "study . . .[if] nat for her own sake, at the least wyse for her chyldren, that she maye teache them and make them good. . . . For that age [childhood] can do nothynge it selfe but counterfayte and folowe other, and . . . taketh [its] fyrst conditions and information of mynde [from the] mother. . . . Therfore it lyeth more in the mother, than men wene, to make the condi- tions of the chyldren."[6] It was through her own prior learning that the mother would be enabled to fulfill this responsibility; for, as Vives stated with typical humanist fervor, "[t]he study of lerning is such a thing, that it occupieth ones mind holly, and lifteth it up . . . from the remembraunce of such thinges as be foul" (p. 8). These same ideas are expressed in Vives's other writings and in the writings of the other humanists.[7]

William Gouge may be taken as typical of the religious reformers, another group of revolutionary thinkers. In his encyclopedic tract, *Of Domesticall Duties*, Gouge states, "Mothers should teach their children; especially when they are young. . . . For while the children are young, their mother is most in their sight. . . . Her precepts and practise in that respect are best heeded by the children, and she hath the best opportunity to persuade them to what she liketh best, so as what they learn in the younger years, commonly they learr of their mothers—and that which they learn, for the most part sticketh mos close unto them, and is longest retained by them."[8]

The writings on motherhood by English Renaissance mothers are persona even intimate, and are addressed by individual women to individual childre under individual circumstances. However, despite their variations, the tracts considered as a group do yield a consistent accumulation of evidence and suggestion on the thinking of Renaissance English mothers. The fact that all these tracts on child-rearing are expressive of deep feelings, clearly voiced, is beyond question. And the basis for this strong emotion would seem to lie in the integration of natural maternal feeling with the religious and intellectual development of women advanced through the theory of the "new mother."

The development of the role of the "new mother" was central to the expectations and experience of the Renaissance woman, who, in the context of Renaissance reality, would expect one day to find the outlet for her creative, spiritual, and intellectual needs and drives in her experience as a mother. Because educated English mothers of the Renaissance were theoretically restricted to the outlets of child nurture and private religion, there was a potential of incompatibility[9] and conflict between the sense of maternal duty and the need for submission. This conflict is realized by the writers of tracts who wrote knowing that they overstepped themselves by writing. Their writings on motherhood illuminate the intimate connection, during the English Renaissance, between the development of woman's spirituality and her application of her increased spiritual resources to her domestic, and particularly to her maternal, role. They represent the essence of the thinking of the "new mother," who was the most liberated female developed in the English Renaissance in what was still a family-centered, religiously oriented time.[10]

ELIZABETH (BERNYE) GRYMESTON (d. 1603)

Elizabeth Grymeston was the daughter of Martin Bernye of Gunton, Norfolk, and became the wife of Christopher Grymeston of Yorkshire. Her work, which was addressed to her only son, Bernye, and first printed after her death, is a specimen of a counseling tract to a child that portrays the writer very clearly. Indeed, Charlotte Kohler has stated that the tract is the "first autobiography of an Elizabethan woman's mind."[11] Certainly it is a transparent medium for Mrs. Grymeston's maternal solicitude, which is the explicit motive for her composition of the work. The tract is divided into fifteen short chapters, which are heavily laden with quotations chiefly from the church fathers and the classics, and often from contemporary English authors (particularly Catholics like herself). Most impressive as advice are two chapters of Pollonian adages: chapter 1, entitled "A short line how to levell your life," and chapter 15, the "Memoratives."

Among the most appealing qualities of Mrs. Grymeston's style are her directness and simplicity, her frequent use of arresting, concrete images, and her ability to assimilate and even to alter quotations from many sources for her own purposes. She is almost certainly the greatest writer among the women considered in this chapter; indeed, Kohler notes that the tract is similar to Burton's *Anatomy* on a smaller scale.[12] Its great strength, like that of the other tracts on motherhood, lies in the strong maternal feelings of the author, which, through the impetus of her sense of maternal responsibility and religious duty, are given eloquent expression by Mrs. Grymeston. That eloquence is amply demonstrated by the following selections, taken from *Miscelanae, Meditations, Memoratives* (London: Printed by M. Bradford for F. Norton, 1604).

from *Miscelanae, Meditations, Memoratives*

To her loving sonne Bernye Grymeston

My dearest sonne, there is nothing so strong as the force of love; there is no love so forcible as the love of an affectionate mother to hir naturall childe: there is no mother can either more affectionately shew hir nature, or more naturally manifest hir affection, than in advising hir children out of hir owne experience, to eschue evill, and encline them to do that which is good. Out of these resolutions, finding the libertie of this age to be such, as that *quicquid libet licet*, so men keep themselves from criminall offenses; and my mother's undeserved wrath so virulent, as that I have neither power to resist it, nor patience to endure it, but must yeeld to this languishing consumption to which it hath brought me: I resolved to breake the barren soile of my fruitlesse braine, to dictate something for thy direction, the rather for that as I am now a dead woman among the living, so stand I doubtfull of thy father's life; which albeit God hath preserved from eight severall sinister assaults, by which it hath been sought; yet for that I see that *Quem saepe transit casus, aliquando invenit*, I leave thee this portable *veni mecum* for thy counseller, in which thou maiest see the true portraiture of thy mothers minde, and finde something either to resolve thee in thy doubts, or comfort thee in thy distresse, hoping, that being my last speeches, they will be better kept in the conservance of thy memorie; which I desire thou wilt make a Register of heavenly meditations.

For albeit, if thou provest learned (as my trust is thou wilt; for that without learning man is but as an immortal beast) thou maiest happily thinke that if every Philosopher fetched his sentence, these leaves would be left without lines, yet remember withall, that as it is the best corne that is of greatest value in fewest pieces, so is it not the worst booke that hath moste matter in least words.

> The gravest wits, that most grave works expect,
> The qualitie, not quantitie respect.

And the spiders webbe is neither the better because woven out of his owne brest, nor the bees hony the worse, for that gathered out of many flowers; neither could I ever brooke to set downe that haltingly in my broken stile, which I found better expressed by a graver authority.

> God send thee too, to be a wits Camelion,
> That any author's colour can put on.

I have prayed for thee that thou mightest be fortunate in two houres of thy life time: In the houre of thy marriage, and at the houre of thy death. Marrie in thine owne ranke, and seeke especially in it thy contentment and preferment: let her neither be so beautifull, as that every liking eye shall levell at her; nor yet so browne, as to bring thee to a loathed bed. Deferre not thy marriage till thou commest to be saluted with a God speed you Sir, as a man going out of the world after fortie; neither yet to the time of

God keepe you Sir, whilest thou art in thy best strength after thirtie; but marrie in the time of you are welcome Sir, when thou art comming into the world. For seldome shalt thou see a woman out of hir owne love to pull a rose that is full blowen, deeming them alwaies sweetest at the first opening of the budde. It was *Phaedra* her confession to Hippolitus, and it holdes for trueth with the most. *Thesei vultus amo illos priores quostulit quondam iuvenis.* Let thy life be formall, that thy death may be fortunate: for he seldome dies well that liveth ill. To this purpose, as thou hast within thee Reason as thy Counsellor to perswade or disswade thee, and thy will as an absolute Prince with a *Fiat Vel Evitetur*, with a *Let it be done or neglected*; yet make thy conscience thy *censormorum*, and chiefe commander in thy little world. Let it call Reason to account whether she have subjected hir selfe against reason to sensuall appetites. Let thy *Will* be censured, whether hir desires have been chaste, or as a harlot she have lusted after hir owne delights. Let thy thoughts be examined. If they be good, they are of the spirit (quench not the spirit) if bad, forbid them entrance; for once admitted, they straight-waies fortifie; and are expelled with more difficultie, than not admitted.

> *Crush the serpent in the head,*
> *Breake ill egges yer they be hatched.*
> *Kill bad chickens in the tread*
> *Fledge [sic] they hardly can be catched.*
> *In the rising stifle ill,*
> *Lest it grow against thy will.*

For evill thoughts are the Divels harbingers; he never resteth, but where they provide his entertainment. These are those little ones whose braines thou must dash out against the rocke of true judgement   [Ps. 137:9]: for

> *As a false lover that thicke snares hath laide,*
> *T'intrap the honour of a faire yoong maid,*
> *When she (though little) listning eare affoords.*
> *To his sweet, courting, deepe affected words,*
> *Feeles some asswaging of his freezing flame,*
> *And sooths himselfe with hope to gain his game,*
> *And rapt with joy, upon this point persists,*
> *That parleing citie never long resists:*
> *Even so the serpent that doth counterfeit*
> *A guileful call t'allure us to his net,*
> *Perceiving us his flattering gloze disgest,*
> *He prosecutes, and jocund doth not rest,*
> *Till he have tri'd foot, hand, and head, and all,*
> *Upon the breach of this new battered wall.*

I could be content to dwell with thee in this argument: but I must confine my selfe to the limits of an epistle, *Quae non debet implere sinistram manum.* To which rule I doe the more willingly submit my selfe, for that the discourses following are motives to the same effect: which I pray thee use to peruse, even in that my affectionate love, which diffused amongst nine children which God did lend me, is now united in thee, whom God hath onely left for my comfort. And because God hath traduced thee with so

/iolent a spirit, as that *quicquid vis valdè vis*; therefore by so much the more it behoveth hee to deliberate what thou undertakest: to which purpose my desire is, that thou night be seasoned with these precepts in thy youth, that the practice of thy age may ave a taste of them. And because that it is incident to quicke spirits to commit rash ttempts: as ever the love of a mother may challenge the performance of her dutifull iilde; be a bridle to thy selfe, to restraine thee from doing that which indeed thou maiest doe: that thou maiest the better forbeare that which in trueth thou oughtest not to doe; for *haud cito progreditur ad maiora peccata, qui parua reformidat*; hee seldomest commits deadly sinne, that makes a conscience of a veniall scandall.

Thou seest my love hath carried me beyond the list I resolved on and my aking head and trembling hand have rather a will to offer than abilitie to go afoord further discourse. Wherefore with as many good wishes to thee, as good will can measure, I abruptly end, desiring God to blesse thee with sorrow for thy sinnes, thankfulnesse for his benefits, feare of his judgement, love of his mercies, mindfulnesse of his presence; that living in his feare thou maiest die in his favour, rest in his peace, rise in his power, remaine in his glorie for ever and ever.

Thine assured loving mother,
Elizabeth Grymeston   [pp. 1-5]

from *Chapter 1. A short line how to levell your life*

When thou risest, let thy thoughts ascend, that grace may descend: and if thou canst not weepe for thy sinnes, then weepe, because thou canst not weepe.

Remember that prayer is the wing wherewith thy soule flieth to heaven; and Meditation the eye wherewith we see God; and Repentance the Supersedea that dischargeth all bond of sinne.

Let thy sacrifice be an honest heart: offer it dayly at set houres, with that devotion that well it may shew, thou both knowest and acknowledgest his greatnesse before whom thou art. So carrie thy selfe as woorthie of his presence.

. . . .

Arme your selfe with that modestie that may silence that untemperate tongue, and controll that unchaste eye, that shall aime at passion.

Be mindfull of things past; Carefull of things present; Provident of things to come.

Goe as you would be met.

Sit as you would be found.

Speake as you would be heard: And when you goe to bed, read over the carriage of your selfe that day. Reforme that is amisse; and give God thanks for that which is orderly: and so commit thy selfe to him that keepes thee.   [sig. B2]

from *Chapter VIII. That feare to die is the effect of an evill life.*

Johannes Patriarch of Alexandria, whose frequent deeds of charity gave him this Epithete, to be called *Johannes Eleemosmarius*, having his tombe in building, gave his people in charge, that it should be left unfinished, and that everie day one should put him in minde to perfect it. His meaning was, that by the meanes having his thoughts fixed of the doore of death, he might the better prepare himselfe for the passage through it. The Pope—that day he is chosen, hath one comes to him with foure marble stones, as patterns to choose of which his tombe shall be built. . . . [H]e whose life was a studie to die, well knowes that death hath lost his tartenesse by passing through the veines of life: he feares not his cold sweats, nor forgoing gripes, but taketh them as throwes in childe-bed, by which our soule is brought out of a lothsome body into eternall felicitie. He heares not the divels, whose temptations he hath valiantly resisted: the grave is no horror to him, for he knowes he sowes the body in corruption to reape it againe in immortalitie. He that liveth well, shall make a good end, and in the day of death his decease shall be blessed, for he rests from his labours, and his works doe follow him. But to him that liveth ill, death is an ever dying death: he lies tormented with the pangues of the dying flesh, amazed with the corrosive fittes of the minde, frighted with terror of that is to come, grieved with remorse of that which is past, stung with the gnawing of a guiltie conscience, terrified with the rigor of a severe judge, vexed with approch of a lothsome sepulchre. They made their prison their paradise, their bellie their God, their appetite their guide: so sowing sinne, they reape miserie, trafficing vanities, they gaine griefe: detestable was their life, and damnable is their decease.   [sigs. D2-D3]

DOROTHY (KEMP) LEIGH (n.d.)

The motherly solicitude that had prompted Elizabeth Grymeston to write also was responsible for the composition of a work by Dorothy Leigh, a "Gentle-woman, not long deceased." The tract was intended as counsel for her sons, whose father had died, and it is divided into four parts. Part I is a dedication to the Princess Elizabeth, daughter of James I, asking that she preserve and protect the work so that Mrs. Leigh's sons might benefit from it.[13] Part II is a letter to her sons explaining the intentions behind her publication. This section is signed, "Your fearefull, faithfull, and carefull Mother, D.L." [sig. A6] Part III is a poem counseling the boys to model themselves on the pattern of the bee. Part IV, the largest section of the work, consists of forty-five chapters concerned with different areas of personal behavior about which Mrs. Leigh was "fearefull." Among Mrs. Leigh's stated objectives are the following: to teach her sons religion, to inspire her sons to write when they are older, and to inspire other women to be careful mothers. Indeed, Mrs. Leigh was intrepid enough to write that women should not "be ashamed to shew their infirmities, but . . . give men the first and chiefe place: yet let us labor to come in the second" (pp. 16-17).

Mrs. Leigh treats many of the subjects of the religious reformers, such as the choice of godly wives of the proper status, just treatment of the wife, the choice of proper names for one's children, and the inculcation of religious thought in them and in one's servants. There are several personal duties that are urged at great length; chief among these is the need for prayer (discussed at great length and in many chapters), the need for discussion of religion, for thankfulness for any of God's blessings, and for proper observance of the Sabbath. Mrs. Leigh expresses a hope that at least some of her sons will become preachers—if, that is, they will undertake that grave trust properly.

Her tract ends with a prayer for her sons: "And the blessing of God Almighty, the Father, the Son and the Holy Ghost be with you all, from this time, even to the end of the world. Amen" (p. 271).

The following selections are taken from *The Mothers Blessing . . .* (London: for John Budge, 1616).

from *The Mothers Blessing*

TO MY BELOVED Sonnes, George, John, and William Leigh, all things pertaining to life and godlinesse.
My children, God having taken your father out of this vale of teares, to his everlasting mercie in Christ, my selfe not onely knowing what a care hee had in his lifetime, that you should bee brought up godlily, but also at his death beeing charged in his Will, by the love and dutie which I bare him, to see you well instructed and brought up in knowledge, I could not choose but seeke (according as I was in dutie bound) to fulfill his will in all things, desiring no greater comfort in the world, then to see you grow in godlinesse, that so you might meete your father in Heaven, where I am sure he is, my selfe being a witnesse of his faith in Christ. And seeing my selfe going out of the world and you but comming in, I know not how to performe this dutie so well, as to leave you these few lines, which will shew you as well the great desire your Father had, both of your spirituall and temporall good, as the care I had to fulfill his will in this; knowing it was the last duty I should performe unto him. But when I had written these things unto you, and had (as I thought) something fulfilled your Fathers request, yet I could not see to what purpose it should tend, unlesse it were sent abroad to you: for should it bee left with the eldest, it is likely the yongest should have but little part in it. Wherfore, setting aside all feare, I have adventured to shew my imperfections to the view of the world, not regarding what censure for this shall bee laid upon me, so that herein I may shew my selfe a loving Mother and a dutifull wife. And thus I leave you to the protection of him that made you, and rest till death:
Your fearefull, faithfull, and carefull Mother,

D.L.   [sigs. A5-A7]

Chap. 2. *The first cause of writing, is a motherly affection.*

But lest you should marvell, my children, why I doe not according to the usual custome of women, exhort you by words and admonitions, rather then by writing: a thing so unusuall among us, and especially in such a time, when there bee so many godly bookes in the World, that they mould in some mens Studies, while their Masters are mard, because they will not meditate upon them; as many mens garments moth-cate in their Chests, while their Christian Brethren quake with cold in the street for want of covering; know therefore that it was the motherly affection that I bare unto you all, which made mee now (as it often hath done heretofore) forget my selfe in regard of you: neither care I what you or any shall thinke of me, if among many words I may write but one sentence, which may make you labour for the spiritual food of the soule, which must bee gathered every day out of the Word, as the children of Israel gathered Manna in the Wilderness [Exod. 16:16-21]. . . . For as the children of Israel must needs starve, except they gathered every day in the Wildernesse and fed of it: so must your soules, except you gather the spirituall Manna out of the Word every day, and feed of it continually: for as they by this Manna comforted their harts, strengthned their bodies, and preserved their lives; so by this heavenly Word of God, you shall comfort your soules, make them strong in faith, and grow in true godlinesse, and finally preserve them with great joy, to everlasting life, through faith in Christ; whereas, if you desire any food for your souls, that is not in the written Word of God, your soules dye with it even in your hearts and mouthes; . . . and there is no recovery for you.

[pp. 1-6]

ELIZABETH (KNEVET) CLINTON, COUNTESS OF LINCOLN (1574?-1630?)

The Countess, daughter of Sir Henry Knevet of Charlton, Wiltshire, married Thomas Clinton, who became the third earl of Lincoln. He predeceased her, and she was dowager-countess when she wrote her *Nurserie*. In this work, she states that she was the mother of eighteen children, and she also styles this tract "the first work of mine that ever came in print" (sig. A2), a comment suggesting that she wrote other works which were not published.

Essentially, the treatise consists of a series of justifications for breast-feeding. It is addressed by the Countess to her daughter-in-law, Briget, who did fulfill that responsibility, while the Countess herself did not (sig. A2, sigs. C4-D). Breast-feeding by the natural mother had been advocated with fervor by humanists and reformers alike. Their claim was that the child was influenced by the nature of the milk it imbibed.[14] The intense arguments of the Countess reflect the influence of these theorists.

Attention should be directed to the modesty of the Countess and to her hesitancy to publish her tract (sigs. C2-C3). An introductory verse by Thomas Lodge justifies her intentions:

> Blest is the land where Sons of Nobles raigne
> Blest is the land where Nobles teach their traine.
> To Church for blisse Kings, Queenes, should Nurses be.
> To state its blisse great Dames Babes nurse to see.
> Go then Great booke of Nursing plead the Cause.
> Teach High'st, low'st, all, its Gods and Natures lawes. (sig. A5)

The following selections are taken from *The Countesse of Lincolnes Nurserie* (Oxford: John Lichfield and James Short, 1622).

from *The Countesse of Lincolnes Nurserie*

To the Right Honourable and approved vertuous Lady: Briget Countesse of Lincolne.

For the better expressing & keeping in memore my Love, and your Worthiness; I doe offer unto your Ladyship: the first worke of mine that ever came in Print; because your rare example, hath given an excellent approbation to the matter contained in this

3ooke; for you have passed by all excuses, and have ventured upon, and doe goe on vith that loving act of a loving mother; in giving the sweete milke of your owne breasts, ɔ your owne childe; wherein you have gone before the greatest number of honourable .adies of your place, in these latter times. But I wish many may follow you, in this ood worke, which I desire to further by my kind perswasion. And such women as will . ouchsafe to read this little short treatise; may be put in minde of a duty, which all mothers are bound to performe; and I shall be glad if any will consider, and put into practice, that which is both naturall and comfortable. I hope they will at the least commend me such as do this good deede, and no more speake scornefully of that which is worthy of great praise; and for my part I thinke it an honour unto you, to doe that which hath proved you to be full of care to please God, and of naturall affection, and to bee well stored with humility, and patience, all which are highly to be praised; to give praise to any person or thing deserving praise, I dare doe it, & for this lovely action of yours I can with much thankefulnesse praise God, for all his gracious guifts of grace and Nature, wherby he hath inabled you, to doe the same: desiring also with my heart, that you may ever, and every way honour God, who hath honoured you many wayes, above many women; and I rejoyce, that I can beare witnesse, that God hath adorned you with fayre tokens of his love and mercy to your soule: As the practise of true Christian religion; dedicating your selfe to Gods service; answerablenesse to all holy commands of the holy God, which are Testimonies of Gods love, and doth challenge a very great esteeme from me, amongst the rest, that can truly judge and rightly discerne what is best; I am full of thoughts in this kinde, or of this matter: yet I say no more but this, Goe on and prosper, Hold fast all that is good, Trust in God for strength to grow and continue in faithfull obedience to his glorious Majesty; And I wil not cease to intreat the Lord of Heaven, to powre aboundantly all Blessings of heaven and earth upon you, and your children, as they increase in number.

> Your Ladyship's in the best and fastest love,
> Elizabeth Lincolne   [sigs. A2-A4]

Because it hath pleased God to blesse me with many children, and so caused me to observe many things falling out to mothers, and to their children; I thought good to open my minde concerning a speciall matter belonging to all childe-bearing women, seriously to consider of: and to manifest my minde the better, even to write of this matter, so farre as God shall please to direct me; in summe, the matter I meane, *Is the duty of nursing due by mothers to their owne children.*

In setting downe whereof, I wil first shew, that every woman ought to nurse her owne childe; and secondly, I will endeavour to answere such objections, as are used to be cast out against this dutie to disgrace the same.

The first point is easily performed. For it is the expresse *ordinance* of God that mothers should nurse their owne children, & being his ordinance they are bound to it in conscience. This should stop the mouthes of all replyers, for *God is most wise*, and therefore must needs know what is fittest and best for us to doe:

By his word it is proved, first by *Examples*, namely the example of *Eve* [Gen. 4:1-2] . . . . Next the example of Sarah [Gen. 21:1-8] . . . [and] another worthy example, namely that excellent woman *Hannah* [1 Sam. 1:20-24] . . . one example more . . . the *blessed Virgin* [Luke 2:6-7].

And so much for proofe of this office, and duty to be Gods ordinance, by his own *Word* according to the argument of *Examples*: I hope I shall likewise prove it by the same word from plaine *Precepts*. First from that *Precept*, which willeth the younger women to marry, and to *Beare* children [1 Timothy 5:14] . . . also . . . at their breasts: . . . [A]nd to inforce it the better upon womens consciences, it is numbred as the first of the good workes, for which godly women should be well reported of.

. . . .

And thus I come to a second *Precept*. I pray you, who that judges aright; doth not hold the suckling of her owne childe the part of a true mother, of an honest mother, of a just mother, of a syncere mother, of a mother worthy of love, of a mother deserving good report, of a vertuous mother, of a mother winning praise for it? All this is assented to by any of good understanding. Therefore this is also a *Precept*, as for other duties, so for *This* of mothers to their children. . . .

I adde to this *the worke that God worketh in the very nature of mothers*, which proveth also that he hath ordained that they should nurse their owne children: for by his secret operation, the mothers affection is so knit by natures law to her tender babe, as she findes no power to deny to suckle it, no not when shee is in hazard to lose her owne life, by attending on it, for in such a case it is not said, let the mother fly, and leave her infant to the perill, as if she were dispensed with: but onely it is said *woe to her*, as if she were to be pittied, that for nature to her child, she must be unnaturall to her selfe.

Now another *worke* of God, proving this point is the *worke of his provision*, for every kinde to be apt, and able to nourish their own fruit: there is no beast that feeds their young with milke, but the Lord, even from the first ground of the order of nature; *Growe, and multiplie* [Gen. 1:28; 9:1]: hath provided it of milke to suckle their owne young, which every beast takes so naturally unto, as if another beast come toward their young to offer the office of Damme unto it, they shew according to their fashion, a plaine dislike of it: as if nature did speake in them, and say it is contrary to Gods order in nature . . .

Oh consider, how comes our milke? is it not by the direct providence of God? Why provides he it, but for the child? The mothers then that refuse to nurse their owne children, doe they not despise Gods providence? Doe they not deny Gods will? Doe they not as it were say, *I see, O God, by the meanes thou hast put into me, that thou wouldst have me nurse the child thou hast given me, but I will not doe so much for thee.* Oh impious, and impudent, unthankfulnesse; both to their own natural fruit borne so neare their breasts, and fed in their owne wombes, and yet may not be suffered to sucke their own milke. . . .

. . . I beseech all godly women to remember how we *elder* ones are commaunded to instruct the *younger* [Titus 1:4-5], to love their children, now therefore love them so as to do this office to them when they are borne, more gladly for *love* sake, then a *stranger*, who bore them not, shall do for *lucre* sake. Also I pray you to set no more so light by Gods blessing in your owne breasts, which the holy Spirit ranketh with other excellent blessings.

. . . .

I doe knowe that the Lord may deny some women, either to have any milke in their breasts at all, or to have any health, or to have a right minde: and so they may be letted from this duty, by *want*, by *sicknesse*, by *lunacy*, &c. But I speake not to these: I speake to you, whose *consciences* witnesse against you, that you cannot justly alleage any of those impediments. . . . [F]eare God, bee diligent to serve him; approve all his ordinances; seeke to please him; account it no trouble, or paine to doe any thing that hath the promise of his blessing: and then you will, no doubt, doe this *good, laudable, naturall, loving duty* to your children. If yet you be not satisfied, inquire not of such as refuse to doe this: consult not with your owne conceit advise not with flatterers: but aske counsell of syncere, and faithfull Preachers. If you be satisfied; then take this with you, to make you doe it cheerefully. Think alwaies that having the child at your breast, and having it in your armes, you have *Gods blessing* there. For children are Gods blessings. Thinke againe how your babe crying for your breast, sucking hartily the milke out of it, and growing by it, is the *Lords owne instruction*, every houre, and every day, that you are suckling it, instructing you to shew that you are his new borne *Babes* by your earnest desire after his word, & the syncere doctrine thereof, and by your daily growing in grace and goodnesse therby, so shall you reape pleasure and profit. Againe you may consider, that when your child is at your breast it is a fit occasion to move your heart to pray for a blessing upon that worke and to give thanks for your child, and for ability and freedome unto that which many a mother would have done and could not; who have tried & ventured their health, & taken much paines, and yet have not obtained their desire. But they that are fitted every way for this *commendable act*, have certainely great cause to be thankfull: and I much desire that God may have glory and praise for *every good worke*, and you much comfort, that doe seeke to honour God in all things. Amen.   [sig. B—p. 21]

ELIZABETH (BROOKE) JOCELINE (1596-1622)

Elizabeth Brooke was raised by her maternal grandfather, Bishop Caderton of London, after her parents separated. Bishop Caderton shared the ideas on education of his friends William Cecil and Anthony Cooke and educated Elizabeth in religion, languages, history, and art. Myra Reynolds calls her "one of the most notable young women of the time of James I."[15] She died in 1622, after six years of marriage to Towrell Joceline of Cambridgeshire and just a few days after her only child was born. To this anticipated child of unknown sex she left her tract as a legacy. The treatise was first printed in 1624, with a preface by her husband, who commends his wife's saintliness and learning. Mrs. Joceline's own writing begins with a letter addressed to her husband in which she expresses her joy at the prospect of bearing and raising his child (thereby inadvertently revealing the closeness of their relationship) and her fear of dying in childbirth (an unfortunately realistic fear for this period and one that proved prophetic). She explains that she has realized that she can leave written instructions for their child, even if she does not survive its birth.[16] She asks her husband to choose a wet nurse carefully for the baby and thereby recalls for us Elizabeth Clinton's *Nurserie.*

The body of the work (which is addressed to the child) is Mrs. Joceline's legacy. She is another mother imbued with an acceptance of the duty to instruct her children in religion. She reminds the child to pray (p. 10), to arm itself against temptation (p. 10), to guard against sloth and pride (p. 15), to pray privately and publicly (p. 15), to guard its speech (p. 15), to avoid "prevalent vices" (pp. 73-74), to keep the Sabbath and the golden rule (p. 80), and to be charitable (p. 80). She even appends a daily schedule of religious observances (pp. 52-75).

Mrs. Joceline's legacy is perhaps the most illuminating of all the tracts on motherhood by English Renaissance mothers because, since it is addressed to both a son and a daughter, it reveals the author's differing approaches to the rearing of a son and a daughter. The reader will note the ambivalence in Mrs. Joceline's instructions about a daughter and will, perhaps, be justified in assigning this ambivalence to a desire, on Mrs. Joceline's part, to protect her unborn daughter from a potentially difficult and uncomfortable way of life.

Finally, the reader will certainly agree with Reynolds's comment that the tract was "deservedly popular because it was so genuine in its forecast of sorrow, so pathetically eager in plans and hopes for her husband and child."[17] It is the most moving of all the monuments to dutiful motherhood presented in this chapter.

The following selections are taken from *The Mothers Legacie* . . . (London: John Haviland, 1624).

from *The Mothers Legacie* . . .

Having long, often and earnestly desired of God, that I might bee a mother to one of his children, and the time now drawing on, which I hope hee hath appointed to give thee unto mee: It drew me into a consideration both wherefore I so earnestly desired thee, and (having found that the true cause was to make thee happy) how I might compasse this happinesse for thee.

I knew it consisted not in honour, wealth, strength of body or friends (though all these are great blessings) therfore it had beene a weake request to desire thee onely for an heire to my fortune. No, I never aimed at so poore an inheritance for thee as the whole world: Neither would I have begged of God so much paine, as I know I must endure, to have only possest thee with earthly riches, of which to day thou maist bee a great man, to morrow a poore begger. Nor did an hope to dandle thy infancy move mee to desire thee. For I know all the delight a Parent can take in a childe is hony mingled with gall.

But the true reason that I have so often kneeled to God for thee, is, that thou mightest bee an inheritour of the Kingdome of Heaven. To which end I humbly beseech Almightie God thou maist . . . serve him as his Minister, if he make thee a man.

It is true that this age holds it a most comtemptible office, fit only for poore mens children, younger brothers, and such as have no other meanes to live. But for Gods sake bee not discouraged with these vaine speeches; but fortifie your selfe with remembring of how great worth the winning of one soule is in Gods sight, and you shal quickly finde how great a place it is to be a Priest unto the living God. If it will please him to move your heart with his holy Spirit, it will glow and burne with zeale to doe him service. The Lord open thy lips, that thy mouth may shew forth his praise [Ps. 51:15].

If I had skill to write, I would write all I apprehend of the happy estate of true labouring Ministers: but I may plainly say that of all men they by their calling are the most truly happy; they are familiar with God, they labour in his Vineyard, and they are so beloved of him, that hee gives them abundance of knowledge. Oh bee one of them, let not the scorne of evill men hinder thee. Look how GOD hath provided for thee sufficient meanes; thou needest not hinder thy study to looke out for living, as the Israelites hindred their worke to looke for strawe [Exod. 5:7-18]: If thou beest not content with this, thou wilt not bee with more; GOD deliver thee from covetousnesse.

I desire thee that though thou takest a spirituall calling, thou wilt not seeke after the livings of the Church, nor promotions, though I honour them as I have great cause, but I would have thee so truly an humble and zealous Minister, that thy onely end should bee to doe God service, without desire of any thing to thy selfe, save the Kingdome of Heaven. Yet as I would not have thee seeke these things, so I would have thee as carefull not to neglect Gods blessings, but with all thankfulnesse to receive what hee bestowes, and to bee a carefull steward, distributing it to those that have need.

I could not chuse but manifest this desire in writing, lest it should please God to deprive me of time to speake.

And if thou beest a daughter, thou maist perhaps thinke I have lost my labour; but reade on, and thou shalt see my love and care of thee and thy salvation is as great, as if thou wert a sonne, and my feare greater.[18]

It may peradventure when thou comest to some discretion, appeare strange to thee to receive these lines from a Mother that died when thou wert borne; but when thou seest men purchase land, and store up treasure for their unborne babes, wonder not at mee that I am carefull for thy salvation, being such an eternall portion: and not knowing whether I shall live to instruct thee when thou art borne, let mee not bee blamed though I write to thee before. Who would not condemne mee if I should bee carelesse of thy body while it is within me? Sure a farre greater care belongs to thy soule; to both these cares I will endeavour my selfe so long as I live.

Againe, I may perhaps bee wondred at for writing in this kinde, considering there are so many excellent bookes, whose least note is worth all my meditations. I confesse it, and thus excuse my selfe. I write not to the world, but to mine owne childe; who it may be, will more profit by a few weake instructions comming from a dead mother (who cannot every day praise or reprove it as it deserves) than by farre better from much more learned. These things considered, neither the true knowledge of mine owne weakenesse, nor the feare this may come to the worlds eie, & bring scorne upon my grave, can stay my hand from expressing how much I covet thy salvation.

Therefore, deare childe, reade here my love, and if God take mee from thee, be obedient to these instructions, as thou oughtest to bee unto mee, I have learnt them out of Gods Word, I beseech him that they may be profitable to thee.   [pp. 1-12]

EZ. W. (n.d.)

There is no definitive information on Ez. W., whose tract takes the form of a rather stylized and learned dialogue between a Protestant mother and her Roman Catholic son, each of whom considers the other damned. The arguments of both parties are intense, precise, and involved, and they demonstrate the impassioned religious partisanship of the time. The text boasts anguished quotations of biblical incidents and parallels and includes a model dialogue between mother and son. The work is rather different from the other tracts considered in this chapter, because it is a remonstrance after the fact rather than simple instruction.

The following selections are taken from *The Answere of a Mother . . .* (Amsterdam, 1627).

from *The Answere of a Mother . . .*

Deare Mother,

It is not the first time since my departure that I have writ unto you, neither shall it bee the last. Nature will find a way to vent her duty were shee ever so hard opprest. Out of sight is not out of mind, for were you but as mindefull of your selfe as I am of you, I doubt not but by the effects you should find mee a dutifull sonne. But as the blind who see not themselves, thinke all other not to see them likewise, so you forgetting your self thinke mee forgetfull of you to. God knowes before whom one daye I am to give an account of my duty towards you, how that there passeth not a day, or night either, when you and yours take your rest, wherein there is not intercession made for you. If I knew what els in this my state a childs naturall obligation could effect, in the behalf of a mother, I would with what indeavour I could accomplish it. But alas, Deare Mother, when your request is unreasonable, nay unnaturall, as the forsaking my religion, Gods Church, his truth, nay himselfe, it standes not with the duty of a sonne any waye to yeald in the least to so unjust demaunds of a Mother. . . . I will add no more least I should seeme rather to preach you a sermon, then to wright you a Letter. Deare Mother, see & bee acquainted with those who both of this faith & life lives amongst you. I am sure their good wayes will better informe you in this kinde then my letters.

. . . .

[W]hat I have wrot unto you Deare Mother, is likewise written to my poore brethren, and sisters whom with your selfe, I commend in my most earnest prayers unto the safe protexion of God almighty who I hope hath brought mee heather to provide for your

poore deceaved soules. In one Lord and Saviour farewell, bee mindefull of your selves
that your soules perish not in that heavie daye of the Lord.

Your ever obedient & dutyfull Sonne

I. MADD   [pp. 3-4]

from *The Answere of a Grived Mother to Hir Seduced Sonnes Letter.*

Thy letter came to my hands (my deare Child) like JOSEPHS partye-culloured
coate [Gen. 37:31-35], to his father JACOB, in many things there holds much
proportion; This is my Sons coate saith the good old man; a wicked beast hath
devoured him: JOSEPH is surely torne in pieces. I cannot say so altogether; but this is
my sons letter, doth your poore aged Mother say, I know it is the great beast, hath set
his marke upon him, & appointed him for the prey. . . .

What there my Son? Now lett hir, who is acquainted with the deare name of a child,
say, whether there houlds not much proportion, betweene JACOBS sorrow and
mine, I goe downe to the grave mourning, I shall lye downe in sorrow. . . . O returne
my son, returne my Son: returne my Son, my Son.

Son. Returne, how readily should a dutifull child come, when a deare mother calls?
how soone would hee doe, what the Mother bidds? . . . But alas! my Mothers request
is unreasonable, nay unnaturall, as the forsaking my Religion, Gods Church, his trueth,
himselfe.

Mother. And is it so my Son? an unreasonable request indeed, and unnaturall; O but
harken my child, and if it bee so, let thy owne Mother bee hated: O harken my child! I
beseech thee, even by the throwes of thy first birth harken! & the Lord give thee an
open eare, while the true Mother pleads with the harlot for hir son [1 Kings 3:16-28],
and hee that is wiser then Solomon bee judge betwixt us, even he bee judge.

. . . .

. . . And now let the harlot speake, for I know shee told thee what thou shouldest
say; what could I have done unto my son, that I have not done, for his better keeping
of these, even all these? Yet would I not seeme a proud Justiciary; for how few are
those HANNAHS? who give their children backe to the Lord, who present them first in
the Temple? who breed their children as they ought; as they are bound to doe [1 Sam.
1:11-2:11]? as the Grandmother LOIS and the Mother EUNICE bred Timothy [2 Tim.
1:5]?

. . . .

Sonne. O my Deare Mother you have almost perswaded me to returne.
Mother. Almost my son? why not altogether? What a cake halfe baked [Exod. 12:34]?
Altogether my son or it is nothing. Thou must make straight steppe, & cast of that
which hangs on so fair, least that which is halting bee turned out of the way. The Lord

calls for thy heart, give it him my son; & follow him wholy, or else thou shalt never with Caleb and Joshuah, come unto that good Land [Josh. 1:1-2; Num. 13:30].

. . . .

Sonne. Ho mother, why what mine eyes have seene, the lives of your Ministers and Professours, why your very lights seeme to bee darknesse: your Seers see not: your Watchmen keepe not sentinell; your Ambassadors for Christs honourable name! . . . [T]hey are as abominable in their practise many of them, as NADAB and ABIHU [Lev. 10:1-2] or ELIES two sones [1 Sam. 2:12], are these the fruits of truth amongst you?

. . . .

Can here bee truth? I tell you (Mother) I know it, you have many who will bee counted children of the light, yet walke in palpable darknesse, doing the deeds of it, can here bee truth Mother? *Mother.* O child take heede you wound not a holy profession, through the vizard of it. . . . And first my Son, I know thou didest not publish this in gath, nor tell it in the streets of ASKELON [2 Sam. 1:20]. If wee had not carried our wickednesse in our foreheads, my child would not have uncovered our skirts. I know thou wouldst perserve the credit of thy owne nest. But the Harlot cannot but know these things.

. . . .

[W]hy Child did I not tell thee, what havock the whore hath made of the Churches, what threatnings she hath breathed forth, what rivers of blood she hath shed, how she hath killed and scourged & persecuted the Saints and Martyrs, of the Lord Jesus that upon hir may come all the righteouse blood shed upon the earth. . . . Come forth from hir, my Child, my sweet Child, come forth, for living there thou must partake of hir sins, & then must thou receive of hir plagues, & how canest thou stand in that burning? . . .[W]hy dost thou linger? my deare Child, consider, other sins speake, blood cryes & here is not Abels blod alone [Gen. 4:8-11] he was but one, here is the voice of bloods, even of all, which were slaine for the word of God. . . . [O]ne thing I begg of thee, and since the Son will have the old Mother crouch and bend to him, why see child, a Mother will not stand upon hir points, shee will doe any thing to have hir Son againe, I doe begg one thing of thee, & I begg it on my knees, it is this, that thou wouldst rouse up thy selfe, for there is a great matter in hand. . . . O come away . . . my deare Child—come hastily linger not, throue thy dowe [i.e., dough] upon thy shoulders, there is no time to leaven it, & trudge away [Exod. 12:34], & the Lord which can perswade JAPHETH to dwell in the tents of SHEM [Gen. 1:27], & if LOTH will prolonge the time in so eminent a danger, canst in mercy to him, cause him to come out of SODOME, before the brimstone and the fire shall fall [Gen. 19:15-25], extend his mercy unto thy servant, seeke him out, who is gon astray & cause him to returne to thee, who art the sheepheard & Bishop of his soule, so shall I ever praise thy name, who hast given mee my Son againe, in whom I may have comfort here, & through they [sic] mercy, joy with him hereafter.

FINIS.   [pp. 3-23]

M.R (n.d.)

The identity of M. R. is unknown. Her text shows her to have been a Puritan, and a literary one, since she includes (unacknowledged) quotations from Edmund Spenser's *Faerie Queene* in her tract.[19] Her work is divided into four main sections on chastity, temperance, beauty, and humility. Each section contains a subsection on maintaining one of these standards (living within compass), and a second subsection on violating the same standard (or living out of compass). Each subsection consists of a series of independent paragraphs and several verses on the virtue or vice described.

The following selections are taken from *The Mothers Counsell . . .* (London: John Wright, 1630?).

from *The Mothers Counsell . . .*

Good Counsell to the Christian Reader:
1. That you keepe a narrow watch over your heart, words, and deedes continually.
2. That with all care the time be redeemed that hath been idly, carelessly, and unprofitably spent.
3. That once in the day at least, private prayer, and meditation be made.
4. That care be had to doe, and receive good in company.
5. That your family be with all diligence and regard, watched over, and Christianly governed.
6. That no more care bee spent in matters of this world, than must needs.
7. That you stirre up your selve to liberalitie to Gods Saints.
8. That you prepare your selves to beare the Crosse, by what meanes soever it shall please God to exercise you.
9. That you give not the least bridle to wandring thoughts.
10. That you bestow some time in mourning, not onely for your owne sinnes, but for the time and age wherein you live.
11. That you looke daily for the comming of our Lord Jesus Christ, for your full deliverance out of this world.
12. That you acquaint your selves with some godly person, with whom you may. conferre of your Christian estate, and open your doubts, to the quickning of Gods grace in you.   [sigs. A2-A3]

.   .   .   .

from "Chastite"

First my Daughter understand, that Chastity is the beautie of the soule, and puritie of life, which refuseth the corrupt pleasures of the flesh; only possessed of those who keep cleane and undefiled; and it consisteth either in sincere virginitie, or in faithfull Matrimony.

.   .   .   .

Chastity is the Seale of Grace, the staffe of devotion, the marke of the Just, the crowne of virginity, the glory of life, and a comfort in Martyrdome.

.   .   .   .

Amongst all the conflicts of a Christian soule, none is more hard than the warres of a chaste minde, for the fight is continuall, and the victorie rare.   [pp. 1-3]

. . . .

from "Wantonesse"

Wantonesse is an enemy to the purse, a foe to the person, a canker to the minde, a corrosive to the conscience, a weakner of the wit, a besotter of the senses, and lastly, a mortall bane to all the bodie.

. . . .

Corrupt company is more infectious than corrupt aire; therefore let women be houised [sic] in their choice; . . . for . . . if those which are neither good nor evill accompany with those that are good, they are transformed into their vertue. If those that are neither good nor evill consort with those that are evill, they are incorporated to their vice. If the good companie with the good, both are made the better; if the evill with the evill, both the worse .   [pp. 6-9]

. . . .

from "Temperance"

Live temperately and vertuously, that thou mayst dye patiently; for who lives most honestly, will dye most willingly: and for thy long dayes and better health on earth, afflict not thy body with too much unnecessary Physicke, but furnish thy minde in time of plentie to lay up for it selfe and others in the time of want; for surely her end shall be easie and happie that death finds with a weake body, but a strong Soule.

Grieve not to groane under the hand of sicknesse: for as sometimes it purgeth the body from intemperate humors, so doth it oftentimes the Soule from more dangerous securitie, and the rather, since there is no perfect health in this world, but a newtralitie betweene sicknesse and health.   [pp. 11-12]

. . . .

from "Madnesse"

A mad woman is like a rough stirring horse, and as he must have a sharp bit, so must shee have a sharp restraint.

. . . .

The tongue of a mad woman is a slipperie instrument, nimble to doe mischiefe; for commonly by it friendship is decayed, worldly riches diminished, the life most miserably wasted, and infamy and immortall paine purchased.

. . . .

As the body being alwayes opprest with labour loseth his strength, and so perisheth; so doth the minde of a woman oppressed with passions and pleasures of this world, lose the force, lust, and desire which shee had to the rest of eternall life to come.

[pp. 15-19]

. . . .

from "Beautie"

There is nothing harder for a woman than to know her selfe; for blinded with beautie and selfe-love, they flatter themselves in all things.

There is in every woman two powers, which draw and conduct her; a desire of pleasure bred in the beautie of the body and a good opinion coveting onely good thinges: betweene these two there is continuall strife in women, and when the opinion hath the maistry, it maketh a woman sober, chaste, discreet, & quiet: but when desire getteth the upper hand, it makes her lustfull, riotous, covetous, & unquiet. . . . Let then the eyes of every womans inward minde first respect the beautie of her soule, then the comelinesse of her body, and lastly, the necessitie of riches.   [pp. 21-22]

.   .   .   .

from "Odiousnesse"

To exceed Nature or thy condition, is a ryotous excesse in lust, apparell, or other ornament, it is also a part of pride, and contrary to decency and comlinesse.

.   .   .   .

A painted womans sorrowes, howsoever extreme, ought not to be redressed: for being trimmed up with dissimulation, she should not be beleeved.

.   .   .   .

A painted womans face is a liver smeared with carrion, her beauty baits of dead wormes, her lookes nets, and her words inticing charmes.   [pp. 27-30]

.   .   .   .

from "Humilitie"

Shee that gathereth vertues without humilitie, casteth dust against the winde, and loseth her labour.

.   .   .   .

Since the Countrey which a woman desires to dwell in, is high and heavenly, and the way thither Lowlinesse and Humilitie, why then desiring this Countrey, should they refuse the way?

.   .   .   .

She only may properly be called a woman that in her behaviour governeth her selfe like a woman, that is to say, conformable to such things as reason willeth, and not as the motions of sensualitie requireth.   [pp. 32-35]

.   .   .   .

from "Pride"

Pride perceiving humilitie to be honourable, desires oftentimes to bee covered with her garment, for feare least appearing alwayes in her owne likenesse she should be little regarded.

.   .   .   .

Pride is alwayes accompanied with Folly, Audacitie, Rashnesse, Impudency, and Solitarinesse: as if one would say that the proud woman is abandoned of all the world, ever attributing that to her selfe which is not, having much more boast than matter of worth.

.   .   .   .

A proud woman is like Theocritus his fisherman: shee onely feeds the vanitie of her fancy with dreames of gold.   [pp. 37-39]

LETTERS AND DIARIES

The personal letters and diaries collected in this chapter have been selected for presentation for three reasons: they demonstrate the relatively spontaneous thinking of the women who wrote them; they throw light on the underlying status or situation of these writers; and they also illuminate, for unforeseen readers of later times, the relationship of these writers to some of the important events of their time.[20]

For the most part, these letters indicate a widespread assimilation by the writers of the domestic, social, and religious teaching inculcated by humanists and religious reformers. They often show an acceptance of the ideal of the "new mother."

In his *Office and duetie of an husband* (1553), Vives stated,

The woman is even as man, a reasonable creature, and hath a flexible witte both to good and evill, the whiche with use and counsell maye be altered and turned. . . . [A] woman oughte to know . . . howe she shoulde honoure God & love her neighboure. . . . and . . . howe she oughte to love and honor her husbande, . . . what her duetye & office is at home, and what is her husbandes, . . . If the husbande be the womans head . . . he ought to execute the office to suche a man belongying, and to teache the woman.[21]

Of equal importance here are Vives's belief in woman's own ability to understand (and to act on her understanding) and the unquestioned positioning of the husband as her "head."

The chief exception to an assimilation of these teachings among the letters of Renaissance Englishwomen are the disputed love letters, called the Casket letters, of Mary Stuart (discussed in Part II). In this present section, the first letter by Anne Boleyn also deviates from the norm. But such were the realities of Renaissance life that even those women who failed to accept the moral teachings of the humanists and the reformers were aware of their need to submit to the authority of man.

Perhaps the most disturbing aspect of these letters is the light they throw on the subordinated legal and social position of women in the English Renaissance. This position is exemplified by Margaret, countess of Richmond, mother of Henry VII, who, despite the authority vested in her by Henry, addressed her son subserviently, and by Brilliana Harley, who conjured up the figure of her husband to enforce her requests to her obviously beloved son. Moreover, both these women had to hide, or distort, their actions from their husbands, or "Lords." For, in the English Renaissance, the legal personality of the married woman was a powerless one, submerged legally in the identity of a male protector. Even those few rights accorded single women were easily and commonly subverted. On the other hand, the domineering

Anna Bacon, addressing her son with great authority, illustrates the status of the widow, who was perhaps the only woman in Tudor England who could conduct herself with some legal power. Catherine of Aragon, queen of England and scion of proud Spanish royalty, was isolated and maltreated by her husband, and her daughter, Princess Mary, was brought to her knees by her father and forced to proclaim her own illegitimacy. The cringing and dependent posture is that most common to the writers of these letters.

The misery often attendant on the dependent and insecure position of even those Tudor women famous today is clearly demonstrated by these letters. The plight of Catherine of Aragon, the Princess Elizabeth, and the Lady Jane Grey, and the manipulations of Anne Boleyn form a backdrop to the important events of the time—the Anglicizing of the English church and the scurrying for the English throne. The by-blows of these events often caused suffering to the weak, and the weak very often were women.

The three diaries presented here—by Lady Grace Mildmay, Lady Margaret Hoby, and Lady Anne Clifford—are the only extant diaries by English women of the early seventeenth century; the diary of Lady Margaret Hoby is the earliest known in English. While Lady Clifford clearly chafes at her unhappy married life, she does not subvert it, and all three of these writers act within the limits prescribed for women of the English Renaissance; Lady Mildmay and Lady Hoby are rigid Puritans, while Lady Clifford, though less confined to an interest in religion, is nevertheless devout.

MARGARET (BEAUFORT) STANLEY, COUNTESS OF RICHMOND (1441-1509)

The mother of Henry VII is the first royal lady in England who left evidence of an interest in the advancement of learning. However, she predated the Renaissance interest in the education of women characterizing the "Age of Catherine of Aragon," [22] and her interest in learning did not extend itself to the education of women. Nor was the Lady Margaret erudite; indeed, she often bewailed her imperfect knowledge of Latin. However, she knew French well enough to translate two religious works from that language into English, [23] and she commissioned the translation of other works from Latin into English. [24] Because her love for reading was known to her circle, books were often left as legacies for her, and on her own initiative, as well as through these gifts, the countess amassed a sizable library. [25] After her death, the countess was commemorated in a long elegy by John Skelton. [26]

Lady Margaret's forceful personality and achievements lend great interest to the tone of the following letter, in which she resorted to pleading with her son, the king, and to subterfuge in dealing with her husband. [27]

The following selection is taken from *Letters of Royal and Illustrious Ladies of Great Britain* . . . , ed. May Anne Everett Green, 3 vols. (London: Henry Colburn, 1846).

1501 to her son, Henry VII

My dearest and only desired joy in this world,

With my most hearty loving blessings and humble commendations I pray our Lord to reward and thank your grace, for that it hath pleased your highness so kindly and lovingly to be content to write your letters of thanks to the French king, for my great matter, that so long hath been in suit, as Master Welby hath shewed me your bounteous goodness is pleased. I wish, my dear heart, an my fortune be to recover it, I trust you shall well perceive I shall deal towards you as a kind, loving mother; and, if I should never have it, yet your kind dealing is to me a thousand times more than all that good I can recover, an all the French king's might be mine withal. My dear heart, an it may please your highness to license Master Whitstone, for this time, to present your honourable letters, and begin the process of my cause . . . it should be greatly to my help, as I think: but all will I remit to your pleasure. And if I be too bold in this, or any my desires, I humbly beseech your grace of pardon, and that your highness take no displeasure.

My good king, I have now sent a servant of mine into Kendall, to receive such annuities as be yet hanging upon the account of Sir William Wall, my lord's chaplain, whom I have clearly discharged; and if it will please your majesty's own heart, at your leisure, to send me a letter, and command me that I suffer none of my tenants be retained with no man, but that they be kept for my lord of York, your fair sweet son, for whom they be most meet, it shall be a good excuse for me to my lord and husband; and then I may well, and without displeasure, cause them all to be sworn, the which shall not after be long undone. . . . And, my dear heart, I now beseech you of pardon of my long and tedious writing, and pray Almighty God to give you as long, good, and prosperous life as ever had prince, and as hearty blessings as I can ask of God.

At Calais town, this day of St. Anne's, that I did bring into this world my good and gracious prince, king, and only beloved son.

By your humble servant, beadwoman, and mother,

Margaret R. [I, 118-20]

ANNE BOLEYN, QUEEN OF ENGLAND (1507-1536)

Queen Anne Boleyn, Henry VIII's second wife and successor to the pious and erudite Catherine of Aragon, was (and remains) the subject of considerable controversy. The daughter of a gentleman, Sir Thomas Boleyn, she spent her early years in the French court.[28] She returned to England from France in 1522 and was much admired at the English court, most dramatically by the king himself. She attained the height of her ambition in marrying Henry VIII, who changed the course of English history as a result of his infatuation; however, his growing distaste for his new queen became clear within a few months of their marriage in 1533. The birth of a daughter (later Elizabeth I), followed by a miscarriage and a stillbirth, did nothing to improve the king's attitude. The queen was eventually accused of adultery and incest

—charges she denied—was found guilty of incest and executed. According to the *DNB*, "she met her fate with singular cheerfulness and courage."[29]

The letters of Anne Boleyn clearly trace the revolution of the wheel of fortune. The earliest of the letters presented here is a bold and straightforward effort to ingratiate herself with Henry VIII. The two contrasting letters to Henry's secretary, Cardinal Wolsey, show her changed attitude to this powerful courtier, whom she first thought would help advance her, and whom she later helped to destroy because he failed to do so. These letters support a characterization of Anne Boleyn as a consistent opportunist[30] and illustrate the behind-the-scenes manipulation characteristic of dependent types.

The following letters are taken from *Letters of Royal and Illustrious Ladies of Great Britain* . . . , ed. Mary Anne Everett Green, 3 vols. (London: Henry Colburn, 1846).

1527 to King Henry VIII

Sire,

It belongs only to the august mind of a great king, to whom Nature has given a heart full of generosity towards the sex, to repay by favours so extraordinary an artless and short conversation with a girl. Inexhaustible as is the treasury of your majesty's bounties, I pray you to consider that it cannot be sufficient to your generosity; for if you recompense so slight a conversation by gifts so great, what will you be able to do for those who are ready to consecrate their entire obedience to your desires? How great soever may be the bounties I have received, the joy that I feel in being loved by a king whom I adore, and to whom I would with pleasure make a sacrifice of my heart, if fortune had rendered it worthy of being offered to him, will ever be infinitely greater.

The warrant of maid of honour to the queen induces me to think that your majesty has some regard for me, since it gives me the means of seeing you oftener, and of assuring you by my own lips (which I shall do on the first opportunity) that I am,

Your majesty's very obliged and very obedient servant,
without any reserve,
Anne Boleyn.   [II, 14-16]

1529 to Cardinal Wolsey

My lord,

After my most humble recommendations, this shall be to give unto your grace, as I am most bound, my humble thanks for the pain and travail that your grace doth take in studying . . . how to bring to pass honourably the greatest wealth that is possible to come to any creature living, and in especial remembering how wretched and unworthy I am in comparing to his highness. And for you, I do know myself never to have deserved by my deserts that you should take this great pain for me. . . .

Now, good my lord, your discretion may consider as yet how little it is in my power to recompense you, but all only with my good-will, the which I assure you, that after this matter is brought to pass you shall find me, as I am bound in the mean time, to owe you my service, and then look what thing in this world I can imagine to do you pleasure in, you shall find me the gladdest woman in the world to do it. And next unto the king's grace, of one thing I make you full promise to be assured to have it, and that is my hearty love unfeignedly during my life; and being fully determined, with God's grace, never to change this purpose, I make an end of this my rude and true-meaning letter, praying our Lord to send you much increase of honour, with long life.

Written with the hand that beseeches your grace to accept this letter as proceeding from one that is most bound to be

Your humble and obedient servant,
Anne Boleyn   [II, 45-47]

1529 to Cardinal Wolsey

My lord,

Though you are a man of great understanding, you cannot avoid being censured by every body for having drawn on yourself the hatred of a king who had raised you to the highest degree to which the greatest ambition of a man seeking his fortune can aspire. I cannot comprehend, and the king still less, how your reverend lordship, after having allured us by so many fine promises about divorce, can have repented of your purpose, and how you could have done what you have, in order to hinder the con-summation of it. . . . I acknowledge that I have put much confidence in your profes-sions and promises, in which I find myself deceived.

But, for the future, I shall rely on nothing but the protection of Heaven and the love of my dear king, which alone will be able to set right again those plans which you have broken and spoiled, and to place me in that happy station which God wills, the king so much wishes, and which will be entirely to the advantage of the kingdom. The wrong you have done me has caused me much sorrow; but I feel infinitely more in seeing myself betrayed by a man who pretended to enter into my interests only to discover the secrets of my heart. I acknowledge that, believing you sincere, I have been too precipitate in my confidence; it is this which has induced, and still induces me, to keep more moderation in avenging myself, not being able to forget that I *have* been

Your servant,
Anne Boleyn   [II, 48-49]

CATHERINE OF ARAGON, QUEEN OF ENGLAND (1485-1536)

Although she left no formal writings behind her, the embattled Catherine of Aragon, the first wife of Henry VIII, must be credited with the introduction to England and the sponsorship there of advanced Renaissance ideas concern-ing the education of women. She brought these ideas with her from Spain, particularly from her mother, Isabella of Castille. Catherine was also noted in her time for her conscientious attention to the education of her own daughter, the Princess Mary.[31]

As a result of Henry's infatuation with Anne Boleyn, and Catherine's refusal to accede to his demand for a divorce, the queen was isolated from the court and denied proper treatment as queen of England over a long period of time. It should be noted that Catherine's refusal was a defense of her own marriage and of the legitimacy and hereditary rights of her daughter. The pious and dignified deportment with which this Spanish princess bore the grave injustices of Henry VIII, no doubt propped by her training and her faith, is noteworthy because it aroused the esteem of the English people for her character and learning.[32]

The following letters amply show the extent to which she suffered during those unhappy years. They are taken from *Letters of Royal and Illustrious Ladies of Great Britain . . .* , ed. Mary Anne Everett Green, 3 vols. (London: Henry Colburn, 1846).

1535 to Dr. John Forest

My reverend father,

Since you have ever been wont in dubious cases to give good counsel to others, you will necessarily know all the better what is needed for yourself, being called to combat for the love of Christ and the truth of the Catholic faith. If you will bear up under these few and short pains of your torments which are prepared for you, you will receive, as you well know, the eternal reward. . . . But O happy you, my father, to whom it has been graciously granted that you . . . should happily fulfil the course of your most holy life and fruitful labours. But woe to me, your poor and wretched daughter, who, in the time of this my solitude and the extreme anguish of my soul, shall be deprived of such a corrector and father, so loved by me in the bowels of Christ. And truly, if it were lawful for me freely to confess what is my most ardent desire in reference to this, to your paternity, to whom I have always hitherto revealed (as was my duty) all the secrets of my heart and conscience, I confess to you that I am consumed by a very great desire to be able to die, either together with you or before you; which I should always seek, and would purchase by any amount of the most heavy and infinite torments of whatever sort, provided it were not a thing repugnant to the Divine will, to which I always willingly submit all my life and my every affection and desire: so much do I dislike, and so greatly would it displease me, to allow myself any joy in this miserable and unhappy world, those being removed of whom the world is not worthy.

But perhaps I have spoken as a foolish woman. Therefore, since it appears that God has thus ordained, go you, my father, first with joy and fortitude, and by your prayers plead with Jesus Christ for me, that I may speedily and intrepidly follow you through the same wearisome and difficult journey; and, meanwhile, that I may be able to share in your holy labours, your torments, punishments and struggles. I shall have all this by your last blessing in this life, but when you have fought the battle and obtained the crown, I shall expect to receive more abundant grace from heaven by your means. As to the rest, I think it would be an extravagant thing in me to exhort you to desire above all other things that immortal reward, . . . you being of such noble birth, gifted with such excellent knowledge of divine things, and (what I ought to mention first) brought up from youth in a religion so holy, and in the profession of the most glorious father St. Francis. Nevertheless, . . . I shall always supplicate his Divine Majesty with continual prayers, with passionate weeping, and with assiduous penitence, that you may happily end your course, and arrive at the incorruptible crown of eternal life. Farewell, my revered father, and on earth and in heaven always have me in remembrance before God.

Your very sad and afflicted daughter,
Catherine [II, 196-200]

1535 to ?

Mine especial friend,

You have greatly bound me with the pains that you have taken in speaking with the king my lord concerning the coming of my daughter unto me. The reward you shall trust to have of God; for (as you know) in me there is no power to gratify that you have done, but only with my good will. As touching the answer which hath been made you, that his highness is contented to send her to some place nigh me, so as I do not see her, I pray you vouchsafe to give unto his highness mine effectual thanks for the goodness which he showeth unto his daughter and mine, and for the comfort that I have thereby received. . . .

Howbeit, you shall always say unto his highness that the thing which I desired was to send her where I am; being assured that a little comfort and mirth, which she should take with me, should undoubtedly be half a health unto her. I have proved the like by experience, being diseased of the same infirmity, and know how much good it may do that I say. And, since I desired a thing so just and reasonable, and (that) so much touched the honour and conscience of the king my lord, I thought not it should have been denied me.

Let not, for my love, to do what you may that this may be yet done. Here have I, among others, heard that he had some suspicion of the surety of her. I cannot believe that a thing so far from reason should pass from the royal heart of his highness; neither can I think that he hath so little confidence in me. If any such matter chance to be communed of, I pray you say unto his highness that I am determined to die (without doubt) in this realm. And that I, from henceforth, offer mine own person for surety, to the intent that, if any such thing should be attempted, that then he do justice of me, as of the most evil woman that ever was born.

The residue I remit to your good wisdom and judgment as unto a trusty friend, to whom I pray God give health. [II, 201-7]

ELIZABETH TUDOR, QUEEN OF ENGLAND (1533-1603)

The following letter, addressed to Catherine Parr, recalls Catherine's kindness to the powerless Princess Elizabeth; the second recalls the queen's zeal for reformed religion and the interest she took in the training of her stepchildren; the third, written to Elizabeth's stepsister, Mary, after Henry's death, reflects the uncertainties and difficulties his daughters faced during that unsettled period.

The following letters are taken from *Letters of Royal and Illustrious Ladies of Great Britain . . .*, ed. Mary Anne Everett Green, 3 vols. (London: Henry Colburn, 1846).

1544 to Catherine Parr

Inimical fortune, envious of all good and ever revolving human affairs, has deprived me for a whole year of your most illustrious presence, and, not thus content, has yet again robbed me of the same good; which thing would be intolerable to me, did I not hope to enjoy it very soon. And in this my exile, I well know that the clemency of your highness has had as much care and solicitude for my health as the king's majesty himself. By which thing I am not only bound to serve you, but also to revere you with filial love, since I understand that your most illustrious highness has not forgotten me every time you have written to the king's majesty, which, indeed, it was my duty to have requested from you. For heretofore I have not dared to write to him. Wherefore I now humbly pray your most excellent highness, that, when you write to his majesty, you will condescend to recommend me to him, praying ever for his sweet benediction, and similarly entreating our Lord God to send him best success, and the obtaining of victory over his enemies, so that your highness and I may, as soon as possible, rejoice together with him on his happy return. No less pray I God, that he would preserve your most illustrious highness; to whose grace, humbly kissing your hands, I offer and recommend myself.

From St. James's, this 31st of July.

Your most obedient daughter, and most faithful servant,
Elizabeth.   [III, 176-77]

1544 to Catherine Parr

To our most noble and virtuous queen Catherine, Elizabeth, her humble daughter, wisheth perpetual felicity and everlasting joy.

Not only knowing the effectuous will and fervent zeal, the which your highness hath towards all godly learning, as also my duty towards you, most gracious and sovereign princess, but knowing also, that . . . the wit of a man or a woman wax dull and unapt to do or understand any thing perfectly, unless it be always occupied upon some manner of study. Which things considered, hath moved so small a portion as God hath lent me, to prove what I could do. And, therefore, have I . . . translated this little book out of French rhyme into English prose, joining the sentences together, as well as the capacity of my simple wit and small learning could extend themselves.

The which book is entitled or named, "The Mirror, or Glass, of the Sinful Soul," wherein is contained, how she (beholding and contemplating what she is), doth perceive how, of herself and her own strength, she can do nothing that good is, or prevaileth for her salvation, unless it be through the grace of God. . . . Trusting also that, through his incomprehensible love, grace, and mercy, she (being called from sin to repentance), doth faithfully hope to be saved. And although I know that, as for my part which I have wrought in it (as well spiritual as manual), there is nothing done as it should be, . . . yet do I trust also . . . that the file of your excellent wit and godly learning, . . . shall rub out, polish, and mend (or else cause to mend) the words (or rather the order of my writing), the which I know, in many places, to be rude, and nothing done as it should be. But I hope that, after to have been in your grace's hands, there shall be nothing in it worthy of reprehension, and that in the mean while no other (but your highness only), shall read it, or see it, lest my faults be known of many. Then shall they be better excused (as my confidence is in your grace's accustomed benevolence), than if I should bestow a whole year in writing or inventing ways for to excuse them.

Praying God Almighty, the Maker and Creator of all things, to grant unto your highness the same New Year's day, a lucky and prosperous year, with prosperous issue, and continuance of many years in good health and continual joy, and all to his honour, praise, and glory.

From Ashridge, the last day of the year of our Lord God, 1544. [III, 177-79]

1547 to Princess Mary

Princess and very dear sister,

You are very right in saying, in your most acceptable letters, which you have done me the honour of writing to me, that our interests being common, the just grief we feel in seeing the ashes, or rather the scarcely cold body of the king, our father, so shamefully dishonoured by the queen, our stepmother, ought to be common to us also. I cannot express to you, my dear princess, how much affliction I suffered when I was first informed of this marriage, and no other comfort can I find than that of the necessity of submitting ourselves to the decrees of Heaven; since neither you nor I, dearest sister, are in such a condition as to offer any obstacle thereto, without running heavy risk of making our own lot much worse than it is; at least, so I think. . . . I think, then, that the best course we can take is that of dissimulation, that the mortification may fall upon those who commit the fault. For we may rest assured that the memory of the king, our father, being so glorious in itself, cannot be subject to those stains which can only defile the persons who have wrought them. Let us console ourselves by making the best of what we cannot remedy. If our silence do us no honour, at least it will not draw down upon us such disasters as our lamentations might induce.

These are my sentiments, which the little reason I have dictates, and which guides my respectful reply to your agreeable letter. With regard to the returning of visits, I do not see that you, who are the elder, are obliged to do this, but the position in which I stand obliges me to take other measures; the queen having shown me so great affection, and done me so many kind offices, that I must use much tact in manoeuvring with her, for fear of appearing ungrateful for her benefits. I shall not, however, be in any hurry to visit her, lest I should be charged with approving what I ought to censure.

However, I shall always pay much deference to your instructions and commands, in all which you shall think convenient or serviceable to you, as being your highness's etc, etc. [III, 193-94]

CATHERINE PARR, QUEEN OF ENGLAND (1512-1548)

The kindness of Queen Catherine toward the Princess Mary, demonstrated in the letter presented below, is all the more remarkable when one remembers the zealous Protestantism of the queen and the no-less-intense Catholicism of the princess. That the two women could collaborate on a religious undertaking is undoubtedly a tribute to Catherine's diplomacy and goodwill. Catherine's advice that Mary publish her translation (part of a larger work undertaken under Catherine's sponsorship) under her own name was unusual advice from and for a woman and was not followed by the princess.

The following letter is taken from *Letters of Royal and Illustrious Ladies of Great Britain* . . ., ed. Mary Anne Everett Green, 3 vols. (London: Henry Colburn, 1846).

1544 to Princess Mary

Although, most noble and dearest lady, there are many reasons that easily induce my writing to you at this time, yet nothing so greatly moves me thereto as my concern for your health; which, as I hope it is very good, so am I greatly desirous to be assured thereof.

Wherefore, I despatch to you this messenger, who will be (I judge) most acceptable to you, not only from his skill in music, in which you, I am well aware, take as much delight as myself, but also because, having long sojourned with me, he can give the most certain information of my whole estate and health. And, in truth, I have had it in mind before this to have made a journey to you and salute you in person; but all things do not correspond with my will. . . .

Now, since, as I have heard, the finishing touch (as far as translation is concerned) is given by Mallet to Erasmus's work upon John, . . . I entreat you to send over to me this very excellent and useful work, now amended by Mallet, or some of your people, that it may be committed to the press in due time; and farther, to signify whether you wish it to go forth to the world (most auspiciously) under your name, or as the production of an unknown writer. To which work you will, in my opinion, do a real injury, if you refuse to let it go down to posterity under the auspices of your own name, since you have undertaken so much labour in accurately translating it for the great good of the public, and would have undertaken still greater (as is well known) if the health of your body had permitted.

And, since all the world knows that you have toiled and laboured much in this business, I do not see why you should repudiate that praise which all men justly confer on you. However, I leave this whole matter to your discretion, and, whatever resolution you may adopt, that will meet my fullest approbation.

. . . I pray God, the greatest and best of beings, that He deign to bless you uninterruptedly with true and unalloyed happiness. May you long fare well in him.

From Hanworth, 20th of September,

Most devotedly and lovingly yours,
Catherine the Queen, K.P. [i.e., Katherine Parr]   [III, 180-81]

LADY JANE (GREY) DUDLEY (1538-1554)

The following letters demonstrate the exceptional, never-to-be-realized potential of the "nine days' queen." The first, an uncompromising letter to a reprobate, is notable for its youthful and religious judgments as well as for its clear statement of reformed doctrine. The second letter of shrewd exhortation to her sister bears eloquent testimony to Lady Jane's understanding of her fellows.[33]

The following letters are taken from John Foxe, *Actes and monuments* . . . (London: John Daye, 1563).

1553 to a learned man . . . falne from the truth . . .

So ofte as I call to minde the dreadfull, and fearfull sayinges of god: that he which laith holde upon the plough and looketh backe againe, is not mete for the kingdome of heaven: And on the other syde to remember the comfortable wordes of our saviour Christe, to all those that, forsaking them selves, do folowe him: I cannot but mervell at thee, and lamente thy case: that thou whiche sometyme wast the lyvely member of Christ: but now the defourmed impe of the devil, some tyme the beautifull temple of God: but now the stinking and filthy kenell of Sathan, sometyme the unspotted spouse of Christe, but now the unshame fast paramour of Antichrist, somtime my faythful brother: but now a staunger and Apostate, yea sometime a stout Christen souldier: but now a cowardly runaway. . . . [W] herfore hast thou taken upon thee the testament of the Lorde in thy mouth? . . . [W] herfore hast thou instructed other to be strong in Christ, when thou thy selfe doest nowe so shamefully shrinke, when thy selfe doest so horriblie abuse the testament and lawe of the Lorde? when thou thy self preachest, not to steale, yet moste abominable stealest, not from men, but from God, and as most heinous sacrilege, robbest Christ thy Lorde of his right members, thy body and thy soule, when thou thyselfe doest rather chose to lyve myserably with shame to the world, than to die and gloriously with honour to reigne with Christ, in whom even in death is life. . . .

. . . [W]hat sayth the prophet Baruche, where he reciteth the epistel of Jeremy, written to the captive Jews? Did he not forewarne them, that in Babilon they should se gods, of gold, silver, wood, & stone, borne upon mens shulders, to cast a feare before the heathen: but be not ye afraid of them, (sayth Jeremy) nor do as other do. But when you se other worship them saye you in your hartes: it is thou (O Lorde) that oughtest only to be worshipped: for as for the timber of those gods, the Carpenter framed them and polished them, yea, gylded be they, & layed over with silver, and vayne thinges: and cannot speake. . . . It is written (saith he) thou shalt honour the lord thy god, and him onely shalt thou serve. These and such lyke do prohibite thee and all Christians to worship any other God than which was before all worldes, and layde the foundations both of heaven and earth. And wylt thou honour a detestable idole, invented by Romishe Popes, and the abominable colledge of craftie Cardinalles. . . . [W]ilt thou eyther for feare of death or hope of life, denie and refuse thy God, who enryched thy povertie, healed thy infirmitie, and yelded to thee his victory, if thou couldst have kept it? . . .

. . . Let the two edged sword of Gods holy worde shere asonder the sewed together sinowes of worldly respectes, even to the very mary of thy carnall harte, and embrace Christ. . . . [F]ight manfully, come life, come death, the quarrel is gods. And undoubtely the victory is ours. . . .

[L]ette the lively rememberaunce of the last day be alwaies afore your eyes, remembring the terrour that such shallbe in at that tyme, with the runnagates and fugitives from Christ, which settinge more by the world, then by heaven, more by their life, then by hym that gave them their life, did shrinke, yea did cleane fall awaye from him that never forsoke them. And contrary wise the inestimable joys prepared for them that feared no perel, nor dreading death, have manfully fought, and victoriously triumphed over all power of darknes, over hell, death, and damnacion, through their most redoubted captain Christ, who nowe stretcheth out his armes to receave you, ready to fal upon your necke and kisse you, and laste of all, to feaste you with the deinties and delicates of hys owne precious bloud, which undoubtedly, if it mighte stande with hys determinate purpose, he wold not let to shed againe, rather than you should be lost. To whome with the father and the holy ghost, be honour, prayse, and glorye everlastingly. Amen.

    Be constant, be constant, feare not for payne,

    Christ hath redemed the, and heaven is thy gayne.   [pp. 920-22]

1554 to Lady Katherine Grey

I have here sente you (good sister Katherin) a booke, which although it bee not outwardlye trimmed with golde, yet inwardly it is more worth then precious stones: it is the boke (deare Sister) of the lawe of the Lorde. It is his testament and last wil, which he bequethed unto us wretches, which shall lead you to the pathe of eternall joye: and if you with a good mind read it, and with an earnest minde do folow it, it shal bring you to an immortal and everlasting life. It wil teache you to live, and learne you to die. It shal winne you more then you shoulde have gained by the possession of your wofull fathers lands. for, as if god had prospered him, you shuld have inherited his lands: so if you apply diligently this boke, sekyng to directe your life after it, you shalbe an inheritor of such riches, as nether the covetous shal withdraw from you, neither thefe shal steale, nether yet the mothes corrupt. Desyre with David, good sister, tunderstand the law of the lord your god. live stil to die, that you (by death) may purchase eternal lyfe. And truste not that the tenderousness of your age shal lengthen your life. For as soone (if God call) goeth the yong as the olde: & labour alwayes to learn to die, defie the worlde, denye the devill, and despise the fleshe and delite your-selfe onely in the Lord. Be penitent for your sinnes, and yet despaire not: be strong in faith, & yet presume not, and desire with saint Paule to be dissolved, and to be with Christ, with whom even in death ther is life. Be like the good servaunt, & even at midnight be waking, lest when death commeth and stealeth upon you like a thefe in the nighte, you be with the evyll servaunt, found sleping [Luke 12:38-39] & leste, for lacke of oyle, you be founde like the five foolish women [Matt. 25:1-13], and lyke hym that had not on the weddyng garment, and then ye be cast out from the mariage [Matt. 22:1-14]. Rejoyce in Christ, as I trust I do. Follow the steppes of your maister Christ, and take up your crosse, lay your sinnes on his back, and alwaies embrace him. And as touchyng my death, rejoyce as I doe, (good Sister,[)] that I shal be delivered of this corruption, and put on incorruption. For I am assured, that I shall for losyng of a mortall lyfe, winne an immortal lyfe, the whiche I pray God graunt you, sende you of his grace to live in his feare, and to die in the true christian fayth, from the whiche (in Gods name) I exhort you, that you never swarve, neither for hope of life, nor for feare of death. For if ye wyl deny his truth for to lengthen youre lyfe, God wyll denye you, and yet shorten youre dayes. And if you will cleave unto him, he will prolong your dayes to your comforte and hys glory, to the whiche glory, god bring me nowe, and you hereafter when it pleaseth hym to call you. Fare you well (good Sister) and put your onely trust in god, who onely muste helpe you.   [pp. 918-19]

LADY ANNA (COOKE) BACON (1528-1610)

The second of Sir Anthony Cooke's daughters, Anna was the most acclaimed scholar among the five sisters and was said to have acted as cotutor with her father to Edward VI. At the age of twenty-two she published a translation of Italian sermons by Bernadine Ochyne, which deal mainly with the subject of predestination.[34]

After her marriage to Nicholas, Lord Bacon, Lady Bacon translated Bishop Jewel's *Apology* into English from Latin. The translation was so perfect that not a word was revised when she presented it to the bishop.

Lady Bacon became the mother of Francis Bacon, the lord chancellor, and of his brother, Anthony. Her painstaking care of her sons is generally acknowledged. Her great solicitude for them is evinced by the correspondence she maintained with them. A request in Francis Bacon's will also demonstrates the strong feeling between mother and sons: "For my burial," he wrote, "I desire it may be in Saint Michael's Church, near St. Albans—there my mother was buried."[35]

The following letter is typical of Lady Bacon's correspondence. The reader's attention is directed to the proverbial advice (rather similar to Francis Bacon's style in his *Essays*), and to the Latin and Greek quotations illustrative of Lady Bacon's great erudition.

The letter is taken from the *Works of Francis Bacon: VIII, Letters and Life*, ed. James Spedding (1862; Rpt. New York: Garret Press, 1968).

1591-2 to Anthony Bacon

The grace of God be daily multiplied in you, with mercy in Christ our Lord.

That you are returned now at length I am right glad. God bless it to us both. But when I heard withal that Lawson, who I fore-suspected, stale hence unto you, and so belike hath wrought upon you again to your hurt, to serve his own turn as heretofore; how welcome that could be to your long-grieved mother, judge you. I can hardly say whether your gout or his company were the worse tidings. I have entertained this gentleman, Mr. Fant, to do so much kindness for me as to journey towards you, because your brother is preparing your lodging at Gray's Inn very carefully for you. I thank God that Mr. Fant was willing to do so, and was very glad, because he is not only an honest gentleman in civil behaviour, but one that feareth God indeed, and as wise withall having experience of our state, and is able to advise you both very wisely and friendly. For he loveth yourself, and needeth not yours, . . . Use him therefore, good son, and make much of such, and of their godly and sound friendly counsel. This one chiefest counsel your Christian and natural mother doth give you even before the Lord, that above all wordly respects you carry yourself ever at your first coming as one that doth unfeignedly profess the true religion of Christ, and hath the love of the truth now by long continuance fast settled in your heart, . . . *In hoc noli adhibere fratrem tuum ad consilium aut exemplum. Sed plus dehinc.* If you will be wavering (which God forbid, God forbid), you shall have examples and ill encouragers too many in these days, and that αϱϛη Βιοι   [sic; apparently should read αϱχιεπισϰσπος] since he was   Βουλευτης, εστι απολεια της εϰϰλησιας μεθ ημων, Φιλει γαϱ την εαντον δοΕαν πλεον της δοΕης τον Χϱιστον.

Beware therefore and be constant in godly profession without fainting, and that from your heart: for formality wanteth none with us, but too common. Be not speedy of speech nor talk suddenly, but where discretion requireth, and that soberly then. For the property of our world is to sound out at first coming, and after to contain. Courtesy is necessary, but too common familiarity in talking and words is very unprofitable, and not without hurt-taking, *ut nunc sunt tempora.* Remember you have no father. And you have little enough, if not too little, regarded your kind and no [sic] simple mother's wholesome advice from time to time. And as I do impute all most humbly to the grace of God whatsoever he hath bestowed upon me, so dare I affirm that it had been good for you every way if you had followed it. . . .

Let now Lawson, that fox, be acquainted with my letters. I disdain both it and him. He commonly opened underminingly all letters sent to you from counsel or friends. I know it, and you may too much, if God opens your eyes as I trust he will. . . . So fare you well, and the Lord bless you and keep you for ever.

Your mother,
A. Bacon

3 Febr.   [pp. 112-13]

LADY BRILLIANA (CONWAY) HARLEY (1600?-1643)

Lady Brilliana Harley was born in the Netherlands and became a naturalized British citizen in April, 1606. She married Sir Robert Harley in 1623 and, according to the *DNB*, "devoted herself to the care of her children, three sons and four daughters."[36] She was very devout and surrounded herself with a circle of Puritan preachers.

Two hundred and five of Lady Harley's letters, written between 1625 and 1643, have been collected and published. With the exception of the first eight, addressed to her husband, they were written to Edward Harley, her oldest son, while he was at Oxford and are chiefly (and adequately) interesting for their marks of motherly affection.

The following letter is typical of those in the collection. Aside from its genuine charm, it holds interest because of the subterfuge with which it ends. It is taken from *Letters of the Lady Brilliana Harley*, ed. T. T. Lewis (London: Camden Society, 1854).

1638 to Edward Harley

Good Ned—I have a nwe wellcome for every letter you send, and a nwe thankes to you for it. I bless God that you are well; the Lord in mercy continue your health, for shure I am, if you be well, I counte it upon my owne score and think meself so. My deare Ned, be still watchfull over your self, that custome in seeing and heareing of vice doo not abate your distaste of it. . . . I remember you in my prayers, as I do my owne soule, for you are as deare to me as my life. I hope in a speciall maner, we shall remember you at the fast; and, deare Ned, thinke upon that day, howe your father is used to spend it, that so you may have like affections to joyne with us. . . .

Deare Ned, be carefull to use exercise; and for that paine in your backe, it may be caused by some indispocion of the kidnes. I would have you drinke in the morning beare boyled with licorisch; it is a most excelent thinge for the kidnes. For the booke, if you can not have it in French, send it me in Inlisch: and I will, if pleas God, send you mony for it. Deare Ned, it is very well doun, that you submite to your fathers desire in your clothes; and that is a happy temper, both to be contented with plaine clothes, and in the weareing of better clothes, not to thinke one selfe the better for them, nor to be trubelled if you be in plaine clothes, and see others of your rancke in better. Seneque had not goot that victory over himselfe; for in his cuntry howes he lived privetly, yet he complaines that when he came to the courte, he founde a tickeling desire to like them at court. I am so unwilling that you should goo to any place without your worthy tutor, that I send this mesenger expresly to your tutor, with a letter to intreate him, you may have the happines of his company, wheather souer you goo. . . . If you should goo to my brothers, I heare theare is a dangerous passage; I desire you may not goo that way but aboute. The Lord in much mercy bles you, and presarve you from all evell, especially that of sinn: and so I rest

Your most affectinat mother,

Brilliana Harley

Your father dous not knowe I send. Thearefore take no notis of it, to him, nor to any.

Decem. 14, 1638

Nobody in the howse knowes I send to you.   [pp. 16-17]

LADY GRACE (SHERRINGTON) MILDMAY (1522-1620)

The second of Sir Henry Sherrington's three daughters, Grace, Lady Mildmay, was raised at Laycock Abbey (Wiltshire), where her upbringing was rigorous. Her governess, carefully chosen by her mother, was a poor relation who emphasized religiosity, chastity, and sobriety, and taught Grace an abbreviated Puritan program of reading, writing, arithmetic, needlework, and music. At fifteen, Grace married Anthony Mildmay, son of a Puritan official at Elizabeth's court. She then moved to Apelthorpe (Northamptonshire), where she busied herself with music, religious occupations, and varied good works in the neighborhood, eventually becoming engrossed chiefly in the rearing of her daughter, Mary, her only child. Mary married Sir Francis Fane of Mereworth in Kent (later the first earl of Westmoreland). The upbringing of their children concerned their grandmother deeply, and her diary, actually a journal of reminiscences written late in Lady Mildmay's life, was addressed to her daughter. The long preface to the journal is entitled "Experience I conned to my child"; it contains Lady Mildmay's most intimate thoughts on the question of the education of the young and constitutes evidence of the interest in and concern about the education of children that was developing among mothers of the Renaissance.

Portions of the journal appeared in an essay by Rachel Wiegall, "An Elizabethan Gentlewoman," *QR*, 215 (1911): 119-35. Unfortunately, Wiegall does not mention the location of the journal, described as "a thick black volume filled with writing, so neat that it seems to spell refinement," and the diary has never been wholly published.

from *Lady Mildmay's Journal*

I have found by observation this to be the best course to sett ourselves in from the beginning unto the end of our lives. First to begin with the Scriptures, to read them with all diligence and humility every day. The Holy Sacraments, Baptism and the Lord's Supper, confirme the faith within us and seale it up for ever betwixt God and our conscience, never to be altered, that we are His selected people to doe His wille, to bless His Name and do His Prayse. Also we should make ourselves expert in the understanding and knowledge of the chronicles of the land. What matters of moment have passed from the beginning under the Government of our Royall and Annoyted Princes, whereby we may be instructed to imitate and follow the good example of true and faithfull subjects, and to have theyr worthy acts and exployts in memory, whereby we may avoyd and shun all treasons and treacherous attempts and all unfaithful combinations with plotters and devisers of evill.

Alsoe the wise and wittie sayings of philosophers being heathen men, without the knowledge of God, are worthie books, sometimes to be read for recreation. It is certaine that there is foundation and ground of many great and ensueing evills when the nobilitie and great personages have no regard nor forecast what governors they sett over theyr children, nor what servants they appoynt to attend upon them. Whereby it cometh to pass too often and too universally that the myndes of children are taynted and corrupted even from theyr infancy and made capable of every lewd and evill conversation, and are made impudent and bold, so that no counsell, example nor reproof can retaigne them.

Many gentlemen and theyr wives are desirous to place theyr sonnes and daughters in honourable services, but they take no care to furnish theyr minds with true religion and virtue and other good parts fitt for such preferment. But if they were putt off and not received into service for want of a better education, everyone would endeavour to amend that fault lest theyr children should be upon theyr hands unpreferred.

Parents have much to answer for before God, who neglect theyr duty in bringing up theyr children or prefere any other labour or delight in the world before that naturall and most necessary employment: for God is displeased, themselves are punished, and theyr children are utterly spoyld thereby, and an infamous memory remaineth of them and theyr generation after them. For it is not possible for those parents to be good, or to have any virtue in them, who seeke not to make theyr children good. And the seedes of goodness being tymely sown, God himself will water, increase and blesse it to the honour and praise and good edification one of another.

All that are conceived and born into this worlde shall either be saints in Heaven, electe children of God, or be damned, reprobated, cast out from God into Hell to be the children of the devill and to dwell with him and his infernal spiritts forever. Wherefore it is a matter of great importance to bring up children unto God, and to cause them to foresake the vanities and follies of this short and momentary lyfe, to performe the worke and lyfe of grace; and in the exercise of that teaching we teach and instruct ourselves unto the same end, which is life everlasting.   [pp. 119-35]

LADY MARGARET (DAKINS) HOBY (1571-1633)

Lady Margaret Hoby was married three times by the age of thirty; her third husband, Thomas Posthumous Hoby, was the son of Elizabeth (Cooke) Hoby and the grandson of Sir Anthony Cooke.

Lady Hoby's rather impersonal diary records her life between 1599 and 1605, and shows it to have been limited to an interest in religion and homemaking. Therefore, it is a valuable record of the occupations of a country woman who shows no concern with broader areas of knowledge or action. Lady Hoby's religious habits were sternly Puritan. Kohler suggests that Lady Hoby kept the "earliest known diary extant in English . . . for the sake of religious discipline." [37]

The following selections are taken from *The Diary of Lady Hoby*, ed. Dorothy M. Meads (London: G. Routledge and Sons, 1930).

from *The Diary of Lady Hoby*

August, 1599
(the Lordes day 12)
after I was redie, I went to privatt praiers, then to breakfast: then I walked tell church time Mr. Hoby, and after to dinner: after which I walked and had speech of no serious maters tell :2: a clock: then I wrett notes into my bible tell :3: and after :4: I came againe from the church, walk, and medetated a Litle, and againe wrett som other notes in my bible of that I had Learned tell :5: att which time I retourned to examenation and praier: and after I had reed some of bond of the suboth, I walked abroad: and so to supper, after to praers, and Lastly to bed.

.   .   .   .

Wensday 15
In the morning at :6: a clock I praied privatly: that done, I went to awiffe in travill of child, about whom I was busey . . . tell :1: a Cloke, about which time, She bing delivered and I havinge praised god, returned home and betook my selfe to privat praier :2: severall times upon occasion: then I wrett the most part of an examenation or triall of a christian, framed by Mr. Rhodes, in the doinge where . . . I againe fell to praier, and after continewed writing . . . after 3: a cloke: then I went to work tell after 5, and then to examenation and praier: the Lord make me thankfull, who hath hard my

praiers and hath not turned his face from me: then I taked with Mrs. Brutnell tell supper time, and after walked a litle into the feeldes, and so to prairs, and then to bed:

.   .   .   .

September, 1599, 1 Saterday
After praier in the morninge, I, beinge not well, did heare Mr. Rhodes read of Gyffard upon the songe of Sallemon: sone after . . . I came in, and praied, and so to dimer: after which I walked about the house, barne, and feeldes, and, when I came home, I praied privat with Mr. Rhodes, wherin I had more comfort then ever I received in my Life before, I praise god; then I went to take my Beesse and, after that, I returned to privat praier my selfe and examenation: then I went to se my Honnie ordered, and so to supper; after which I went to lector, and soone after to bed:

.   .   .   .

[Jan, 1600] The 8: day
After privatt praier I dined, and sonne after, I went to walsingams house, wher I saw my lady Rich, my lady a Ruttland, and my lady walsingame: after I Cam home I was pained in the toothach which Continewed with me 4 days after, in which time I exercised prainge & readinge as I was able, and tooke phisike of Doctor Lister, who, coming to se me the 4 day after my paine, beinge the :12: of this moneth, tould me of my lady of Bedfords death the night before, which was the Lordes day, who was well at the sarmon in the after none, and dead that night.

.   .   .   .

[Feb, 1602] The :4: day
I was sent for to Trutsdall to the travill of my Cossine Isons wiffe, who that Morninge was brought to bed of a daughter: the same day, at night, I hard of a fish that was taken up att Yarmoth, 53 foott Long and 23 broade.

.   .   .   .

[October, 1603] The :5: day
Mr. Hoby, my mother, and my selfe, went to the dalls this day: we had in our Gardens a second sommer, for Hartechokes bare twisse, whitt Rosses, Read Rosses; and we, havinge sett a musk Rose the winter before, it bare flowers now. I thinke the Like hath seldom binn seene it is a great frute yeare all over.

.   .   .   .

[Oct., 1603] The 23 day
this day I hard the plauge was so great at whitbie that those which were cleare shutt themselves up, and the infected that escaped did goe abroad: Likewise it was reported that, at London, the number was taken of the Livinge and not of the deed: Lord graunt that these Jugmentes may Cause England with speed to tourne to the Lord.

[pp. 62-207]

LADY ANNE (CLIFFORD) HERBERT (1590-1676)

Lady Anne was the daughter of George Clifford, earl of Cumberland, and his wife, Margaret Russell, countess of Cumberland. Like her mother, Lady Anne was known for her interest in literature, expressed in support for institutions and individuals rather than in her own writing. Her first husband was Richard Sackville, earl of Dorset. After his death, she married Shakespeare's patron, Philip Herbert, earl of Pembroke and Montgomery. Both marriages were unhappy, perhaps because Lady Anne was an unyielding personality. In her later years, Lady Anne, a rich and unencumbered widow, delighted in supervising her enormous properties. The diary she kept in 1603 and 1616 records her unsettled domestic life and gives some clue to her interest in the management of her own estate, and to her rather broad reading in literature, philosophy, and religion.[38]

The following selections are from *The Diary of the Lady Anne Clifford*, ed. V. Sackville-West (London: William Heinemann, Ltd., 1923).

from *The Diary of the Lady Anne Clifford*

[from] May 1616

Upon the ninth I received a letter from Mr. Bellasis how extreme ill my Mother had been and in the afternoon came . . . letters that my Mother was exceeding ill and as they thought in sore danger of death. . . . At night was brought to me a letter from my Lord to let me know his determination was, the Child should go live at Horseley and not come hither any more so as this was a very grievous and sorrowful day to me.

Upon the 10th Rivers came from London and brought me word from Lord William that she was not in such danger as I fear'd. . . .

All this time my Lord was in London where he had all and infinite great resort coming to him. He went much abroad to Cocking, to Bowling Alleys, to Plays and Horse Races, and commended by all the world. I stayed in the country having many times a sorrowful and heavy heart, and being condemned by most folks because I would not consent to the agreements, so as I may say, I am like an owl in the desert.

Upon the 13th being Monday, my Lady's footman . . . brought letters out of Westmoreland, by which I perceived how very sick and full of grievous pains my dear Mother was, so as she was not able to write herself to me. . . .

Upon the 29th Kendall came and brought me the heavy news of my Mother's death which I held as the greatest and most lamentable cross that could have befallen me. . . .

[from] Jan., 1617

Upon the 22nd the Child had her 6th fit of the ague in the morning. . . . Upon the 25th I spent most of my time in working and in going up and down to see the Child. About 5 or 6 o'clock the fit took her, which lasted 6 or 7 hours.

[from] April 1617

The 5th my Lord went up to my closet and said how little money I had left contrary to all they had told him. Sometimes I had fair words from him, and sometimes foul, but I took all patiently and did strive to give him as much content and assurance of my love as I could possibly, yet I told him that I would never part with Westmoreland upon any condition whatever. Upon the 6th after supper because my Lord was sullen and not willing to go into the nursery I made Mary bring the child to him into my chamber, which was the first time she stirred abroad since she was sick.

. . . .

The 16th my Lord and I had much talk about these businesses, he urging me . . . to go to London to sign and seal but I told him that my promise so far passed to my brother and to all the world that I would never do it, whatever became of me and mine.

. . . .

[from] April, 1617

The 19th I signed 33 letters with my own hand which I sent by him to the tenants in Westmoreland. The same night my Lord and I had much talk of and persuaded me to these businesses, but I would not, and yet I told him I was in perfect charity with all the world. All this Lent I eat flesh and observed no day but Good Friday.

The 20th being Easter Day my Lord and I and Tom Glenham and most of the folk received the Communion by Mr. Ran, yet in the afternoon my Lord and I had had a great falling out, Mathew continuing still to do me all the ill office he could with my Lord. All this time I wore my white satin gown and my white waistcoat. . . .

. . . .

The 24th my Lord went to Sen'noak again. After supper we played at Burley Break upon the Green. This night my Lord came to lie in my chamber.

. . . .

The 26th I spent the evening in working and going down to my Lord's Closet where I sat and read much in the Turkish History and Chaucer.   [pp. 46-66]

3 SECULAR WRITINGS

IT WAS noted earlier that the humanist and religious reform movements in England were intertwined. This combination had peculiar effects on the writings of Renaissance Englishwomen: most of the materials by English-women in this period which were printed were religious in nature, while nonreligious materials were usually left in manuscript. As a result, Ruth Willard Hughey concluded that "women in sixteenth-century England were disciples of the Reformation rather than of the Renaissance."[1] However, the validity of this conclusion is open to serious objection on several bases.

First, it would have to be shown that women differed from men in publishing predominantly religious works and in circulating nonreligious materials in manuscript form. Hughey does not raise this question. But one thinks of such circulated manuscripts as Sidney's *Arcadia* and wonders if there was not a general tendency to suppress nonreligious materials; certainly there is no question as to the proliferation of published religious works by men. It would be necessary to tabulate published and nonpublished religious and secular materials by men and women, and to determine whether the proportions of writings in each category varied by sex, in order to determine whether the discrepancy among women noted by Hughey is significant.

However, even if such a tabulation indicated that the proportions of secular works published by men and women differed significantly, one could still question the basis Hughey ascribes to such a phenomenon. A hypothetically high number of religious works published by women, in proportion to those left in manuscript, could reflect a sense of propriety rather than a degree of personal involvement and interest in one area of knowledge at the expense of the other. Certainly the moral climate of the time in England was conducive to female reticence on nonreligious subjects.

In evaluating the works of Renaissance Englishwomen, one must consider the intensity of religious fervor and ferment; religion carried more than a strictly personal significance for men and women. In G. M. Trevelyan's words, "The Reformation in England was at once a political, a religious and a social event."[2] Religious tutelage often was geared to political goals and tied to partisan strife. Indeed, after Elizabeth had been settled on the throne for more than a decade, more secular literature by women began to appear, in contrast to earlier, more turbulent times. Therefore, it could be misleading to calculate the interests of Renaissance women on a quantitative basis. Indeed, one could argue that the secular manuscript writings by women argue for a high degree of interest and hard-won erudition on their part, which was garnered despite the religious climate of the times and despite the fact that women apparently were hesitant to publish secular works.

Perhaps it is more worthwhile to trace cycles of concentration on one or another type of writing.

In 1548, in a preface to Princess Mary's translation of Erasmus' *Paraphrase of the Gospel of St. John*, Nicholas Udall made the famous remark that,

It was now no news in England to see young damsels in noble houses and in the courts of princes, instead of cards and other instruments of idle trifling, to have continually in their hands either psalms, homilies and other devout meditations, or else Paul's epistles, or some book of holy scripture matters, and as familiarly both to read or reason thereof in Greek, Latin, French or Italian, as in English. It was now a common thing to see young virgins so trained in the study of good letters, that they willingly set all other vain pastimes at naught, for learning sake. It was now no news at all, to see Queens and ladies of most high estate and progeny, instead of courtly dalliance, to embrace virtuous exercises of reading and writing, and with most earnest study both early and late, to apply themselves to the acquiring of knowledge, as well in all other liberal artes and disciplines, as also most especially of God and his most holy word.[3]

This was an accurate description of the erudite Tudor women of the early sixteenth century, a coterie of women of noble birth who were exceedingly pious, grave, and learned, primarily as a result of home tutelage. These women were occupied with materials like Erasmus' *Paraphrase*.

By 1564, Thomas Becon, a Puritan reformer, was advocating an extension of the education of less privileged young women:

[I]f it be thoughte conveniente, . . . that scholes should be . . . set up for the right education and bringing up of the youthe of the male kynde: why shoulde it not also be thought convenient, that scholes be built for the godly institucion and vertuous bringing up of the youth of the female kynde? Is not the woman the creature of God, so well as the man? . . . [H]ave not we all oure beginning of her? . . . Can that woman govern her house godly, which knoweth not one poynt of godlynes? Who seeth not now then howe necessarye the vertuous education and bringinge up of the woman-kinde is? Which thinge canne not be conveniently brought to passe except scholes for that purpose be appoynted.[4]

By 1581, in his *Positions*, Richard Mulcaster, the foremost champion of education for females among the educators of the latter part of the sixteenth century, was advocating the extension of the education of women, "toothe and naile," partly because it was, he said, already customary in England to educate young girls.[5]

The extension of women's education, which works such as these espouse and demonstrate, brought about a leveling of educational goals from a high standard of great individual tuition to a more practical, less erudite standard; the new ideal was to provide less socially privileged women with a basic education in addition to training in the domestic arts.

As feudalism evolved into a stable capitalistic and monarchical system under the popular Tudor rulers, the middle class developed into a vital part of English life. Middle-class women benefited socially and intellectually from the programs addressed to and absorbed by this urban group.[6] Like women of the upper classes, they enjoyed increased respect as women and greater scope within the home, engaged in increased religious activity, and continued to participate in business.[7] Their writings reflect this vitality.

From 1570 to 1600, under the relatively secure and settled rule of Elizabeth, there was an increase in secular writings by women, attributable in part to this shift in and extension of the educational program for women. In the leaner years for women immediately following Elizabeth's death, there was a reaction against the intellectual aspirations of women; James I is said to have asked of one erudite maiden, "But can she spin?" Perhaps it is to this reaction that the decrease in the number of published secular works by women after 1600, the spate of idealizations of the rule of Elizabeth, and the group of spirited tracts in defense of women (written by women) can be ascribed.

WRITINGS ON SOCIETY

In *The Lawes Resolutions of Womens Rights* (1632), T. E. stated that,

[W]omen have no voice in Parliament, they make no laws, they abrogate none. All of them are understood either married or to be married, and their desires are subject to their husbands. I know no remedy, though some women can shift it well enough.[8]

After her own summary of the limitations of the rights of Elizabethan women under law, the late Pearl Hogrefe attempted to minimize the significance of these limitations by citing the discrimination against some men under the Tudors. "Tudor society was patriarchal," stated Hogrefe (p. 10), listing such inequities as the system of primogeniture and the control imposed over the marriage choice of even an heir. But an argument such as this serves merely to distort the facts. For while some men may be discriminated against some of the time under patriarchy, all women under this system are automatically disadvantaged. In the Elizabethan world only a widow could, under favorable circumstances, function with a significant degree of autonomy. The real and significant enhancement of the status of the Renaissance English-woman was limited to the confines of her home. The rule of even an heiress to the throne was questioned by a public that distrusted female leadership at any level. Queen Elizabeth's accession to the throne was sharply, though inadvertently, greeted by John Knox's First Blast of the Trumpet (1558), which had actually been directed against her Catholic stepsister, Queen Mary, "[t]hat horrible monster Jesabel of England."[9] Efforts by other Protestants to appease the new Protestant queen, such as John Aylmer's Harborowe for Faithfull and Trewe Subjects . . . (1559), dwelt more on Elizabeth's excep-tional qualities than on the general worth of women. Thus they evinced an underlying distrust of women.[10]

It is in part a reflection of the esteem in which Elizabeth came to be held that public opinion concerning the abilities of women was raised during her reign. An example of this tendency to generalize from the queen to women in general is found in Mulcaster's Positions; he advocates the education of women for several reasons, and one developed at great length is the example of the English "diamond" Elizabeth, living proof of the wonderful results of such training (p. 173). Elizabeth's qualities were reflected in her rule, and respect for her was extended to other women in reflected glory.

However exaggerated the homage paid to Elizabeth—as Diana, Cynthia, or Faerie Queene,—there is no question that her power was real and her genius for rule genuine. The memorial praises by Diana Primrose are sincere, since they were first printed after Elizabeth's death. The virtues she celebrates are not only political and diplomatic but also the religious and personal virtues advocated for Elizabethan women (though actually undercut in life by Elizabeth).

The need of hangers-on to flatter in a system in which reward is determined by favor, the need of writers, for example, for patronage, leads also to a cruder kind of homage represented in this chapter by the writings of Mary Fage and Aemilia Lanyer, two women of the middle class. Their obsequious-ness is obvious, and their praise celebrates the conventional virtues they ascribe to their would-be patrons.

Despite their need to flatter for favor (a need felt by male writers, too), these women evince a pride in their own sex through their praises of other women. In Aemilia Lanyer's work this pride asserts itself as a major theme, in straightforward defenses of womankind and in praises of a particular model of feminine virtues, the countess of Cumberland, to whom Lanyer's poem is addressed.

There is a further group of writings constituting spirited feminist arguments asserting the humanity and nobility of women. These tracts also can be seen as demonstrations of a growing sense of confidence and spirit on the part of Renaissance Englishwomen, and they are consistent with the considerable advances made by the male theorists in admitting women to a stronger position in private life. By the early seventeenth century, Englishwomen were beginning to develop an increased confidence in their own humanity. However, there was as yet no Marie du Gournay in England to call for the equal education of men and women and for the right of women to engage in any work, as that French writer did in her *Egalité des hommes et des femmes* (1622). The earliest, even faintly comparable, argument by an Englishwoman appeared in 1640 in a pamphlet entitled *The womens sharpe revenge . . .*, written under a pseudonym; in it, Mary Tattlewell (pseud.) and Joane hit him-home (pseud.) argued against the poor education of women and the harsher judgments meted out to them for sexual indiscretions. The early seventeenth-century tracts were moderate and well within the acceptable English limits, but their very existence bespoke the future upheaval these first advances presaged. By the end of the century, writers such as Bathsua Makin, author of *An essay to revive the antient education of gentlewomen* (1673), were beginning to sound clarion calls like those of du Gournay.

ELIZABETH TUDOR, QUEEN OF ENGLAND (1533-1603)

The following poem seems to respond to a sonnet addressed to Elizabeth by her cousin, Mary Stuart, after the queen of Scots had escaped imprisonment in Scotland and had fled to England for refuge. The term "daughter of debate" apparently refers to Mary, and Elizabeth's conventional image of the ship in port recalls Mary's imagery. (See Part II). The apparent callousness on Elizabeth's part should be balanced by the fact that Elizabeth, who had been branded a bastard, ascended a shaky throne in 1558, and that fears of a Catholic invasion to seat Mary on the English throne were strong until the Scottish queen's execution in 1587 ended her strong claim to English rule—a claim realized by her son, James.

Elizabeth's point of view is more assertively masculine, or more expansively Machiavellian, than that of the other women writers on society; this fact is understandable, since she wrote from within the power base and could assert her aims straightforwardly.

The text of Elizabeth's poem is taken from Leicester Bradner, ed., *Poems of Queen Elizabeth I* (Providence, R.I.: Brown University Press, 1964).

THE DOUBT OF FUTURE FOES

The doubt of future foes exiles my present joy,
And wit me warns to shun such snares as threaten mine annoy;
For falsehood now doth flow, and subjects' faith doth ebb,
Which should not be if reason ruled or wisdom weaved the web.
But clouds of joys untried do cloak aspiring minds,   [5]
Which turn to rain of late repent by changed course of winds.
The top of hope supposed the root upreared shall be,

And fruitless all their grafted guile, as shortly ye shall see.
The dazzled eyes with pride, which great ambition blinds,
Shall be unsealed by worthy wights whose foresight falsehood finds.   [10]
The daughter of debate that discord aye doth sow
Shall reap no gain where former rule still peace hath taught to know.
No foreign banished wight shall anchor in this port;
Our realm brooks not seditious sects, let them elsewhere resort.
My rusty sword through rest shall first his edge employ   [15]
To poll their tops that seek such change or gape for future joy.   [p. 4]

ANNE (EDGCUMBE) TREFUSIS (fl. 1589)

Anne Trefusis was the daughter of Peter Edgcumbe (d. 1607). Her first
marriage was to the Reverend Hugh Dowriche of Devonshire; her second
was to Richard Trefusis of Cornwall.[11] The long poem (approximately 2400
lines) for which she is most known was composed during her first marriage,
and she accordingly is referred to most frequently as Anne Dowriche. The
author states her philosophical and esthetic reasons for writing her *Historie* in
the prefatory materials. However, despite Dowriche's interest in poetry, her
effort is not a successful poem; one need only compare her Devil's Council
with Book II of *Paradise Lost* to see this. It is of society, viewed nationalisti-
cally and devoutly, that she is writing; therefore, her *Historie* has been placed
among the other writings on society by Renaissance women. Anne Dowriche's
piety and cultivated tastes place the work well within the permitted areas for
women. Moreover, she is conventional in excusing her work on the ground
"that it is a womans doing." Despite her disclaimer, she was sufficiently
audacious to compose and expose her *Historie*, although she is far from the
type of pleader for women's rights who is conspicuous among the writers in
this chapter.

The following selection is taken from *The French Historie* . . . (London: T.
Orwin for T. Man, 1589).

from THE FRENCH HISTORIE . . .

As walking on a daie, the woods and forrests nie:
In shrillyng voyce, and mournfull tunes, me thought I heard one crie.
Which sodaine feare so dasht my blood and senses all,
That as one in a traunce I staid to see what would befall.
A thousand thoughts opprest my fearfull wavering braine,   [5]
In musing what amid the woods that fearful voice shuld mean
I feard least theeves had robd and cast some man aside:
Because it was the common waie where men did use to ride.
Among the savage beasts that in these woods remaine,

I doubted least some travler stood in danger to be slaine.   [10]
But casting feare apart, I ranne toward the place,
To see the wight that did lament, and waile his wofull case.
Alone, no perill nigh, within a bushie dale,
A stranger sate: I got aside to heare his dolefull tale.

. . . .

[The narrator is spied by the Frenchman and a conversation and discourse follow]

[Fr.] I am a stranger wight, and *France* my native soyle,
       From which, of late, by luckles chance, & need, am forst to toyle: [110]
       Such troubles and such warres of late have there befell,
       That such as feare the Lord aright no suretie have to dwell
       Within that wofull Land: so God me hether sent.
       To live with you in happie state, which he this Land hath lent.
[N.]   Oh happie then am I: my frend I thee desire   [115]
       Come goe with me, for of these warres I greatly long to hear.

. . . .

       Therefore my frend I praie, thy wit and tongue prepare,
       The cause of all these bloodie broiles in verse for to declare.   [120]
       And first of all describe the matter and the man,
       The place, the time, the manner how this Civill warre began.
[Fr.] O Sir, but this request doth pierce my wounded hart,
       Which gladly would forget again my woful countries smart.

. . . .

       But sith it is your will to know the wofull state
       Of Christs afflicted Church in *France*, which Antichrist doth hate.   [130]
       Come rest you here a while, and marke what I shall tell,
       Great warres & broiles I must declare, God grant it may be wel.
       And first to pitch the plot that you doo so desire,
       I will unfolde the cheefest cause that kindled first this fire.

       About the verie yeere of Christ his Incarnation   [135]
       A thousand five hundred fiftie seven by just computation:
       Henrie ware the Crowne the second of that name,
       In whose unhappie Reigne began this fearfull fierie flame.
       For now in *France* began Gods truth for to appeare,

Whose joiful beames in Germanie at this time shone ful cleer.   [140]
But as the *Jewes* sometimes Gods Prophets did despise,
And as the Scribes and Pharisies did set their whole devise
To shade the shining light, which God to them had sent:
So France in furie blindlie set against Gods truth is bent.
Which truth but latelie sowen, and scant appearing greene,   [145]
They seeke by force, by fire and sword, to roote & raze it cleene.
But though proud Pharao did Gods chosen long oppresse,
Yet still amiddes the fierie broiles his people did increase.
So now amiddes the flame Gods word a passage found,
Which did increase his chosen flocke by force of silver sound.   [150]
Which sound in Gods elect did worke such sodaine change
In all estates, that at the first in *France* it seemed strange.
Gods mightie Spirite did worke his mercie still was prest,
That some of all estates were calde their blindnesse to detest.
Though riches be a let, and noble birth some staie,   [155]
That verie few of these (saith Christ) do finde the perfect way:
Yet God to bring to passe the worke he did intend,
Did also raise some Noble men the poorer to defend.
So now they fall at square, now here began the strife:
For Sathan could not beare to see a new reformed life.   [160]
That Prophesie is true (for Christ did speak the word)
I came not to give peace to mine, but strife, debate & sword.
The sonne against the sire, one frend against another,
The word shal brothers part, & set the daughter gainst the mother.
So fel it out in *France*, his word did now devide   [165]
His chosen, from the rest of those that tooke the adverse side.
The Land devided thus, two parts there fell at first,
Gods people were in number least, the greater was the worst.
Now Sathan was afraid, for now he strived sore
To keepe the King and chiefest States in blindnes as of yore.   [170]
It pincht him to the quicke to lose his kingdome so,
It greevde him to the hart that he should let his servants go.
He sits not idle now, he calls his wits in place,
Some cunning knacke for to contrive to help him in this case.
His wilie wilfull craft by long experience bred   [175]
Hath taught him now an ancient feat to crush the gospels head.
Now summons he his men and servants to appere;
Now help me at this need (quoth he) my frends & felows deer:
Now is the time to stirre while matters yet be newe,
While blinded mindes in doubting hang, not knowing what is true.   [180]
For if the word of God do once begin to shine,

Then farewell all, I shalbe faine my kingdome to resigne.
But if you will agree and follow mine advise,
We shall cut off this sowen word, as fast as it shall rise.   [pp. 1-4]

AEMILIA (BASSANO) LANYER (1570?-1640?)

Although superficially Lanyer's work may seem to be a religious poem lacking proportion, a careful reading serves to establish its cohesion and good sense. She states that her purpose in writing is to "applie my Pen to write [the] . . . never dying fame," of the countess of Cumberland, her former employer and the mother of Anne Clifford (see chapter 2). Therefore, the countess is Lanyer's center of interest, but she enhances her praises for the countess and enlarges her theme by depicting her as an example of feminine virtues. These virtues are set forth in accounts of Eve, the daughters of Jerusalem, and the Virgin Mary, as well as in tales of less exalted women and in repeated praises of the countess. Christ's passion is recounted, however briefly, because it is a subject in which the countess is interested and because she approves time spent on it; it is introduced into the poem in relation to the countess, who is a model of godliness who will enjoy eternal bliss because of the sacrifice of Christ. Once one appreciates the fact that the subject of this poem is the commendable qualities of women such as the countess of Cumberland, then the account of the life of Christ and the supportive materials concerning commendable women fall into perspective. Once the poem's axis is so established, the amount of attention given these subjects is reasonable.

Similarly, a shorter piece, appended to the main poem, has a legitimate place within such a frame. This piece is "A Description of Cookeham," a residence of the countess in which Lanyer lived when she was in her service; the emphasis in this description is on Cookeham's conduciveness to meditation and withdrawal from earthly things.

Finally, Lanyer's smooth style and skillful paraphrasing of biblical texts should be noted, and this writer should be placed on the periphery of the group of women writers who composed defenses of women.

The following selections are taken from *Salve Deux Rex Judaeorum . . .* (London: Valentine Simmes for Richard Bonian, 1611).

from *SALVE DEUX REX JUDAEORUM . . .*

Sith Cynthia [Elizabeth Tudor] is ascended to that rest
Of endlesse joy and true Eternitie,
That glorious place that cannot be exprest
By any wight clad in mortalitie,
In her almightie love so highly blest,   [5]

And crown'd with everlasting Sov'raigntie;
Where Saints and Angells do attend her Throne,
And she gives glorie unto God alone.

To thee great Countess now will I applie
My Pen, to write thy never dying fame;   [10]
That when to Heav'n thy blessed Soule shall flie,
These lines on earth record thy reverend name:
And to this taske I meane my Muse to tie,
Though wanting skill I shall but purchase blame:
Pardon (deere Ladie) want of womans wit   [15]
To pen thy praise, when few can equall it.

    . . . .
. . . thou, the wonder of our wanton age
Leav'st all delights to serve a heav'nly King: [170]
Who is more wise? or who can be more sage,
Than she that doth Affection subject bring;
Not forcing for the world, or Satans rage,
But shrowding under the Almighties wing;
Spending her yeares, moneths, daies, minutes, howres,   [175]
In doing service to the heav'nly powres.

[Many more praises of the countess follow, then an account of the Passion,
emphasizing the guilt of Pilate, who failed to follow his wife's sage advice.
This failure reverses the male and female roles in the Garden of Eden, when
Eve misguided Adam. And even in Paradise, Lanyer asserts, Adam sinned
more than Eve.]

Let not us Women glory in Mens fall,
Who had power given to over-rule us all.   [760]

Till now your indiscretion sets us free,
And makes our former fault much less appeare;
Our Mother *Eve*, who tasted of the Tree,
Giving to *Adam* what she held most deare,
Was simply good, and had no powre to see,   [765]
The after-comming harme did not appeare:
The subtile Serpent that our Sex betraide,
Before our fall so sure a plot had laide.

That undiscerning Ignorance perceav'd
No guile, or craft that was by him intended: [770]

For, had she knowne of what we were bereavid,
To his request she had not condiscended.
But she (poore soule) by cunning was deceav'd,
No hurt therein her harmlesse Heart intended:
For she alleag'd Gods word, which he denies   [775]
That they should die, but even as Gods, be wise.

But surely *Adam* cannot be excus'd,
Her fault, though great, yet he was most too blame;
What Weaknesse offerd, Strength might have refus'd,
Being Lord of all, the greater was his shame: [780]
Although the Serpents craft had her abus'd,
Gods holy word ought all his actions frame:
For he was Lord and King of all the earth,
Before poore *Eve* had either life or breath.

Who being fram'd by Gods eternall hand,   [785]
The perfectst man that ever breath'd on earth,
And from Gods mouth receiv'd that strait command,
The breach whereof he knew was present death:
Yea having powre to rule both Sea and Land,
Yet with one Apple wonne to loose that breath;   [790]
Which God hath breathed in his beauteous face,
Bringing us all in danger and disgrace.

And then to lay the fault on Patience backe,
That we (poore women) must endure it all;
We know right well he did discretion lacke,   [795]
Beeing not perswaded thereunto at all;
If Eve did erre, it was for knowledge sake,
The fruit beeing faire perswaded him to fall:
No subtill Serpents falshood did betray him,
If he would eate it, who had powre to stay him? (See milton)   [800]

Not *Eve*, whose fault was onely too much love,
Which made her give this present to her Deare,
That what shee tasted, he likewise might prove,
Whereby his knowledge might become more cleare;
He never sought her weaknesse to reprove,   [805]
With those sharpe words, which he of God did heare:
Yet men will boast of Knowledge, which he tooke
From *Eves* faire hand, as from a learned Booke.

If any Evill did in her remaine,
Beeing made of him, he was the ground of all,   [810]
If one of many Worlds could lay a staine
Upon our Sexe, and worke so great a fall
To wretched Man, by Satans subtill traine;
What will so fowle a fault amongst you all?
Her weaknesse did the Serpents words obay,   [815]
But you in malice Gods deare Sonne betray.

Whom, if unjustly you condemne to die,
Her sinne was small, to what you doe commit;
All mortall sinnes that doe for vengeance crie,
Are not to be compared unto it: [820]
If many worlds would altogether trie,
By all their sinnes the wrath of God to get;
This sinne of yours, surmounts them all as farre
As doth the Sunne, another little starre.

Then let us have our Libertie againe,   [825]
And challendge to your selves no Sov'raigntie;
You came not in the world without our paine,
Make that a barre against your crueltie;
Your fault beeing greater, why should you disdaine
Our beeing your equals, free from tyranny?   [830]
If one weake woman simply did offend,
This sinne of yours hath no excuse, nor end.

To which (poore soules) we never gave consent,
Witnesse thy wife (O *Pilate*) speakes for all;
Who did but dreame, and yet a message sent,   [835]
That thou should'st have nothing to doe at all
With that just man; which, if thy heart relent,
Why wilt thou be a reprobate with *Saul*?
To seeke the death of him that is so good,
For thy soules health to shed his dearest blood.   [840]

. . . .

[A similar strain of defense is evident in the description of the daughters of Jerusalem.]

Most blessed Daughters of *Jerusalem*,   [985]
Who found such favor in your Saviours sight,

To turne his face when you did pitie him;
Your tearefull eyes beheld his eyes more bright;
Your Faith and Love unto such grace did clime,
To have reflection from this Heav'nly light: [990]
Your eagles eies did gaze against this Sunne,
Your hearts did thinke, he dead, the world were done.

When spitefull men with torments did oppresse
Th'afflicted body of this innocent Dove,
Poore women seeing how much they did transgresse,   [995]
By teares, by sighs, by cries, intreate, nay prove,
What may be done among the thickest presse,
They labour still these tyrants hearts to move:
In pitie and compassion to forbeare

Their whipping, spurning, tearing of his haire,   [1000]
But all in vaine, their malice hath no end,
Their hearts more hard than flint, or marble stone;
Now to his griefe, his greatnesse they attend,
When he (God knowes) had rather be alone;
They are his guard, yet seeke all meanes t'offend;   [1005]
Well may he grieve, well may he sigh and groane;
Under the burden of a heavy crosse
He faintly goes to make their gaine his losse.

[The description of the Virgin Mary is sympathetic and realistic.]

His wofull Mother waiting on her Sonne,
All comfortlesse in depth of sorrow drownd;   [1010]
Her griefs extreame, although but new begunne,
To see his bleeding Body oft she swouned:
How could she choose but thinke her selfe undone,
He dying, with whose glory she was crowned?
None ever lost so great a losse as shee,   [1015]
Being Sonne, and Father of Eternitie.

Her teares did wash away his pretious blood,
That sinners might not tread it under feet
To worship him, and that it did her good
Upon her knees, although in open street,   [1020]
Knowing he was the Jessie floure and bud,
That must be gath'red when it smell'd most sweet:
Her Sonne, her Husband, Father, Saviour, King,
Whose death killd Death, and tooke away his sting.

Most blessed Virgin, in whose faultlesse fruit,   [1025]
All Nations of the earth must needes rejoyce,
No Creature having sence though ne'r so brute,
But joyes and trembles when they heare his voyce;
His wisedome strikes the wisest persons mute,
Faire chosen vessel, happy in his choyce: [1030]
Deere Mother of our Lord, whose reverend name,
All people Blessed call, and spread thy fame.

          .   .   .   .
What wonder in the world more strange could seeme,
Than that a Virgin could conceive and beare
Within her wombe a Sonne, That should redeeme
All Nations on the earth, and should repaire   [1100]
Our old decaies: who in such high esteeme,
Should prize all mortals, living in his feare;
As not to shun Death, Povertie, and Shame,
To save their soules, and spread his glorious Name.

          .   .   .   .
Who on his shoulders our blacke sinnes doth beare
To that most blessed, yet accursed Crosse;
Where fastning them, he rids us of our feare,
Yea, for our gaine he is content with losse,
Our ragged clothing scornes he not to weare,   [1125]
Though foule, rent, torne, disgracefull, rough and grosse,
Spunne by that monster Sinne, and weav'd by Shame,
Which grace it selfe, disgrac'd with impure blame.

How canst thou choose (faire Virgin) then but mourne,
When this sweet of-spring of thy body dies,   [1130]
When thy faire eies beholde his bodie torne,
The peoples fury, heares the womens cries;
His holy name prophan'd, He made a scorne,
Abusde with all their hatefull slaunderous lies:
Bleeding and fainting in such wondrous sort,   [1135]
As scarce his feeble limbes can him support.

          .   .   .   .

[After her description of the sacrifice of Christ, Lanyer returns to her praises of
the countess, to whom she attributes a true appreciation of the essential
message of Christianity.]

Loe Madame, heere you take a view of those,   [1825]
Whose worthy steps you doe desire to tread,
Deckt in those colours which our Saviour chose;

The purest colours both of White and Red,
Their freshest beauties would I faine disclose,
By which our Saviour most was honoured: [1830]
But my weake Muse desireth now to rest,
Folding up all their Beauties in your breast.

Whose excellence hath rais'd my sprites to write,
Of what my thoughts could hardly apprehend;
Your rarest Virtues did my soule delight,   [1835]
Great Ladie of my heart: I must commend
You that appeare so faire in all mens sight:
On your Deserts my Muses doe attend:
You are the Articke Starre that guides my hand,
All what I am, I rest at your command.   [1840]
FINIS.   [sigs. A-E4]

JANE ANGER (PSEUD.) (fl. 1589)

The individual who wrote under this pseudonym apparently is the earliest woman to have written a feminist pamphlet in England. Her work appeared in 1589, in answer to a misogynist tract she describes as "the newe surfeit of an olde lover . . . which came by chance to my handes"; her concern is limited to men's sexual trickery. Jane exemplifies the woman from the lower ranks of society who was moved to answering such attacks and defending her sex. As Kohler states, "no set piece of defense . . . has been traced to the pen of a woman of noble or even of exceptionally gentle birth."[12] Despite the temerity of Jane Anger and of the other writers who defended women, only one, Rachel Speght, used her own name.

The following selection is taken from *Jane Anger, her Protection for Women* . . . (London: Richard Jones and Thomas Orwin, 1589).

from *Jane Anger, her Protection for Women* . . .

The greatest fault that doth remaine in us women is, that we are too credulous, for could we flatter as they [men] can dissemble, and use our wittes well, as they can their tongues ill, then never would any of them complaine of surfeiting. But if we women be so so perillous cattell as they terme us, I marvell that the Gods made not Felicitie as well a man, as they created her a woman, and all the morall vertues of their masculine sex, as of the feminine kinde, except their Deities knewe that there was some soveraity in us women, which could not be in them men. . . . The Gods knowing that the mindes of mankind would be aspiring, and having thoroughly viewed the wonderfull vertues wherewith women are inriched, least they should provoke us to pride, and so con-found us with Lucifer, they bestowed the supremacy over us to man, that of that Cockscombe he might onely boast, and therfore for Gods sake let them keepe it.

.   .   .   .

Wee are contrary to men, because they are contrarie to that which is good: because they are pur blind, they cannot see into our natures, and we too well (though we had but halfe an eie) into their conditions, because they are so bad: our behaviours alert daily, because mens vertues decay hourely.

. . . .

  Esteeme of men as of a broken Reed,
  Mistrust them still, and then you wel shall speede.

[L]et us secretlye our selves with our selves, consider howe and in what, they that are our worst enemies, are both inferiour unto us, & most beholden unto our kindenes.

  The creation of man and woman at the first, hee being formed In principio of drosse and filthy clay, did so remaine until God saw that in him his workmanship was good, and therfore by the tranformation of the dust which was loathsome unto flesh, it became putrified. Then lacking a help for him, GOD making woman of mans fleshe, that she might bee purer then he, doth evidently showe, how far we women are more excellent then men. Our bodies are fruitfull, wherby the world increaseth, and our care wonderful, by which man is preserved. From woman sprang mans salvation. A woman was the first that beleeved, & a woman likewise the first that repented of Sin. In women is onely true Fidelity. . . . They confesse we are necessarie, but they would have us likewise evil. . . . [L] east some should snarle on me, barking out this reason: that none is good but God, and therfore women are ill. I must yeeld that in this respect we are il, & affirm that men are no better, seeing we are so necessarie unto them.

. . . .

  I have set downe unto you (which are of mine owne sex) the subtil dealing of untrue meaning men: not that you should contemne al men, but to the end that you may take heed of the false hearts of al & stil reproove the flattery which remaines in all: for as it is reason that the hennes should be served first, which both lay the egs & hatch the chickins: so it were unreasonable that the cockes which tread them, should be kept clean without meat. As men are valiant, so are they vertuous: and those that are borne honorably, cannot beare horrible dissembling heartes. But as there are some which cannot love hartely, so there are many who lust uncessantly, & as many of them wil deserve wel, so most care not how il they speed so they may get our company. Wherin they resemble Envie, who will be contented to loose one of his eies that another might have both his pulled out. And therefore thinke well of as many as you may, love them that you have cause, heare every thing that they say, (& affoord them noddes which make themselves Noddies) but beleeve very little therof or nothing at all; and hate all those, who shall speake any thing in the dispraise or to the dishonour of our sex.

[sigs. B3-D1]

RACHEL SPEGHT (fl. 1617-1621)

  In 1615, a particularly virulent and poorly written attack on women was issued by one Joseph Swetnam under the title *The Arraignment of Lewd, Idle, Froward and unconstant women*.[13] In 1617, three responses appeared to this attack, which then had been reissued for the fourth time. There is a slight possibility that the attack and the responses to it were part of a scheme to make profits. However, this is unlikely.[14]

The earliest of the responses entered on the Stationer's *Register* was by Rachel Speght (see chapter 1), who issued a fairly subdued rejoinder. Her work is composed of two main parts, and the arguments, reminiscent of those of the early humanists and reformers, are mainly biblical and occasionally classical. The first section of her work is an eloquent, mature, and sustained argument for the nobility of women. It is well organized and excellently written, and its intensity places it above even serious tracts by male theorists. The second portion of the pamphlet, entitled *Certaine Quaeries to the Bayter of Women* [Swetnam] . . ., is placed in an epilogue and attacks specific points in Swetnam's tract. This section is more argumentative and lively than the first; however, it has no unity beyond the fact that the thrusts are aimed at Swetnam's points. It is closer than the first part to the polemic associated with such Elizabethan pamphleteers as Nashe, Greene, and Harvey.

The following selections are taken from *A Mouzell for Melastomus* . . . (London: Nicholas Okes for Thomas Archer, 1617).

from *A Mouzell for Melastomus* . . .

If lawfull it bee to compare the Potter with his Clay, or the Architect with the Edifice, then may I, in some sort, resemble that love of God towards man, in creating woman, unto the affectionate care of *Abraham* for his sonne *Isaac*, who that hee might not take to wife one of the daughters of the *Cannanites*, did provide him one of his owne Kindred [Gen. 24:1-67].

. . . the resplendent love of God toward man appeared, in taking care to provide him an helper before hee saw his owne want, and in providing him such an helper as should bee meete for him. Soveraignety had hee over all creatures, and they were all serviceable unto him; but yet afore woman was formed, there was not a meete helpe found for *Adam*. Mans worthineese not meriting this great favour at Gods hands, but his mercie onely moving him thereunto: I may use those words which the *Jewes* uttered when they saw Christ weepe for *Lazarus, Behold how hee loved him* [John 11:36]: Behold, and that with good regard, Gods love; yea his great love, which from the beginning hee hath borne unto man: which, as it appeares in all things; so next his love in Christ Jesus apparantly in this; that for mans sake, that hee might not be an unite, when all other creatures were for procreation duall, hee created woman to bee a solace unto him, to participate of his sorrowes, partake of his pleasures, and as a good yokefellow beare part of his burthen. Of the excellencie of this Structure, I meane of Woman, whose foundation and original of creation, was Gods love, do I intend to dilate.

. . . .

[Speght proceeds to answer some traditional objections against women and offer some traditional retorts as well as some individual ones.]

. . . [W]oman was made . . . to be a Companion and *helper* for man; and if she must be an helper, and but an helper, then are those husbands to be blamed, which lay the whole burthen of domesticall affaires and maintenance on the shoulders of their wives. For, as yoake-fellowes they are to sustayne part of ech others cares, griefs, and calamities: . . . So that neither the wife may say to her husband, nor the husband unto his wife, I have no need of thee, no more then the members of the body may so say each to other, betweene whom there is such a sympathie, that if one member suffer, all suffer with it. . . .

Marriage is a merri-age, and this worlds Paradise, where there is mutuall love. Our blessed Saviour vouchsafed to honour a marriage with the first miracle that he wrought [John 2:1-11]. . . .

And not a few, but many times, doth our blessed Saviour in the Canticles, set forth his unspeakable love towards his Church under the title of an Husband rejoycing with his Wife; and often vouchsafeth to call her his Sister and Spouse, by which is shewed that with *God is no respect of persons*, Nations, or Sexes: for whosoever, whether it be man or woman, that *doth beleeve in the Lord Jesus, such shall bee saved*. And if Gods love even from the beginning, had not beene as great toward woman as to man, then would hee not have preserved from the deluge of the old world as many women as men; nor would Christ after his Resurrection have appeared unto a woman first of all other, had it not beene to declare thereby, that the benefites of his death and resurrection, are as available, by beleefe, for women as for men; for hee indifferently died for the one sex as well as the other: Yet a truth ungainesayable is it, that the *Man is the womans Head*; by which title yet of Supremacie, no authoritie hath hee given him to domineere, or basely command and imploy his wife, as a servant; but hereby is he taught the duties which hee oweth unto her: For as the head of a man is the imaginer and contriver of projects profitable for the safety of his whole body; so the Husband must protect and defend his Wife from injuries. . . . Secondly, as the Head doth not jarre or contend with the members, which *being many*, as the Apostle saith, *yet make but one bodie*; no more must the husband with the wife. . . . Thirdly, and lastly, as hee is her Head, hee must, by instruction, bring her to the knowledge of her Creator, that so she may be a fit stone for the Lords building. Women for this end must have an especiall care to set their affections upon such as are able to teach them. . . .

Thus if men would remember the duties they are to performe in being heads, some would not stand a tip-toe as they doe, thinking themselves Lords & Rulers. . . . But least I should seeme too partiall in praysing women so much as I have (though no more then warrant from Scripture doth allow) I adde to the premises, that I say not, all women are vertuous, for then they should be more excellent then men, sith of *Adams* sonnes there was *Cain* as well as *Abel*, and of *Noahs*, *Cham* as well as *Sam*; so that of men as of women, there are two sorts, namely, good and bad, which in *Mathew* the five and twenty chapter, are comprehended under the name of *Sheepe* and *Goats*. And if women were not sinfull, then should they not need a Saviour: but the Virgin *Mary* a patterne of piety, *rejoyced in God her Saviour: Ergo*, she was a sinner. In the *Revelation* the Church is called the Spouse of Christ; and in *Zachariah*, wickednesse is called a woman, to shew that of women there are both godly and ungodly: for Christ would not *Purge his Floore* if there were not Chaffe among the Wheate; nor should gold need to be fined, if among it there were no drosse. But farre be it from any one, to condemne the righteous with the wicked, or good women with the bad (as the Bayter of Women doth:) For though there are some scabbed sheepe in a Flocke, we must not therefore conclude all the rest to bee mangie: And though some men, through excesse, abuse Gods creatures, wee must not imagine that all men are Gluttons, the which wee may with as good reason do, as condemne all women in generall, for the offences of some particulars. Of the good sort is it that I have in this booke spoken, and so would I that all that reade it should so understand me: for if otherwise I had done, I should have incurred that woe, which by the Prophet *Isaiah* is pronounced against them that *speake well of evill*, and should have *justified the wicked, which thing is abominable to the Lord.*   [sigs. C-E2]

ESTER SOWERNAM (PSEUD.) (fl. 1617)

The second of the responses to Swetnam is by an author, presumably a woman, who called herself Ester Sowernam. Nothing can be said of this woman beyond the strong possibility that she was from the middle class, since her dedicatory remarks were addressed to London apprentices. She refers to Speght's pamphlet and states that she is writing to complete "the maid's" arguments. Her writing is more lively than Speght's, and her work is more replete with classical references. It is composed of several parts, some of which are quite inventive: an estimation of women in antiquity and in British history; an arraignment of Swetnam before the bar of justice, and two jaunty poems (not included here), besides the usual scriptural defenses of the nobility of women.

The following selections are taken from *Ester hath hang'd Haman . . .* (London: Printed for Nicholas Bourne, 1617).

from *Ester hath hang'd Haman . . .*

If the author of this *Arraignment* had performed his discourse either answerable to the Title, or the Arguments of the Chapters; hee had been so farre off from being answered by me, that I should have commended so good a labour, which is imployed to give vice just reproofe, and vertue honourable report. But at the very first entrance of his discourse, in the very first page, he discovereth himselfe neither to have truth in his promise, nor religious performance. . . .

I am not onely provoked by this Authour to defend women, but I am more violently urged to defend divine Majestie in the worke of his Creation.

. . . .

The Argument of the first Chapter is, *to shew to what use Women were made*; it also sheweth, *That most of them degenerate from the use they were framed unto, etc.*

Now, to shew to what use woman was made, hee beginneth thus. *At the first beginning a Woman was made to bee an helper to Man: And so they are indeed, for they helpe to consume and spend, etc.* This is all the use, and all the end which the Authour setteth downe in all his discourse for the creation of woman. Marke a ridiculous jeast in this: Spending and consuming of that which Man painfully getteth, is by this Authour the use for which Women were made. And yet (saith hee in the Argument) *most of them degenerate from the use they were framed unto.* Woman was made to spend and consume at the first: But women doe degenerate from this use, *Ergo, Midasse doth contradict himselfe. . . .*

He runneth on, and saith, *They were made of a Rib, and that their froward and crooked nature doth declare, for a Rib is a crooked thing, etc.*

Woman was made of a crooked rib, so she is crooked of conditions. *Joseph Swetnam* was made as from *Adam* of clay and dust, so he is of a durty and muddy disposition: The inferences are both alike in either; woman is no more crooked, in respect of the one; but he is blasphemous in respect of the other.

. . . .

. . . having examined what . . . *Joseph Swetnam* hath wrested out of Scriptures, to dishonour and abuse all women: I am resolved . . . to collect and note out of Scriptures . . . what incomparable and most excellent prerogatives God hath bestowed upon women, . . . what choyse God hath made of women, in using them as instruments to worke his . . . designes for the generall benefit of man-kind . . . [and] what excellent and divine graces have beene bestowed upon our Sexe . . . in the worke of Redemption.

. . . .

It appeareth by that Soveraignty which God gave to *Adam* over all the Creatures of Sea and Land, that man was the end of Gods creation, whereupon it doth necessarily, without all exception follow, *Adam* being the last worke, is therefore the most excellent worke of creation: yet *Adam* was not so absolutely perfect, but that in the sight of God, he wanted an *Helper.* . . .

It is furthermore to be considered, as the Maide, in her *Mussell for Melastomius* hath observed: that God intended to honour woman . . . in that he created her out of a subject refined. . . .

That delight, solace, and pleasure, which shall come to man by woman, is prognosticated by that place wherein woman was created: for she was framed in Paradice, . . .

When woman was created, God brought her unto *Adam*, and then did solempnise that most auspicious Marriage betwixt them. . . .

Joseph Swetnam, having written his rash, idle, furious and shamefull discourse against Women . . . it was concluded . . . as he had arraigned women at the barre of fame and report, . . . at the same barre where he did us the wrong to arraigne him, that thereby wee might defend our assured right. . . .

So that wee brought him before two Judgesses, *Reason*, and *Experience.* . . .

[W]ee . . . were well pleased that his five Senses and the seaven deadly sinnes should stand for his Jury. . . .

. . . [A]ll things being accordingly provided, the prisoner was brought to the barre, where he was called and bid hold up his hand, which hee did, but a false hand God he knowes, his enditement was red, which was this which followeth. . . .

. . . As *Eve* did not offend without the temptation of a Serpent; so women doe seldome offend, but it is by provocation of men. Let not your impudencie, nor your consorts dishonestie, charge our sexe hereafter, with those sinnes of which you your selves were the first procurers. . . . [Y]ou charge women with clamorous words, and bring no proofes; I charge you with blasphemie, with impudencie, scurilitie, foolery and the like. I shew just and direct proofe for what I say. . . .

Now, . . . to draw to an end, let me aske according to the question of *Cassian*, *Cui bono?* what have you gotten by publishing your Pamphlet; good I know you can get none. You have (perhaps) pleased the humors of some giddy, idle, conceited persons: But you have died your selfe in the colours of shame, lying, slandering, blasphemie, ignorance, and the like. [pp. 1-47]

CONSTANTIA MUNDA (PSEUD.) (fl.1617)

The third response to Swetnam's broadside is perhaps the closest to a professional and journalistic pamphlet of the three. Constantia Munda, presumably a woman, wrote with scrupulous attention to diction and the proper attribution of quotations, curious in a user of near-scurrilous invective. One point of attack on Swetnam concerns his careless diction and lack of precision. Possibly Munda was the most educated and most knowledgeable of the three authors of these feminist pamphlets, since she uses quotations from several languages and draws on information relating to the higher professions. Like Ester Sowernam, she refers to the defenses of her predecessors, and apparently she is attempting to bolster their arguments. She seems less intensely religious than the other writers of these feminist pamphlets.

The following selection is taken from *The Worming of a madde Dogge . . .* (London: Printed for Lawrence Hayes, 1617).

from *The Worming of a madde Dogge . . .*

The itching desire of oppressing the presse with many sottish and illiterate Libels stuft with all manner of ribaldry, and sordid inventions, when every foule-mouthed male-content may disgorge his *Licambaen* poyson in the face of all the world, hath broken out into such a dismall contagion in these our dayes, that every scandalous tongue and opprobious witte, like the Italian Mountebankes will advance their pedling wares of detracting virulence in the publique *Piazza* of every Stationers shoppe. And Printing that was invented to be the store-house of famous wits, the treasure of Divine literature, the pandect and maintainer of all Sciences, is become the receptacle of every dissolute Pamphlet. . . . To call that imperfect, froward, crooked and perverse to make an arraignment and Beare-baiting of that which the Pantocrator would in his omniscient wisedome have to be the consummation of his blessed weekes worke, the end, crowne, and perfection of the never-sufficiently glorified creation. What is it but an exorbitant phrensie, and wofull taxation of the supreme deitie. Yet woman the greatest part of the *lesser world* is generally become the subject of every pendanticall goose-quill. . . . Though feminine modesty hath confin'd our rarest and ripest wits to silence, wee acknowledge it our greatest ornament, but when necessity compels us, tis as great a fault and folly *loquenda tacere, ut contra gravis est culpa tacenda loqui*, being too much provoked by arrainments, baytings, and rancarous impeachments of the reputation of our whole sex, *stulta est clementia—peritura parcere carta*, opportunity of speaking slipt, by silence, is as bad as importunity upheld by babling. . . . Know therefore that wee will cancell your accusations, travers your bils, and come upon you for a false inditement. . . . What if you had cause to be offended with some (as I cannot excuse all) must you needs shoot your paper-pellets out of your potgun-pate at all women?

. . . .

[A] private abuse of your owne familiar doxies should not breake out into open slanders of the religious matron together with the prostitute strumpet; of the nobly-descended Ladies, as the obscure base vermine that have bitten you; of the chaste and modest virgins, as well as the dissolute and impudent harlot. . . . In the commemorations of founders and benefactors, how many women have emulated your sex in bountifull exhibitions to religious uses and furtherance of pietie? I might produce infinite examples, if neede were: but bray a foole in a morter . . . yet he will not leave his foolerie. . . . [I]t may be you have a further drift, to make the world beleeve you have an extraordinary gift of continencie; soothing your selfe with this supposition, that this open reviling is some token and evidence you never were affected with delicate and effeminate sensualitie, thinking this pamphlet should assoile thee from all manner of levie and taxation of a lascivious life. . . . I would make this excuse for you, but that the crabbednesse of your stile, the unsavory periods of your broken-winded sentences perswade your body to be of the same temper as your minde. . . . Ile take the paines to worme the tongue of your madnesse, and dash your rankling teeth downe your throat. . . . [T]hou that acknowledgest thy selfe to be madde, in a rough furie, your wits gon a woolgathering that you had forgot your selfe (as I think) Nero-like in ripping up the bowels of thine owne Mother for I have learnt so much Logicke to know . . . whatsoever is spoken or praedicated on the kinde is spoken of every one in the same kinde. . . . Is it not a comely thing to heare a Sonne speake thus of his mother: . . . Doe you not blush to see what a halter you have purchased for your owne necke? . . . [I]s this the requitall of all her cost, charge, care, and unspeakable paines she suffered in the producing of such a monster into the light? If she had cram'd gravell downe thy throat when shee gave thee sucke, or exposed thee to the mercy of the wilde beasts in the wildernesse when she fed thee with the pap, thou couldst not have showen thy selfe more ungratefull then thou hast in belching out thy nefarious contempt of thy mothers sexe. . . . Although thou art not apprehended and attached for thy villany I might say fellonie, before a corporall judge, yet thine owne conscience if it be not seared up, tortures thee, and wracks thy tempestuous minde with a dissolution and whurring too and fro of thy scandalous name, which without blemish my penne can scarce deigne to write.

.   .   .   .

Your indiscretion is as great in the laying together & compiling of your stolne ware, as your blockishnesse in stealing. . . . Sometimes your dogrill rhymes make mee smile. . . . Sometimes you make me burst out with laughter. . . . Doest thou not blush . . . to pervert . . . the strait wayes of God, by prophaning the Scriptures . . . besides thy pitifully wronging of the Philosophers . . . whom your illiterate and clownish Muse never was so happy to know whether they wrote any thing or no. . . . But you that will traduse the holie Scriptures, what hope is there but you will deprave humane authors. . . . I would runne through all your silly discourse, and anatomize your basery, but as some have partly beene boulted out already, and are promised to be prosecuted, so I leave them as not worthy rehearsall or refutation.   [pp. 1-31]

DIANA PRIMROSE (fl. 1630)

Diana Primrose was the composer of a competent memorial, in rimed couplets, to Elizabeth I. She praises ten conventional and accepted virtues (religion, chastity, prudence, temperance, clemency, justice, fortitude, science, patience, and bounty) which she ascribes to Elizabeth and recommends to "All Noble Ladies and Gentlewomen." These virtues parallel some of the virtues described in Spenser's *Faerie Queene*. The praise of Diana

Primrose, in the dedicatory poem by Dorothy Berry, echoes the sentiments of the entire work.

The following selection is taken from *A Chaine of Pearle* . . . (London: for Thomas Paine, 1630).

from *A CHAINE OF PEARLE* . . .

TO ALL NOBLE LADIES, AND GENTLE-WOMEN.
To You the Honour of our Noble Sex,
I send this CHAINE, with all my best Respects:
Which if you please to weare, for her sweet sake,
For whom I did this slender POEM make.   [5]
You shall erect a Trophie to her Name,
And crowne your selves with never-fading fame.
                        Devoted to your Vertues,
                        Diana P.   [sig. A2]

TO THE EXCELLENT LADY, THE COMPOSER OF THIS WORKE.
Shine forth (Diana) dart thy Golden Raies,
On her blest Life and Raigne, whose Noble Praise
Deserves a Quill pluckt from an Angels wing,
And none to write it but a Crowned King.
Shee, shee it was, that gave us Golden Daies,   [5]
And did the English Name to Heaven raise:
Blest be her Name! blest be her Memory!
That *England* crown'd with such Felicity.
And thou, the *Prime-Rose* of the *Muses* nine,
(In whose sweete Verse ELIZA'S Fame doth shine,   [10]
Like some resplendent Star in frosty night)
Hast made thy Native Splendor far more bright,
Since all thy PEARLES are peerles-orient,
And to thy selfe a precious Ornament.
This is my censure of thy ROYALL CHAINE   ] 15]
Which a far better Censure well may claime.
                        Dorothy Berry.   [sig. A3]

The Induction

As Golden Phoebus with his radiant face
Enthron'd in his Triumphant Chaire of State,
The twinkling Stars and Asterismes doth chase
With his Imperiall Scepter, and doth hate
All consorts in his Starry Monarchy,   [5]

As prejudiciall to his Soveraignty.
So Great ELIZA, England's brightest Sun,
The Worlds Renowne and everlasting Lampe,
Admits not here the least Comparison;
Whose Glories, doe the Greatest Princes dampe.   [10]
That ever Sceptor swaid or Crown did weare,
Within the Verge of either Hemispheare.
Thou English Goddesse, Empresse of our Sex,
O Thou whose Name still raignes in all our hearts,
To whom are due our ever-vowd Respects!   [15]
How shall I blazon thy most Royall parts?
Which in all Parts did so divinely shine,
As they deserve APOLLO'S Quill (not mine.)
Yet, since the GODS accept the humble Vowes
Of Mortalls, daigne (O Thou Star-crowned Queen)   [20]
T'accept these ill-composed Pearly-Rowes:
Wherein, thy Glory chiefly shall be seene:
For by these Lines so black and impolite,
Thy Swan-like Lustre shall appeare more white.
            Thy Emperiall Majesties eternall Votary,
                    DIANA.   [sig. A4]

The fift Pearle
Clemency

Her Royall *Clemency* comes next in view,
The Vertue which in her did most renew
The image of *Her* Maker, who in that
Exceeds himselfe, and doth commiserate
His very Rebells, lending them the light   [5]
Of Sunne and Moone, and all those Diamonds bright.
So did ELIZA cast *Her* Golden Rayes
Of *Clemency*, on those which many wayes
Transgrest *Her* Lawes, and sought to undermine
The Church and State, and did with Spaine combine.   [10]
And though by Rigor of the Law *Shee* might
Not wronging them, have taken all *Her* right
Yet *Her* Innate and princely *Clemencie*
Mov'd Her to pardon their Delinquencie,
Which sought Her Gracious Mercy, and repented   [15]
Their Misdemeanors, and their Crimes lamented.
So doth the Kingly Lyon with his foe,
Which once prostrate, he scornes to worke his woe.
So did this Vertues sacred Auri flame,
Immortalize our Great ELIZA's Name.   [p. 7]   [20]

MARY FAGE (fl. 1637)

From remarks in the dedication to her composition, it can be inferred that Mary Fage, who describes herself as the "wife of Robert Fage, the younger, Gentleman," was acquainted with the royal family, despite her middle-class status. The many learned allusions and Latin quotations throughout the work suggest that she was well educated. Therefore, she is another example of the educated woman of the middle class. Her text consists of four hundred and twenty clumsily written acrostic verses formed from the names or titles of royalty and nobility, and written in the rhetoric of praise. However, it would be a mistake to say, with Ruth Hughey, that "any significance [of *Fames Roule*] lies in the fact that it was another attempt at verse making by a woman from the middle ranks."[15] An equally significant point is the ease with which this female hanger-on could beg for sustenance; the attitude and tone of her work are those of one accustomed to and comfortable with the production of excessive flattery; the rather obvious motive for this flattery is supplied in the last verse. One wonders whether Mary Fage attempted to support herself through her writing, and whether she can be included in the rather small number of Renaissance Englishwomen who were professional writers. Certainly the dedicatory letter by Esther Kello, included below, is less offensively cloying only because it is addressed to just one person.

The following selections are taken from *Fames Roule* . . . (London: Richard Oulton, 1637).

from *FAMES ROULE* . . .

To the Kings Most Excellent Majestie: Carolus Stuarte. Anagramma.

Av: Sol's Tru Trace.

>   CHARLES our great Monarch, on my bended knee,
>   AV! much-admiring at your Majesty!
>   R   ender I to your sacred Personage
>   O   f your most Princely vertues, this true gage:
>   L   ustrous your beames of brightnes, like true *Sol*,   [5]
>   V   ailes the beholders eyes, or dazels all,
>   S   hining in glory over all the Earth;
>   S   hewing your light unto the greatest birth:
>   T   he severall planets of our firmament,
>   V   ertues nobility, their lustre lent,   [10]
>   AV! have from you, our true and lively Sunne,
>   R   eleeving with your heat, where ere you come.
>   T   hus just true fervour in your person pace,
>   E   nliv'ning all things in your *SOL'S TRU TRACE.*   [pp. 1-2]

Sun, Moone, and Stars, yee rare Birds of the skie,
That in your thought, to vertues heav'n do flie;
Riches of Heaven and Earth, I doubt if rich
At all there be, beyond your glorious pitch:
Pardon the portrait of your handmaids Pen,   [5]
Presuming you to paint, the Worthiest Men:
Take it as what shee had, shee hath no better,
Accept it kindly, shee'l abide your debtor:
And your rich natures so will richly shine
For kind acceptance is a thing divine.   [10]

M.F.

FINIS   [p. 297]

IMAGINATIVE LITERATURE

During the late Middle Ages, writers in the courtly love tradition attributed to women the encouragement and inspiration for their literary efforts about love. The association of actual women with the production of works of art was refined by Dante and Petrarch into an attribution of the inspiration for their highest creative activities to Beatrice and Laura.

After the introduction of the printing press in England, women there acted as sponsors of written works; the encouragement by Margaret Stanley, countess of Richmond, of the earliest works of William Caxton, Wynkyn de Worde, and Richard Pynson has been noted (see chapter 2). The growing erudition of Renaissance Englishwomen and the increasing interest they took in the intellectual and literary works of their time are reflected in the dedication of works to them by poets and scholars; these writers often sought support or patronage for their efforts in dedications ranging from the dignified acknowledgment of past and present favors to excessive flattery in hope of future support. The dedications often note the creative work of the women to whom they are addressed; sometimes poems are written to or about these supporters of the muse.[16]

Generally, Renaissance Englishwomen made little effort to publicize or even print their own literary efforts. Possibly this failure is a result of the negative attitude taken by the male arbiters of the time regarding works by women on subjects outside the spheres of religion and domesticity, which were considered the province of women. Interesting light is shed on this question in an unusual preface by Margaret Tyler, who translated the Spanish romance *The mirrour of princely deedes and knighthood* in 1578. In her prefatory letter to the reader, Tyler attempts to justify her work:

. . . [M]y defence is by example of the best, amongst which many have dedicated their labours, some stories, some of warre, some phisick, some lawe, some as concerning government, some divine matters, unto divers ladies & gentlewomen. And if men may & doe bestow such of their travailes upon gentlewomen, then may we women read such of their works as they dedicate unto us, and if we may read them, why not farther wade in them to the serch of a truth. And then much more why not deale by translation in such arguments, especially this kinde of exercise being a matter of more heede then of deep invention or exquisite learning, & they must needs leave this as confessed, that in their dedications they minde not only to borrow names of worthy personages, but the testimonies also for their further credit, which neither the one may demaund without ambition, nor the other graunt without overlightnes: if women be excluded from the view of such workes as appeare in their name, or if glory onely be sought in our common inscriptions, it mattereth not whether the parties be men or women, whether alive or dead. . . . [M]y perswasion hath bene thus, that it is all one for a woman to pen a story, as for a man to addresse his story to a woman. But amongst al my il willers, some I hope are not so straight that they would enforce me necessarily either not to write or to write of divinitie. . . . And thus much as concerning this present story, that it is neither unseemly for a woman to deale in, neither greatly requiring a lesse staied age then mine is. But of these two points gentle reader I thought to give thee warning, least perhaps understanding of my name & yeares, thou mightest be carried into a wrong suspect of my boldnesse and rashnesse, from which I would gladly free my selfe by this plain excuse, & if I may deserve thy good favour by lyke labour, when the choice is mine owne I will have a speciall regard of thy liking.[17]

Almost nothing is known of this bold translator besides the detail mentioned in her other dedicatory letter (to Lord Thomas Howard); in it Tyler says that she was once a servant to Lord Howard's parents.

Some information also should be given concerning two other women translators, whose contributions lie in the drama. The two are Lady Joanna Lumley and Lady Mary Herbert. Their translations constitute two of the three complete works in drama by Renaissance Englishwomen; the third effort is an original drama by Elizabeth Cary, Lady Falkland, and is considered in Part II.

The earlier of the two translators is Lady Joanna Lumley, née Fitzalan (1534-1576), the older of the daughters of Henry Fitzalan, earl of Arundel. She married John, Lord Lumley, in 1549. Harold Child, the editor of her translation of Euripides' Iphigenia at Aulis, dates the translation of the tragedy as closely subsequent to her marriage. The translation was transcribed into a handwritten notebook, and the drama is the only item in the book in English; the rest is in Latin. Although the play is translated into prose and is completely lacking in gracefulness, it is also, in Child's words, "the earliest attempt to render into English a work of one of the Greek dramatists."[18] Furthermore, the translation was made at a time when a knowledge of Greek was rare among Elizabethans. Since Lady Lumley's effort remained unpublished until 1909, it had no impact on the drama of her time. Its significance lies, first, in its demonstration of the remarkable erudition of its young translator; second, in its subject, which could be expressed as the abuse of two females in a patriarchal society; and, third, in Lady Lumley's interest in this subject. For

Clytemnestra and Iphigenia are the only personages in the drama who are depicted as admirable individuals. Therefore, the choice of *Iphigenia at Aulis* for translation is suggestive, since this drama sympathetically portrays women as victims, as maids, wives, and mothers.

Although it must be conceded that there is no historical influence to be attributed to Lady Lumley's unpublished translation, the same cannot be said for the translation of Garnier's *Antonie* by Lady Mary Herbert, countess of Pembroke. According to her editor, Alice Luce, the countess's translation, called *The Tragedie of Antonie*, was "the first of that series of pure Seneca plays which appeared in the last decade of Elizabeth's reign . . . it afterwards became the model of the only two plays in the literature which are written wholly in the style of the French Seneca drama."[19] Thus the countess is associated with a type of drama which, although originally elitist, eventually filtered into such popular plays as Kyd's *Spanish Tragedy* and Shakespeare's *Titus Andronicus*.

The translation of Garnier by the countess, while differing in minor details from the French, is very close to the text as it appears in the 1595 reprint of Garnier's works; the countess uses rhyme schemes systematically related to Garnier's for the choruses, and blank verse for most of the remainder of the text, which Garnier wrote in French Alexandrines. Altogether, Luce notes, the translation demonstrates the countess's "command of form and metre."[20] Of interest is her choice of the subject of the fidelity of Cleopatra and the love of Antony. One might even speculate that it was Garnier's interpretation of the character of Cleopatra that stimulated the countess to translate his play; for Garnier's Cleopatra is strikingly dependent and certainly cast as a victim. In a reversal of conventional thought, Cleopatra is not the ultimate charmer or seducer, but rather the hapless mother, unable to effect what she strives for despite her seemingly exalted position and powerful personality. If she is not tantalizing in the same sense as Shakespeare's Cleopatra, she is nevertheless intriguing to the student of the Renaissance by virtue of her interest for Lady Herbert. The work also is important as a finished, artful translation and as a "begetter" of similar works.

Other translators of literary materials among Renaissance Englishwomen include Queen Elizabeth, who translated such classical materials as a letter by Seneca, a dialogue by Xenophon, and two orations by Isocrates,[21] and Lady Mary (Fitzalan) Howard, sister of Lady Lumley, who translated *Certain Ingenious Sentences . . .*[22] from Greek to Latin.

The need to analyze and group materials in order to provide an intelligible account of the writings of Renaissance Englishwomen has dictated the inclusion of many literary materials in other sections of this study. Such works as Lady Colville's *Godlie Dreame*, Anne Dacre's elegy, and Elizabeth Grymeston's tract could have been assembled under the heading of imaginative literature, which they are, had the scheme of this anthology not required that they be included elsewhere. Therefore, this section is the poorer for want of works lending themselves primarily to religious or domestic classifications; any reader who has read the materials in the preceding sections will realize that many of the selections are not only social documents of importance but are also literary creations deserving of recognition. Some of the works in Part II have greater literary worth than those grouped in this section. Conversely, the works in this section are not all of the first rank, but all are worthy of notice and all are imaginative rather than domestic or religious. The reader's attention is directed particularly to the very unusual materials by Isabella Whitney, which are of an assertive and buoyant nature uncommon among the writings of Renaissance Englishwomen.

ELIZABETH TUDOR, QUEEN OF ENGLAND (1533-1603)

The following poem is generally considered to be Elizabeth's, although Leicester Bradner considers it among the "doubtful" poems attributed to the queen and notes that its "facile wit" is unlike her other poems.[23] The text is taken from Leicester Bradner, ed. *The Poems of Queen Elizabeth I* (Providence, R.I.: Brown University Press, 1964).

WHEN I WAS FAIR AND YOUNG . . .

When I was fair and young, then favor graced me.
Of many was I sought their mistress for to be,
But I did scorn them all and answered them therefore:
Go, go, go, seek some other where, importune me no more.

How many weeping eyes I made to pine in woe,   [5]
How many sighing hearts I have not skill to show,
But I the prouder grew and still this spake therefore:
Go, go, go, seek some other where, importune me no more.

Then spake fair Venus' son, that brave victorious boy,
Saying: You dainty dame, for that you be so coy,   [10]
I will so pluck your plumes as you shall say no more:
Go, go, go, seek some other where, importune me no more.

As soon as he had said, such change grew in my breast
That neither night nor day I could take any rest.
Wherefore I did repent that I had said before: [15]
Go, go, go, seek some other where, importune me no more.   [p. 7]

ISABELLA WHITNEY (fl. 1567-1573)

It is unfortunate that virtually nothing is known of this rather unusual Elizabethan writer, apparently the first declared professional woman poet in England. She may have been related to Geoffrey Whitney of Cheshire, who was the author of an early emblem book entitled *A Choice of Emblemes* (1586).[24] She is an early woman writer of secular materials and an important example of the type who produced a relatively high number of secular works from 1570 to 1600. Her simple themes and restrained language are similar to those of George Gascoigne, Barnebe Googe, and George Turberville. Her many allusions are classical rather than biblical, her verse is fluent, and her point of view is secular. Furthermore, she is jocose, almost carefree. From remarks in her works we can infer that she was of the middle class; her sisters are servants, and she herself has lost a position. She shows an easy familiarity with and affection for the city of London; in general, she seems to be the type of Elizabethan woman of letters Virginia Woolf mistakenly thought to have no existence in Elizabethan days.[25]

Portions of several of Whitney's works follow. The earliest is a verse letter to a false lover, written in the tradition of Ovid's *Heroides*,[26] and joined, when it was issued, to two other poems on the theme of faithlessness in love.

Her collection or "nosegay" of one hundred and ten verses of advice were written in the manner of George Gascoigne's *Hundreth sundrie Flowres* (1572). More interesting, perhaps, than the individual rhymes are the appended verse epistles directed to her brothers, sisters, and cousins, some of which follow; these letters contain autobiographical information and clarify Whitney's secularized point of view. The publication concludes with a truly remarkable document—a will or testament to her beloved London, a poem that brings the city to life in its sixteenth-century form and reminds the reader if not in its tone, then in its vividness, of Nashe's descriptions of the sprawling life of the metropolis. The carefree, almost vagabond tone, which occasionally becomes strongly emotional, the incessant common sense, which sometimes is incisively bright, and, most of all, the sense of self-reliance set Whitney's work apart from that of the other women writers of her time.

The following selections are taken from works by Whitney: *The Copy of a Letter* . . . (London: Richarde Jhones, 1567?) and *A sweet Nosegay* . . . (London, 1573).

from *A LETTER . . . TO HER UNCONSTANT LOVER*

As close as you your wedig [sic] kept
    yet now the trueth I here:
which you (yer now) might me have told
    what nede you nay to swere?

          .   .   .   .

And if you cannot be content
    to lead a single lyfe.
(Although the same right quiet be)
    then take me to your wife.

So shall the promises be kept,   [25]
    that you so firmly made:
Now chuse whether ye wyll be true,
    or be of SINONS* trade.   [*Sinon tricked the Trojans into bringing
                                 the wooden horse into Troy.]

Whose trade if that you long shal use,
    it shal your kindred stayne: [30]
Example take by many a one
    whose falshood now is playne.

As by ENEAS* first of all   [*i.e., Aeneas]
    who dyd poore Dido leave,
Causing the Quene by his untroeth   [35]
    with Sword her hart to cleave,

Also I finde that THESEUS* did,   [*Theseus was the unfaithful lover of
    his faithfull love forsake: Ariadne.]
Stealyng away within the night
    before she dyd awake.   [40]

     .   .   .   .

Now may you heare how falsenes is   [65]
    made manyfest in time:
Although they that comit the same,
    think it a veniall crime.

For they, for their unfaithfulness,
    did get perpetuall fame: [70]
Fame? wherefore dyd I terme it so?
    I should have cald it shame.

Let Theseus be, let Jason* passe,   [*Jason deserted Medea for Glauce]
    let Paris* also scape: [*Paris eloped with Helen]
That brought destruction unto Troy   [75]
    All though the Grecian Rape.

And unto me a Troylus* be,   [*Troilus was faithful to the faithless
    if not you may compare: Cressida]
With any of these parsons that
    above expressed are.   [80]

But if I can not please your mind
    for wants that rest in me:

Wed whom you list, I am content,
  your refuse for to be.
    . . . .
And when you shall this letter have
  let it be kept in store: [110]
For she that sent it hath sworne the same,
  As yet to send no more.

And now farewel, for why at large
  my mind is here exprest.
The which you may perceive, if that   [115]
  you do peruse the rest.

              Finis.   [sigs. A2-A6]

from A SWEET NOSEGAY . . .

The Auctor to the Reader.
This harvest tyme, I harvestlesse,
  and serviceless also:
And subject unto sicknesse, that
  abrode I could not go.
Had leasure good, (though learning lackt)   [5]
  some study to apply:
To reade such Bookes, wherby I thought
  my selfe to edyfye.
    . . . . . .
[Good Fortune] me brought
  where fragrant flowers abound.
The smell whereof prevents ech harme,
  if yet your selfe be sound.   [90]
    . . . . . .
And now I have a Nosegay got,
  that would be passing rare:
Yf that to sort the same aright,   [125]
  weare lotted to my share.
But in a bundle as they bee,
  (good reader them accept:)
It is the gever: not the guift,
  thou oughtest to respect,   [130]
And for thy health, not for thy eye,
  did I this Posye frame:

Because my selfe dyd safety finde,
   by smelling to the same.   [sigs. A5-A6]

. . . .

The I. Flower.
Such freendes as have ben absent long
   more joyful be at meeting
Then those which ever present are
   and dayly have their greetyng.

. . . .

The. VI.
For to abound in every thing,
   and not their use to know:
It is a pinching penury:
   wherfore, thy goods, bestow.

. . . .

The. 34.
She that is an Adulteresse
   of evylles is a sea:
Her wickednesse consumes her selfe
   and Husband doth decay.

. . . .

The 62.
The angry lover flattereth
   himselfe with many lyes:
And fondly feedeth on such toyes
   as fancy doth devise.
The 63.
Ech lover knoweth what he lykes
   and what he doth desire.
But seld, or never doth he know,
   what thing he should require.

. . . .

The 81.
Of worldly things, the chiefest is seld,
   a well contented mind:
That doth dispise for to aspyre,
   nor gapeth gifts to fynde.

. . . .

A soveraigne receyt.
The Juce of all these Flowers take,
and make thee a conserve:

And use it firste and laste: and it
    wyll safely thee preserve.   [sigs. A6-C5]

from *AN ORDER PRESCRIBED BY IS. W. TO TWO OF HER YONGER SISTERS SERVINGE IN LONDON*

Good sisters mine, when I shal further from you dwell:
Peruse these lines, observe the rules
which in the same I tell.
So shal you wealth posses,
    and quietnesse of mynde: [5]
And al your friends to se the same:
a treble joy shall fynde.
In mornings when you ryse,
    forget not to commende:
Your selves to God, beseeching him   [10]
    from dangers to defende.
Your soules and boddies both,
    your Parents and your friends:
Your teachers and your governers
    so pray you that your ends,   [15]
May be in such a sort,
    as God may pleased bee:
To live, to dye, to dye to live,
With him eternally.

            . . . .
Your busines soone dispatch,
    and listen to no lyes:
Nor credit every fayned tale,
    that many wyll devise.   [35]
For words they are but winde
    yet words may hurt you so:
As you shall never brook the same,
    yf that you have a foe.
God shyld you from all such,   [40]
    as would by word or Byll.
Procure your shame, or never cease
tyll they have wrought you yll.

            . . . .
Your Masters gon to Bed,
    your Mistresses at rest.

Their Daughters all do hast above
    to get themselves undrest.
See that their Plate be safe,   [80]
    and that no Spoone do lacke,
See Dores & Windowes bolted fast
    for feare of any wrack.
Then help yf neede ther bee,
    to doo some housholde things   [85]
Yf not to bed, referring you,
    unto the heavenly king.
Forgettyng not to pray
    as I before you taught;
And geveing thanks for al that he   [90]
hath ever for you wrought.   [sigs. C7-D1]

from *TO HER SISTER MISTERIS A. B.*

Because I to my brethern wrote,
    and to my Sisters two:
Good Sister Anne, you this might note,
    yf so I should not doo
To you or ere I parted hence,   [5]
You vainely had bestowed expence.

Yet is it not for that I write,
    for nature dyd you bynde:
To doo me good: and to requight,
    hath nature mee inclynde: [10]
Wherfore good Sister take in gree,
These simple lynes that come from mee.

Wherin I wish you Nestors dayes,
    in happy health to rest:
With such successe in all assayes,   [15]
    as those which God hath blest:
your husband with your prety Boyes,
God keepe them free from all annoyes.

And graunt if that my luck it bee,
    to linger heere so long: [20]
Til they be men: that I may see,
    for learning them so strong:

That they may march amongst the best,
Of them which learning have possest.

. . . .

Good Sister so I you commend,
   to him that made us all:
I know you huswyfery intend,
   though I to writing fall:
Wherfore no longer shal you stay,   [35]
From businesse, that profit may.

Had I a husband, or a house,
   and all that longes therto
My selfe could frame about to rouse   [?]
   as other women doo: [40]
But til some houshold cares mee tye,
My bookes and Pen I wyll apply.
             Your loving sister. Is. W.   [sig. D1-D2]

THE AUCTHOUR . . . MAKETH HER WYLL AND TESTAMENT

The time is come I must departe,
From thee ah famous Citie:
I never yet to rue my smart,
did finde that thou hadst pitie.
Wherefore small cause ther is, that I   [5]
should greeve from thee to go:
But many women foolyshly,
lyke me and other moe
Doe such a fyxed fancy set,
on those which least desarve,   [10]
That long it is ere wit we get,
away from them to swarve,
But tyme with pittie oft wyl tel
to those that wil her try:
Whether it best be more to mell   [15]
or utterly defye.
And now hath time me put in mind,
of thy great cruelnes:
That never once a help wold finde,
to ease me in distres.   [20]
Thou never yet, woldst credit geve
to boord me for a yeare:

Nor with Apparell me releve
except thou payed weare.
No, no, thou never didst me good,   [25]
nor ever wilt I know:
Yet am I in no angry moode,
but wyll, or ere I goe
In perfect love and charytie,
my Testament here write: [30]
And leave to thee such Treasurye,
as I in it recyte.
Now stand a side and geve me leave
to write my latest Wyll
And see that none you do deceave,   [35]
of that I leave them tyl.   [sigs. E2-E3]

from *THE MANER OF HER WYLL, & WHAT SHE LEFT TO LONDON: AND TO ALL THOSE IN IT: AT HER DEPARTING.*

I whole in body and in minde,
but very weake in Purse:
Do make, and write my Testament
for feare it wyll be wurse.
And fyrst I wholy doo commend,   [5]
my Soule and Body eke:
To God the Father and the Son,
so long as I can speake.
And after speach: my Soule to hym,
And Body to the Grave: [10]
Tyll time that all shall rise agayne,
their Judgement for to have.

   . . . .
And now let mee dispose such things,
as I shal leave behinde:
That those which shall receave the same,
may know my wylling minde.
I first of all to London leave   [25]
because I there was bred:
Brave buildyngs rare, of Churches store,
and Pauls to the head.
Betweene the same: fayre streats there bee,
and people goodly store: [30]
Because their keeping craveth cost,

I yet wil leave him more.
First for their foode, I Butchers leave,
that every day shall kyll:
By Thames you shal have Brewers store,   [35]
and Bakers at your wyll.
And such as orders doo observe,
and eat fish thrice a weeke:
I leave two Streets, full fraught therwith
they neede not farre to seeke.   [40]

   . . . .

For Women shall you Taylors have,
by Bow, the chiefest dwel:
In every Lane you some shall finde,
can doo indifferent well.   [80]
And for the men, few Streetes or Lanes,
but Bodymakers bee:
And such as make the sweeping cloakes,
with Gardes beneth the knee.

   . . . .

Now when thy folke are fed and clad
with such as I have namde: [90]
For daynty mouthes, and stomachs weake
some Junckets must be framde.
Wherfore I Poticaries leave,
with Banquets in their Shop:
Phisicians also for the sicke,   [95]
Diseases for to stop.

   . . . .

Yf they that keepe what I you leave,
aske Mony: when they sell it: [110]
At Mint there is such store, it is
unpossible to tell it.

   . . . .

Now for the people in thee left,
I have done as I may:
And that the poore, when I am gone,   [135]
have cause for me to pray.
I wyll to prisons portions leave,
what though but very small:
Yet that they may remember me,
occasion be it shall: [140]

   . . . .

Now London have I (for thy sake)
within thee, and without:
As coms into my memory,   [255]
dispearsed round about
Such needfull thinges, as they should have
herre left now unto thee,
When I am gon, with conscience
let them dispearsed bee.   [260]
And though I nothing named have,
to bury mee withall:
Consider that above the ground,
annoyance bee I shall.

    .   .   .   .

Rejoice in God that I am gon,
out of this vale so vile.
And that of ech thing, left such store,   [275]
as may your wants exile,
I make thee sole executor, because
I lov'de thee best.
And thee I put in trust, to geve
the goodes unto the rest.   [280]

    .   .   .   .

And (though I am perswade) that I
shall never more thee see: [310]
Yet to the last, I shal not cease
to wish much good to thee.
This xx, of October,
in ANNO DOMINI
A thousand: v hundred seventy three   [315]
as Alminacks descry.
Did write this Wyll with mine owne hand
and it to London gave:
In witnes of the standers by,
whose names yf you wyll have,   [320]
Paper, pen and Standish were:
at that same present by:
With Time, who promised to reveale,
so fast as she cold hye
The same: least of my nearer kyn,
for any thing should vary: [325]
So finally I make an end
no longer can I tary.
Finis. by Is. W.   [sigs. E3-E9]

E. D. (ELIZABETH DOUGLAS?) (fl. 1587)

Petrarch's *Triumphs* were translated by two Renaissance Englishwomen: Mary Herbert, countess of Pembroke, and Anna Hume, daughter of David Hume of Godscroft.[27] They were of sufficient interest to a third, unfortunately known to us only as E. D.,[28] to inspire her to write two sonnets, placed at the beginning of Fowler's 1587 translation of Petrarch's work. E. D. reveals herself to have been widely read and deeply conversant with literature.

The text of the following poem is taken from the *Works of William Fowler Secretary to Queen Anne, wife of James VI*, ed. Henry W. Meikle, 3 vols. (Edinburgh and London: William Blackwood and Sons for the Scottish Text Society, 1914).

E. D. IN PRAISE OF MR. WILLIAM FOULAR HER FREIND

The glorious greiks dois praise thair HOMERS quill,
The citeis sevin dois strywe quhair he was borne;
The Latins dois of Virgill vant at will,
And Sulmo* thinks her Ovid dois adorne;   [*birthplace of Ovid]
The Spanzoll* laughs (sawe** Lucan) all to scorne,   [*Spaniard]   [5]
And France for RONSARD stands, and settis him owt;   [**save]
The better sort for BARTAS blawis the horne,
And Ingland thinks thair SURRYE first but dout. *   [*without doubt]
To praise their owen these contreis gois about:
Italians lyke PETRARCHAS noble grace,   [10]
Who well deserwis first place amangs that rout.
Bot FOULAR thow dois now thame all deface,
No vanting grece nor Romane now will strywe,
Thay all do yeild Sen foular doith arrywe.   [I, 19]

LADY MARY (SIDNEY) HERBERT, COUNTESS OF PEMBROKE (1561-1621)

The following poem, written by the countess in anticipation of an intended visit by Queen Elizabeth to Wilton House,[29] takes the form of a dialogue between two shepherds, Thenot and Piers. It consists of interlocking tetrameter tercets in eight pairs, and each pair contains a comment and a rejoinder by the two speakers. Both shepherds agree in praising Astrea; their only difference lies in the extravagance of their praise. The use of the pastoral dialogue is an additional testimony to the classical education of the countess and her competence as a poet.

The poem first appeared in Davison's *Poetical Rhapsody* (London: by V. S. for John Baily, 1602). STC 6373. Reel no. 643. It is the only composition by a woman included in that work. The text which follows is taken from Davison.

from *"A DIALOGUE BETWEENE TWO SHEPHEARDS . . ."*

Thenot.   I Sing divine ASTREA'S praise;
          O Muses! help my wittes to raise,
          And heave my Verses higher.

Piers.   Thou needst the truth but plainely tell,
          Which much I doubt thou canst not well,   [5]
          Thou art so oft a lier.

Thenot.   If in my Song no more I show
          Than Heav'n, and Earth, and Sea do know,
          Then truely I have spoken.

Piers.   Sufficeth not no more to name,   [10]
          But being no lesse, the like, the same; —
          Else lawes of truth be broken.

Thenot.   Then say, she is so good, so faire,
          With all the earth she may compare,
          Not *Momus* selfe denying.   [15]

                    .   .   .   .

Piers.   Where chiefest are, there others bee,
          To us none else but only shee;   [35]
          When wilt thou speake in measure?

Thenot.   ASTREA may be justly sayd,
          A field in flowry robe arrayd,
          In Season freshly springing.

Piers.   *That* Spring indures but shortest time,   [40]
          This never leaves *Astreas* clime,
          Thou liest, instead of singing,

Thenot.   As heavenly light that guides the day,
          Right so doth thine each lovely Ray,
          That from *Astrea* flyeth.   [45]

Piers.   Nay, darknes oft that light enclowdes,
          Astreas beames no darknes shrowdes;
          How lowdly Thenot lyeth!

Thenot.   ASTREA rightly terme I may
          A manly Palme, a Maiden Bay,   [50]
          Her verdure never dying.

Piers.   Palme oft is crooked, Bay is lowe,
          Shee still upright, still high doth growe,
          Good *Thenot*, leave thy lying.

Thenot.   Then, *Piers*, of friendship tell me why,   [55]
           My Meaning true, my words should ly,
           And strive in vaine to raise her.

Piers.   Words from conceit doe only rise,
           Above conceit her honour flies;
           But silence, nought can praise her.   [60]
                    [sigs. B5-B6]

RACHEL SPEGHT (fl. 1617-1621)

   Rachel Speght's *Dreame* was printed with her *Mortalities Memorandum* in
1621. One may conjecture that the death of her mother, discussed in the
poem, was the basis for her choice of subject. The two poems, though
published together, differ in treatment and point of view. *The Dreame* is an
allegorical poem that considers Rachel's own interest in learning and her
frustrations in her search for knowledge. The poem is enclosed in a medieval
dream frame; the dream is ended by the news of the death of Rachel's
mother. The theme of death thereby introduced is the link between the
Dreame and the *Memorandum* (see chapter 1), and the news of the death
functions as an effective device for ending the first piece. Rachel's original
motives for writing, expressed in the preface, are of real interest: she states
that she wanted to demonstrate both her ability to write (since many people
considered the earlier *Mouzell* to be her father's work) and her own seriousness, and to benefit the public with edifying materials. She shows continuing
interest in the Swetnam controversy by discussing the sequels to her *Mouzell*,
and she demonstrates her own familiarity with classical materials, particularly
in a roll call of illustrious women of classical times similar to those composed
by English humanists.
   The following selection is taken from *Mortalities Memorandum with a
Dreame Prefixed* . . . (London: by Edward Griffin for Jacob Bloome, 1621).

from THE DREAME

[The narrator begins by recounting that she fell asleep one evening.]
           . . . ere Aurora spread her glittering beames,
           Or did with roabes of light her selfe invest,
           My mentall quiet sleepe did interdict,   [15]
           By entertaining a nocturnall guest.
           A *Dreame* which did my minde and sense possesse,
           With more then I by Penne can well expresse.

           At the appoyntment of supernall power,
           By instrumental meanes me thought I came   [20]

Into a place most pleasant to the eye,
Which for the beautie some did *Cosmus* name,
Where stranger-like on every thing I gaz'd,
But wanting wisedome was as one amaz'd.

Upon a sodeyne, as I gazing stood,   [25]
Thought came to me, and ask't me or my state,
Inquiring what I was, and what I would,
And why I seem'd as one disconsolate;
To whose demand, I thus againe replide,
I, as a stranger in this place abide.   [30]

. . . .

My griefe, quoth I, is called *Ignorance*,
Which makes me differ little from a brute:
For animals are led by natures lore,   [45]
Their seeming science is but customes fruit;
When they are hurt they have a sense of paine;
But want the sense to cure themselves againe.

. . . .

Quoth she, I wish I could prescribe your helpe;
Your state I pitie much, and doe bewaile;
But for my part, though I am much imploy'd,   [75]
Yet in my judgement I doe often faile.
And therefore I'le commend unto your triall
Experience, of whom take no deniall.

. . . .

[Once found, *Experience* offers the following advice:]
The onely medicine for your maladie,
By which, and nothing else your helpe is wrought,
Is *Knowledge*, of the which there is two sorts,
The one is good, the other bad and nought;
The former sort by labour is attain'd,   [95]
The latter may without much toyle be gain'd.

But tis the good, that must effect your cure,
I pray'd her then, that she would further show,
Where I might have it, that I will, quoth shee,
In *Eruditions* garden it doth grow: [100]
And in compassion of your woefull case,
Industrie shall conduct you to the place.

Disswasion hearing her assigne my helpe,
(And seeing that consent I did detect)

Did many remorses to me propose,   [105]
As dulnesse, and my memories defect;
The difficultie of attaining lore,
My time, and sex, with many others more.

    . . . .

[The others counter Disswasion's arguments:]

First quoth *Desire, Disswasion*, hold thy peace,   [115]
These oppositions come not from above:
Quoth *Truth*, they cannot spring from reasons roote,
And therefore now thou shalt no victor prove.
No, quoth *Industrie*, be assured this,
Her friends shall make thee of thy purpose misse.   [120]

For with my sickle I will cut away
All obstacles, that in her way can grow,
And by the issue of her owne attempt,
I'le make thee *labor omnia vincet* know.
Quoth *Truth*, and sith her sex thou do'st object,   [125]
Thy folly I by reason will detect.

Both man and woman of three parts consist,
Which *Paul* doth bodie, soule, and spirit call:
And from the soule three faculties arise,
The mind, the will, the power; then wherefore shall   [130]
A woman have her intellect in vaine,
Or not endevour *Knowledge* to attaine.

The talent, God doth give, must be imploy'd,
His owne with vantage he must have againe:
All parts and faculties were made for use;   [135]
The God of *Knowledge* nothing gave in vaine.
'Twas *Maries* choyce our Saviour did approve,
Because that she the better part did love.

    . . . .

When *Truth* had ended what shee meant to say,
Desire did move me to obey her will,
Whereto consenting I did soone proceede,
Her counsell, and my purpose to fulfill;
And by the helpe of *Industrie* my friend,   [185]
I quickly did attaine my journeyes end.

Where being come, *Instructions* pleasant ayre
Refresht my senses, which were almost dead,
And fragrant flowers of sage and fruitfull plants,
Did send sweete favours up into my head,   [190]
And taste of science appetite did move,
To augment Theorie of things above.

    . . . .

And as I walked wandring with *Desire*,
To gather that, for which I thither came;   [200]
(Which by the helpe of *Industrie* I found)
I met my old acquaintance, *Truth* by name;
Whom I requested briefely to declare,
The vertue of that plant I found so rare.

Quoth shee, by it Gods image man doth beare,   [205]
Without it he is but a humane shape,
Worse then the Devill, for he knoweth much;
Without it who can any ill escape?
By vertue of it evils are withstood;
The minde without it is not counted good.   [210]

Who wanteth *Knowledge* is a Scripture foole,
Against the *Ignorant* the Prophets pray;
And *Hosea* threatens judgement unto those,
Whom want of *Knowledge* made to runne astray,
Without it thou no practique good canst show,   [215]
More then by hap, as blind men hit a Crow.

    . . . .

This true report put edge unto *Desire*,
Who did incite me to increase my store,   [230]
And told me 'twas a lawfull avarice,
To covet *Knowledge* daily more and more.
This counsell I did willingly obey,
Till some occurrence called me away.

And made me rest content with that I had,   [235]
Which was but little, as effect doth show;
And quenched hope for gaining any more,
For I my time must other-wayes bestow.
I therefore to that place return'd againe,
From whence I came, and where I must remaine.   [240]

But by the way I saw a full fed Beast,
Which roared like some monster, or a Devill,
And on *Eves* sex he foamed filthie froth,
As if that he had had the falling evill;
To whom I went to free them from mishaps,   [245]
And with a *Mouzell* sought to binde his chaps.

But as it seemes, my moode out-run [sic] my might,
Which when a selfe-conceited Creature saw,
Shee past her censure on my weake exployt,
And gave the beast a harder bone to gnaw;   [250]
Haman shee hangs, 'tis past he cannot shun it,
For *Ester* in the Pretettense hath done it.

And yet her enterprize had some defect,
The monster surely was not hanged quite
For as the childe of *Prudence* did conceive,   [255]
His throat not stop't he still had power to bite.
She therefore gave to *Cerberus* a soppe,
Which is of force his beastly breath to stoppe.

                . . . .

. . . leaving them I passed on my way,   [265]
But ere that I had little further gone.
I saw a fierce insatiable foe,
Depopulating Countries, sparing none;
Without respect of age, sex, or degree,
It did devoure, and could not daunted be.   [270]
                . . . .

The name of this impartial foe was *Death*,
Whose rigour whil'st I furiously did view,
Upon a sodeyne, ere I was aware;
With perceiving dart my mother deare it slew;   [280]
Which when I saw it made me so to weepe,
That teares and sobs did rouze me from my sleepe.

But, when I wak't, I found my dreame was true;
For *Death* had ta'ne my mothers breath away,
Though of her life, it could not her bereave,   [285]
Sith shee in glorie lives with Christ for aye;
Which makes me glad, and thankefull for her blisse,
Though full bewayle her absence, whom I misse.

A sodeine sorrow peirceth to the quicke,
Speedie encounters fortitude doth try;   [290]
Unarmed men receive the deepest wound,
Expected perils time doth lenifie;
Her sodeine losse hath cut my feeble heart,
So deepe, that daily I indure the smart.

The roote is kil'd, how can the boughs but fade?   [295]
But sith that Death this cruell deed hath done,
I'le blaze the nature of this mortall foe,
And shew how it to tyranize begun.
The sequell then with judgement view aright,
The profit may and will the paines requite.   [300]

Esto Memor Mortis.   [pp. 1-10]

LADY MARY (SIDNEY) WROTH (1586?-1640)

Lady Wroth was the oldest daughter of Robert Sidney, the earl of Leicester,
and the niece of Sir Philip Sidney. She married Robert Wroth in 1604 and
bore him one son, James, in 1613, the same year the earl died. The child
lived two years. Lady Wroth proved a great and sympathetic patroness of the
arts. Ben Jonson's *Alchemist* is dedicated to her, as are his forty-sixth sonnet
and Epigrams 103 and 105 in *Underwoods*. Chapman dedicated a sonnet to
her, and George Wither and William Gamage each dedicated an epigram.
She published her first and only work in 1621 probably in an effort to support
herself, since she had been left an impoverished estate by her husband and
had not succeeded in extricating herself from debt. Her pastoral romance,
which was named for a friend, Susan Herbert, countess of Mountgomery. is a
long prose narrative, varied with interpolated lyrics and written in imitation of
her uncle's *Arcadia*.[30] The narrative consists of a seemingly endless series of
adventures involving misplaced people, mistaken identities, trivial coinci-
dences, lucky meetings, and fortuitous endings to seemingly tragic sets of
circumstances. The romance skirts around the natural human passions and is
far gentler and more courtly than Sir Philip Sidney's work; consequently, it
has the air of an overly long fairy tale that takes place in a vast never-never
land. The ultrarefined quality of the characters makes the work less plausible
than either of the versions of Sir Philip Sidney's *Arcadia*.

Lady Wroth's prose and verse are handled competently; what they lack is a
sense of the genuine, or even of the truly sincere. Verses are interpolated
lavishly throughout the narrative, and a large number are placed at the end.
This number includes an interlocking sonnet sequence, quite an unusual
product from the pen of a Renaissance Englishwoman. Lady Wroth has true

facility and grace; she is lacking in the ability to make her materials moving. Therefore, her achievement must be qualified finally as historical rather than literary; she is, in Kohler's words, "the first English woman to have composed an original romance."[31] The romance itself must be considered derivative, since it adds nothing original to her uncle's contribution to the genre. The spirit of the work is courtly; Lady Wroth gives an attention to human affairs which had been applied only to religious materials by earlier Renaissance women writers in England.

A short section from the end of Book IV is presented here, as well as several of the sonnets from Wroth's "Crowne of Sonnets." The texts are taken from *The Countesse of Mountgomeries Urania* (London: John Marriott and John Grismand, 1621).

from *The Countesse of Mountgomeries Urania*

[Pamphilia, the main heroine, sorrows as a result of her unrequited love for Amphilanthus. At the end of Book IV, however, he changes his disdainful attitude, all is forgiven, and the narrative ends—happily ever after.]

Pamphilia still continued her devout vow, and heart tormenting sorrow, was yet by her servants and Nobles perswaded to ride abroad; she was wonderfull unwilling, knowing it would but trouble her the more, for what pleased others tormented her; what others delighted in vext her to see: what others gloryed and pleasured in, tortured her; when others commended the sweete Ayre, pleasant Fields, Brookes, Meddowes, Springs, Flowres, all these said shee, shew severally to mee my only losse, and serve but as if I wanted remembrance of him, which I should hate my soule for, if shee had not true and multiplicity of worthy matters to glory in the memory of him, and sorrow for his losse; that word losse, made her as if loose her selfe in passion, yet never lost she the use and plenty of her teares; being as if silent, and retyred to spare her breath to spend it in sighs for him, and her thoughts to be exprest in teares; yet abroad she went to satisfie their desires, and as it happened to content her selfe, although had any that morning but spoken that word, as if she should be content, it had bin as ill to her, as meriting her disfavour, but comming into a wood, sweete and delicately pleasing to all but her selfe, to whom nothing could be in that nature, she walked alone, having lighted from her horse, commanding them to attend her returne in that place, they obeyed, and she wandred a good space, her thoughts yet making farther journeyes, yet so farre shee went till shee came to a dainty Spring, issuing out of a stony banke upon pibbles, and making on them a murmuring, sweetely dolefull tune, cleere the water was running on gravell; and such as was fit for her cleere eyes to looke upon, weepe shee did, teares falling into the streame, not much increasing the brightness of it, though abundantly they fell, but certainely inriching it with rare sweetnes, and dropping into it such vertue as appeared after in some that dranke of it, for at that very instant there arrived a Knight armed on horsebacke, the Queene heard his horse, and looking up contrary to her accustomed fashion, had no sudden wit to leave the place, but sat still or lay still as she did, hee saw her not, but seeing the dainty streame alighted to drinke of it, and not knowing a readier way, pulled first his gauntlet off, then his helme to take up some of the water; the Queene lying among the flowres, and some bushes betweene, so as she could better see him, then he discerned her, especially not thinking of any there perceived; O what? nay what? her soule without her selfe, because in an other body returned, she quickly rose up, and as she parted so hoped to meete him, kind to her, she ranne unto him, forgiving, nay forgetting all injuries, he seeing her threw downe his helme, with open armes received her, and withall unfained affection embraced her, and well might hee joyfully doe it, love thus exprest, besides a labour saved of asking pardon, but here such Ceremonies needed not, those are by these lovers thought fit for either false Lovers, that must make up their contents with words, or new or unexperienced Lovers, who talke halfe their time away, but they knew each other, loved, onely happy in each other, and admired each others loves; never was such affection exprest, never so truly felt, to the company, they together returned, he leading her, or rather imbracing her with his conquering armes, and protesting the water he dranke being mixed with her teares, had so infused constancy and perfect truth of love in it, as in him it had wrought the like effect, then were they the best bestowed teares that ever my eyes shed, though till now hardly ever have they bin dry said she; speake not said hee of so sad a busines, we are now againe together, and never so againe, I hope, to part, to her traine thus they arrived, but when knowne by them, they never staid to be called to kisse his hands, but ranne all at once, every one striving to be first, and all casting themselves at his feete, he tooke them up, and with much noble kindnes received them; then they returned to the Cittie, and the next day to the wood againe to see the hell of deceit, but now no more to be abused, thence they brought with them the most loyall servant, and the bravest friend that ever man had, the noble *Polarchos, Amphilanthus* now recovered his Sword, and brought home his Armour, resolving nothing should remaine as witnesses of his former ficklenes, or the property of that place, destroying the monument, the Charmes having conclusion with his recovering; but none but himselfe could have gayned the Sword, because belonging to him, millions had tryed in the meane space, and all lamentably perplext; now all is finished, Pamphilia blessed as her thoughts, heart, and soule wished: *Amphilantus* expressesly contented, *Polarchos* truly happy, and joyfull againe; this still continuing all living in pleasure, speech is of the Germans journey, *Amphilanthus* must goe, but intreates *Pamphilia* to goe as far as *Italy* with him, to visit the matchles Queene his mother, she consents, for what can she denye him? all things are prepared for the journey, all now merry, contented, nothing amisse; griefe forsaken, sadnes cast off, *Pamphilia* is the Queene of all content; *Amphilanthus* joying worthily in her.

[pp. 557-58]

from *A CROWNE OF SONNETS DEDICATED TO LOVE*

In this strange Labyrinth how shall I turne,
Wayes are on all sides, while the way I misse:
If to the right hand, there in love I burne,
Let me goe forward, therein danger is.
If to the left, suspition hinders blisse: [5]
Let mee turne backe, shames cryes I ought returne:

Nor faint, though crosses, which my fortunes kisse.
Stand still is harder, although sure to mourne.
Thus let mee take the right, or left hand way,
Goe forward, or stand still, or back retire: [10]
I must these doubts indure without allay
Or helpe, but travell finde for my best hire.
Yet that which most my troubled sense doth move,
Is to leave all and take the threed of Love.

Is to leave all and take the threed of Love,   [15]
Which line straight leads unto the soules content,
Where choice delights with pleasures wings do move,
And idle fant'sie never roome had lent.
When chaste thoughts guide us, then our minds are bent
To take that good which ills from us remouve: [20]
Light of true love brings fruite which none repent;
But constant Lovers seeke and wish to prove.
Love is the shining Starre of blessings light,
The fervent fire of zeale, the root of peace,
The lasting Lampe, fed with the oyle of right,   [25]
Image of Faith, and wombe for joyes increase.
Love is true Vertue, and his ends delight,
His Flames are joyes, his bands true Lovers might.

            .   .   .   .

He may our Prophet, and our Tutor proove,
In whom alone we doe this power finde,
To joyne two hearts as in one frame to moove
Two bodies, but one soule to rule the minde.
Eyes which must care to one deare Object binde,   [75]
Eares to each others speach as if above
All else, they sweete, and learned were; this kind
Content of Lovers witnesseth true love.
It doth inrich the wits, and make you see
That in your selfe which you knew not before,   [80]
Forcesing you to admire such gifts should be
Hid from your knowledge, yet in you the store.
Millions of these adorne the throane of Love,
How blest are they then, who his favours prove.

            .   .   .   .

He that shuns Love, doth love himselfe the lesse,
And cursed he whose spirit not admires   [100]
The worth of Love, where endlesse blessednes
Raignes, & commands, maintain'd by heav'nly fires.

Made of Vertue, joyn'd by Truth, blowne by Desires,
Strengthned by Worth, renew'd by carefulnesse,
Flaming in never-changing thoughts: bryers   [105]
of Jealousie shall here misse welcomnesse.
Nor coldly passe in the pursutes of Love
Like one long frozen in a Sea of yce:
And yet but chastly let your passions moove,
No thought from vertuous Love your minds intice.   [110]
Never to other ends your Phant'sies place,
But where they may returne with honor's grace.

                    .   .   .   .

Bee from the Court of Love and reason torne,   [155]
For Love in Reason now doth put his trust,
Desert and liking are together borne
Children of Love, and Reason, Parents just.
Reason adviser is, Love ruler must
Be of the State, which Crowne he long hath worne,   [160]
Yet so, as neither will in least mistrust
The government where no feare is of scorn.
Then reverence both their mights thus made of one,
But wantonnesse, and all those errors shun,
Which wrongers be, Impostures, and alone   [165]
Maintainers of all follies ill begunne.
Fruit of a sower, and unwholesome grownd.
Unprofitably pleasing, and unsound.   [pp. 36-41]

MARY OXLIE OF MORPET (n.d.)

All that can be said with certainty about Mary Oxlie is that she was a Scottish friend of Drummond's who tried her hand at verse making, and who contributed a poem in praise of that poet which appeared in the 1656 edition of his poems. She professed the familiar handicaps of the Renaissance woman—domestic cares, lack of tutoring—but it is significant that she compares herself in these qualities to a man. For this shows that there were some Renaissance women who were able to consider their position in relation to men and not to assume their own inferiority.

The following poem is taken from *Poems by that most Famous Wit, William Drummond of Hawthornden*, ed. Edward Phillips (London: R. Tomlins, 1656). Wing 2202.

TO WILLIAM DRUMMOND OF HAWTHORNDEN

I Never rested on the Muses bed,
Nor dipt my Quill in the Thessalian Fountaine,

My rustick Muse was rudely fostered,
And flies too low to reach the double mountaine.

Then do not sparkes with your bright Suns compare,   [5]
Perfection in a Womans worke is rare;
From an untroubled mind should Verses flow;
My discontents makes mine too muddy show;
And hoarse encumbrances of houshold care
Where these remaine, the Muses ne're repaire.   [10]

If thou dost extoll her Haire,
Or her Ivory Forehead faire,
Or those Stars whose bright reflection
Thrals thy heart in sweet subjection:
Or when to display thou seeks   [15]
The snow-mixt Roses on her Cheekes,
Or those Rubies soft and sweet,
Over those pretty Rows that meet.
The Chian* Painter as asham'd   [*from Scio, an island in the
Hides his Picture so far fam'd;   Aegean]   [20]
And the Queen he car'vd it by,
With a blush her face doth dye,
Since those Lines do limne a Creature,
That so far surpasst her Feature.
When thou shew'st how fairest Flora   [25]
Prankt* with pride the banks of Ora,   [*bedecked, decorated]
So thy Verse her streames doth honour,
Strangers grow enamoured on her,
All the Swans that swim in Po
Would their native brooks forgo,   [30]
And as loathing Phoebus beames
Long to bath in cooler streamos [sic].
Tree-turn'd Daphne would be seen,
In her Groves to flourish green,
And her Boughs would gladly spare   [35]
To frame a garland for thy haire,
    That fairest Nymphs with finest fingers
    May thee crown the best of singers.

But when thy Muse dissolv'd in show'rs
Wailes that peerlesse Prince of ours,   [40]
Cropt by too untimely Fate,

Her mourning doth exasperate
Senselesse things do see thee moane,
Stones do weep and Trees do groane,
Birds in aire, Fishes in flood,   [45]
Beasts in field forsake their food;
The Nymphs forgoing all their Bow'rs
Teare their Chaplets deckt with Flowers,
Sol himselfe with misty vapor
Hides from earth his glorious Tapor,   [50]
And as movd to heare thee plaine,
Shews his griefe in show'rs of raine.   [sig. A8]

PREFACES

The materials presented in this section were written as public statements of conscious aims. They alternately explain, apologize for, and justify the works they accompany. They are direct expressions of what the writers considered to be unimpeachable—displayable—motivations and goals. Therefore, their range is that of the thinking of the many conforming Renaissance English-women who wrote and left the legacy of their minds and thoughts behind them. This range changes over the years of the English Renaissance.

William Cecil's tribute to Queen Catherine Parr in the 1548 edition of her *Lamentacion* demonstrates the early Tudor justification for publication of women's writing. Cecil states:

Here mayest thou se one, if the kynde may moove the a woman, if degre may provoke thee a woman of highe estate, by byrthe made noble, by mariage mooste noble, by wysedome, godly, . . . refusyng the worlde wherin she was loste, to obteyne heaven, wherin she may be saved: abhorryng synne, whiche made her bonde, to receive grace, whereby she may be free: dispisyng fleshe the cause of corrupcion, to put on the spirite, the cause of sanctificacion: forsakyng ignorance wherin she was blind, to come to knowledge, wherby she may see: remoovyng supersticion, wherwith she was smothered, to enbrace [sic] true regilion [sic], wherwith she may revive.[32]

From this position, which, after all, is identical to the point of view adopted by Catherine Parr herself when she urged Princess Mary to publish work under her own name (see chapter 2), women of the Renaissance had moved quite a distance by 1621. For in that year, a work of serious purpose, Rachel Speght's *Mortalities Memorandum*, was printed with the following prefatory poem, addressed by Speght "To the Reader":

Readers too common, and plentifull be;
For readers they are that can read a, b, c.

And utter their verdict on what they doe view,
Though none of the Muses they yet ever knew.
But helpe of such Readers at no time I crave,   [5]
Their silence, then censure, I rather would have:
For ignorant Dunces doe soonest deprave.

But, courteous Reader, who ever thou art,
Which these my endeavours do'st take in good part,
Correcting with judgement the faults thou do'st finde,   [10]
With favour approving what pleaseth thy minde.
To thee for thy use, and behoofe, I extend
This poore *Memorandum* of our latter end.
Thus wishing thee wellfare, I rest a true friend.[33]

The following dedicatory materials demonstrate the gradual, somewhat uneven widening of the point of view of Renaissance Englishwomen from a virtually total domination by religious interests to a relatively secularized, self-assertive stance.

ELIZABETH TUDOR, QUEEN OF ENGLAND (1533-1603)

The following prefatory letter is taken from the Lady Elizabeth's translation of Queen Margaret of Navarre's *A godly Medytacyon of the christen Sowle* . . . (Wesel: 1548). Perhaps Elizabeth's youth and still uncertain position account for her submissive tone.

from *A godly Medytacyon of the christen Sowle*

If thu do throughly reade thys worke (dere frynde in the lorde) marke rather the matter than the homely speache therof, consyderynge it is the studye of a woman, whych hath in her neyther conynge nor science, but a fervent desyre that yche one maye se, what the gifte of God the creatour doth whan it pleaseth hym to justyfye a hart. For what is the hart of a Man, concernynge hys owne strength, before he hath receyved the gift of faythe? Therby only hath he knowledge of the goodnesse, wysedome, and power of God. And as sone as he through that faythe, knoweth pythely the truthe, hys hart is anon full of charyte and love. So that by the ferventnesse therof, he excludeth all fleshly feare, and fyrmely trusteth in God . . .

O happy and fortunate gifte which causeth a Man to possesse a grace so desyred. Alas, no man coulde thys understande, onles by soch gyfte God had geven it hym. . . . Therfore gentyll reader, with a godly mynde, I besyche the paciently thys worke to peruse whych is but small in quantyte, and taste nothynge but the frute therof. Prayeng to God full of all goodnesse, that in thy harte he wyll plante the lyvely faythe. Amen.

                                                                [sigs. B2-B3]

LADY ANNA (COOKE) BACON (1528-1610)

While single and living in her parents' home, Anna Cooke made a translation into English of fourteen of the Italian sermons of an Italian theologian, Bernadine Ochine. The prefatory letter addressed by Anna Cooke to her mother suggests that the celebrated daughters of Sir Anthony Cooke owed some of their zeal for the new learning to the influence of their mother, Lady Anne (Fitzwilliam) Cooke.

The following selection is prefixed to *Fouretene sermons of Bernadine Ochyne . . . Translated out of Italian in to oure natyve tounge by A. C.* (London: John Daye, 1550?). STC 18767. Reel no. 121.

from *Fouretene sermons*

Since the Orygynal of whatsoever is, or may be converted to ani gooduse in me, hath frelye proceded (thoughe as the minister of GOD) of youre Ladyshypes mere carefull, and Motherly goodnes, as well procurynge all thynges thereunto belongeynge, as in youre many, and most Godly exhortacyons, wherein amonge the rest, it hath pleased you, often, to reprove my vaine studye in the Italyan tonge, accompting the sede thereof, to have bene sowen in barayne, unfruitful grounde . . . I have . . . perceived it my duty to prove howe muche the understandynge of youre wyll could worcke in me towardes the accomplyshynge of the same. And for that I have wel knowen your chyfe delight, to rest in . . . exaltynge wholy the glory of God: . . . I have taken in hande to dedicate unto youre Ladyship this smale number of Sermons . . . to the end it might appere, that your so many worthy sentences touching the same, have not utterly ben without some note in my weake memory. . . . [I]t may please youre Ladyshippe to vouchsafe that thys my smal labor may be alowed at your handes, under whose proteccion only it is committed wyth humble reverence, as yeldyng some parte of the fruite of your Motherly admonicions, in this my wylling servyce. Your Ladyshyppes Daughter most boundenly obedient,

A. C.   [pp. 5-8]

MARGARET (HOWE) ASCHAM (fl. 1535-1590 or 1592)

A debt is owed to Margaret Ascham, widow of the educator Roger Ascham, who, after her husband's death in 1568, insured that his tract on education, *The Scholemaster*, was published. When the work appeared in 1570, it contained a short dedicatory letter to Sir William Cecil by Mrs. Ascham, who acknowledged at great length a sense of obligation to Sir William. She also showed her sense of the significance of her husband's work and of the fitness of its dedication to a man of Sir William's interests.

The following "Dedicatory Letter" is taken from Roger Ascham, *The Scholemaster . . .* (London: John Daye, 1570). STC. 832. Reel no. 1019.

from *The Scholemaster*

To the honourable Sir William Cecill Knight, principall Secretarie to the Quenes most excellent Majestie.

Sondry & reasonable be the causes why learned men have used to offer and dedicate such workes as they put abrode to some such personage as they thinke fittest, either in respect of abilitie of defense or skill for jugement, or private regard of kindenesse and dutie. Every one of those considerations, Syr, move me of right to offer this my late husbands M. Aschams work unto you. For well remembryng how much all good learnyng oweth unto you for defense therof, as the Universitie of Cambrige, of which my said late husband was a member, have in chosing you their worthy Chaunceller acknowledged, and how happily you have spent your time in such studies & caried the use therof to the right ende, to the good service of the Quenes Majestie and your contrey to all our benefites, thyrdly how much my sayd husband was many wayes bound unto you, and how gladly and comfortably he used in hys lyfe to recognise and report your goodnesse toward hym, leavyng with me then his poore widow and a great sort of orphanes a good comfort in the hope of your good continuance, which I have truly found to me and myne, and therfore do duely and dayly pray for you and yours: I could not finde any man for whose name this booke was more agreable for hope & protection, more mete for submission to judgement, nor more due for respect of worthynesse of your part and thankefulnesse of my husbandes and myne. Good I trust it shall do, as I am put in great hope by many very well learned that can well judge therof. Mete therfore I compt it that such good as my husband was able to do and leave to the common weale, it should be received under your name, and that the world should owe thankes therof to you to whom my husband the authour of it was for good recyved of you, most dutiefully bounden. And so besechyng you, to take on you the defense of this booke, to avaunce the good that may come of it by your allowance and furtherance to publike use and benefite, and to accept the thankefull recognition of me and my poore children, trustyng of the continuance of your good memorie of M. Ascham and his, and dayly commendying the prosperous state of you and yours to God whom you serve and whose you are, I rest to trouble you.

Your humble
Margaret Ascham   [p. 2]

MARGARET TYLER (fl. 1578)

The following selection is taken from the prefatory letter to Tyler's translation of Diego Ortunez de Calahorra's *A mirrour of princely deedes and knighthood* (London: T. East, 1578). Although a small part of Margaret Tyler's prefatory letter was quoted earlier, the letter holds sufficient interest to be quoted more fully in this section.

from *A mirrour of princely deedes and knighthood*

M.T. to the Reader.

Thou hast heere, gentle Reader, the historie of Trebatio an Emperour in Greece: whether a true storie of him in deede, or a famed fable, I wot not, neither dyd I greatly

seeke after it in the translation, but by me it is done into English for thy profit & delight.
. . . For I take the grace thereoff to be rather in the reporters device then in the truth of
this report, as I would that I could so well impart with thee the delight which my selfe
findeth in reading the Spanish: but seldome is the tale carried cleane from an others
mouth. Such delivery as I have made I hope thou wilt friendly accept, the rather for
that it is a womans work, though in a story prophane, and a matter more manlike then
becometh my sexe. But as for the manlinesse of the matter, thou knowest that it is not
necessary for every trumpettour or drumstare in the warre to be a good fighter. They
take wage onely to incite others though themselves have privy maimes, and are thereby recurelesse. So Gentle Reader if my travaile in Englishing this Authour, may bring
thee to a liking of the vertues heerin commended, and by example therof in thy princes
& countries quarrel to hazard thy person & purchase good name, as for hope of well
deserving my selfe that way, I neither bend my selfe therto nor yet feare the speach of
people if I be found backward. I trust every man holds not the plow, which would the
ground were tilled: & it is no sinne to talke of Robinhood though you never shot in his
bow: Or be it that the attempt were bolde to intermeddle in armes, so as the auncient
Amazons did, and in this story Claridiana doth, & in other stories not a fewe, yet to
report of armes is not so odious but that it may be borne withal, not onely in you men
which your selves are fighters, but in us women, to whom the benefit in equal part
apperteineth of your victories, either for that the matter is so commendable that it
carrieth no discredit from the homelinesse of the speaker, or for that it is so generally
knowen that it fitteth every man to speake thereoff. . . . The invention, disposition,
trimming, & what els in this story, is wholy an other mans, my part none therein but
the translation. . . . So that the question now arriseth of my choice, not of my labour,
wherfore I preferred this story before matter of more importance. For answere
whereto gentle Reader, the truth is, that as the first motion to this kinde of labour came
not from my selfe, so was this peece of worke put upon me by others, & they which
first counsailed me to fall to worke, tooke upon them also to be my taskemasters and
overseers least I should be idle, and yet bicause the refusall was in my power, I must
stand to answere for my easy yelding. . . . But my defence is by example of the best,
amongst which many have dedicated their labours, some stories, some of warre, some
phisick, some lawe, some as concerning government, some divine matters, unto divers
ladies & gentlewomen. And if men may & doe bestow such of their travailes upon
gentlewomen, then may we women read such of their works as they dedicate unto us,
and if we may read them, why not farther wade in them to the serch of a truth. And
then much more why not deale by translation in such arguments, especially this kinde
of exercise being a matter of more heede then of deep invention or exquisite learning,
& they must needs leave this as confessed, that in their dedications they minde not
only to borrow names of worthy personages, but the testimonies also for their further
credit, which neither the one may demaund without ambition, nor the other graunt
without overlightnes: if women be excluded from the view of such workes as appeare
in their name, or if glory onely be sought in our common inscriptions, it mattereth not
whether the parties be men or women, whether alive or dead. But to retourn whatsom-
ever the truth is, whether that women may not at al discourse in learning, for men lay
in their claim to be sole possessioners of knowledge, or whether they may in some
maner that is by limitation or appointment in some kinde of learning, my perswasion
hath bene thus, that it is all one for a woman to pen a story, as for a man to addresse

his story to a woman. But amongst al my il willers, some I hope are not so straight that they would enforce me necessarily either not to write or to write of divinitie. Whereas neither durst I trust mine owne judgement sufficiently, if matter of controversy were handled, nor yet could I finde any booke in the tongue which would not breed offence to some, but I perceive some may be rather angry to see their Spanish delight tourned to an English pastime, they could wel alow the story in Spanish, but they may not afford it so chepe, or they would have it proper to themselves. What Natures such men be off, I list not greatly dispute, but my meaning hath ben to make other parteners of my liking, . . . And thus much as concerning this present story, that it is neither unseemly for a woman to deale in, neither greatly requiring a lesse staied age then mine is. But of these two points gentle reader I thought to give thee warning, least perhaps understanding of my name & yeares, thou mightest be carried into a wrong suspect of my boldnesse and rashnesse, from which I would gladly free my selfe by this plaine excuse, & if I may deserve thy good favour by lyke labour, when the choice is mine owne I will have a speciall regard of thy liking.

So I wish thee well,

Thine to use, M.T.   [sigs. A3-A6]

ANNE WHEATHILL (n.d.)

All that is known of Anne Wheathill is that she was of the middle class, that she was concerned with religion to the exclusion of other interests, and that, in Ruth Hughey's words, "she was an apt imitator of a current vogue,"[34] for collections of prayers and meditations entitled like hers. Wheathill's dedication to A handfull of holesome . . . hearbes is entirely in keeping with the tone of the work. Her combined willingness to publish and her diffident comments on her work are typical of those of her fellow writers.

The following preface, addressed "To all Ladies," is from A handfull of holesome (though homelie) hearbs, . . . (London: H. Denham, 1584).

from A handfull of holesome (though homelie) hearbs . . .

To all Ladies, Gentlewomen, and others, which love true religion and vertue, and be devoutlie disposed; Grace, mercie, and peace, in Christ Jesus.

For a testimoniall to all the world, how I have and doo (I praise God) bestowe the pretious treasure of time, even now in the state of my virginitie or maidenhood; lo heare I dedicate to all good Ladies, Gentlewomen, and others, . . . a small handfull of grose hearbs; which I have presumed to gather out of the garden of Gods most holie word. Not that there is anie unpurenes therein, but that (peradventure) my rudenes may be found to have plucked them up unreverentlie, and without zeale.

Whereupon of the learned I may be judged grose and unwise; in presuming, without the counsell or helpe of anie, to take such an enterprise in hand; nevertheless, as GOD doth know, I have doone it with a good zeale, according to the weaknes of my knowledge and capacitie. And . . . yet doo I trust, thys small handfull of grosse hearbs, holesome in operation and workeing, shall be no lesse acceptable before the majestie of almightie God than the fragrant floures of others, gathered with more understanding.

But without presumption I may boldie saie, they have not sought them with a more willing hart and fervent mind; nor more to the advancement of Gods glorie, & the desire of acceptation, then I have doon. Which if I may obtaine, with the good judgement and liking of all my brethren and sisters in the Lord, I shall thinke my time most happilie bestowed: for that thereby I did avoid idlenes, to the pleasing of almightie God; and have gained those, whom I know not, as well strangers to me, as my acquaintance, to be my friends, that shall taste these grose hearbs with me.

The Lord Jesus Christ, who moisteneth all his elect with his most precious blood, give us all a sweete taste in him. . . .

Amen, Amen,
Yours in Christ,
Anne Wheathill,
Gent. [n.p.n.]

ANNE (EDGCUMBE) TREFUSIS (fl. 1589)

We note the juxtaposition, in Anne Dowriche's work, of an interest in literary effect and in theology. Her belittling of her ability to write poetry (in the first letter, addressed to her brother) contradicts her meaning in the second letter.

The following selections are prefixed to *The French Historie* . . . (London: T. Orwin, for T. Man, 1589).

from *The French Historie . . .*

To the right worshipfull her loving Brother Master Pearce Edgecombe, of Mount Edgecombe in Devon, Esquier, Mercie and peace from Jesus Christ.

Right worshipfull, and my loving Brother, I have heard it often & truelie reported; that Lawes maie be broken, but Nature cannot be forgotten. . . . When I had ended this present Pamphlet, I saw that the simplicite of it required a Patron; and the often remembrance of your former curtesies inforced me to make bolde with you. . . . This Booke which proceedes under your protection, if you consider the matter, I assure you it is most excellent and well worth the reading: but if you weigh the manner, I confesse it is base & scarce worth the seeing. This is therefore my desire; that the simple attire of this outward forme, maie not discourage you from seeking the comfortable tast of the inward substance. You shall finde here manie things for comfort worthie the considering, and for policie the observing. This hath beene my ordinarie exercise for recreation at times of leasure for a long space togeather: If I were sure that you would take but halfe so much pleasure in reading it, as I have in collecting and disposing it: I should not neede anie farther to commend it. If you finde anie thing that fits not your liking, remember I pray, that it is a womans doing. The thinge it selfe will sufficientlie proove this to be true. Thus committing the patronage of this my recreation unto your protection, and you with my good sister in law your wife, and all your children to the Lords tuition, I cease to trouble you: Honiton, the 25 day of Julie 1589.

Your loving Sister,
Anne Dowriche.   [sigs. A2-A3]

To the Reader

Amongst manie excellent precepts which Saint Paul gave unto the Church, this is to be considered; Let al things be done unto edifying. . . . That my onelie purpose in collecting & framing this worke, was to edifie, . . . you shall easilie perceive by the chusing and ordering of these singular examples which hereafter insue. In which these speciall circumstances are to be considered. First, the great furie and rage of Sathan liklie to bee displaced from his Kingdome of error and blindnes; the franticke madnes of the ignorant possessed people, delighting in darkenesse, and striving to upholde the Kingdome of their Master; and the prompt facilitie and readines of Sathans ministers to put in execution anie kinde of wickednesse: . . . Secondlie, the power, majestie, & dignitie of the Divell, possessing the chiefest States of the earth, & seeming to the outward appearance to weild the Truth unto his obedience, in suppressing the strongest that dared openly to withstand him: . . . Thirdlie, the policie and crafte of Sathan and his members in devising by subtiltie to circumvent the godlie; under the shadow of trust, to exercise tyrannie; under the colour of courtesie to practise crueltie; and under the vaile of a sacred oath, to cover most shamefull villanie. . . . We had need therefore to be watchfull, strong, and wise: . . . We are to learn also, what trust we ought to repose in the promises and oaths of professed Papists, what shewe so ever they make of love and frendship. . . . Wheresoever thou shalt finde the Divel brought in Poeticallie to make any oration to the King and States of France, as in manie places he is: then understand, that under those speeches are expressed all the subtilties, villanies, cruelties, and policies that were devised, and by devilish meanes put in practise against the godly, more lively to set them down in their colors, as if it came from the divels owne mouth, as no doubt it came from his spirite. Againe, in all the orations of the Martirs, & of the King, the Queene, the Guise, and all other that have speaches in this booke, marke that of purpose the nature both of the person that speaks and also of the matter that is spoken, are lively set down: so that here are not bare examples of vertue and vice, but also the nature and qualities of those vertues or villanies are manifestly depainted to them that will seeke for it. . . .

The causes why I have described it in verse are 3. First for mine owne exercise, being a learner in that facultie; Secondlie, to restore againe some credit if I can unto Poetrie, having beene defaced of late so many waies by wanton vanities. Thirdlie, for the more noveltie of the thing, and apt facilitie in disposing the matter framed to the better liking of some mens fantasies, because the same Storie in effect is alreadie translated into English prose. . . . To speake trulie without vaine glorie, I thinke assuredlie, that there is not in this forme anie thing extant which is more forceable to procure comfort to the afflicted, strength to the weake, courage to the faint hearted, and patience unto them that are persecuted, than this little worke, if it be diligentlie read and well considered. So wishing that all the excellent and rare Wits that now flourish in England, and shew them selves manie times in vaine devises, would all learne to consecrate their singular giftes to the glorie of God, the edifying of his Church, and the salvation of the soules of Gods chosen. . . .

So I commit thee to Gods protection, and commend this my pleasant exercise to thy good liking: which, if I perceive to be accepted, thou shalt incourage mee to proceede,

to make thee acquainted with more excellent actions. Honiton in Devon. this xxv of
July. 1589.

A. Dowriche

TO THE READER THAT IS FRENDLIE TO POETRIE.

What so thou be that readst my Booke,
Let wit so weigh my will;
That due regard maie here supplie
The want of learned Skill.

A: D: [sigs. A4-B]

JANE ANGER (PSEUD.) (fl. 1589)

The following letter "To the Gentlewomen of England . . .," is taken from
Jane Anger, her Protection for Women . . . (London: Richard Jones and
Thomas Orwin, 1589). The tone of the preface to Anger's *Protection* is
angrier than that of the work itself—perhaps because it is more straightforward.

from *Jane Anger, her Protection for Women . . .*
To the Gentlewomen of ENGLAND, health.

Gentlewomen, though it is to be feared that your setled wits wil advisedly condemne
that which my cholloricke vaine hath rashly set downe, and so perchance ANGER shal
reape anger for not agreeing with diseased persons: Yet, (if with indifference of
censure, you consider of the head of the quarrell) I hope you will rather shew your-
selves defendantes of the defenders title, then complainantes of the plaintifes wrong. I
doubt judgement before trial, which were injurious to the Law, and I confesse that my
rashnesse deserveth no lesse, which was a fit of my extremitie. I will not urge reasons
because your wits are sharp and will soone conceive my meaning, nor will I be tedious
least I proove too too troublesome, nor over darke in my writing, for feare of the name
of a Ridler. But (in a worde) for my presumption I crave pardon, because it was
ANGER that did write it. committing your protection and my selfe to the protection of
your selves, and the judgement of the cause to the censures of your just mindes.

Yours ever at commandment,
Ja: A.

To all women in generall, and gentle Reader whatsoever.

Fie on the falshoode of men, whose minds go oft a madding, & whose tongues can
not so soone bee wagging, but straight they fal a railing. Was there ever any so abused,
so slaundered, so railed upon, or so wickedly handeled undeservedly as are we women?

Will the Gods permit it, the Goddesses stay their punishing judgements, and we ourselves not pursue their undoinges for such devilish practices? O Paules steeple and Charing Crosse! A halter hold al such persons! Let the streames of the channels in London streates run so swiftly as they may be able alone to carrie them from that sanctuarie! Let the stones be as Ice, the soales of their shooes as glasse, the wayes steep like AEtna & every blast a whirlwind puffed out of Boreas his long throat, that these may hasten their passage to the Devils haven. Shal surfeiters rayle on our kindnes, you stand stil & say nought, and shall not Anger stretch the vaines of her braines, the stringes of her fingers, and the lists of her modestie to answere their surfeitings? Yes, truely. And herein I conjure all you to aide and assist me in defence of my willingnes, which shall make me rest at your commands. Fare you well.

Your friend,

Ja.A.   [n.p.n.]

LADY ELIZABETH (COOKE) RUSSELL (1529-1609)

The following selections are from the prefaces to Lady Russell's translation of John Poynet's *Way of Reconciliation . . . Touching the Trueth, Nature, and Substance of the Body and Blood of Christ in the Sacrament . . .* (London: Printed by R. B., 1605). They demonstrate Lady Russell's imposing personality.[35]

from *A Way of Reconciliation . . .*

The Author to the Reader

To seeke the attonement of men is to be commended, and it hath a sure promise of God: *Blessed bee the peacemakers.* But I feare me, lest in greedily following the same, it happen to me which chanceth to them that part fraces, while they seeke others safetie, they beare the blowes themselves. And I, while I study to make enemies friends, perhaps shall have small thankes of them. Which if it happen, the example of him shal comfort me, which said, *If I should please men, I should not be the servant of Christ.* Farewell, and indeavour thy selfe to please Christ.

To the Right Honourable, My most entierly beloved and onely daughter, the Lady Anne Herbert, wife to the Lord Henry Herbert, sonne and heire apparent to Edward the most noble Earle of Worcester.

Most vertuous and worthilie beloved daughter, Even as from your first birth and cradle I was most careful, above any worldly thing, to have you sucke the perfect milke of sincere Religion: So willing to ende as I beganne, I have left to you, as my last Legacie, this Booke. A most precious Jewell to the comfort of your Soule . . . [n]ow naturalized by mee into English, like to his learned Author, to whom, from my part most Honour and Service is due. Surely at the first I meant not to have set it abroad in Print, but my selfe onely to have some certaintie to leane unto, in a matter so full of controversie, and to yeeld a reason of my opinion. But since by my lending the Copie of mine owne hand to a friend, I am bereft thereof by some; And fearing lest after my death it should be Printed according to the humours of others, and wrong of the dead, who in his life approved my Translation with his owne allowance: Therefore dreading, I say, wrong to him above any other respect, I have by Anticipation prevented the worst. I meant this to you, good daughter, for a New-yeeres gift, but altered by griefe for your Brothers broken arme. Farewell my good sweet Nanne. Good blesse thee with the continuance of the comfort of his holy Spirit, that it may ever worke in you, and persevere with you to the ende, and in the ende.

IN ANNAM FILIAM.

Ut veniens Annus tibi plurima commodet Anna,
Voce pia Mater, supplice mente precor,
Ut valeas, pariterque tuo cum Coniuge, Proles,
Officijs iunctis, vita serena fluat.
                    Elizabetha Russella,
                    Dowager.   [sigs. A2-A3]

ESTHER (INGLIS) KELLO (1571-1624)

Esther Kello wrote professionally, but her professionalism, as the following dedicatory letter shows, was that of a dependent writer. The following letter is the "Dedicatory Epistle," to *Octonaries upon the vanitie and Inconstancie of the World . . .* (The First of Janyer, 1609).

from *Octonaries*

In all Piety, Vertue and trew nobility to the right puissant and honorable Lord, my Lord Peter, etc.

My Lord, my humble duety first remembred. It may appear straunge to your honor: that I a stranger unknowen to you, should present you with any thing proceeding from me: yet having consecrated sum labours of my pen and pensill to the highest and nobils of this land, assweell to sundrie of the Peers of this Realme, as to the Kings Majestie and to the Prince his Grace unto whom they have bene very gratious and acceptable. And synce it hath pleased Almighty God to bring me in thir parts hard by your Honor: I have presumed altho unacquainted with your Honor: to prepare and dedicat this work to present you with. Trusting your Honor: will accept of it with ass good will as I have doone it for your saike, and let it have sum secreit corner in your Honors: cabinet, and so much the rather because it is the handy work of a woman, who beseeches God to graunt you many good yeers, in health, honour and prosperitie, and who shall allwayse remaine as one,

                    Most ready to serve and honnour your Lordship:
Jan. 1; 1609.   Esther Inglis   [n.p.n.]

RACHEL SPEGHT (fl. 1617-1621)

The following selections are from the prefaces to Rachel Speght's two publications. The earlier, addressed "To all vertuous Ladies, . . .," is prefixed to *A Mouzell for Malestomus* . . . (Nicholas Okes for Thomas Archer, 1617). The second, addressed "To the Worshipfull Gentlewoman, . . . Marie Mound-ford," is prefixed to *Mortalities Memorandum* . . . (London: Edwin Griffin for Jacob Bloome, 1621).

from *A Mouzell for Malestomus* . . .

To all vertuous Ladies Honourable or Worshipfull, and to all others of Hevahs [Eve's] sex fearing God, and loving their just reputation, grace and peace through Christ, to eternall glory.

It was the simile of that wise and learned Lactantius, that if fire, though but with a small sparke kindled, bee not at the first quenched, it may worke great mischiefe and dammage: So likewise may the scandels and defamations of the malevolent in time prove pernitious, if they bee not nipt in the head at their first appearance. The consideration of this (right Honourable and Worshipfull Ladies) hath incited me (though yong, and the unworthiest of thousands) to encounter with a furious enemy to our sexe, least if his unjust imputations should continue without answere, he might insult and account himselfe a victor. . . . Secondly, if . . . [he] should have had free passage without any answere . . . the vulgar ignorant might have beleeved his Diabolicall infamies to be infallible truths, not to bee infringed; . . . A third reason why I have adventured to fling this stone at vaunting *Goliah* is, to comfort the mindes of all *Hevahs* sex, both rich and poore, learned and unlearned, with this Antidote, that if the feare of God reside in their hearts, maugre all adversaries, they are highly esteemed and accounted of in the eies of their gracious Redeemer. . . . Worthy therefore of imitation is that example of *Seneca*, who when he was told that a certaine man did exclaime and raile against him, made this milde answere; Some dogs barke more upon custome then curtnesse. . . . This I alleage as a paradigmatical patterne for all women, noble & ignoble to follow, that they be not enflamed with choler against this our enraged adversarie, but patiently consider of him according to the portraiture which he hath drawne of himselfe, his Writings being the very embleme of a monster.

This my briefe Apologie (Right Honourable and Worshipfull) did I enterprise, not as thinking my selfe more fit then others to undertake such a taske, but as one, who . . . did no whit dread to combate with our said malevolent adversarie. And if in so doing ﹐ shall bee censured by the judicious to have the victorie, and shall have given content unto the wronged, I have both hit the marke wherat I aymed, and obtained that prize which I desired. But if *Zoilus* shall adjudge me presumptuous in Dedicating this my *Chirograph* unto personages of so high ranke; both because of my insufficiency in literature and tendernesse in yeares: I thus Apologize for my selfe; that . . . in regard of my imperfection both in learning and age, I need so much the more to impetrate patronage from some of power to sheild mee from the biting wrongs of *Momus*, who oftentimes setteth a rankling tooth into the sides of truth. . . . And so not doubting of the favourable acceptance and censure of all vertuously affected, I rest

> Your honours and worships
> Humbly at commandement,
> Rachel Speght.   [sigs. A3-A6]

from *Mortalities Memorandum* . . .

TO THE WORSHIPFULL AND VERTUOUS Gentlewoman, her most respected Godmother Mrs Marie Moundford, wife unto the worshipfull Doctour Moundford Physitian.

Amongst diversitie of motives to induce the divulging of that to publique view, which was devoted to private Contemplation, none is worthy to precede desire of common benefit. . . . These premises have caused the Printing presse to expresse the subsequent *Memorandum of Mortalitie*, by which if oblivious persons shall bee incited to premeditation off, and preparation against their last houre, when inevitable *Death* seazing on them, shall cease their beeing upon earth, I shall with *Jacob* say, I have enough: . . . I know these populous times affoord plentie of forward Writers, and criticall Readers; My selfe hath made the number of the one too many by one; and having bin toucht with the censures of the other, by occasion of my *mouzeling Melastomus*, I am now, as by a strong motive induced (for my rights sake) to produce and divulge this of spring of my indevour, to prove them further futurely who have formerly deprived me of my due, imposing my abortive upon the father of me, but not of it. . . .

Unto your worthy selfe doe I dedicate the sequel as a testimonie of my true thankefulnesse for your fruitfull love, ever since my beeing, manifested toward me, your actions having beene the Character of your affection. . . . I would not have any one falsly to thinke that this *Memorandum* is presented to your person to implie in you defect of those duties which it requires; but sincerely to denote you as a paradigma to others. . . . Thus presenting unto God my supplication, and unto you my operation, the former to him for your safetie, the latter to you for your service, I ever remaine.

> *Your God daughter in dutie obliged*
> Rachel Speght.   [sigs. A2-A4]

ESTER SOWERNAM (PSEUD.) (fl. 1617)

The following selection is taken from *Ester hath hang'd Haman* . . . (London: Printed for Nicholas Bourne, 1617). This preface has interest for its focus: the goodwill of young men of the working class who are prospective husbands and defenders of women. It reminds us of the world of such domestic drama as Dekker's *Shoemaker's Holiday.*

from *Ester hath hang'd Haman* . . .

TO ALL WORTHY AND HOPEfull young youths of Great-Brittaine: But respectively to the best disposed and worthy Apprentices of LONDON.

Hopefull and gallant youths of Great-Brittaine, and this so famous a Cittie. There hath been lately published a Pamphlet entituled The Arraignment of lewd, idle, froward and inconstant Women. . . .

The Author of the Arraignment, and my selfe, in our Labours doe altogether disagree; he raileth without cause, I defend upon direct proofe: He saith, women are the worst of all Creatures, I proove them blessed above all Creatures. . . . [H]e saith, women are the cause of mens overthrow, I proove if there by any offence in a woman, men were the beginners. Now, in that it is farre more woman-like to maintaine a right, than it is man like to offer a wrong, I conceived that I could not erre in my choyse, if I did direct a labour well intended to worthy young youths, which are well disposed.

When you have past your minority, or served your Apprenticeships under the government of others, when you begin the world for your selves, the chiefest thing you looke for is a good Wife.

.   .   .   .

Now my selfe presuming upon your worthy and honest dispositions, I have entred into the Garden of Paradise, and there have gathered the choysest flowers which that Garden may affoord, and those I offer to you.

If you beleeve our adversary, no woman is good, howsoever she be used: if you consider what I have written, no woman is bad, except she be abused.

If you believe him that women are so bad Creatures, what a dangerous and miserable life is marriage?

If you examine my proofes to know directly what women are, you shall then finde there is no delight more exceeding then to be joyned in marriage with a Paradisian Creature . . . answerable to the Countrey whence she commeth . . .

There can be no love betwixt man and wife but where there is a respective estimate the one towards the other. How could you love? nay, how would you loath such a monster, to whom Joseph Swetnam poynteth?

Whereas in view of what I have described, how can you but regardfully love with the uttermost straine of affection so incomparable a Jewell.

.   .   .   .

You my worthy youths are the hope of Manhoode, the principall poynt of Man hoode is to defend, and what more man-like defence then to defend the just reputa-tion of a woman. I know that you the Apprentices of this Citie are as forward to main-taine the good, as you are vehement to put downe the bad.

.   .   .   .

Let not the title of this Booke in some poynt distaste you, in that men are arraigned, for you are quit by Non-age. None are here arraigned, but such olde fornicators as came with full mouth and open cry to Jesus and brought a woman to him taken in adultery, who when our Saviour stoopt downe and wrote on the ground, they all fled away [John 8:1-11]. Joseph Swetnam saith, A man may finde Pearles in dust. . . . But if they who fled had seene any Pearles, they would rather have stayed to have had share, then to flye and to leave the woman alone, they found some fowle reckoning aginst themselves in our Saviour's writing, as they shall doe who are heare arraigned. . . . Yet this is an hard case. If a man raile against a woman and know no lewdnesse by any, he shall prove himselfe a compound foole, If he rayle at women who in his owne experienced tryall had made many bad, he shall shew himselfe a decompounded K [i.e., Knave]. I doe not meane Knight: The best way is, he that knoweth none bad, let him speake well of all: he who hath made more bad then he ever intended to make good, let him hold his peace least hee shame himselfe. Farewell.

Ester Sowernam.   [sigs. A4-A5]

CONSTANTIA MUNDA (PSEUD.) (fl. 1617)

The following selection is taken from *The Worming of a madde Dogge . . .* (London: Printed for Lawrence Hayes, 1617). The tone of Munda's poem to her mother is in sharp contrast to her remarks to Joseph Swetnam.

from *WORMING OF A MADDE DOGGE*

TO THE RIGHT WORSHIPFUL LADY her most deare Mother, the Lady PRUDENTIA MUNDA . . .

As first your paines in bearing me was such
A benefit beyond requitall, that twere much
To thinke what pang of sorrow you sustain'd
In child-birth, when mine infancy obtain'd
The vitall drawing in of ayre, so your love   [5]
Mingled with care hath shewen it selfe, above
The ordinary course of Nature: seeing you still
Are in perpetuall Labour with me, even untill
The second birth of education perfect me,
You travaill still though Churched oft you be.   [10]
    In recompence whereof what can I give,
But what I take, ever that I live,
Next to the heavens 'tis yours. Thus I pay
My debt by taking up at interest, and lay
To pawne that which I borrow of you: so   [15]
The more I give, I take, I pay, I owe.
Yet lest you thinke I forfait shall my bond
I here present you with my writing hand.
Some trifling minutes I vainely did bestow
In penning of these lines that all might know   [20]
The scandals of our adversarie, and
I had gone forward had not Hester hang'd
Haman before: yet what here I wrote
Might serve to stop the curs wide throat,
Until the haltar came, since which I ceast   [25]
To prosecute what I intended, lest
I should be censur'd that I undertooke

A worke that's done already: so his booke
Hath scapt my fingers, but in like case
As a malefactor changeth place   [30]
From Newgate unto Tiburne, whose good hope
Is but to change his shackels for a rope.
   Although this be a toy scarce worth your view,
Yet deigne to reade it, and accept in lieu
Of greater dutie, for your gracious looke   [35]
Is a sufficient Patrone to my booke.
This is the worst disgrace that can be had.
A Ladies daughter worm'd a dog that's mad.
                        Your loving Daughter
                        Constantia Munda.   [n.p.n.]

LADY ELEANOR (TOUCHET) DOUGLAS (d. 1652)

   The fruits of the learning of Eleanor Douglas, the youngest daughter of
George Touchet, Baron Audeley, were to prove singular after her marriages
first to Sir John Davies and later Sir Archibald Douglas, both of whom were
unable to tolerate her peculiar ideas. Lady Douglas, who has been termed a
"seventeenth century prophetess," claimed to embody the spirit of the
Prophet Daniel, with whose name she formed an anagram to her own
(Eleanor Audeley—Reveale O Daniel). Lady Eleanor prophesied early
deaths for both her unbelieving husbands, as well as dire events for the king
and the degraded kingdom of England. These ideas gained for Lady Eleanor
the displeasure of King Charles I, and she was, at different times, imprisoned,
fined, and exiled; in addition, her works were ordered burned. Consequently, most of her pamphlets were printed surreptitiously. Most of Lady Eleanor's
works appeared in the 1640s and 1650s. However, A Warning to the
Dragon, which expresses most of her important themes, appeared in 1625.
Like her other works (including one long poem that appeared under several
different titles and in varying lengths, this tract lacks total coherence.[36] Lady
Eleanor was certainly unbalanced, and she lived at a time when humane
treatment for a person like herself was unknown.
   The following selection is taken from A Warning to the Dragon and all his
angels (London, 1625).

from A Warning to the Dragon . . .

A GENERALL EPISTLE, to the fold and Flocke of Christ, and to them that are gone
astray, that say they are Apostles, and Catholiques and are not, etc.

Grace be to you and Peace from God the Father, and from our Lord Jesus Christ, who
gave himselfe for our Sinnes, and in the absence of his Body for a remembrance the

Blessed Supper, till his second appearing. As often as we taste thereof, he takes it as a token we are not unmindfull of his tender mercy that tasted Death it selfe for us; . . . To him be glory and dominion for ever and ever. Amen.

It seemed good unto me, having a perfect understanding given mee in these things, and the dispensation of them, an office not a trade; to . . . present this Visitation to your view, joyning you together of the first Arke, and universali great House, vessels of Honor and dishonour, some cleane and purified, others having need of purging.

. . . .

Pressed and constrained with obedience to him, and Duty towards you; saying no other things then the Prophets and Apostles did say should come to passe, that yee might know the certainty of those things, wherein yee have beene instructed, whether you will heare or whether you will forbeare.

It is a salve to annoint and open the eyes of the blinde, to bring them that sit in darknesse a light. . . . Unto me is given this stone to polish, unto me this grace is given.

It is as it were a new Song to be sung before the everlasting Throne, a salutation for Strangers and the Brethren. . . .

Finally, to those that require a Signe, or thinke this Confidence; Boasting that high stiles are not steps for the declining age of this weake world to climbe, my defence is no shorter then free.

Least any should thinke of me above or better then he seeth me to be, as others to suspect a forged passe; To present you with Pearles of that sort or holy things, I forbeare at this time.

. . . .

. . . O Lord remember thy servants Abraham, Isaac, & Jacob, & looke not to the stubbornnes, nor to the wickednes of this People, turne their harts, preserve thy Church, and his victorious Majestie to tread downe the power of his enemies, our Soveraigne gratious Lord and the Queene, annoint them with thy holy Spirit, Crowne them with Grace; and forren Princes, especially the Kings excellent sister, with a happie life here, and eternall life hereafter. Be gratious to the remnant of JOSEPH, heare I beseech thee the Prayer of thy servant.

> The Servant of Jesus Christ:
> O A SURE DANIEL.
> DANIEL, — — — I END AL   [sigs. A3-A10]

ALEXIA GREY (1606-1640)

Alexia Grey, baptized "Magarit," was the daughter of Edward Grey, Esquire, a Catholic.[37] Her upbringing was more frivolous than pious, but, at about the age of twenty, she experienced a "wonderfull dream or vision" that "turned her hart wholy towards" God. She was professed on June 24, 1631, at the Benedictine Abbey of the Immaculate Conception in Ghent. There she undertook the publication of an English translation of the *Rule of the Most Blessed Father Saint Benedict Patriarke of all Munkes* (Gant, 1632). STC 1860. Reel no. 1090. The following selection is taken from this edition.

from *The Rule of the . . . Munkes*

TO THE HONOURABLE; RIGHT REVERENDE AND HER MOST RESPECTED
LADY THE LADY EUGENIA POULTON, ABBESSE OF THE ENGLISH MONAS-
TERY OF THE HOLY ORDER OF S. BENEDICT IN GANT.

Honourable and Right Reverende Madame

Never doe the newe risinge sunne spreede forth his beames, without a newe comfort
to the behoulders; neither doth the splendours yealded to so many dayes, yeares, and
ages, any whitt deminish the accustomed solace taken by the newe Spectatours. And
can I doubt this glorious sunne, our Rule, a bright beame of divine light, newely raised
to shine in this place, by your lady shipps predicessour and your indevour, bringe lesse
them [sic] wonted joy to the injoyers, and though itt hath illustrated the worlde, for
many dayes, yeares, and ages, with so clere beames of Illustrious sanctity,
cannonizinge with glorious triumph more then 300 sainctes, brought from the
obscurity of idolitry, to the light of faith, 33 nations; adorned the Church with 15000
Bishopps 7000 Archbishops 200 Cardinalls, and twentyefour Popes, most of which
shine unto the world, as brightest starres havinge taken ther lustre and light, as from
the sunne, from this glorious Rule. Not to number the innumerable flourishinge
monasteryes, the shininge and illustrious Doctours, and writters, the intyre and purest
Virgines, fruites, which this holy rule, as a most comfortable sunne, hath produced,
fostered, and brought up to inlighte and illustratt, both with word, writinges, and
examples, of singular sanctitye, the whole Occidentall church, Can I (as I say) yet
doubt, that the vigour ther of, is any whitt deminished, butt rather as an experienced
and an eye wittnesse can I avere, newe comfort, joy, and solace, raysed in the mindes,
and harts, of the newe Embracers, who under your Ladyshipps goverment, happely
doe a newe injoy the splendour of that light, and most comfortably do pertake the fire
of charity, which with herbeames, she doth inkindle in our hartes. Give mee therfore
leave, most Respected Madame, though after many ages, to lett this so holy a rule
spreed her rayes abroade in our English tonge, under your ladishippes protection, that
as you instill the love of it in our hartes, so you would make itt obvious to our Eyes, and
amonge the rest to hers, who desires to remaine as she this day is become.

Your Ladishipps.
Professed and vowed child,
Alexia Gray.   [pp. 2-4]

JANE OWEN (d. before 1634)

The following selection is taken from the *Antidote against Purgatory* . . .
(1634). This is another serious work by a member of the Catholic minority,
published only after the author's death.

from *Antidote against Purgatory* . . .

TO THE WORTHY AND CONSTANT CATHOLICKES OF ENGLAND: And more
particularly, to such, who be of the best temporall Meanes.

WORTHY and noble Catholiks: My charity towards the advancing of the spiritual good
of your soules, is the maine Allective, inviting me to write this small Treatise, (pardon I

pray the boldnes of my Sexe heerin.) The subject therof is, First, to inculcate, & make deep impressions in your minds, of the horrour, and most dreadfull torments of Purgatory: Secondarily, to set before your eyes, the best meanes to prevent, at least to assuage, and mitigate them. . . . That you believe there is a Purgatory, your owne Catholike Faith teacheth you; therefore presuming that you rest immoveable therein, without the least fluctuation of judgment, I hould it were but lost labour, to spend any time in prooffe thereof. . . .

Touching the terriblenes of the Torments of Purgatory, I have insited [sic, possibly meaning engrafted] in the authority of the most Blessed Cardinall Bellarmine; out of one of whose spirituall bookes I have translated a whole passage concerning this subject, as hereafter I shall more fully shew. Thus I make him the foundation or groundworke of this my ensuing Discourse; and the rest following I do build, and erect upon this foundation: so as this Miscelene worke of myne, may perhaps resemble the statua [sic] of Nabuchodonozor, of which, part was gould, part silver, and part of baser mettall. So I am sure, that what is taken out of the learned Cardinalls writings in this my Treatise, is perfect gould or silver; what is adjoyned thereto by me, must (I willingly yield) endure the touch of the learned, to prove what mettall it is.

. . . .

Well, I humbly beseech you to have a setled eye upon your soules good, for the preventing of future punishments; and remember, that our Saviour in the Ghospell . . . commended the unjust Steward for hoording up for the tyme to come; and shall then the slouthfull carelessnes of Catholikes be unbrayded with that unjust stewards diligence?

. . . .

And with this (Worthy & deare Catholickes) I remit you to the perusing of this litle Treatise; Humbly beseeching his Mercy, that the reading of it may beget great and worthy effects in you; And then I shall hope, that you will vouchsafe me now and then, your charitable prayers; not only for the remitting of the guilt of eternall damnation, due for my infinite sinnes; but also, if so his Divine Majesty would vouchsafe me, (though most unworthy) so much favour and grace, that I may escape this most dreadfull fyer of Purgatory.

Your soules well-wishing Admonisher,
Jane Owen. [pp. 2-11]

SUZANNE DU VEGERRE (fl. 1639)

No information is available on the life of Suzanne du Vegerre, an example of the enduring pious type whose attitude toward secular romances is in marked contrast to Margaret Tyler's. The following selection is taken from "The Authors Epistle to the READER," prefixed to du Vegerre's translation of *Admirable Events, selected out of four bookes, written in French by John Peter Camus* . . . (London: T. Harper for W. Brooks, 1639)

from *Admirable Events* . . .

The enterprise which I have taken in hand, is to wrastle, or rather to encounter with those frivolous books, which may all be comprized under the name of Romants, which would require the hands which fables attribute unto *Briarius*, or the strength which

Poets give unto *Hercules*; the hands of that Gyant to handle so many pens, and the vigour of that *Heroe* to undergoe so painefull a labour; but what cannot a courage do, animated by a zeale of pleasuring his neighbour, and provoked by desire to advance the light of vertue, and to lessen vice. O why hath not my pen the vertue to cure the wounds that these wicked books cause in this world? or at least why cannot it devoure these monsters, which the writers of those aforesaid workes, meere inchanters of mindes, cause to appeare in the formes of bookes? . . . [A]t least if these my labours could cure those who are miserably infected with often viewing these Pamphlets: if the losse of so much time may be called imployment, I should not thinke my labour spent in vaine, nor my pen unprofitable. But when I see this mischievous tree, which I strive to cut down, casting forth so many branches, as I lop off, and doing like the vine, which never sprouts so well, as when it is cut, it makes me feare a labour like unto that of *Danaides*, or of *Sisyphus*. . . .

Now to overthrow so many fabulous Bookes, I undertake not my combat directly, as if I were confuting heresies, for it is not needfull that I should trouble my self to prove the obscurity of darknesse, nor to shew the falshood of these Romants, Adventures, Chivalries, and other such trash. . . . By what manner doe I then labour to overcome my adversaries? it is by diversion, setting relations true and beneficiall, in the place of those that are prophane, . . . to the end that those whose great leisure causeth to seeke wherewith to imploy their time, may finde wherewithall to entertaine their desires.

Even as truth is constant, so falshood is wavering and differing, & is capable of more different formes, then the *materia prima*, or the Proteus of Poets, which is the cause that these Authors, who love vanity, and follow after lyes, set forth their works in as many fashions, as they please. . . . [I]n briefe, they stuffe them with so many baits, that the licourishnesse of the sawce makes them loose the taste of the meat, which of it selfe is without favour or relish, and most commonly hurtfull: whereas narrations of things, which have truely happened, are tyed to more subjection, for . . . conscience obliges to keep faithfully to the ground and body of the History: . . . the Author is strictly tyed to the bounds of probability, out of which he may not swerve a nailes breadth, without discrediting the whole worke. For although fables, parables, and poeticall fictions, do sometimes hide in them good precepts, and many serious examples, yet the instructions loose much of their credit when they are mixed amongst vaine inventions. . . .

Now amongst the multitude of these writings, which like unto Reeds, have nothing but a pleasing verdure, and a faire shew of stately words, hollow and empty without any solid substance, there are one kinde which may be called an Ants nest, a seed-plot or nursery of these wanton inventions, and that is it which beares the title of tales and novels . . . full of so much licentiousnesse and dishonesty, that it is pitty to see these Bookes in the hands of youth, who sucke this Heraclian honey (sweet but venemous) through the sight. . . .

. . . But to say in generall what mine opinion is of these and all such like confused heapes of frivolous relations, I cannot better compare them then to dainty garden knots & borders which have Serpents hidden under their flowers, or unto fine fields: pleasing unto the eye, but full of Hemlocke and Aconitum, or unto Sallets, wherein are poysonous hearbs, or unto those fine Gold-Smiths workes, wherein are inferred base mettals, and counterfeite stones . . . or unto the horse of *Troy*, out of which came armed souldiers, by whom that beautifull City was turned into ashes. I say not this so much to disgrace my adversaries as to give testimony to truth.

Now (my deare reader) it is this kinde of bookes which I strive to supplant by these singular Events, which I heare offer unto thy view. . . . [T]hou shalt here finde naturall beauties without art, I meane, examples which borrow all their grace and worth from the force of truth which upholds them, and whose testimonies are seene in the times, places, and persons:

All these Events, which I call singular, as well for being rare and notable, as for having no connexion the one with the other, each one making its body, hath as it were undertaken, either to cry downe a vice, or to extoll a vertue. The end I ayme at, as being (also the end of all good history) to withdraw from evill, and to excite unto good, . . . adding a few words, short, but pressing, like to so many spurres, which pricke forward to well doing, and so many Bits which hold backe from the doing of evill, sometimes shewing the recompence of goodnesse, and sometimes the punishment of vice, to the end that love and feare may support the good, and retaine the bad in their endeavours. . . .

As for the manner I am to advertise thee, that I study as much as I can for brevity, . . . I keep close to the matter, & give little liberty unto my thoughts, to spread into digressions, if they be not necessary, and as it were bred in the subject, by reason whereof I have weaned my self from the sweet milke of poesie, and have abstained from putting any verses in these Events. I have also taken away the other graces, as Apostrophes, dialogismes, complaints, speeches, conferences, letters, orations; in briefe, all that might enlarge or embellish so that in comparison of our other relations, these are but abridgements, of histories, and as it were Skeletons, nothing remaining but the bones of each Event, stript of the ornaments which might have set forth their bodies in a far fairer hew. There be mindes which soyle in reading a history of great length, humane patience being not of any great extent: but when Events are set downe in such a manner as the end is not farre from the beginning, this is it which incourageth the reader, and both giveth him a desire of seeing further, and also eases him in reading. . . .

This booke of Events is a Garland made of many flowers, a honey composed of many hearbs, whose juyces are different, a treacle made of divers ingredients, and wherein the Serpent of vice is seasoned with so many antidotes, that in liew of hurting, it will doe good. . . .

If I did write these Histories rather to please men, then to benefit my neighbour, it may bee I should be faine to feare their censures, and seeke to conjure or appease their bad humours. But should I entertaine such a thought, as to purchase reputation in this world, then would I set my selfe in another posture, and would give unto my pen a subject more flashing and ranging. . . .

Examples of good and evill have a like vertue (provided) they meet with a disposition according in the soules of them that see them. For many reade books for curiosity, others for variety, or to passe time, and for want of other imployment, another with envy, few with sincerity, few with a desire to profit, and to put in practise the good instructions they finde therein. . . .

But let them say on, some good soules (neverthelesse) whose dispositions are inclined to vertue, will be glad to finde profitable admonitions set downe, and sweetly mingled with varieties of pleasures fitting their humour. And therefore I have strove by the helpe of my pen to publish examples worthy to be noted, to the end that wee may grow wise by the good or evill hap of others. This is the marke aymed at by all these Events, which I have gathered in the great field of the world. It is your part, deare

Reader, to extract honey out of the hardest stone, oyle out of the flint, studying a reformation of manners in this schoole of humane actions; Remembring alwaies that the secret (and if I may so say) the great worke of prudence and justice, is to avoyd evill, and to imbrace good.   [sigs. a-a8]

MARY TATTLEWELL (PSEUD.) AND JOANE HIT HIM-HOME (PSEUD.) (fl. 1640)

The following selection is taken from *The womens sharpe revenge . . .* (London: I. Okes for Ja. Becket, 1640). Perhaps the good humor of this preface can serve as a barometer of an increased self-confidence on the part of its unidentified authors, presumably women.

from *The womens sharpe revenge . . .*

The Epistle of the Female Frailty, to the Mal-Gender, in Generall.
Reader,

If thou beest of the Masculine Sexe, we meane thee and thee onely: . . . *Affable, Loving, Kinde* and *Courteous: Affable* we call thee, because so apt (I will not say to prate but) to prattle with us: *Loving*, in regard that the least grace being from us granted, you not onely voew to love us, but loath to leave us: *Kinde*, that you will not meete with us, without Congies, not part from us without Kisses: and *Courteous*, because so willing to bring your selves upon your Knees before us: more prone to bow unto *Beauty*, than to *Baal*; and to idolatrize to us, rather than unto any other Idoll: and therefore our hope is, that what you use to protest in private, you will not now blush to professe in publicke: Otherwise in clearing our Cause, and vindicating our owne vertues wee shall not doubt to divulge you, for the onely dissemblers.

And in this case we appeale unto your owne Consciences, even to the most crabbed and censorious, the most sowre and supercilious, which of you all hath not solicited our Sexe? . . . [U]se Women to Court men? [O]r have wee at any time complained of their Coynesse? Have we bribed them with our Bounties? Troubled them with our Tokens? . . . [O]r rather they to us? . . .

Yet suffer you us to be reviled, and railed at, taunted & terrified, undervalu'd, and even vilified, when among you all wee cannot find one Champion to oppose so obstinate a Challenger, but that wee are compelled to call a Ghost from her Grave, to stand up in the defence of so proud a defiance. Since then you will not be Combatants for us in so just a cause, wee intreat you to become competant Judges, to censure indifferently betwixt the Accuser, and the Accused. . . .

So, if you shall give our defamer his due, and that we gaine the Honour of the Day: If you be young men, we wish you modest Maides in marriage; if Batchellours, beautifull Mistresses; If Husbands, handsome wives, and good huswifes: If widdowers, wise, and wealthy widowes; if young, those that may delight you: if old, such as may comfort you: and so we women bequeath unto you all our best wishes.

Mary Tattlewell
Joane hit him-home.
Spinsters.

THE EPISTLE TO THE READER.

Long Megge of Westminster, [38] *hearing the abuse offered to Women,*
riseth out of her grave, and thus speaketh:

Why raise you quiet soules out of the grave?
To trouble their long sleep? what peevish Knave
Hath wakned my dead ashes? . . .

. . . .

I Margery, and for my upright stature
Sirnam'd Long Megge: of well disposed nature,
And rather for mine honour, then least scorne
Titled from Westminster, because there borne.   [20]
And so Long Megge of Westminster; to heare
Our fame so branded, could no way forbeare
But rather then digest so great a wrong,
Must to my ashes give both life and tongue.
And then (poore Poet) whatsoere thou beest,   [25]
That in my now discovery, thy fault seest.
Confesse thine errour, fall upon thy knees,
From us, to begge thy pardon by degrees.

. . . .

'Tis knowne the service that I did at Bulloigne,
Beating their French armes close unto their wollein: [40]
They can report, that with my blows and knocks
I made their bones ake, worse then did the Pocks.
Of which King Henry did take notice then,
And said, amongst my brave and valiant men,
I know not one more resolute, or bolder,   [45]
And would have laid his sword upon my shoulder,
But that I was a woman: And shall I
Who durst so proud an Enemie defie?
So fam'd in field, so noted in the Frenches,
A president to all our Brittish Wenches,   [50]
Feare to affront him; or his soule to vexe,
Who cares in any termes, thus taunt our sex?
Therefore relent thine errour I advise thee
Else in what shape soere thou shalt disguise thee,
I shall inquire thee out: nay, if thou should,   [55]
Take on all thee all those figures Proteus could,
It were in vaine: nay (which the more may daunt thee)
Even to the grave, I vow my ghost shall haunt thee.
Therefore, what's yet amisse, strive to amend,
Thou knowest thy doom, if farther thou offend.   [60]

[sigs. A3-A11]

Part II Writings by Exceptional Figures

4 ANNE (ASKEW) KYME (1521-1546)

THERE were many women martyrs in Renaissance England. John Foxe compiled the names of at least forty-six women who were executed because of their religious principles.[1] Besides the Protestants, in whom, of course, Foxe was interested, there were also Catholic martyrs. Perhaps the most notable of the women among this group was Margaret Clitherow, the martyr of York (d. 1586), who was pressed to death after refusing to divulge the names of others, and who was canonized in recent years as St. Margaret.

Of the large number of women martyrs in Renaissance England, Anne Askew, the Protestant martyr, is the only woman to have left records of her experiences. Her life and writings clearly and dramatically illustrate the milieu of the early Renaissance Englishwoman. It is the hallmark of her greatness that she evinced so early the attitudes that would characterize later English-women.

For although the subordination of women under law continued throughout the English Renaissance, the status of Englishwomen rose. For women, as for men, the significance accorded to religious questions during the period led to perhaps disproportionate education in religion and concern over religious questions.[2] Because women were affected equally with men by the doctrine of the priesthood of all believers, their religious experiences became a matter of concern and interest. Such concern underlies works such as Bessie Clerk-sone's *Conflict* (see chapter 1), the experiences of even poor women like Bessie being worthy of the prolonged attention of both her minister and the reading public. Ultimately, the theory that, in William and Malleville Haller's words, "God communicated . . . with wives as with husbands[,] . . . was the camel's head of liberty within the tent of masculine supremacy."[3] But this concession came after many years of Protestant activity and had not yet been made in Anne Askew's lifetime.

Concurrently, during the Renaissance there was a rise in the respect ac-corded to the state of marriage and, consequently, to the married woman, as well as to home life and the vocation of raising God-fearing children. By

1622, William Gouge, writer of perhaps the most encyclopedic of all the domestic conduct books, was writing of "that small inequality which is betwixt the husband and the wife: for of all degrees wherein there is any difference betwixt person and person there is the least disparity betwixt man and wife."[4] The writers of the many domestic conduct books discussed the custom of forced marriages, or the constraint of marriage choice by parents. Even those writers who argued for parental choice of mate usually counseled parents to consider their children's preferences.[5] This advice represents an advance over the practice of earlier times and contrasts with Margaret Paston's accounts of the severe beatings administered to her daughter, and the nips and taunts complained of by Lady Jane Grey, which were in accord with the belief that parents should choose their children's mates.[6] But the growth in the belief in the right to choice of mate and in the ideal of companionate marriage also developed in England after the time of Anne Askew.

Anne Askew, who came of an old Lincolnshire family, was the second daughter of Sir William Askew, a knight. She was educated as a girl and given to biblical study; the extent of her education is undetermined, but it equipped her to know the Bible intimately enough to dispute it with clergymen. Anne fell victim to the unfeeling conduct of her father, who forced her to marry Thomas Kyme of Kelsey after her sister, who had been engaged to him, died. Askew's motive, of course, was to retain the financial gains that were attendant on the match.

According to John Bale, who assembled and published her writings after her death, Anne Askew, although unwilling to marry Kyme, was "compelled agaynst her wyll or fre consent to marrye with hym. Notwithstandynge, the marryage ones past, she demeaned herselfe lyke a Christen wyfe, and had by him (as I am infourmed) ii chyldren."[7] However, problems set in following the marriage. Anne's intense interest in religious questions led first to her intense study of the Bible and finally to her becoming a Protestant. Her Catholic husband drove her out of the house, because, according to the *DNB*, she had "offended the priests."[8] The fate of her two children is not known; possibly they had died as infants.[9] In 1545, Anne went to London, probably seeking a formal separation or divorce on the basis of St. Paul's words that, "if the unbelieving depart let him depart. A brother or sister is not under bondage in such cases" [1 Cor. 7:15]. Divorce on such grounds became a tenet of the Protestant reformers later on.[10]

In London, Anne may have served as a waiting woman to Queen Catherine Parr.[11] By June 1545, she was arrested and examined for heresy concerning the sacrament, very possibly at the instigation of her husband and his family.[12] However, after her arraignment at Guildhall on June 14, 1545, she was released because no witnesses appeared to testify against her. The following year, on June 18, 1546, she was again arraigned. This time, following her arraignment, Anne was subjected to torture in the Tower. She remained steadfast to her beliefs, incriminated no others, and was burned at the stake on July 16, 1546.

John Foxe describes Anne Askew's death as follows:

. . . [I]t remaineth that we touch somwhat as touching her end & martyrdom. She, beyng borne of such stock & kyndred, that she might have lyved in great wealth & prosperitie, if she wold rather have folowed the world then Christ, but now she was so tormented, that she could neither live long in so great distres, neither yet by the adversaries be suffred to die in secret, wherfor the daie of her execution was appointed, & she was brought into Smithfielde in a chayre, because she could not go on her feete, by meanes of her great tormentes when she was brought unto the stake, she was tied by the middle with a chaine that helde up her body, when all thinges were thus prepared to the fire, the kinges letters of pardon were brought, wherby to offer her safe garde of her life, if she would recant, which she would neither receave, neither yet vouchsafe once to look upon. Shaxton also was there present who openly that day recanting his opinions, went about with a long oration to cause her also to turne, against whome she stoutly resisted. Thus she being troubled so many maner of waies, having now ended the long course of her agonies, being compassed in with flames of fire, as a blessed sacrifice unto God, she slept in the Lorde, in An. 1546 . leaving behind her a singular example of Christen constancie for all men to folowe.[13]

Anne Askew's own accounts of her interrogations are limited to religious questions, especially to questions concerning the doctrine of transubstantiation, which she denied. However, it is quite possible that her torture and death had larger political implications. Note has already been made of the intensity of religious training in the period. But this training had an areligious side. Charlotte Kohler has stated that,

the emphasis on religion covered more than an interest in the welfare of the soul, since then religious opinion was also political opinion, so inextricably intertwined that many minds were religiously educated to serve political ends. The reverse was also true and equally responsible for such results as the fires of Smithfield, and the strict surveillance of all outward expression of personal thought, which was not easily relaxed or given up by those in authority.[14]

Henry VIII, an acute, brilliant Tudor ruler, was well aware of the problems caused by his break from Rome. He was very sensitive to the delicacy of his position. His great personal popularity was undermined to some extent by his mistreatment of Catherine of Aragon and his subsequent execution of some dissident, or seemingly disloyal, courtiers. But while Henry was relatively secure as the legitimate and accomplished king of England who was the pride of the English people, courtiers who depended on Henry for support in their seemingly unassailable posts were often viewed with great resentment and even hatred by citizens on whom they enforced unpopular and oppressive policies, and these courtiers had much less reason to feel secure than did King

Henry. Their dependence was only on the king, a rather unpredictable, mercurial, and undependable patron. Therefore, they had the personal need to suppress unsettling ideas in order to maintain their own positions. Needless to say, calculations of this type were pragmatic and political, not doctrinal.

Anne Askew was a threat in her own right to the position of Henry VIII and the conservative elements in British society. For she did not accept Henry's strictures on transubstantiation. And she, a woman no less, also attempted to gain freedom from her husband on grounds not sanctioned by the emerging English church.[15] As head of the new English church, Henry had justified his separation from Catherine on the grounds that his marriage was invalid on the basis of consanguinity and should be annulled; he did not recognize the right to divorce for desertion or cruelty. Thus, ideas like Anne Askew's were inherently subversive of the social and political fabric. Ironically, by the time of Elizabeth Tudor, these ideas had gained more currency and would certainly not have resulted in martyrdom, for they no longer represented as great a political threat.[16]

But Anne Askew's martyrdom was not an isolated event, nor was she an isolated figure. Perhaps the full truth behind her story will never be known, but it is very likely that she was persecuted in an effort to attack more influential and powerful figures with whom she was associated—Queen Catherine Parr and her circle of ardent religious supporters.[17]

There was certainly a strong effort, on the part of powerful ministers of Henry's court, to discredit and topple Queen Catherine Parr because of her ardent and rather extreme religious views. She was seen as a threat to courtiers of different ideologies because of her great influence over Henry VIII. Accordingly, they schemed to discredit her with the king (see chapter 1). But Anne Askew was apparently a member of the queen's entourage after she first traveled to London, and her torture during her second examination, administered by ministers of Henry VIII, apparently was aimed at eliciting the names of influential zealots. It is a fact that the torture of a person like Anne Askew was uncommon. The questioners broached the names of many of Catherine Parr's close associates to Anne Askew, although she refused to incriminate any. Therefore while they escaped, this "small fish" was caught in the net of the conspirators, and, as stated above, "she could neither live long in so great distres, neither yet by the adversaries be suffred to die in secret." The substantial truth of this torture and of many other aspects of her narrative have been largely verified.[18] Thus, the reader is left with the impression of an oppressive, self-serving regime that denied freedom of conscience to those intrepid enough to express their beliefs openly and to live in accordance with them. The first impression given by Anne Askew's narratives is that these accounts could not possibly be true. But petty doubts as to how this or that particular could have been written out or remembered are allayed by the independent corroboration found to support this material.[19] Then, too, as

Pearl Hogrefe suggests, the maid mentioned by Anne Askew, whose begging was her source of support while in prison, could easily have transported or transcribed materials from the prison.[20]

A more studied reaction to the narrative brings some of the qualities of Anne Askew to the fore; first, her taciturnity. While she was very voluble concerning her beliefs, she had little to say on some subjects which arouse the interest and sympathy of the reader. Concerning her torture, she says only, "Then they ded put me on the racke, bycause I confessed no ladyes nor gentyllwomen to be of my opynyon, and theron they kepte me a longe tyme. And bycause I laye styll and ded not crye, my lorde Chauncellour and mastre Ryche, toke paynes to racke me their owne handes, tyll I was nygh dead."[21] When removed from the rack, Anne "swounded, and then they recovered me agayne." Following further interrogation, on the bare floor of the Tower, she was "brought to an howse, and layed in a bed, with as werye and payneful bones, as ever had pacynct Job, I thanke my lorde God therof" (p. 49). That is all she has to say on the subject. Similarly, when questioned about her husband, she says only, "I answered, that my lorde chancellour knewe all redye my mynde in that matter. They with that answere were not contented, but sayd, it was the kynges pleasure, that I shuld open the matter to them. I answered them playnely that I wolde not so do" (p. 15). More poignantly, she ends a letter, written shortly before her death, with the commands, "[F]are wele dere frynde, and praye, praye, praye" (p. 49). Finally, the complaint by one of her inquisitors that she "had so fewe wordes" is answered, "God hath geven me the gyfte of knowlege, but not of utteraunce. And Salomon sayth, that a woman of fewe wordes, is a gyfte of God."[22]

Another outstanding quality is her quick wit, evinced both in her replies themselves and in her asides concerning events. Thus she writes, "But he sayd agayne unto me. I sent one to geve yow good counsell, and at the first worde ye called hym papyst. That I denyed not, for I perceyved, he was no lesse, yet made I non answere unto it" (p. 33). Similarly, when she is asked whether a mouse that eats the consecrated wafer "receyved God or no? Thys questyon ded I never aske, but in dede they asked it of me, wherunto I made them no answere, but smyled" (p. 9). To a protest by a questioner to one of her answers, she replies, "Though it were but meane (sayd I) yet was it good ynough for the questyon" (p. 30).

Probably the most amazing of her qualities has already been demonstrated in part by the foregoing remarks—fearlessness. Her courage united with the strength of her convictions to support her. Despite her efforts to avoid antagonizing her judges, the reader is left with no doubt that she was unafraid to speak her mind whenever tact would not carry the day. Thus, in answer to the first accusation at her first examination that she did not believe in transubstantiation, she "demaunded [rather than answering] thys questyon of hym, wherfore S. Steven was stoned to deathe: And he sayd, he coulde not tell.

Then I answered, that nomore walde I assoyle hys vayne questyon" (p. 2).
This was hardly an auspicious or a timid beginning. When told that "a woman
ought not to speake in the congregacyon . . . [she] asked hym how manye
women he had seane, go into the pulpett and preache. he sayde, he never
sawe non. Then I sayd, he ought to fynde no faute in poore women, except
they had offended the lawe" (p. 11). Were the stakes not so deadly and
earnest, the sport would indeed have been great! Anne Askew's utter intrepi-
dity is displayed very clearly in the letter she sent to her "fire fellow," John
Lascels, who had been her instructor in religion. He had been told that she
had recanted after her torture, and to his anxious inquiries on that score she
replied: "I marvele not a lyttle, what shuld move yow, to judge in me so
slendre a faythe, as to feare deathe, whych is the ende of all myserye. In the
lorde I desyre yow, not to beleve of me soch wyckednesse."[23] Finally, she did
not hesitate to try to put her case to King Henry himself. With a naiveté that
causes the reader to pity her all the more, she refused to answer some of the
questions of her interrogators, but offered "that if it were the kynges pleasure
to heare me, I wolde shewe hym the truthe." When told that she was too
insignificant to be heard by the king, she answered, "that Salomon was
reckened the wysest kynge that ever lyved, yet myslyked not he to heare ii.
poore comon women, moch more hys grace a symple woman and hys
faythfull subject" (p. 15). When one of the king's officials told her that Christ
was present "in that bread . . . in a boxe" and "compared it unto the kynge,
and sayd, that the more hys majestees honour is set forth, the more commendable it is. Then sayd I, that it was an abhomynable shame unto hym, to
make no better of the eternall worde of God, than of hys slenderlye con-
ceyved fantasye" (p. 23). Finally, she did not hesitate to request that she be
allowed to present her case to King Henry (p. 36).

Perhaps the greatest proof of the respect felt by others for Anne Askew is
the fact that they addressed her and spoke of her as Anne Askew, that is, by
her maiden name, thus according recognition to her independence.

The materials written by Anne Askew are contained in the examinations or
records of her two arrests. These records are introduced, interpolated, and
summarized by John Bale, who sets his own statements apart from those by
Anne Askew by prefacing them with his own name and those of Anne Askew
with hers, and by the use of different typefaces. He breaks up her statements
at times with material he thinks should be interpolated. Bale's comments are
omitted from the selections below. The examinations include letters written by
Anne Askew to several persons, her confession of faith, her prayer before her
death, her translation of Psalm 54,[24] and an original ballad.

The ballad places her among the minor poets of the sixteenth century, and
marks her as the first woman to have composed original verses in English.[25]
Furthermore, it is informed, as are her examinations, with the force of her
faith, and both documents are striking and moving. "Not oft use I to write,"[26]
she states, and this fact gives special force to lines she felt impelled to write

after having undergone torture. The powerful image of displaced justice and her strong religious feelings are demonstrated by her somber drawing of religious bigotry. Her sufferings are recaptured skillfully and movingly. The reader can only admire the caliber of a woman who can, when being tortured for following her convictions, wish mercy for her tormentors. The strength of the last verses of her ballad leaves the reader with profound respect for the intellect, independence, and courage of Anne Askew.

The following selections are taken from *The first examinacyon of Anne Askewe, latelye martyred in Smythefelde, . . .* (Wesel: D. van der Straten, 1546), and *The lattre examinacyon of Anne Askewe, . . .* (Wesel: D. van der Straten, 1547).

from *The first examinacyon . . .*

A. To satisfie your expectation, good people (sayth she) this was my first examynacyon in the yeare of oure Lorde M. D. xlv and in the moneth of Marche, first Christofer dare examyned me at Sadlers hall, beynge one of the quest, and asked yf I ded not beleve that the sacrament hangynge over the aultre was the verye bodye of Christ realye. Then I demaunded thys questyon of hym, wherfore S. Steven was stoned to deathe: And he sayd, he coulde not tell. Then I answered, that no more wolde I assoyle hys vayne questyon.

. . . .

A. Secondly he sayd, that there was a woman, whych ded testyfye, that I shulde reade, how God was not in temples made with handes. Then I shewed hym the vii and xvii chaptre of the Apostles actes, what Steven & Paule had sayd therin. Wherupon he asked me, how I toke those sentences: I answered, that I wolde not throwe pearles amonge swyne, for acornes were good ynough.

. . . .

A. Thirdly he asked me, wherfor I sayd, that I had rather to reade fyve lynes in the Bible, than to heare fyve masses in the temple. I confessed, that I sayd no lesse. Nor for the dysprayse of eyther the Epistle or Gospell. But bycause the one ded greatlye edyfye me, & the other nothinge at all. . . .

. . . .

A. Fortlye he layed unto my charge, that I shuld saye, If an yll prest mynystred, it was the devyll and not God. My answre was, that I never spake soche thynge. But thys was my sayenge, That what so ever he were, whych mynystred unto me, hys yll condycyons coulde not hurte my faythe. But in sprete I receyved never the lesse, the bodye and bloude off Christ.

. . . .

A. Fiftly he asked me, what I sayd concernynge confession: I answered hym my meanynge, whych was as Saynt James syth, that everye man ought to acknowlege hys fautes to other, & the one to praye for the other.

. . . .

A. Sixtly he asked me, what I sayd to the kynges boke: And I answered hym, that I could saye nothynge to it, bycause I never sawe it.

. . . .

A. Seventhly he asked me, if I had the sprete of God in me: I answered if I had not, I was but a reprobate or cast awaye.

. . . .

A. Then he sayd, he had sent for a prest to examyne me, whych was there at hande. The prest asked me, what I sayd to the Sacrament of the aultre: & requyred moche to knowe therin my meaninge. But I desyred hym agayne, to holde me excused concernynge that matter. Non other answere wolde I make hym, because I preceyved hym a papyst.

. . . .

A. Eyghtly he asked me if I ded not thynke, that pryvate masses ded helpe sowles departed. And I sayd, it was great Idololatrye to beleve more in them, than in the deathe whch Christ dyed for us.

. . . .

A. Then they had me from thens, unto my lorde Mayre. And he examyned me, as they had before, and I answered hym dyrectlye in all thynges, as I answered the qweste afore.

. . . .

A. Besydes thys my lorde mayre layed one thynge unto my charge, which was never spoken of me, but of them. And that was, whether a mouse eatynge the hoste, receyved God or no: Thys questyon ded I never aske, but in dede they asked it of me, wherunto I made them no answere, but smyled.

. . . .

A. Then the Byshoppes chaunceller rebuked me, & sayd, that I was moche to blame for utterynge the scriptures. For S. Paule (he sayd) forbode women to speake or to talke of the worde of God. I answered hym, that I knewe Paules meanynge so well as he, whych is, i Corinthiorum xiiii, that a woman ought not to speake in the congregacyon by the waye of teachynge. And then I asked hym, how manye women he had seane, go into the pulpett and preache, he sayde, he never sawe non. Then I sayd, he ought to fynde no faute in poore women, except they had offended the lawe.

. . . .

A. Then my Lorde mayre commaunded me to warde. I asked hym, if suretees wolde not serve me, And he made me short answere, that he wolde take non. Then was I had to the Countre, and there remayned xii dayes, no frynde admytted to speake with me.

. . . .

A. But in the meane tyme where was a prest sent to me, whych sayd that he was commaunded of the byshopp to examyne me, & to geve me good counsell, whych he ded not. But first he asked me for what cause I was put in the Counter: And I tolde hym I coulde not tell. Then he sayd, it was great pytie that I shulde be there without cause, and concluded that he was verye sorye for me.

. . . .

A. Secondly he sayd, it was tolde hym, that I shuld denye the sacrament of the aultre. And I answered hym agayne, that that I had sayd, I had sayd.

. . . .

A. Thirdly he asked me, if I were shryven, I tolde hym no. Then he sayd, he wolde brynge one to me, for to shryve me. And I tolde hym, so that I myght have one of these iii, that is to saye, doctor Crome, syr Gyllam, or Huntyngton, I was contented, bycause I knewe them to be men of wysdome. As for yow or anye other, I wyll not dysprayse, bycause I knowe ye not.

. . . .

A. Fortly he asked me, if the host shuld fall, and a beast ded eate it, whether the beast ded receyve God or no: I answered, Seynge ye have taken the paynes to aske thys questyon, I desyre yow also to take so moche payne more, as to assoyle it your selfe. For I wyll not do it, bycause I perceyve ye come to tempte me. And he sayd, it was agaynst the ordre of scoles, that he whych asked the questyon, shuld answere it. I tolde hym, I was but a woman, & knewe not the course of scoles.

. . . .

A. Fyftly he asked me, if I intended to recyve the sacrament at easter, or no: I answered, that els I were no Christen woman, and that I ded rejoyce, that the tyme was so nere at hande.

. . . .

A. And the xxiii daye of Marche, my cosyne Brittayne came into the Counter to me, and asked there, whether I myght be put to bayle or no: Then went he immedyat-lye unto my lorde Mayre, desyerynge of hym to be so good lorde unto me, that I myght be bayled. My lorde answered . . . requyrynge hym to go and speake with the chauncellour of London. For he sayd, lyke as he coulde not commytt me to pryson without the consent of a spirytuall offycer, nomore coulde he bayle me without consent of the same.

. . . .

A. So upon that he went to the chancellour, requyrynge of hym as he ded afore of my lorde mayre. He answered hym, that the matter was so haynouse, that he durst not of hymself do it, without my Lorde of London were made prevye therunto. But he sayd, he wolde speake unto my lorde in it. And bad hym repare unto hym the next morowe and he shuld wele knowne my lordes pleasure.

. . . .

A. And upon the morowe after, he came thydre, and spake both with the chaun-cellour, & with lorde byshopp of London. My lorde declared unto hym, that he was verye wele contented that I shuld come forth to a comunycacyon. And appoynted me to apere afore hym the next daye after, at iii of the clocke, at after none. More over he sayd unto hym, that he wolde there shulde be at that examynacyon, soche lerned men as I was affeccyoned to. That they might se, and also make report, that I was handeled with no rygour. He answered hym, that he knewe no man that I had more affeccyon to than other. Than sayd the byshopp. Yes, as I understande, she is affeccyoned to Doctor Crome, Sir Gyllam, Whyteheade, and Huntyngton, that they myght heare the matter, for she ded knowe them to be lerned, and of a godlye judgement.

. . . .

A. Also he requyred my cosyne Bryttayne, that he shulde ernestlye persuade me to utter, even the verye bottom of my harte, And he sware by hys fydelyte, that no man shuld take anye advauntage of my wordes. Neyther yet wolde he laye ought to my charge, for anye thynge that I shuld there speake. But if I sayd anye maner of thynge amys, he with other more wolde be glad to reforme me therin, with most godlye counsell.

. . . .

A. On the morowe after, my lorde of London sent for me, at one of the clocke, hys houre beynge appoynted at thre. And as I came before hym, he sayd, he was verye sorye of my trouble, & desyred to knowe my opynyon in soche matters, as were layed agaynst me. He requyred me also in anye wyse, boldelye to utter the secretts of my harte, bydynge me not to feare in anye poynt. For what so ever I ded saye within hys house, no man shuld hurte me for it. I answered, For so moche as your Lordeshypp appoynted iii of the clocke, and my fryndes shall not come tyll that houre, I desyre yow to pardon me of gevynge answere tyll they come.

. . . .

A. Then sayd he, that he thought it mete, to sende for those iiii men whych were afore named, & appoynted. Then I desyred hym, not to put them to the payne. For it shuld not nede, bycause the ii gentylmen whych were my fryndes, were able ynough to testyfye that I shuld saye.

. . . .

A. Immedyatelye after came my cosyne Bryttayne in with dyverse other, as Mastre Hawe of Grayes inne, & soche other lyke. Then my lorde of London persuaded my cosyne Bryttayne, as he had done oft before, which was, that I shuld utter the bottom of my harte in anye wyse.

. . . .

A. My lorde sayd after that unto me, that he wolde I shuld credyte the counsell of my fryndes in hys behalfe, whych was, that I shuld utter all thynges that burdened my conscyence. For he ensured me that I shuld not nede to stande in doubt to saye any thynge. For lyke as he promysed them (he sayd) he promysed me, & wolde perfourme it. Whych was, that neyther he, nor anye man for hym, shuld take me at advauntage of anye word I shuld speake. And therfor he bad me, saye my mynde without feare. I answered hym, that I had nought to saye. For my conscyence (I thanked God) was burdened with nothynge.

. . . .

A. Then brought he fourth thys unsaverye symylytude, That if a man had a wounde, no wyse surgeon wolde mynystre helpe unto it, before he had seane it un-covered. In lyke case (sayth he) can I geve yow no good counsell, unlesse I knowe wherwith your conscyence is burdened. I answered, that my conscyence was clere in all thynges. And for to laye a playstre unto the whole skynne, it might apere moche folye.

. . . .

A. Then ye dryve me (sayth he) to laye to your charge, your owne report, whych is thys. Ye ded saye he that doth receyve the sacrament by the handes of an yll prest or a synner, he receyveth the devyll, & not God. To that I answered, that I never spake soche wordes. But . . . that the wyckednesse of the prest shuld not hurte me, but in sprete and faythe I receyved no lesse, the bodye and bloude of Christ. Then sayd the byshopp unto me, what a saynge is thys: In sprete. I wyll not take yow at that advaun-tage. Then I answered, My lorde without faythe and sprete, I can not receyve hym worthelye.

. . . .

A. Then he layed unto me, that I shuld saye, that the sacrament remaynynge in the pixte was but breade. I answered that I never sayd so: But in dede the qwest asked me soche a qwestion, wherunto I wolde not answere (I sayd) tyll soche tyme as they had assoyled me thys question of myne. Wherfor Steven was stoned to deathe. They sayd, they knewe not Then sayd I agayne, nomore wolde I tell them what it was.

. . . .

A. Then layd it my Lorde unto me, that I had alleged a serten text of the scripture. I answered that I alleged non other but S. Paules owne saynge to the Athenianes, in the xvii chaptre of the Apostles actes. That God dwelleth not in temples made with handes. Then asked he me what my faythe and beleve was in that matter: I answered hym. I beleve as the scripture doth teache me. . . . And upon thys argument he tarryed a great whyle, to have dryven me to make hym an answere to hys mynde. Howbeit I wolde not, but concluded thus with hym, that I beleved therin and in all other thynges, as Christ and hys holye Apostles ded leave them.

. . . .

A. Then he asked me, whye I had so fewe wordes? And I answered God hath geven me the gyfte of knowlege, but not of utteraunce. And Salomon sayth, that a woman of fewe wordes, is a gyfte of God, Prover. 19.

. . . .

A. Thirdlye my lorde layed unto my charge, that I shuld saye, that the Masse was ydolatrye. I answered hym. No, I sayd not so. Howbeyt (I sayd) the qwest ded aske me, whether pryvate Masses ded releve sowles departed, or no? Unto whome than I answered, O Lorde what ydolatrye is thys? that we shuld rather beleve in pryvate masses, than in the helthsom deathe of the dere sonne of God Than sayd my lorde agayne, What an answere was that? Though it were but meane (sayd I) yet was it good ynough for the questyon.

. . . .

A. And then doctor Standish desyered my lorde, to byd me saye my mynde, concernynge that same text of S. Paule. I answered, that it was agaynst saynt Paules lernynge, that I beynge a woman, shuld interprete the scriptures, specyallye where so manye wyse lerned men were.

. . . .

A. Then my lorde of London sayd he was infourmed, that one shulde aske of me, if I wolde receyve the Sacrament at Easter, and I made a mocke of it. Then I desyered that myne accuser myght come fourth, whych my lorde wolde not. But he sayd agayne unto me. I sent one to geve yow good counsell, and at the first worde ye called hym papyst. That I denyed not for I perceyved, he was no lesse. yet made I non answere unto it.

. . . .

A. Then he rebuked me, and sayd, that I shuld report, that there were bent agaynst me, thre score prestes at Lyncolne. In dede (quoth I) I sayd so. For my fryndes tolde me, if I ded come to Lyncolne, the prestes wolde assault me and put me to great trouble, as therof they had made their boast. And whan I hearde it, I went thydre in dede, not beynge afrayd, because I knewe my matter to be good. More over I remayned there vi dayes, to se what wolde be sayd unto me. And as I was in the mynster, readynge upon the Byble, they resorted unto me by ii and by v & by vi. myndynge to have spoken to me, yet went they theyr wayes agayne with out wordes speakynge.

. . . .

A. Then my lorde asked, if there were not one that ded speake unto me. I tolde hym, yeas, that there was one of them at the last, whych ded speake to me in dede. And my lorde then asked me, what he sayd? And I tolde hym, hys wordes were of so small effecte, that I ded not now remembre them.

. . . .

A. Then sayd my lorde, There are manye that reade & knowe the scripture, & yet do not folow it, nor lyve therafter. I sayd agayne. My lorde, I wolde wyshe, that all men knewe my conversacyon and lyvynge in all poyntes, for I am so sure of my selfe thys houre, that there are non able to prove anye dyshonestie by me. If you knowe anye that can do it, I praye yow brynge them fourth.

. . . .

A. Then my lorde went awaye, and sayd, he wolde entytle sumwhat of my meanynge. And so he writte a great cyrcumstaunce. But what it was, I have not all in memorye. For he wolde not suffre me to have the coppie therof. Onlye do I remembre thys final porcyon of it.

. . . .

A. Be it knowne (sayth he) to all men, that I Anne Askewe, do confesse thys to be my faythe and beleve, notwithstandynge my reportes made afore to the contrarye. I beleve that they whych are howseled at the handes of a prest, whether hys conversacyon be good or not, do receyve the bodye and bloude of Christ in substaunce. . . . . I do beleve in thys and in all other sacramentes of holye churche, in all poyntes accordynge to the olde catholyck faythe of the same. In witnesse wherof, I the seyd Anne have subscrybed my name. There was sumwhat more in it, whych because I had not the coppie, I cannot now remembre.

. . . .

A. Then he redde it to me, and asked me, if I ded agre to it, And I sayd agayne, I beleve so moche therof, as the holye scripture doth agre to. Wherfor I desyre yow, that ye wyll adde that therunto. Then he answered, that I shuld not teache hym what he shuld write. With that, he went forth into hys great chamber, and redde the same byll afore the audyence, whych envegled and wylled me to sett to my hande, saynge also that I had faver shewed me.

. . . .

A. Then sayd the Byshopp, I myght thanke other & not my selfe, of the faver I founde at hys hande. For he consydered (he sayd) that I had good fryndes, and also that I was come of a worshypfull stocke. Then answered one Christofer, a servaunt to mastre Denye. Rather oughte ye (my lorde) to have done it in soche case. for Gods sake than for mannys.

. . . .

A. Then my lorde sate downe, and toke me the wrytynge to sett therto my hande, and I writte after thys maner, I Anne Askewe do beleve all maner thynges contayned in the faythe of the Catholyck churche. Then because I ded adde unto it, the Catholyck churche, he flonge into hys chambre in a great furye. With that my cosyne Brittayne folowed hym, desyrynge hym for Gods sake to be good lorde unto me. . . . .

. . . .

A. Then went in unto hym doctor weston and said, that the cause whye I ded write there the Catholyck churche, was, that I understode not the churche written afore. So with moche ado, they persuaded my lorde to come out agayne, & to take my name with the names of my suerties, which were my cósyne Brittayne and mastre Spylman of Grayes inne.

. . . .

A. Thys beynge done, we thought that, I shuld have bene put to bayle immedyat-lye, accordynge to the order of the lawe. Howbeit he wolde not so suffre it, but commyted me from thens to preson agayne untyll the next morowe. And than he wylled me to apere in the guylde halle, & so I ded. Not withstandynge they wolde not put me to bayle there neyther, but redde the Byshoppes witynge [sic] unto me as before, and so commaunded me agayne to prison.

. . . .

A. Then were my suerties appoynted to come before them on the next morowe in Paules churche, whych ded so in dede. Not withstandynge they wolde ones agayne have broken of with them, bycause they wolde not be bounde also for an other woman at their pleasure. whom they knewe not, nor yet what matter was layed unto her charge. Notwithstandynge at the last, after moche ado & reasonynge to and fro, they toke a bonde of them of recognysaunce for my fourth commynge. And thus I was at the last, delyvered. Written by me Anne Askewe. [pp. 2-41]

from *The lattre examinacyon* . . .

[Bale prefaces, besides his own remarks, a letter which "out of the preson she wrote unto a secrete frynde of hers, . . ."]

. . . .

A. The summe of my examynacyon afore the kynges counsell at Grenewyche.

Your request as concernynge my preson fellawes, I am not hable to satysffye, bycause I hearde not their examynacyons. But the effect of myne was thys. I beynge before the counsell, was asked of mastre kyme. I answered, that my lorde chancellour knewe all redye my mynde in that matter. They with that answere were not contented, but sayd, it was the kynges pleasure, that I shuld open the matter to them. I answered them playnely that I wolde not so do. But if it were the kynges pleasure to heare me, I wolde shewe hym the truthe. Then they sayd, it was not mete for a kynge with me to be troubled. I answered, that Salomon was reckened the wysest kynge that ever lyved, yet myslyked not he to heare. ii. poore common women, moch more hys grace a symple woman and hys faythfull subject. So in conclusyon, I made them non other answere in that matter.

. . . .

A. Then my lorde chauncellour asked me of my opynyon in the sacrament. My answere was thys. I beleve, that so oft as I in a Christen congregacyon, do receyve the breade in remembraunce of Christes deathe, & with thankes gevynge acordynge to hys holye instytucyon, I receyve therwith the frutes also of hys most gloryouse passyon. The Byshopp of wynchestre had me make a dyrect answere. I sayd, I wolde not synge a newe songe to the lorde in a straunge lande   [Ps. 137:4].

. . . .

A. Then the Byshopp sayd, I spake in parables. I answered it was best for hym. For if I shewe the open truthe (quoth I) ye wyll not accept it. Then he sayd I was a paratte. I tolde hym agayne, I was ready to suffre all thynges at hys handes. Not onlye hys rebukes, but all that shuld folowe besydes, yea, and that gladlye. Then had I dyverse rebukes of the counsell, bycause I wolde not expresse my mynde in all thynges as they wolde have me. But they were not in the meane tyme unanswered for all that, whych now to rehearce, were to moche. For I was with them there above fyve houres. Then the clerke of the counsell conveyed me from thens to my ladye Garnyshe.

              . . . .

A. The next day I was brought agayne before the counsell, Then wolde they nedes knowe of me, what I sayd to the sacrament. I answered, that I alredye had sayd that I coulde saye. Then after diverse wordes, they bad me, go by, Then came my lorde Lyle, my lorde of Essexe, and the Byshopp of wynchestre requyrynge me ernestlye, that I shuld confesse the sacrament to be fleshe, bloude and bone, Then sayd I to my lorde Par and my lorde Lyle, that it was great shame for them to counsell contrarye to their knowlege. Wherunto in fewe wordes they ded saye, that they wolde gladlye all thynges were wele.

              . . . .

A. Then the Byshopp sayd, he wolde speake with me famylyarlye. I sayd, so ded Judas whan he unfryndelye betrayed Christ. Then desyered the Byshopp to speake with me alone. But that I refused. He asked me, whye? I sayd, that in the mouthe of two or thre wytnesses everye matter shuld stande, after Christes & Paules doctryne. Math. 18. and 2 Cor. 13.

              . . . .

A. Then my lorde chauncellour begane to examyne me agayne of the sacrament. Then I axed hym, how longe he wolde halte on both sydes? Then wolde he nedes knowe, where I founde that? I sayd in the scripture 1. Reg. 18. Then he went hys waye.

              . . . .

A. Then the Byshopp sayd, I shuld be brente. I answered that I had serched all the scriptures yet coulde I never fynde there that eyther Christ or hys Apostles put anye creature to deathe. Well, well, sayd I, God wyl laughe your thretenynges to scorne, Psal. 2. Then was I commaunded to stande a syde.

              . . . .

A. Then came to me doctor Coxe, and doctor Robynson. In conclusyon we coulde not agree. Then they made me a byll of the sacrament, wyllynge me to set my hande therunto, but I wolde not. Then on the sondaye I was sore sycke, thynkynge no lesse than to dye. Therfor I desyred to speake with Latymer it wolde no [sic] be. Then was I sent to Newgate in my extremyte of syckenesse. For in all my lyfe afore, was I never in soch payne. Thus the lorde strengthen yow in the truthe. Praye, praye, praye.

              . . . .

A. The confessyon of me Anne Askewe, for the tyme I was in Newgate, concern-ynge my beleve.

I fynde in the Scriptures (sayth she) that Christ toke the breade, and gave it to hys dyscyples, saynge. Eate, Thys is my bodye, whych shall be broken for yow, meanynge in substaunce hys owne verye bodye, the breade beynge therof an onlye sygne or sacrament. For after lyke maner of speakynge, he sayd, he wolde breake downe the temple, & in iii wayes buylde it up agayne, sygnyfyenge hys owne bodye by the temple, as S. Johan declareth it. Joa. 2. And not the stonye temple itselfe. So that the breade is but a remembraunce of hys death, or a sacrament of thankes gevynge for it. wherby we are knytt unto hym by a communyon of Christen love.

. . . .

A. For it is playneleye expressed in the hystorye of Bel in the Bible, that God dwelleth in nothynge materyall. O kynge (sayth Daniel) be not decyved Daniel 14. for God wyll be in nothynge that is made with handes of men, Acts. 7. Oh what styff-necked people are these, that wyll alwayes resyst the holye Ghost. But as their fathers have done, so do they, bycause they have stonye hartes. Written by me Anne Askewe, that neyther wyshe deathe, nor yet feare hys myght, and as merye as one that is bowne towardes heaven. Truthe is layed in pryson. Luce 21, The lawe is turned to wormewood, Amos 6. And there can no ryght judgemente go forth, Esaie 59.

. . . .

A. Oh forgeve us all our synnes & receyve us gracyouslye. As for the workes of our handes, we wyll nomore call upon them, for it is thu lorde that arte our God. Thu shewest every mercye unto the fatherlesse. Oh if they wolde do thys (sayth the lorde) I shuld heale theyr sores, yea with all my harte wolde I love them.

. . . .

A. Salomon (sayth S. Steven) buylded an howse for the God of Jacob. Howbeyt the hyest of all dwelleth not in temples made with handes. As sayth the prophete, Esa. 66. Heaven is my seate & the earthe is my fote stole. What howse wyll ye buylde for me? sayth the lorde, or what place is it that I shall rest in? hath not my hande made all these thynges? Acts. 7. . . . Laboure not (sayth Christ) for the meate that perysheth, but for that endureth unto the lyfe everlastynge. whych the sone of man shall geve yow. for hym god the father hath sealed, Joan, 6.

. . . .

A. The summe of the condempnacyon of me Anne Askewe, at yelde hawle.

They sayd to me there, that I was an heretyke and condempned by the lawe, if I wolde stande in my opynyon. I answered that I was no heretyke, neyther yet deserved I anye deathe by the lawe of God. But as concernynge the faythe whych I uttered and wrote to the counsell, I wolde not (I sayd) denye it, bycause I knew it true. Then wolde they nedes knowe, if I wolde denye the sacrament to be Christes bodye and bloude: I sayd, yea. for the same sonne of God, that was borne of the vyrgyn Marie, is now gloriouse in heaven, and wyll come agayne from thens at the lattre daye lyke as he went up. Acts. 1. And as for that ye call your God, is but a pece of breade, for a more profe therof marke it whan ye lyst lete it lye in the boxe but iii monthes, and it wyll be moulde, and so turne to nothynge that is good. Wherupon I am persuaded, that it can not be God.

. . . .

A. After that they wylled me to have a prest. And than I smyled. Then they asked me, if it were not good? I sayd, I wolde confesse my fawtes to God. for I was sure that he wolde heare me with faver. And so we were condempned without a quest.

. . . .

A. My beleve whych I wrote to the counsell was thys. That the sacramentall breade was left us to be receyved with thankes gevynge, in remembraunce of Christes deathe,

the onlye remedye of our sowles recover. And that therby we also receyve the whole benefyghtes and frutes of hys most gloryouse passion.

. . . . . .

A. Then wolde they nedes knowe, whether the breade in the boxe were God or no? I sayd, God is a sprete, and wyll be worshypped in sprete and truthe. Joan. 4. Then they demaunded Wyll you planelye denye Christ to be in the sacrament? I answered that I beleved faythfullye the eternall sonne of God not to dwell there . . . concludynge thus. I neyther wyshe deathe, nor yet feare hys myght, God have the prayse therof with thankes.

. . . .

A. My lettre sent to the lorde Chauncellour.
The lorde God, by whome all creatures have theyr beynge, blesse yow with the lyght of hys knowlege, amen. My dutye to your lordshyppe remembred &c. It myght please yow to accepte thys my bolde sute, as the sute of one, whych upon due consyderacyons is moved to the same and hopeth to obtayne. My request to your lordeshypp is only that it may please the same to be ameane for me to the kynges magestie, that hys grace maye be certifyed of these fewe lynes whych I have written concernynge my beleve. Whych whan it shall be trulye conferred with the harde judgement geven me for the same, I thynke hys grace shall wele perceyve me to be wayed in an uneven payer of balaunces. But I remytt my matter and cause to almyghtye god, whych ryghtlye judgeth all secretes. And thus I commende your lordeshypp to the governaunce of hym, and felyshypp of all sayntes. Amen. By your handemayde Anne Askewe.

. . . . . .

A. My faythe brevelye written to the kynges grace.
I Anne Askewe of good memorie although God hath geven me the breade of adversyte and the water of trouble, yet not so moch as my synnes have deserved, desyre thys to be knowne to your grace. That for as moch as I am by the law condepned [sic] for an evyll doer, Here I take heaven and earthe to recorde, that I shall dye in my innocencye. And accordynge to that I have sayd first, and wyll saye last, I utterlye abhorre and detest all heresyes. And as concernynge the supper of the lorde, I beleve so moch as Christ hath sayd therin, whych he confirmed wyth hys most blessyd bloude. I beleve also so moch as he wylled me to folowe & beleve, and so moch as the catholyck churche of hym doth teache. for I wyll not forsake the commaundement of hys holye lyppes. But loke what God hath charged me with hys mouthe, that have I shutte up in my harte. And thus brevelye I ende, for lacke of lernynge. Anne Askewe.

. . . .

The effect of my examynacyon and handelynge, sens my departure from Newgate.
On tewesday I was set from newgate to the sygne of the crowne where as mastre Ryche and the Byshopp of London with all their power and flatterynge wordes went aboute to persuade me from God. But I ded not esteme their glosynge pretenses. Then came there to me Nicolas Shaxton, and counselled me to recant as he had done. Then I sayd to hym, that it had bene good for hym, never to have bene borne with manye other lyke wordes.

. . . .

A. Then mastre Riche sent me to the tower, where I remayned tyll thre of the clocke. Then came Riche and one of the counsell, chargynge me upon my obedyence, to shewe unto them, if I knewe man or woman of my secte. My answere was, that I knewe none. Then they asked me of my ladye of Sothfolke, my ladye of Sussex, my ladye of Hertforde, my ladye Dennye, and my ladye Fitzwyllyams. I sayd, if I shuld pronounce anye thynge agaynst them, that I were not hable to prove it.

. . . .

A. Then commaunded they me to shewe, how I was mayntayned in the Counter, and who wylled me to stycke by my opynyon. I sayd that there was no creature, that therin ded strengthen me. And as for the helpe that I had in the Counter, it was by the meanes of my mayde. For as she went abroade in the stretes, she made to the prentyses, and they by her ded sende me moneye. But who they were, I never knewe.

. . . .

A. Then they sayd, that there were dyverse gentylwomen, that gave me moneye. But I knewe not their names. Then they sayd that there were dyverse ladyes, whych had sent me moneye. I answered that there was a man in a blewe coate, whych delyvered me, x shyllynges, and sayd that my ladye of Hertforde sent it me. And an other in a vyolet coate ded geve me viii shyllynges, and sayd that my ladye Dennye sent it me. Whether it were true or no, I can not tell. For I am not suer who sent it me, but as the men ded saye.

. . . .

A. Then they sayd, there were of the counsell that ded maynteyne me. And I sayd, no. Then they ded put me on the racke, bycause I confessed no ladyes nor gentyllwomen to be of my opynyon, and theron they kepte me a longe tyme. And bycause I laye styll and ded not crye, my lorde Chauncellour and mastre Ryche, toke paynes to racke me their owne handes, tyll I was nygh dead.

. . . .

A. Then the lyetenaunt caused me to be loused from the racke. Incontynentlye I swounded, and then they recovered me agayne. After that I sate ii. longe houres reasonynge with my lorde Chauncellour upon the bare floore, where as he with manye flatterynge wordes, persuaded me to leave my opynyon. But my lorde God (I thanke hys everlastynge goodnesse) gave me grace to persever, and wyll do (I hope) to the verye ende.

. . . .

A. Then was I brought to an howse, and layed in a bed, with as werye and payneful bones, as ever had pacynt Job, I thanke my lorde God therof. Then my lorde Chauncellour sent me worde if I wolde leave my opynyon, I shuld want nothynge If I wolde not, I shuld fourth to Newgate, and so be burned I sent hym agayne worde, that I wolde rather dye, than to breake my faythe. Thus the lorde open the eyes of their blynde hartes, that the truthe maye take place. fare wele dere frynde, and praye, praye, praye.

. . . .

Anne Askewes answere unto Johan Lassels letter.
Oh frynde most derelye beloved in God. I marvele not a lyttle, what shuld move yow, to judge in me so slendre a faythe, as to feare deathe. whych is the ende of all myserye. In the lorde I desyre yow, not to beleve of me soch wyckednesse. for I doubt it not, but God wyll perfourme hys worke in me, lyke as he hath begonne.

. . . .

I understande, the counsell is not a lyttle dyspleased, that it shulde be reported abroade, that I was racked in the towre they saye now, that they ded there, was but to fear me. Wherby I perceyve, they are ashamed of their uncomelye doynges, and feare moch least the kynges mageste shulde have infourmacyon therof. Wherfor they wolde no man to noyse it. Well, their crueltye God forgeve them. Your hart in Christ Jesu. fare wele, and praye.

. . . .

A. The confessyon of her faythe whych Anne Askewe made in Newgate afore she suffered.
I Anne Askewe, of good memorye, although my mercyfull father hath geven me the breade of adversyte, & the water of trouble, yet not so moch as my synnes hath deserved, confesse my selfe here a synner before the trone of hys heavenly mageste desyrynge hys eternall mercye. And for so moch as I am by the law unryghtouslye condempned for an evyll doer concernynge opynyons, I take the same most mercyfull God of myn, whych hath made both heaven and earthe, to recorde, that I holde no opynyons contrarye to hys most holye worde.

. . . .

A. And I trust in my mercyfull lorde, whych is the gever of all grace, that he wyll gracyouslye assyst me agaynst all evyll opynyons, whych are contrarye to hys blessed veryte. for I take hym to witnesse, that I have, do, and wyll do unto my lyves ende, utterlye abhorre them to the uttermost of my power. But thys is the heresye whych they report me to holde, that after the prest hath spoken the wordes of consecracyon, there remayneth breade styll.

. . . .

A. But they both saye, and also teache it for a necessarye artycle of faythe, that after those wordes be ones spoken, there remayneth no breade, but even the selfe same bodye that hynge upon the crosse on good frydaye, both fleshe, bloude, and bone. To thys beleve of theirs, saye I naye. for then were our commen Crede false, whych sayth that he sytteth on the ryght hande of God the father almyghtye, and from thens shall come to judge the quyck & the dead. Loo, thys is the heresie that I holde, and for it must suffer the deathe.

. . . .

A. But as touchynge the holye and blessyd supper of the lorde, I beleve it to be a most necessarye remembraunce of hys gloryouse sufferynges and deathe. More over I beleve as moch therin, as my eternall & onlye redemer Jesus Christ wolde I shuld beleve. fynallye I beleve all those scriptures to be true whom he hath confirmed with hys most precyouse bloude.

. . . .

A. Yea, and as S. Paule sayth, those scriptures are suffycyent for our lernynge and salvacyon, that Christ hath lefte here with us. So that I beleve, we nede no unwritten verytees to rule hys churche with. Therfor loke what he hath layed unto me with hys owne mouthe, in hys holye Gospell, that have I with Gods grace, closed up in my harte. And my full trust is (as David sayth) that it shall be a lanterne to my fote steppes, Psalme 118.

. . . .

A. There be some do saye, that I denye the Eucharystye or sacrament of thankes gevynge. But those people do untrulye report of me. for I both saye and beleve it, that if it were ordered lyke as Christ instytuted it and left it, a most syngular confort it were unto us all. But as concernynge your Masse, as it is now used in our dayes, I do saye & beleve it, to be the most abhomynable ydoll that is in the worlde.

    . . . .

A. O lorde, I have more enemyes now, than there be heeres on my heade. Yet lorde lete them never overcome me with vayne wordes. But fyght thu lorde, in my stede. for on the cast I my care. With all the spyght they can ymagyne, they fall upon me whych am thy poore creature. Yet swete lorde, lete me not set by them whych are agaynst the. for in the is my whole delyght.

    . . . .

A. And Lorde I hartelye desyre of the, that thu wylte of thy most mercyfull good-nesse, forgeve them that vyolence, whych they do & have done unto me. Open also thu their blynde hartes, that they maye herafter do that thynge in thy syght, whych is onlye acceptable before the. And to sett fourth thy veryte aryght, without all vayne fantasyes of synneful men. So be it, O lorde, so be it. By me Anne Askewe.

                                                           (pp. 11-63)

THE BALADE WHYCH ANNE ASKEWE MADE AND SANGE WHAN SHE WAS IN NEWGATE

    Lyke as the armed knyght
        Appoynted to the fielde
    With thys world wyll I fyght
        And fayth shall be my shielde.

    Fayth is that weapon strong   [5]
        Whych wyll not fayle at nede
    My foes therfor amonge
        Therwith wyll I procede.

    As it is had in strengthe
        And force of Christes waye   [10]
    It wyll prevayle at lengthe
        Though all the devyls saye naye.

    Faythe in the fathers olde
        Obtayned ryghtooysnesse
    Whych makes me verye bolde   [15]
        To feare no worldes distresse.

    I now rejoyce in hart
        And hope byd me do so
    For Christ wyll take my part
        And ease me of my wo.   [20]

Thu sayst lorde, whoso knockes
   To them wylt thu attende
Undo therfor the locke
   And thy stronge power sende.

More enmyes now I have,   [25]
   Than heeres upon my heed
Lete them not me deprave,
   But fyght thu in my steed.

On the my care I cast
   For all their cruell spyght   [30]
I sett not by their hast
   For tho art my delyght.

I am not she that lyst
   My anker to lete fall,
For everye dryslynge myst   [35]
   My shyppe substancual.

Not oft use I to wryght
   In prose nor yet in ryme,
Yet wyll I shewe one syght
   That I sawe in my tyme.   [40]

I sawe a ryall trone
   Where Justyce shuld have sytt,
But in her stede was one
   Of modye cruell wytt.

Absorpt was rygtwysnesse   [45]
   As of the ragynge floude,
Sathan in hys excesse,
   Sucte up the gyltlesse bloude.

Then thought I, Jesus lorde
   Whan thu shalt judge us all   [50]
Harde is it to recorde
   On these men what wyll fall.

Yet lorde I the desyre
   For that they do to me
Lete them not tast the hyre   [55]
   Of their inyquyte.   [pp. 63-64]

5 MARY STUART (1542-1587)

ALTHOUGH she was a center of political and religious controversy in her life-time and still remains a mystery, the following circumstances of Mary Stuart's life are unquestioned: Mary Stuart, queen of Scotland, was the daughter of James V of Scotland and his French queen, Mary of Guise. She was raised and educated in the court of Henry II of France. Exercises she wrote show her knowledge of Latin; she wrote also in French, Italian, and English. In addition, Mary knew Scots, Greek, and Spanish, and the library she formed in her palace in Scotland included volumes in all the above languages.[1] Her first marriage, on August 20, 1558, to the French dauphin, ended after just eighteen months, on his death, at which time the Catholic Mary chose to return to Protestant, tumultuous Scotland, rather than to remain in France in the secure possession of a large income as dowager. Her second marriage, in July, 1564, was to Lord Robert Darnley. Mary's son James (later James VI of Scotland and James I of England) was born of this union, a fact strengthening Mary's already strong claim to the English throne (as the great-granddaughter of Henry VII). Mary and Darnley soon became adversaries. Darnley was murdered on February 9, 1567. Mary's third marriage, on May 15, 1567, was to the adventurous John Hepbonine, earl of Bothwell, an important actor in the murder of Darnley, and a powerful and ambitious figure among the Scottish nobles. This marriage was facilitated by a cynical annulment of Bothwell's first marriage by the same authority who had originally granted a dispensation for it. After her third marriage, Mary lost the support of her nobles, who briefly imprisoned her in Scotland. After escaping to England, she was tried and imprisoned by Elizabeth I, and spent the remaining nine-teen years of her life in prison, until her second trial and execution in 1587.

The facts recounted above have been variously embellished by opposing explanations of Queen Mary's character and actions. The gulf between Mary Stuart's supporters and critics is indicated by such questions as the following: Was Mary's upbringing seriously devout or tainted by dissolution?[2] What were her studies and predilections?[3] Was Mary passionately in love with Bothwell?[4] Did she knowingly consent to the murder of Darnley by her nobles to facilitate separation from Darnley and marriage to Bothwell?[5] Or was she, rather, unaware of the plot?[6] More fundamentally, was her nature sensual or strait-laced?[7] Was she unmoved by cruelty or, alternately, unable to tolerate brutality?[8] These questions are closely related to a study of Mary's writings because some materials attributed to her, including a remarkable mini-sequence of love sonnets unique for the period, are considered forgeries by her apologists.

Moreover, despite the many volumes written concerning Mary Stuart, the writings of the queen of Scots have never been seriously evaluated as litera-ture. Those incomplete efforts made to collect and examine her writings have been based on an interest in Mary Stuart's political, religious, or moral atti-tudes and not on the merits of the writings themselves. Furthermore, the queen herself has been seen only in stark relief as either a martyr, according to her partisans, or a fiend, according to her detractors. The complexity of the woman Mary Stuart, her talent, and the historical originality of her point of view have been neglected; blindness toward the queen's complex character has been coupled with a blindness toward her extraordinary writings. For, in the context of her time, and in terms of both point of view and esthetics, Mary Stuart's poetry, and particularly her love sonnets, should be accorded a recognition they have not previously secured.

To understand how Queen Mary's poetry came to be neglected, it is neces-sary to examine the queen's poems and career in the context of the Renais-sance background.

Alone among Mary's poetry, copies of the love sonnets (together with copies of a group of love letters) were presented as evidence against the queen at her first trial.[9] The letters implicate Mary in the murder of Darnley, and have been stated to have been fabricated by her enemies as evidence against her; however, the sonnets do not implicate the queen in the conspiracy. They do indicate that she was genuinely and deeply in love with Bothwell; however, her love for Bothwell was not the crime for which she was tried.[10] In a palpably balanced consideration of the sonnets, Mrs. P. Stewart-MacKenzie-Arbuthnot, a partisan of the queen's and the compiler of the most complete anthology of her poetry yet published, states that the sonnets,

are far more serious and less open to suspicion than the Casket letters. . . . [I]f impres-sions . . . are of any value, I must admit that I do not feel the same conviction that the Mary Stuart touch is absent as I do in the case of most of the letters. . . . The metre is the same as in many of her authentic poems, and what is perhaps of more significance, the spelling in the contemporary copy . . . seems to follow Mary's usual method. The i instead of í the u instead of v in the centre of words . . . which Father Pollen notices to be so characteristic, and then the play on the word subject . . . all this, though by no means conclusive, may seem to make the theory of forgery less possible. . . . Skelton allows the probability of the sonnets being genuine, and if they prove anything, they prove that at one time in her life—apparently after the 21st of April, 1567—Mary did fall under the influence of a fatal affection for the man who had ruined her: a neutral theory, which leaves untouched the murder question, and which . . . is rather implied, I think, in the memoirs of her old friend, Sir James Melville, and in the extracts of contemporary Catholic opinion quoted by Father Pollen.[11]

In addition, although it is true that the sonnets are much simpler than those of Mary's more usual model, Ronsard, and that they are characterized by such non-Ronsardian qualities as the run-on line, it is also true that the subject matter and obvious emotion of the poet are more suited to this less exalted style. Furthermore, these qualities are typical of the work of another member of the Pléiade, Du Bellay.[12] And we know of Mary Stuart's love for the poetry of Du Bellay.[13]

Enough has been said to show the plausibility of Mary's authorship of the sonnets. It is time to consider the poems themselves and to appreciate the emotion animating them and reaching across the centuries to convince the reader of its truth.

It is probably no small part of the fascination the sonnets exert that they allude so clearly to the difficult, conflicted, and tenuous position in which her feelings had placed the queen: her separation from her son (whom, in fact, she was never to see after the age of ten months), her renunciation of the respect of both her nobles and her humbler subjects, and her conscious lowering of her sense of personal independence and of political sovereignty. These references add "a certain realism,"[14] in Ellen Moers's words, to the situation outlined in the sonnets.

The dramatic behavior of the queen of Scots was an anomaly at a time in which even royal matrons were the subordinates of their husbands. The changes in woman's status that did occur in the Renaissance were not revolutionary enough for a figure like Mary Stuart. For she knowingly set aside all considerations of conventional morality. No other woman of her milieu was willing to cast aside the moral and conventional underpinnings of Renaissance life, as Mary stated her willingness to do and as she suffered for doing. There is certainly great pathos in the cringing posture of Mary Stuart, who had been crowned queen of Scotland at the age of one week and had been the pampered darling of the court of France. However, Mary could not take the direction of her affairs altogether into her own hands; for example, it is a fact that Bothwell did not divorce Jean Gordon until twelve days before his marriage to Mary. As a woman in the complex, semifeudal society of sixteenth-century Scotland, Mary Stuart was, in fact, unable to be unrestrainedly self-directing and sexually unconventional. The time was not yet ripe for the degree of freedom or equality to which she, a woman, aspired. Although a queen, she was expected to conform to social mores.

Presumably some event in the dramatic and stormy series of events marking her romance with Bothwell interrupted Mary's writing, for the last of her sonnets is incomplete. This fragment clearly expresses Queen Mary's vigorous realism, her awareness of the distance between her station in life and her behavior, her commitment to her lover, and her jealousy. In expressing these motifs, and even by virtue of its fragmented, interrupted state, this sonnet therefore is typical of the entire series of Queen Mary's love sonnets.

Queen Mary's other poetry, as Julian Sharman (her earliest editor) notes, is also occasional: "Produced on occasions of extraordinary grief or emotion, each poem is allied to some passage in that turbulent career."[15] Mary Stuart's poetry reflects her exposure in her youth to the brilliant culture of the French Renaissance. Her early memorial verses, written at the French court, are in the grand style of Ronsard, a fact that is not surprising when one recalls that poet's strong influence on his contemporaries.[16] The memorial verses seem rather superficial or even spurious in emotion, although they are competent examples of their type. But there is a significant shift from this superficiality to a mature resignation and patience under trial in the later, meditative verses. If these are less gripping than the love sonnets, they are nevertheless graceful and sincere. Undoubtedly, misfortunes served to strengthen Mary Stuart's character and self-control, in addition to bringing her closer to the conventional values of her day. The final refinement of her thought is expressed in her last poems, which are actually prayers.

Queen Mary's sense of doomed fate permeates even her earliest verses. Another recurring theme is her strong sense of guilt. These motifs appear not only in her poetry, but also in her essay on adversity, which begins movingly but deteriorates in vitality and organization and seems unfinished. Much of Queen Mary's voluminous correspondence has been collected and published; the letters express her concern for her son and her interest in politics, as well as in the subjects of religion and love, so prominent in the poetry. Some letters of particular interest follow: a letter to the mother of the murdered Darnley, a letter to the countess of Arundel (imprisoned like the queen), and the queen's poignant last letter to her brother-in-law, the king of France.

Moers has noted the "striking correlation between strong-mindedness and love writing in the history of women's literature."[17] This phenomenon is exemplified in the life and diversified writings of the fascinating Mary Stuart, which record the channeling of the queen's early passion into strong, religious devotion in her later life. Queen Mary comes closer in affliction than in passion to the spirit of the women of her age, but never does she lose her strong, if changed, sense of herself as a full human being.

Indeed, Mary Stuart stands apart from the other women of her time by virtue of a rounded, multidirected, and assertive nature. Perhaps she has remained a puzzle because she could not actually be cut to fit either the martyr's or the villain's role. Leaving aside the question of her foreknowledge of Darnley's murder, a moot point which the most meticulous scholarship of centuries has been unable to determine, her behavior is perplexing because it seems to follow so many different bents. She is at once an accomplished poet, a charming court figure, a passionate lover, a concerned mother, and a devout Catholic. It is certainly to her liberal continental background, as well as to her sense of herself as a royal personage, that her unique desire for self-realization through both power and sexuality can be attributed. John Stuart Mill, in describing female rulers, asserted that,

princesses, being more raised above the generality of men by their rank than placed below them by their sex, have never been taught that it was improper for them to concern themselves with politics; but have been allowed to feel the liberal interest natural to any cultivated human being, in the great transactions . . . in which they might be called on to take a part. The ladies of reigning families are the only women who are allowed the same range of interests and freedom of development as men.[18]

It was Mary Stuart's misfortune that, after having been raised with expectations of such freedom of action, she found herself in a milieu in which she, a woman, could not order her married life with the same freedom as men. Indeed, Antonia Fraser has stated that, "The consort was . . . the perennial problem of the female ruler in this century: it is significant that the one queen who emerged in the eyes of the people as having never made a mistaken match was Queen Elizabeth,"[19] who retained her independence by remaining single. Juliet Dusinberre has compiled a list of "notorious female sovereigns"[20] of the sixteenth century; interestingly, this is a list of women who ruled effectively, if cruelly, when independent of men. In fact, Mill observes that the competent women rulers he cites "retained the supreme direction of affairs in their own hands."[21]

Despite their enjoyment of a greater freedom for intellectual development, Renaissance Englishwomen were still socially and legally disfranchised by modern standards, particularly once they had become incorporated into the legal personality of a man through marriage. It was the tragedy of the talented Mary Stuart that her sense of personal purpose and desire, developed in her through her education, led her to follow the predictable dictates of her mind and emotions in courses overstepping the permitted limits in England, and resulting in tragedy. And it has been a misfortune for our literary tradition that the partisan controversy engulfing her name has led to the neglect of her literary contribution until now.

Mary Stuart made no effort to publish her writings. Some scattered works were published by contemporaries, but the first publication of her collected French, Italian, and Latin poetry was edited by Julian Sharman (*Poems of Mary Queen of Scots* [London: Basil Montague, 1873]). Doubts exist as to Mary's authorship of some of this poetry, most notably of the love sonnets to Bothwell (the Casket sonnets). A large collection of Mary's correspondence and other documents was published by Prince Alexander Labanoff (*Recueil des Lettres et Memoires de Marie Stuart*, 7 vols. [London: Charles Dolman,

1844]). A collection of prose and verse in both the original French, Latin, or Italian of Mary, and in English translation was edited by Mrs. P. Stewart-Mackenzie-Arbuthnot *(Queen Mary's Book, A Collection of Poems and Essays* [London: George Bell and Sons, 1907]). Arbuthnot's basis for selection is rather arbitrary: she includes some doubtful pieces but excludes the love sonnets, apparently because she prefers not to think of Mary as Bothwell's mistress.

The following writings are arranged chronologically. The original text of the sonnets appears in the notes to facilitate literary evaluation. The notes also furnish information on the provenance of each piece.

from VERSES ON THE DEATH OF FRANCIS II (1560)

I

The voice of my sad song
  With mournful sweetness guides
My piercing eye along
  The track that death divides; —
  Mid sharp and bitter sighs,   [5]
  My youth's bright morning dies.

II

Can greater woes employ
  The scourge of ruthless fate?
Can any hope, when joy
  Forsakes my high estate?   [10]
  My eye and heart behold
  The shroud their love enfold.

          . . . .

VI

For me, sad stranger here,
  There is no resting place:
And blest would change appear
  If change might grief efface.
  My bliss is now my woe—   [35]
  All drear where'er I go.

          . . . .

X

I see no other thing,   [55]
  Or beautiful or bright,
Save that which love's fond memories bring
  Before my mental sight; —
  And ne'er from this sad heart
  Its presence can depart.   [60]

XI

My song, —these murmurs cease,
  With which thou hast complained.
Thine echo shall be peace:
  Love, changeless and unfeigned,
  Shall draw no weaker breath,   [65]
  In parting or in death.[22]

SONNETS TO BOTHWELL (1567?)

I

Oh you High Gods, have pity, and let me find
Somehow some incontestable way to prove
(So that he *must* believe in it) my love
And this unwavering constancy of mind!
Alas, he rules already with no let   [5]
A body and a heart which must endure
Pain and dishonour in a life unsure,
The obloquy of friends and worse things yet.
For him I would account as nothing those
Whom I named friends, and put my faith in foes: [10]
For him I'd let the round world perish, I
Who have hazarded both conscience and good fame,
And, to advance him, happily would die. . . . [sic]
What's left to prove my love always the same?[23]

II

Into his hands, utterly into his power,   [15]
I place my son, my life, my honour and all
My subjects and my country, being in thrall

To him so fast that daily, hour by hour,
My all-surrendered soul hath no intent
But, despite any trouble which may ensue   [20]
To make him see that my great love is true,
And that my constancy is permanent.
Storm or fair weather, let come what may!
My soul has found its bourne and there shall stay.
Soon will I give him proof beyond all fears   [25]
That I am one faithful with no disguise,
And not by feigned submission or false tears,
As others use, but in quite different wise.[24]

III

Folk honour her because she does your will
While I, obedient too, get blame and strife,   [30]
Not being (to my sore grief), like her, your wife,
But yet in duty I will outdo her still.
Faithful she is, and profits much thereby—
For fine it is to queen it in your house;
Whereas what scandal doth my love arouse;   [35]
Albeit she'll never serve you better than I!
She thinks not of the dangers that beset you;
I have no rest, such are my fears thereof:
All her friends smiled upon her when she met you,
But against all men's wish I brought you love;   [40]
Yet nonetheless you doubt if I be true
And make no question of *her* faith to you.[25]

IV

By you, my Heart, by winning you for mate,
Once more the fortune of her House ascends:
By you she has enjoyed a high estate   [45]
Beyond all expectation of her friends.
She had your fast affection, O my Treasure,
And for a time she held your heart bewitched;
With you she tasted all sweet amorous pleasure,
And by your fame her own was thrice enriched,   [50]
Nor did she suffer any loss beyond
A dull fool's joy of whom she once was fond.
Wherefore I'll not grudge aught that she may give
One who for steadfastness, goodness of heart,

Courage and brain and beauty, stands apart,   [55]
Unparalleled. And in that faith I live![26]

V

When you so wildly loved her, she was cold;
And when your suffering brought you near to madness,
As comes to all whose love is uncontrolled,
She did but counterfeit a little sadness   [60]
That—she could catch no joy from your fierce fire.
Her dresses proved that in her own proud view
No imperfections, howsoever dire,
Could blot her image from a heart so true.
I saw in her no right and proper dread   [65]
Lest such a husband, such a man, should die.
You gave her all she is; and she, instead
Of glorying in the hour that sealed your fate,
Has never prized it at its own just rate:
Yet you can say you loved her desperately![27]   [70]

VI

And now does she begin to comprehend
How foolishly she let herself despise
The love of such a lover! Now she tries
To wheedle, flatter, and deceive my friend
With writings that are so astutely done   [75]
That never in *her* brain were they conceived
But, rather, from some splendid writer thieved,
Thus hiring eloquence though having none.
Nevertheless these writings, false in hue,
Her tears, her cries, her bitter lamentation   [80]
And her shrill grief, though mere dissimulation.
Have worked so well that you suppose them true,
And hold her letters under lock and key,
And both believe and love her more than me.[28]

VII

That you trust her, alas, is plain enough   [85]
And that you doubt my truth is all too plain.
O my Sole Wealth and my One Only Love,
I strive to make you sure of me—in vain:

You think me light, as far too well I see,
And watch me with suspicion all day long   [90]
Though without cause: whereby you do to me,
Dear heart, a very great and grievous wrong.
You little know what love to you I bear;
You even fear lest someone else may win me;
You look upon my words as empty air,   [95]
And think my heart is weak as wax within me;
You count me a vain woman without sense:
Yet all you do makes my love more intense.[29]

VIII

Still my love grows and, while I live, must grow
Because of my great joy in having part—   [100]
Even though it be some corner—of that heart
To which at last my loyal love will show
So luminously that all his doubt shall go.
For him would I contend with bitterest fate,
Seek out high honours to enhance his state,   [105]
And do for him so much that he will know
How all my hopes of true content or wealth
Do in obedience and in service lie.
For him I covet fortune and bright fame;
For him I value mine own life and health;   [110]
For him it is that I do shoot so high:
And he will find me evermore the same.[30]

IX

For him what countless tears I must have shed:
First, when he made himself my body's lord
Before he had my heart: and afterward   [115]
When I became distraught because he bled
So copiously that almost life went out:
And at that sight fear seized my heart and head
Both for the love I bore him and the dread
Of losing my sole rampart and redoubt [sic].   [120]
For him I turned my honour to disgrace,
Though honour is our one sure joy and pride:
For him bade Conscience find a humbler place

Chilled my most-trusted friends, and set aside
Every consideration! . . . What would I do?   [125]
Make a love-compact, Love of my heart, with you!³¹

X

I seek but one thing—to make sure of You
Who are the sole sustainer of my life;
And if I am presumptuous so to do,
In spite of all their bitterness and strife,   [130]
It is because your gentle Love's one thought
Is both to love and serve you loyally,
To count the worst that fate can do as naught,
And to make *my* will with *your* will agree.
Someday you certainly will comprehend   [135]
How steadfast is my purpose, and how real,
Which is to do you pleasure until death,
Only to you, being subject: in which faith
I do indeed most fervently intend
To live and die. To this I set my seal.³²   [140]

XI

My Heart, my Blood, my Soul, my chiefest Care,
You promised that we two should taste the pleasure
Of planning the fair future at our leisure;
Yet all night long I lie and languish here
Because my heart is sore beset with fear,   [145]
Seeing that it beats so far off from its treasure.
At times I am afraid beyond all measure
That you forget me utterly, Most Dear:
Sometimes I dread lest gossip, all-untrue,
May harden your kind thoughts from love to hate,   [150]
Or I am chilled with terror lest some new
And troublous throw of chance or shaft of fate
May swerve away from me my Dearest Love. . . .
O God, drive Thou all evil omens off!³³

XII

Not seeing you, despite your word to me,   [155]
I take up pen and paper, and indite,

Concerning a hard case of wrong and right,
Much wondering also what your view may be:
But which of us loves better, I know well;
And easily may you measure which gains most. . . .[34]   [160]

SONNET TO ELIZABETH (1568)

A longing haunts my spirit, day and night,
Bitter and sweet, torments my aching heart;
'Twixt doubt and fear, it holds its wayward part,
And, while it lingers, rest and peace take flight.

Dear sister, if these lines too boldly speak   [5]
Of my fond wish to see you, 'tis for this—
That I repine and sin, in bitterness,
If still denied the favour that I seek.

Ah! I have seen a ship freed from control
On the high seas, outside a friendly port,   [10]
And what was peaceful change to woe and pain;
Ev'n so am I, a lonely, trembling soul,
Fearing,—not you, but to be made the sport
Of Fate, that bursts the closest, strongest chain![35]

Letter to the Countess of Lennox, her mother in lawe (1570)

from Chatsworth, 10 July, 1570

Madame, if the wronge and false reportes ennemies well knowen for traytors to you,
and alas much trusted of me by your advice, had not so farr sturred against my innocency (and I must saie against all kindnes) that you have not onelie as it were condemned me wrongfullie, but so hated, as your wordes and deedes hath testefied to all
the worlde a manifest misliking in you against your owne blood, I would not have
obmitted thus long my duetie in writing to you, excusing me of those untrew reportes
made of me: but hoping with Goddes grace and tyme to have my innocencie knowen
to you, as I trust it is alreadie to the most part of all indifferent persons, I thought best
not to trouble you for a time, till now that suche a matter is moved that toucheth us
bothe, which is, the transporting of your little sonne and my onelie childe in this
cuntrey, to the which, albeit I were never so willing yet y wolde be glad to have your
advise therein as in all other thinges towching him. I have borne him, and God
knoweth with what danger to him and to me bothe, and of you he is dissended, so I
mene not to forget my duetie to you in showing therein anye unkindnes to you, how
unkindlie that ever you have delt with me, but will love you as my aunte and respect
you as my mother in lawe. And if it please you to know further of my mynde in that
and all other thinges betwixt us, my ambassador the bishopp of Rosse shalbe redie to

conferr with you. And so after my hartlie commendations, remitting me to the saide ambassador and your better consideration, I comitt you to the protection of almightie God, whome I praye to preserve you and my brother Charles, and cause you to knowe my hart better nor you doo.

From Chattsworth, this 10th of julii 1570.

By your loving daughter in lawe.

Au dos: To my ladie Lennox, my mother in lawe.[36]

from *MEDITATION IN VERSE (1573)*

Alas! when others hail the hour of sleep,
And troubles, laid aside, seem all forgot,
For me 'tis then that haunting Memory
Calls up the picture of my bitter lot;
And I recall how swift my life has waned   [5]
From joy to sorrow. Then upon my face,
Gather the bitter drops that joy efface!
And later, when I gently meditate
On subjects neither frivolous nor vain,
Concerning all the world's inconstancy,   [10]
And small assurance in the sons of man,
'Tis then I judge that naught is permanent,
Evil or good, beneath the firmament.—
And this again recalls those counsels sage,
Pronounced long since by Solomon the wise: [15]
I have said he, turned o'er life's every page
That could have warmed my heart or pleased my eyes,
But have found naught in this round, earthy mass
But vanity, as all things come and pass!

    . . . .

Fine clothes and sports, dancing and merry laughter   [30]
Soon pass: while mourning and regret come after.
And beauty, which we learn so well to prize,
Fades, as old age begins to dim the eyes.
To eat and drink and folly's art to sue,
Ends but in sickness and in misery,   [35]
While friends and riches, aye, and learning too,
Are vain the soul's desires to satisfy.
Thus all our blessings in this life of pain
Are hard to win and harder to retain!
—And still we look for happiness below,   [40]
Where all that meets us is an empty show!
Ah! we must seek in a far other place

The true repose, true happiness and grace,
All which is promised us in mercy sweet,
If we but cast us at our Saviour's feet.   [45]
For 'tis not here, but in the distant Heaven,
That our eternal heritage is given.

. . . .

Then O my Saviour, Father, Deity,
Do thou in tender mercy look on me!—
As on that sinful woman long ago,
Who, kneeling at Thy feet, bemoaned her woe,
And Peter was forgiven too,—the same   [60]
Who with a coward's oath denied Thy name.
As unto them, O give me now Thy grace,
And let Thy mercy all my sins efface!
Withdraw my soul from its poor earthly claims,
And in Eternity fix Thou its aims.   [65]

. . . .

Preserve me, gracious Lord, from every sin,
And every day augment the faith wherein
My Mother-Church has reared and cherished me,—
Within whose precincts I alone am free!
Save me from sin and ignorance and pride,   [80]
Which drives us to the mournful gates of death,
And grant, O Lord, that ever at my side
May stand my guardian angel. So my breath
That falters o'er its praises, prayers and tears,
Its sighs and aspirations, hopes and fears,   [85]
May to his care consign all earthly grief,
And find in Thy forgiveness sweet relief.

. . . .

I plead no merit. Witness, on my part,
Thy Passion, deeply graven in my heart.
My God, forsake me not! See, I entreat,   [100]
In that most crucial change, which comes too late
To please my ardent soul, that at Thy feet,
Forgiven, I may claim the hour that now I wait![37]

POEM ON SACRIFICE (1573)

The wrath of God the blood will not appease
Of bulls and goats upon His altars shed,
Nor clouds or fragrant incense upward spread,—
He joyeth not in sacrifice like these.

Those, Lord, who would Thee in their offerings please,   [5]
Must come in faith, by hope immortal led,
With charity to man, and duteous tread
Thy paths, unmurmuring at Thy high decrees.

This the oblation which is sweet to Thee:
A spirit tuned to prayer and thoughts divine,   [10]
Meek and devout, in body chastely pure.
O Thou All-Powerful, grant such grace to me,
That all these virtues in my heart may shine,
And to Thy glory evermore endure.[38]

from *Essay on Adversity (1580)*

He who desires that others should have no right to mock at or to disparage his work,
ought it seems to me, above all things, to make so good a choice of the subject he
proposes to treat, that no one can apply to him the ancient adage: *ne sutor ultra
crepidam.* This is why, leaving philosophy to philosophers, laws to legislators, and to
poets the making of songs, enriched with fictions, metamorphoses, histories, and
profitable teaching, and, briefly, giving to each respectively the opportunity of render-
ing testimony according to his vocation, I have thought that I could not better employ
my time (to avoid indolence, and now that I am deprived of the means of exercising
the charge to which God called me in my cradle) than by discoursing upon the diversity
of human afflictions and the various accidents of mortal life. Nor can anyone, I think,
justly blame me for choosing this theme (to me so familiar!) seeing that no person of
our age, especially of my quality, has had greater experience therein. It will at least
furnish the kindly-disposed with material on which to exercise their charity, in fulfill-
ment of the commandment which enjoins us to "weep with those who weep"—
especially when they come to consider the many daily afflictions to which we who
suffer are subject. And thus they will take occasion to address themselves to God, in
order, by prayer and intercession, to turn away His wrath from us. While those afflicted
like me, who may happen to read this discourse, will learn from the example of
persons who have suffered similar misfortunes before them, that the only remedy lies
in turning to God, who always invites them to do so.

But, since there are various kinds of afflictions,—those on the one hand that concern the inner and nobler side of man, and therefore the most dangerous, on the other
hand, those lesser evils that pertain only to the body, I have resolved, in order to avoid
confusion, to treat of each in turn, commencing with those more serious griefs that
have resulted in tragedy to persons who, obstinate in their resentment, and finding
themselves on that account deserted by God, have allowed the torments of despair to
drive them into the sin of self-destruction. And this, either from the influence of
despair, or from lack of any inclination towards repentance and self-amendment.

Of all these, we shall endeavor to find examples, both in ancient pagan literature and
among distinguished persons in modern times. Then we shall consider, on the contrary, the fate of those who, being afflicted with similar misfortunes, have received
them as just and affectionate chastisement at the hands of that loving God and Father,

whom they confess to having so often and so deeply offended. And for this reason tribulation has been to them as a furnace to fine gold—a means of proving their virtue, of opening their so-long-blinded eyes, and of teaching them to know themselves and their own failings. For this is the beginning of virtue, and the way to learn submission to the good pleasure of the Creator, who has given us, in recompense, blessings both material and spiritual, in which all our happiness should consist.

And then we shall conclude, by the grace of God, with resolution and prayer to Him that it may please Him to give me perfect patience under my sufferings, and grace to amend my life, that I may be worthy to be named with those sufferers, who have willingly carried their crosses in this world.

Following this plan I have mentioned, I shall place in the first rank of afflictions, and as the bitterest that a man can suffer, the torments of an evil and guilty conscience, for this is a worm that gnaws continually, and for which no riches or success can compensate the victim. He can never enjoy repose, or know what it is to sleep in peace, undisturbed by the suspicions of others; for sleep is a blessing denied to tyrants and so many others.

.   .   .   .

How many lose patience under troubles such as these!—and truly they are difficult to endure, for our Saviour Himself showed a curiosity as to His reputation when He asked His disciples: "Whom say men that I am [Matt. 16:13]?"—even showing some anger on the occasion.

But, nevertheless, we must endeavor, through all these afflictions, to guard against the sin of impatience, lest we fall into a worse dishonour than before, for impatience is a very direct road to despair—so much so, that many a one, thinking to guarantee himself against blame, has fallen into far greater sin, and put an end to his own life.

Thus the devil whom men think to expel, may return with seven others worse than himself; and this is illustrated by the example of Cain, who, envious of the honour his brother had received (whose sacrifice was accepted by God with greater favour than his own), instead of amending his own sacrifice, chose to commit a really infamous crime, in shedding his brother's blood. Being reproved on this account by God—always so careful of His children, and so prompt to admonish us in time to enable us to return to Him—instead of confessing his guilt, he refused to humble himself or to ask forgiveness, exclaiming only: "Every one that findeth me shall slay me [Gen. 4:1-14]!"

Oh, heart too proudly conscious of the shadow of honour, for whose sake thou dost sacrifice the true honour—this is to act like the dog, who, holding a piece of flesh in his mouth, (the reflection of which in the water appears to be larger than itself) drops it to snatch at its shadow, which is nothing!

.   .   .   .

For all else, . . . there is a remedy to be found, for God has told us that though our sins be red like scarlet, they shall be as white as snow [Isa 1:18] while the glory of those who are innocent shall be the greater for having patiently supported the cross He has assigned them.

.   .   .   .

O act unworthy of a Christian, to whom not only is it not permitted to murmur at the rod of God, but who must even believe that he has merited far worse! for there is no act or dishonour which cannot be wiped out and effaced by penitence, even as God has told us that though our sins be red like scarlet, they shall be as white as snow, and that if we are innocent, our recompense shall be the greater, and our glory the more excellent for having patiently supported the cross He has only assigned us in order to prove our worth and to increase our merit.

And, nevertheless, O what misery we see daily caused through this notion of honour which men have forged in their own heads! The wisest, best, and greatest of men will lose their lives and hazard their souls on account of some libel, or some reflection lightly made. They thrust the law of God on one side, not only to vaunt their own praises, but to cast away their whole existence for so small a matter as a chance word which is but wind, and which, perhaps, he who pronounced it would willingly retract.

And since this human law is so directly contrary to that of Jesus, alas! how we shall have to answer one day, we who allow the prince of this world such dominion over the flock: having had, moreover, such strict charge on the subject from the great celestial shepherd. God knows that I, for my part, have been a great sinner in this respect.

But it is time now to consider another aspect, and one which, in my opinion, affects very closely every person of a kindly nature and generous disposition. God, like the good father of a family, distributes His talents among His children, and whoever receives them and puts them out at profit is discharged and excused from eternal suffering. These who thus win profit, receive a double reward, and are selected and summoned to infinite joy, as we learn from the parable of the rich man, who, going into a strange land, left to one of his servants three talents, to another two, and to another one. . . . Thus with St. Paul, we may say, "Omnia quae scripta sunt, nostra doctrina scripta sunt."

As humility is the virtue most pleasing to God, and the one in which all others find root and increase in perfection, . . . so is pride its opposite, for pride is the mother and source and augmentation of all vice, misery and sin. But at the same time, we must be careful and with prudent judgment consider that in endeavoring to avoid the latter, we should not fall into the disagreeable and ugly slough of pusillanimity, a thing unworthy of generous souls such as those should be who, by divine provision are called to wield the sceptre, bear rank, and exercise authority over the people of God.[39]

POEM ON RESIGNATION (1583)

> O Lord, my God, do Thou this prayer receive,
> As I submit me to Thy Holy Will;
> And, while my soul to this sad earth shall cleave,
> O grant me power to yield in patience still!

> Alas! I sink, and in my weakness fall,   [5]
> If Thou Thy loving strength do not impart,—
> Strength before which the bonds of sin shall quail,
> Leaving Thee ruler of this weeping heart.

> Ah, make my soul Thy constant dwelling-place;—
> Ever through love and hatred, good and ill,   [10]

Through care and sorrow, through life's perilous race,
Faith and Thy Holy love be with me still!

Give me, dear Lord, the true humility,
And strengthen my too feeble, halting faith:
Let but Thy Spirit shed His light on me,—   [15]
Checking my fever with His purer breath.

Give me the power to meet my fate in love,
In constancy and hope, whate'er it be.
And let me draw sweet comfort from above,
Despising earth's vain pomp and subtlety.   [20]

Deliver me from error, vice and pride,
And prove me, Lord, with sorrow's direst scourge.
Lo! through the ills Thy justice doth provide,
My heart's vain longings Thou shalt wholly purge!⁴⁰

SONNET TO RONSARD (1583)

Ronsard! Perchance a passing note of pain
Speaks sometimes to thy heart of days gone by,
When he who was thy king did not disdain
To do thee honour for thy poesy.

Since pride and hate he knew not, I will claim   [5]
The title of good prince to grace his name.

Ah! write not of his fame and grandeur now,—
Frail offspring these, that will be dead tomorrow;
Lay thou a nobler laurel on his brow:
That he would fain have healed grief and sorrow!⁴¹   [10]

from Letter to the Countess of Arundel (1585)

Right truly and well beloved cousin, we have been informed of your injuries and afflictions, no doubt much increased by those that have happened to your husband, who is so dear to us; nor should we have been the last to signify the same to you, had an opportunity presented, of which we have most unworthily and wrongfully been deprived. We have felt great grief on the one side from your afflictions, and comfort on the other to understand the godly constancy in both of you, for the defence of our faith and religion, a matter for all good christians to hold in precious remembrance. You have been lights of faith and honour to guide the weaker brethren, and to recover others by your godly example, who, through malice or ignorance, have declined from our faith. . . . We have long since thought within ourselves of the afflicted state of you both and considered by what labour of ours we might procure the liberty of your good husband. But, on the one side, the great jealousy of this state, and the promptitude of the same to interpret our actions for the worst, as well as the want of intelligence with you both, have prevented us all this while from putting any thing in execution for the advancement of your cause, lest from zeal to do good, we might have committed some error, and rather have put your case backward than forward; and so, it is necessary we understand from yourself your state, and the hope you conceive of repairing it, whereunto our labours shall not be wanting, but be most ready when the same may honour and profit you both. —You may easily conjecture that it is no small grief to us, that our only son is, by the malice of the time and the wicked practices of some instruments, led to be so backward in matters of his own salvation, and for the consolation of this whole Isle. In which points, as we never omitted the duty of a good mother, when we could recover time to do so, being sequestered from him from his nativity, so shall we never desist hereafter to do him good offices, though the labours of the enemies of God and of this Isle tend to break all intelligence between us, and to divide us with practices. How horrible these practices are both in the sight of God and all good christian people, we refer to God and all the christian world, who learn and see the same, as well as infinite other injuries continually practiced against us. —You will receive some letters enclosed which are to be delivered in Scotland to some good servants of ours, wherein we pray you to give us leave to employ your care and labours to so good a work; and that, by means of your friends and servants upon the borders, this service, grateful to God and us, may be settled and continued secretly by your care, which you know to be requisite at this time. You will also receive herewith a letter to my lord Harry Howard, which we pray you likewise may be well delivered. We have also written herewith a few lines to the lady Cobham, which we likewise desire to be delivered to her; and we pray you further to buy for us of the best silks or velvets that you can find, as much as will serve to make her a couple of gowns, to wear for our sake. Yet because we would be very loath to commit an error, which may easily be in such a jealous time, and not knowing on what terms of friendship you stand with the lady Cobham, we leave you to use your own discretion for the delivery of the said letter and silks; though, perhaps, our service may be someway advanced by the delivery of the same; but, as we said, we remit this matter to your discretion, and to your experience of her and of the time. —Of which charge, as well as of your state, and that of your husband, we desire to be informed by means of the french ambassador, from whom you will receive these our letters. We recommend him and his wife much unto you, as personages of honour, and to us well disposed, for which consideration we know that you will respect them the more. When you shall receive answers to our said letters out of Scotland, which must come by the care of such trusty servants and friends as you shall appoint to this charge, we pray you to send us the same, and all others, by means of the french ambassador, whereby they shall come to our hands by God's grace, to whom we commit both yourself and your husband, with all good affection.

Your very good cousin and friend forever,

Marie R.[42]

POEM ON LIFE (1586?)

Alas! What am I? What has my life become?
A corpse existing when the pulse has fled;

An empty shadow, mark for conflicts dread,
Whose only hope of refuge is the tomb!

Cease to pursue, O friends, with envious hate,   [5]
My share of this world's glories hath been brief.
Soon will your ire on me be satiate,
For I consume and die of mortal grief.

And ye, my faithful friends, who hold me dear,
In dire adversity and bonds and woe,—   [10]
I lack the power to guerdon love sincere;
Wish, then, the close of all my ills below,
That, purified on earth, with sins forgiven,
My ransomed soul may share the joys of heaven.[43]

Letter to Henry III, King of France, Her Brother In Law (1587)

Sir, my good brother, having under God's hand for my sins, as I believe, come to throw me in the arms of this Queen, my cousin, where I have had much trouble and passed nigh to twenty years. I am at last by her and her estates condemned to death, and having claimed my papers, by them confiscated to the end of making my testament, I have been unable to recover aught that would serve me, nor to gain leave freely to make the same, nor that after my death my body should be transported, as I desire, into your realm, where I have had the honour to be queen, your sister, and ancient ally.

This day and afternoon has been pronounced to me my sentence, to be executed to-morrow, as a criminal, at eight o'clock of the morning. I have not had leisure to make you a full discourse of all that has passed, but if it please you to credit my doctor and those others, my heart-broken servants, you will hear the truth; and as, God be thanked, I despise death and in good faith protest that I receive it innocent of all crime, even were I their subject, the Catholic religion and the maintenance of the right that God has given me to this crown are the two points of my condemnation, and yet they will not let me say it is for the Catholic religion that I die, but for the fear of change to their own; and for proof, they have taken from me my almoner, nor, for all he is in the house, can I win them to let him come to confess me or give me sacrament at my death; but they have been very instant with me to receive the consolation and doctrine of their minister, summoned to that end. The bearer and his company, for the most part your subjects, will testify of my carriage in this my latest act. It remains that I beseech you, as King Most Christian, good brother and ancient ally, who have ever protested your love to me, that at this hour you give proof of your goodness, for the one part in charity giving me solace in that which, for easing of my conscience, I cannot without you, which is to recompense my heart-broken servants according to them their wages; for the other, to let pray God for a queen who has been called Most Christian, and dies Catholic, stripped of all her goods. As for my son, I recommend him to you in so far as he shall merit, for I cannot answer for him. I have had the hardi-hood to send you two stones, rare for the health, desiring it for you perfect, with happy and long life. You will receive them as from your most loving sister, who dies giving you witness of her good heart towards you. I recommend to you again my servants. You will order, if it please you, that for my soul, I be paid from part of what you owe me, and that in honour of Jesus Christ, whom I shall pray tomorrow at my death for you, you yield me the wherewithal to found a dead-mass and give the alms required.

This Wednesday, at two hours after midnight, Your most loving and very good sister,

                                                                                              Mari R.

To the Most Christian King my brother and ancient ally.[44]

POEM, COMPOSED ON THE MORNING OF HER EXECUTION (1587)

My Lord and My God, I have hoped in Thee;
O Jesu, sweet Saviour, now liberate me!
I have languished for Thee in afflictions and chains,
Through long years of anguish and bodily pains.
Adoring, imploring, on humbly bowed knee,
I crave of thy mercy to liberate me.[45]   [5]

6 ELIZABETH (TANFIELD) CARY (1585-1639)

BORN Elizabeth Tanfield, and raised so strictly that she was required to converse with her mother on her knees, Elizabeth early became famous for her learning, which included a knowledge of several languages and wide reading. Strong-willed throughout her life, she independently mastered the languages and disciplines appealing to her—a fact demonstrating both her aptitude and her personality. To amass her learning, she was forced to resort to subterfuges and suborning of servants in defiance of first her own mother and later her mother-in-law, following her marriage at fifteen to Sir Henry Cary.

The extent to which Lady Falkland could ignore hindrances to her interests is graphically described by her daughter. It seems that self-adornment annoyed Lady Falkland. However, because she wished to please her husband she acquiesced in the ministrations of her maids, but she could not sit still while they attended her, and they were forced to follow her about and to adjust her costume when she paused in her perambulations.[1] In minor matters, then, she could overcome her own sense of propriety and please her husband. Her biographers describe her strong desire to subordinate her own wishes to her husband's, in the contemporary pattern of the ideal wife. Nevertheless, in 1626, she was finally driven by strong leanings she had not been able to quell over the many years of her marriage to convert to Catholicism. Realizing that her conversion would constitute a serious embarrassment to her husband, who had been appointed lord deputy of Ireland in 1622 and was forced to maintain order in that country between the belligerent sects, Lady Falkland attempted to effect a secret conversion. However, her efforts were undermined by an apparently disloyal friend, Lady Denby, and the facts became known to Lord Falkland. Accordingly, he attempted to force his wife to recant, imposing severe economic and social pressures upon her. However, she remained obdurate, despite the fact that she was separated from her husband and her children and reduced to serious economic straits. As Kenneth Murdoch states, Lady Falkland was not deterred by this sort of "minor martyrdom. . . . [S]he managed . . . to cheat herself into believing that she could make a world in which the ideal might be all . . . the obstacles ignored, and the dangers forgotten. Success came only in so far as blind energy could prevail over petty material hindrances. In her daughter's incisive phrase, 'she always seemed scarce able to do small things, but great ones, by the grace of God, she sometimes did,'"[2] throughout her life.

During this separation from her husband, Lady Falkland began a major project of translation which she continued in her last years and which will be discussed shortly. Before Lord Falkland's death from gangrene in 1633, the quarrel between husband and wife had been at least partially resolved (although not without the intercession of the king and privy council); and Lady Falkland attended her husband throughout his last illness. Her economic position remained the same, however; she was passed over in her father's will, probably because of her faith, and lived after her husband's death on only two hundred pounds per year.

Gradually, Lady Falkland gained the confidence of her seven surviving children. Her oldest daughter had died before Lady Falkland's conversion, but the remaining four daughters, who were finally allowed to live with their mother, became nuns. Two of her three sons eventually became priests after their mother had them kidnapped from their guardian, their oldest brother (Lucius, Lord Falkland), and spirited them into a French monastery. The zeal and character of the young Lord Falkland, if not his specific convictions, are similar to those of his remarkable mother.[3]

Lady Falkland was a translator of primarily religious materials, as well as a composer of original literature which, if not actually religious, is certainly of a serious, almost philosophical cast. While the list of her compositions is long, those that are extant are few, but these are both revealing of and consistent with her character as it is known to us. Her earliest extant work is the translation of a French treatise on geography and was apparently completed when she was still single.

Her most important work is the closet drama *Mariam, Faire Queene of Jewry*, the first original drama in English by an Englishwoman, and "a belated specimen," according to Maurice Valency "of the type of drama advocated by the Pembroke group."[4] A detailed consideration of this play, Lady Falkland's most important literary effort, is deferred until the end of this section; her other works will first be enumerated.

Apparently Lady Falkland wrote a second drama known to her circle and set in Syracuse, because John Davies states that she ". . . in Buskin fine,/ with feete of State, dost make thy [her] Muse to mete/ the scenes of Syracuse and Palestine."[5] However, this play seems to be lost altogether. Another work was found among Lord Falkland's papers and was long attributed to him. However, it has been shown to have been written by Lady Falkland and is apparently an unfinished drama or the work draft of one. This is a half-biographical, half-dramatical *History of King Edward II*, which, in Stauffer's phrase, "marks the wedding, under the Stuarts, of prose and verse, of biography and the drama."[6] The work survives in two versions, both first printed late in the seventeenth century; the longer version is the more nearly playlike of the two; in it many speeches have been developed, but there is a preponderance of narrative over dialogue. There are great differences between this work and the *Mariam*;[7] the latter is a meticulously classical play, following the unities scrupulously; *The History of King Edward II* proceeds over a long period, with many changes in scene and more than three actors. One speculates that, had this work been completed, it would have shown considerable development of Lady Falkland's ability to write living drama. As in the case of the finished *Mariam*, there is a subtle appreciation of the principal female character, in this case the adulterous Queen Isabel. Short sections from both versions appear here, as well as the preface to the work, which bears eloquent and dignified testimony to Lady Falkland's personal sorrows. These three efforts reflect Lady Falkland's love for plays, a love attested to in the biography by her daughter.[8]

The learned Lady Falkland translated all of the works of Jacques Davy, Cardinal Du Perron, but, with one exception, her translations were not printed. The exception, recorded in the *DNB*, is "Cardinal Perron's *Reply* to the attack on his work by King James, but the book was ordered to be burned."[9] A few copies of the translation escaped burning, and the dedication to Queen Henrietta Maria and the epistle to the reader, which indicate Lady Falkland's sense of purpose, are both presented here. The reader will note in them a pride both in the work and in the fact that it was done by a woman.

Lady Falkland also wrote verse lives of Saint Mary Magdalene, Saint Agnes the Martyr, and Saint Elizabeth of Portugal, as well as many hymns in celebration of the Virgin.[10] Despite her eccentricities, and the level of poverty to which she was reduced, Lady Falkland's great scholastic standing aroused the interest of learned people of her time, who often visited her truly miserable dwelling.[11] The 1633 edition of the *Works* of John Marston was dedicated to Lady Falkland, "because Your Honour is well acquainted with the Muses."[12] John Davies's poem in her honor has already been noted.

The authorship of *Mariam, Faire Queene of Jewry* was something of a literary teaser until this century. The title page reads only, "Written by that learned, vertuous, and truly noble Ladie, E.C."[13] E. C. was alternately identified as any of these women: Lady Falkland, or either of two other women, a mother and daughter, both also named Elizabeth Cary, but now both discounted as the playwright.[14] It was A. C. Dunstan, editor of the Malone Society reprint of *Mariam*, who proved that Lady Falkland was the author. Dunstan carefully investigated the different family trees of these women, and he presents proofs for Lady Falkland's authorship which are impressive and convincing. He matches genealogical factors to hints in a dedicatory sonnet, and he notes that there are thematic factors (which will be discussed later) also supporting the ascription of the work to Lady Falkland.[15] The source of *Mariam*, as Dunstan points out, is the *Antiquities* of Josephus, available before the play appeared, in German, French, English, and Latin translations as well as in the original Greek. Dunstan suggests that the English translation may have been used and, on textual evidence also, dates the composition of the play between 1602 and 1604.[16] The central character, as the title indicates, is the Hasmonaeite princess Mariam, who became the adored wife of the notorious Herod and was eventually executed by his orders.

Maurice Valency shows the play to be part of a long tradition of plays based on the historical tragedy of Herod and Mariam. Such plays, he states,

involve three elements—a man loves a woman excessively; he does or has done something which causes her to turn cold towards him; this coldness he is incapable of separating in his mind from the suspicion of infidelity, every circumstance works upon this suspicion, and he is driven to kill the woman he loves.[17]

It is noteworthy that this drama is much closer to Greek drama than to French-Senecan in its construction. With one minor exception—involving a nonspeaking actor—only three actors appear in each scene. Unity of place is observed in that all action takes place in Jerusalem, a fact diverging from the actual history as given by Josephus. It is not impossible for the action to take place within twenty-four hours, though such a day would be a very eventful one. There are no supernatural agencies or ghosts. There is a chorus at the end of the fifth act. Finally, there is true dramatic unity in the sense that the action and characters develop, and there is no use of either inflated or artificial language. The verse form is alternately rhymed pentameter lines, with the exception of rhyme tags at the end of each act, and with more elaborate and varied versification in the choral speeches. However, it should be noted that Valency considers "the plot . . . classical only in its superficial form," because there are three, albeit integrated, "actions"[18] in it.

The play takes place in Palestine at a time of disorder. Herod, originally a usurper, has succeeded in wresting control of the country from its once-powerful Hasmonaeite rulers, and in marrying the beautiful and aristocratic princess Mariam, who has borne him several children. Among the means employed by Herod to secure himself has been the murder of Mariam's young and popular brother, the high priest Aristobulus. As a result of Herod's action, Alexandra, the mother of the murdered priest and queen-mother of Palestine, has corresponded with Cleopatra. She, in turn, has interceded with Antony, on Alexandra's behalf, and has caused the summoning of Herod to

Egypt, to tender an explanation of his conduct. It is interesting to note that, historically, these personally dissimilar, but dependent women, did actually correspond and sympathize with one another. It is also significant that Alexandra enlisted Cleopatra's support by appealing to her maternal feelings. Another very remarkable fact is that Herod was so passionately fond of Mariam that he was completely uninterested in the seductive Cleopatra. This attitude certainly agrees with Valency's requirement for the play. Before the play begins, Herod has been duly summoned to Antony, has won Antony's support, and has returned to Palestine. On his return, he has learned that Joseph, his uncle, who had been left in charge of Mariam and Alexandra, had told the women that the jealous Herod had ordered them killed if he was himself executed by Antony. Naturally, this revelation has led to further resentment of Herod by Mariam, the sister of his young victim. Salome, Herod's sister, who has long been resentful of Mariam's influence and of her aristocratic airs, attempts to arouse Herod's jealousy but succeeds only in having Joseph killed; Mariam remains safe at least temporarily. Before the opening of the drama, this course of events has been repeated, in large measure, a second time, following a second murder by Herod of a close relative of his wife. This time the victim is Hyrcanus, father of Alexandra and grandfather of Mariam.

The events of the drama transpire after the time of Herod's second leave-taking from Jerusalem, and continue past Mariam's execution and Herod's remorse. For this time, Herod's jealousy is indeed provoked beyond endurance and Mariam is executed. Generally, the play follows Josephus' account very closely: some of the action is, in fact, a bit mysterious without reference to that source, while other events are elaborated beyond anything in the original. Valency has shown *Othello* "to be no distant relative"[19] of Mariamne drama; besides the generic similarity of plot, the jealous transports of Lady Falkland's Herod are similar to the Moor's, and both are probably related ultimately to the "tyrannical, bombastic, revengeful and cruel"[20] Herod of the medieval mystery plays. A parallel closer in time to Mariam relates to the exchanges of curses between Lady Falkland's *Mariam* and Herod's first wife, Doris, who is mentioned only in passing in Josephus, but who appears here with her now-banished son, Antipater, seeking to redress his grievance. Doris is of the same stripe as Queen Margaret of Shakespeare's *Henry VI* and *Richard III*. It is significant that Mariam's personal feelings for Herod, which are not mentioned in Josephus, are developed in this drama and shown to be in conflict. Another significant difference between the historical source and the play is the reduction in the drama of Alexandra's historical role in Mariam's condemnation. In Josephus, Alexandra, who was the more active of the women in conspiring against Herod, denounced her daughter once she was condemned:

When Alexandra observed how things went, and that there were small hopes that she herself should escape the like treatment from Herod, she changed her behavior to quite the reverse of what might have been expected from her former boldness, and this after a very indecent manner; for out of her desire to show how entirely ignorant she was of the crimes laid against Mariamne, she leaped out of her place, and reproached her daughter in the hearing of all the people, and cried out that "she had been an ill woman, and ungrateful to her husband, and that her punishment came justly upon her, for such her insolent behavior: for that she had not made proper returns to him who had been their common benefactor." . . . . [A]t the first she [Mariam] gave her not a word, nor was discomposed at her peevishness, and only looked at her; yet did she, out of a greatness of soul, discover her concern for her mother's offense, and especially for her exposing herself in a manner so unbecoming her; but as for herself, she went to her death with an unshaken firmness of mind, and without changing the color of her face.[21]

In the play, this event is not shown; there is simply a quiet report that Alexandra did not bewail Mariam's death, but rather damned her daughter as unfaithful to Herod. This downplaying of Alexandra's perfidy can be argued to indicate sympathy for the queen-mother's position on the part of Lady Falkland.

Josephus describes Mariam as imprudent, saying that she "did not . . . consider seasonably with herself, that she lived under a monarchy, and that she was at another's disposal."[22] He elaborates by saying that Mariam had an

excellent character, both for chastity and greatness of soul; but she wanted moderation, and had too much of contention in her nature . . . she took too unbounded a liberty. . . . Moreover, that which most affected her was what he had done to her relations: and she ventured to speak of all they had suffered by him, and at last greatly provoked both the king's mother and sister till they became enemies to her; and even he himself also did the same, on whom alone she depended for her expectations of escaping the last of punishments.[23]

Valency considers Lady Falkland to have "a low opinion of women in general. None of her female characters are praise-worthy,"[24] he says. However, this observation is off the mark. It is probably closer to the play and to Lady Falkland's meaning to consider her own dilemma at the time she was writing the drama. For at this point in her married life, Lady Falkland was herself attempting, unsuccessfully, to reconcile traditional conceptions of properly submissive, wifely behavior to her "head" (i.e., husband), with her own educated and independent rejection of her husband's religious philosophy. Valency says, "If the play has a general moral, it seems to be that even a tyrant is entitled to a humble, patient and loving wife: in any case it is a woman's duty to preserve appearances."[25] This is a superficial judgment of the drama. A love large enough to accept treacherous murder would be monstrous as the love of Lady Macbeth is monstrous; it is Mariam's changes of heart that, in fact, form the moral center of the play.

Perhaps, Valency's mistake lies in ascribing primary importance, in the Mariamne canon, to the character of Herod;[26] in Lady Falkland's play, written by a woman of independent mind who was troubled by this trait, Mariam's dilemma, as much as Herod's, forms the focal situation. In another manner of speaking, Mariam's and Herod's dilemma is an example of what Leonora Brodwin has shown to be "the tragic liability of preserved sovereignty within a love relationship."[27] Valency minimizes the part of Mariam in this tragic juxtaposition. It is Mariam's undoing that she will not avail herself of the powerful weapon of sexual attraction to retain Herod's favor, since she cannot satisfy herself with merely personal security and ignore Herod's mistreatment of her family. In this portrayal of Mariam, the drama agrees with Josephus, but she is even more complex than this in the play; she is not merely a pawn, married for political reasons, but a woman with genuine feeling for her husband—a woman of independent feelings and ideas, whose independence of mind and heart leads to trouble.

It is fair to say that the four married women in the play are presented sympathetically. The worst of Alexandra's actions are merely alluded to, and while Doris, too, is underhanded, she, like Alexandra, is forced to futile schemes by her impotent place in a male hierarchy, a position leaving her little more than empty curses to relieve her frustration. Salome, who here, as in Josephus, is scheming and lecherous, addresses herself directly to her dilemma by plotting to rid herself of an unloved husband, rather than merely bewailing her inability to initiate divorce proceedings under Jewish law. Her pluck, like that of Shakespeare's Edmund, forces us to unwilling admiration.

Another trait discernible in the play is Lady Falkland's ability to accept a situation on its own terms: there are no anachronisms, no Christianization of the Jewish scene. Rather, as in the case of Salome's divorce, there is an understanding of the position of the woman who wanted to sue for divorce under Jewish law. This is only one of many instances in which Lady Falkland's full appreciation of her materials is made clear to the reader.

Nonetheless, her writing appeals to the intellect rather than to the emotions;[28] *Mariam* was almost certainly intended for reading, rather than for acting, in the tradition of the dramas of the Pembroke group. And it is not actable.[29] However, its importance is not limited to the fact that it is a historical first. Instead, the play is a significant intellectual effort—a most interesting and individual handling of materials by a woman from whom one would expect no less. It is a subtle and penetrating criticism of the arbitrary nature of monarchy, of the intrigue and deceit this state engenders, and, most particularly, of the consequences to even the most seemingly exalted of women of their dependent position in such a society. Therefore, despite Valency's judgment that "the *Tragedie of Mariam* is certainly not to be numbered among the outstanding Mariamne tragedies,"[30] the play is truly significant as the work of a historically independent-minded woman who was herself unable to reconcile her thinking with her role as a dutifully obedient wife and mother. The central issue is the nature of Mariam. *Mariam*, like *Antonie* and *Iphigenia*, is a study of the dependent woman, and each of these works, by a member of the intellectual elite of the time, embodies a sensitive study of the matron and mother, which shows the fascination independent-minded women of the past held for like-minded women of the English Renaissance.

The following selections are taken from: *The History of the Life, Reign, and Death of Edward II* . . . (London: J. C. for Charles Harper, Samuel Crouch, and Thomas Fox, 1680); *The History of the most unfortunate Prince, King Edward the second* . . . in *Harleian Miscellany*, I (London: John White, John Murray, John Harding, 1808); Jacques Davy, Cardinal Du Perron, *Reply of the Cardinall of Perron to the* . . . *King*, trans. Lady Elizabeth Falkland (Douay: M. Bogart, 1630); and *The Tragedie of Mariam, Faire Queene of Jewry* (London: Thomas Creede for Richard Hawkins, 1613; Rpt., Malone Society; London: Charles Wittingham and Co. at the Chiswick Press, 1914).

from *The History of the Life, Reign, and Death of Edward II* . . .

The Author's PREFACE to the Reader

To out-run those weary hours of a deep and sad Passion, my melancholy Pen fell accidentally on this Historical Relation; which speaks a King, our own, though one of the most Unfortunate; and shews the Pride and Fall of his Inglorious Minions.

I have not herein followed the dull Character of our Historians, nor amplified more than they infer, by Circumstance. I strive to please the Truth, not Time; nor fear I Censure, since at the worst, 'twas but one Month mis-spended; which cannot promise ought in right Perfection.

If so you hap to view it, tax not my Errours; I my self confess them.
20 Feb. 1627
                                                                        E.F. (n.p.n.)

Edward the Second, eldest Son of *Edward* the First and *Elenor* the vertuous Sister of the *Castilian* King, was born at *Carnarvan* April 25, 1284; and in the most resplendant pride of his age, immediately after the decease of his noble Father, crowned King of *England* July 1307. . . . If we may credit the most antient Historians that speak of the Princes and Passages of those times, this Royal Branch was of an Aspect fair and lovely, carrying in his outward appearance many promising Predictions of a singular expectation. But the judgment, not the eye, must have the preheminence in point of Calculation and Censure. . . . His story speaks the Morning fair, the Noon-tide eclipsed, and the sad Evening of his Life more memorable by his untimely Death and Ruine. He could not have been so unworthy a Son, of so noble a Father, nor so inglorious a Father of so excellent a Son, if either Vertue or Vice had been hereditary. . . . But the divine Ordinances are inscrutable, and not to be questioned; it may else seem justly worthy admiration, how so crooked a Plant should spring from a Tree so great and glorious. His younger years discovered a softly [sic], sweet, and milde temper, pliable enough to the impressions of Vertue; when he came to write Man, he was believ'd over-liberally wanton, but not extreamly vicious. The Royal honour of his Birthright was scarcely invested in his person, when Time (the Touchstone of Truth) shews him to the world a meer Imposture; in Conversation light, in Condition way-waird, in Will violent, and in Passion furious and irreconciliable.

Edward, his valiant and prudent Father, had, by the glory of his victorious Arms, and the excellency of his Wisdom and Providence, laid him the sure foundation of a happy Monarchy; making it his last and greatest care to continue it so in his succession . . . [leaving] no means unattempted; being confident that Wedlock, or the sad weight of a Crown, would in the sense of Honour call him in time off to thoughts more innocent and noble. Tenderness of Fatherly affection abus'd somewhat his belief, and made him give his disorderly actions the best construction. . . . And to make him more apt and fit to receive and follow his instructions, he takes from him those tainted humours of his Leprosie, that seduced the easiness of his nature, and mis-led his unripe knowledge, too green to master such sweet and bewitching temptations. Gaveston his Ganymede, a man as base in Birth as in Condition, he commandeth to perpetual Exile.

. . . .

The melancholy apparitions of their parting, gave the world a firm belief that this inchanting Mountebank had in the Cabinet of his Masters heart, too dear a room and being. The King knowing such impressions are easily won, but hardly lost, strives to take him off by degrees, and labours to make him wave the memory of that dotage which with a divining Spirit he foresaw in time would be his ruine. But death overtakes him before he could bring this so good a Work to full perfection. . . . When he felt those cold fore-running Harbingers of his nearly-approaching End, he thus intreats his Son and Lords, whose watry eyes ingirt his glorious Death-bed.

Edward, the time draws near that calls me to my Grave, you to enjoy this Kingdom. If you prove good, with happiness 'tis yours, and you will so preserve it; if otherwise, my Pains and Glory will be your Dishonour. To be a King, it is the gift of Nature; and Fortune makes him so that is by Conquest; but Royal Goodness is the gift of Heaven, that blesseth Crowns with an Immortal Glory. Believe not vainly that so great a Calling is given to man to warrant his disorder. It is a Blessing, yet a weighty Burthen, which (if abused) breaks his back that bears it. Your former Errours, now continued, are no more yours, they are the Kings, which will betray the Kingdom. The Soveraigns Vice begets the Subjects Errour, who practise good or ill by his Example. Can you in Justice punish them for that whereof your self are guilty? But you, perhaps, may think your self exempt, that are above the Law. Alas, mistake not; there are Injunctions higher far than are your own, will crave a Reckoning. To be belov'd, secures a sweet Obedience; but fear betrays the heart of true Subjection, and makes your People yours but by Compulsion. Majestick thoughts, like Elemental fire, should tend still upwards; when they sink lower than their Sphere, they win Contempt and Hatred. Advance and cherish those of ancient Bloud and Greatness: Upstarts are rais'd with Envy, kept with Danger. You must preserve a well-respected distance, as far from Pride, as from too loose a Baseness. Master your Passions with a noble temper; such Triumphs makes the

Victor conquer others. See here the Ruines of a dying Scepter, that once was, as you
are, a youthful Blossom. I had not liv'd to see this snowy Winter, but that I wean'd my
heart from vain Temptations; my Judgment, not my Eye, did steer my Compass,
which gave my Youth this Age that ends in Glory. I will not say, you too too long have
wander'd, though my sad heart hath droopt to see your Errour. The time now fitly calls
you home; embrace it: for this advantage lost, is after hopeless, Your First-fruit must
make good your Worth; if that miscarry, you wound your Subjects Hopes and your
own Glory. Those wanton Pleasures of wild Youth unmaster'd, may no more touch
the verge of your affections. The Royal Actions must be grave and steady, since lesser
Lights are fed by their Example: So great a Glory must be pure transparent, that hand
to hand encounters Time and Envy. Cast off your former Consorts; if they sway you,
such an unnoble President will shake your Peace, and wound your Honour. Your
wanton Minion I so lately banisht, call you not back, I charge you on my Blessing: for
his return will hasten your destruction. Such Cankers may not taste your ear or favour,
but in a modest and chast proportion. Let true-born Greatness manage great Employ-
ments; they are most fit that have a native goodness. Mushroms in State that are pre-
ferr'd by dotage, open the Gap to Hate and Civil Tumult. You cannot justly blame the
Great ones Murmur, if they command that are scarce fit to serve them; such sudden
leaps must break his neck that ventures, and shake that Crown which gives his Wings
their motion. And you, my Lords, that witness this last Summons, you in whose Loyal
hearts your Soveraign flourisht, continue still a sweet and vertuous Concord; temper
the heart of my youthful Successor, that he may prove as good, as great in Title. Main-
tain the Sentence was by me pronounced; keep still that Viper hence that harbours
mischief: if he return, I fear 'twill be your Ruine. It is my last Request; I, dying, make it,
which I do firmly hope you will not blemish I would say more, but, ah, my Spirits fail
me.[31] [pp. 1-7]

from The History of the most unfortunate Prince, King Edward the second

Edward the Second, born at Carnarvan, was immediately after the death of Edward
the First, his father, crowned King of England. If we may credit the historians of those
times, this prince was of an aspect fair and lovely, carrying in his outward appearance
many promising predictions of a singular expectation. But the judgment, not the eye,
must have pre-eminence in the censure of human passages; the visible calendar is not
the true character of inward perfection; evidently proved in the life, reign, and
untimely death of this unfortunate monarch.

His story eclipseth this glorious morning, making the noon-tide of his sovereignty full
of tyrannical oppressions, and the evening more memorable by his death and ruin.
Time, the discoverer of truth, makes evident his imposture, and shews him to the
world, in conversation light, in will violent, in condition wayward, and in passion
irreconcileable.

Edward, his father, a King no less wise than fortunate, by his discreet providence,
and the glory of his arms, had laid him the sure foundation of a happy monarchy. He
makes it his last care so to enable and instruct him, that he might be powerful enough
to keep it so. From this consideration he leads him to the Scotish [sic] wars, and brings
him home an exact and able scholar in the art military. He shews him the benefit of

time and occasion, and makes him understand the right use and advantage. He instructs him with the precious rules of discipline, that he might truly know how to obey, before he came to command a kingdom. Lastly, he opens the closet of his heart, and presents him with the politick mysteries of state, and teacheth him how to use them by his own example; letting him know, that all these helps are little enough to support the weight of a crown, if there were not a correspondent worth in him that wears it.

These principles make the way open, but the prudent father had a remaining task of a much harder temper. He beheld many sad demonstrations of a depraved and vicious inclination; these must be purified, or his other cautions were useless, and to little purpose. A corruption in nature, that by practice hath won itself the habit of being ill, requires a more than ordinary care to give it reformation. Tenderness of fatherly love abuseth his belief, and makes him ascribe the imperfections of the son to the heat of youth, want of experience, and the wickedness of those that had betrayed his unripe knowledge and easy nature with so base impressions. He imagines, age and the sad burthen of a kingdom would, in the sense of honour, work him to thoughts more innocent and noble; yet he neglects not the best means to prepare and assure it. He extends the height of entreaty, and useth the befitting severity of his paternal power; making his son know, he must be fit for a sceptre before he enjoys it. He takes from him those tainted humours of his leprosy, and enjoins him by all the ties of duty and obedience, no more to admit the society of so base and unworthy companions. Gaveston, the Ganymede of his affections, a man, as base in birth as conditions, he sentenceth to perpetual exile.

The melancholy apparitions of this *loth to depart*, give the aged father an assurance, that his syren had too dear a room in the wanton cabinet of his son's heart. He strives to enlighten his mind, and to make him quit the memory of that dotage, which he foresaw, in time, would be his destruction. But death overtakes him before he could give it perfection; the time is come, that he must, by the law of nature, resign both his life and kingdom.

He summons his son, and bequeaths him this dying legacy; commanding him as he will in another day answer his disobedience, never to repeal his sentence. To his kindred and peers, that with sad tears, and watery eyes, were the companions of his deathbed, he shortly discourseth the base conditions this parasite, and lets them understand both their own and the kingdom's danger, if they withstood not his return, if it were occasioned. They knew his injunctions were just, and promise to observe them; he is not satisfied till they bind it with an oath, and vow religiously to perform it. This sends him out of the world with more confidence, than in the true knowledge of his son's wilful disposition he had cause to ground on.   [p. 69]

from *Reply of the . . . Cardinall of Perron to the . . . King*

TO THE MAJESTIE OF HENRIETTA MARIA . . . QUEENE OF GREAT BRITTAINE

Your Majestie, MAY please to be informed that I have in this dedication delivered to you that right, that I durst not withhold from you. . . . [H]ad I given it to anie other protection, I had done your Majestie a palpable injurie. You are a daughter of France, and therefore fittest to owne his worke who was in his time, an Ornament of your countrie.

You are the Queen of England, and therefore fittest to patronize the making him an English man, that was before so famous a Frenchman. You are Kinge James his Sonns wife, and therefore, since the misfortune of our times hath made it a presumption, to give the Inheritance of this worke (that was sent to the Father in French) to the Sonne in English, whose proper right it is, you are fittest to receive it for him, who are such a parte of him, as none can make you two, other then one. And for the honour of my Sexe, let me saie it, you are a woeman, though farr above other woemen, therefore fittest to protect a woman's worke, if a plaine translation wherein there is nothing aimed at, but rightlie to expresse the Authors intention, may be called a worke; And last (to crowne your other additions) you are a Catholicke and a zealous one, and therefore fittest to receive the dedication of a Catholicke worke. And besides all this, which doth appropriate it to you, for my particular, your Majestie is she, to whom I professe my selfe.

A most faithfull subject, and a most humble servant.   [sig. a2]

TO THE READER

READER, Thou shalt heere receive a Translation welintended, wherein the Translator could have noe other end but to informe thee aright. To looke for glorie from Translation, is beneath my intention, and if I had aimed at that, I would not have chosen so late a writer, But heere I sawe stored up, as much of antiquitie as would fitlie serve the purpose. I desire to have noe more guest at of me, but that I am a Catholique and a Woman; the first serves for mine honor, and the second, for my excuse, since if the worke be but meanely done, it is noe wonder, for my Sexe can raise noe great expectation of anie thing that shall come from me: Yet it were a great follie in me, if I would expose to the view of the world, a work of this kinde, except I judged it to want nothing fitt, for a Translation. Therefore, I will confesse, I thinke it well done, and so had I confest Sufficientlie in printing it: if it gain noe applause, hee that writt it faire hath lost more labour then I have done for I dare avouch it hath bene fower times as long in transcribing, as it was in translating. I will not make use of that worne-out forme of saying I printed it against my will, mooved by the importunitie of Friends; I was mooved to it by my beleefe that it might make those English that understand not French, whereof there are many even in our universities, reade Perron; And when that is done, I have my End. The rest I leave to Gods pleasure.   [sig. C2]

from *The Tragedie of Mariam, Faire Queene of Jewry*

[In the first act, Mariam's first speech, a monologue, reveals her confusion of mind. This confusion is far more involved than in Josephus, because Mariam is not torn between wifely duty and Hasmonaeite family loyalty, but between her love for Herod and her resentment of both his order to have her killed if he is condemned by Antony, and his murder of her brother and grandfather. Believing Herod to have been killed, she bemoans his death with conflicting emotions.]

[Mariam]   How oft have I with publike voyce runne on?
            To censure Romes last Hero for deceit:

Because he wept when Pompeis life was gone,
Yet when he liv'd, hee thought his Name too great.
But now I doe recant, and Roman Lord
Excuse too rash a judgment in a woman;
My sexe pleads pardon, pardon then afford,
Mistaking is with us, but too too common.
Now doe I finde by selfe Experience taught,
One object yeelds both griefe and joy:

　　　.　.　.　.　.　.　.

When *Herod* liv'd, that now is done to death,
Oft have I wisht that I from him were free:
Oft have I wisht that he might lose his breath,
Oft have I wisht his Carkas dead to see.

　　　.　.　.　.　.　.　.

But now his death to memorie doth call,
The tender love, that he to *Mariam* bore:
And mine to him, this makes those rivers fall,
Which by an other thought unmoistned are.
For *Aristobulus* the lowlyest youth
That ever did in Angels shape appeare:
The cruell *Herod* was not mov'd to ruth,
Why then grieves *Mariam Herods* death to heare?

　　　.　.　.　.　.　.　.

Yet cannot this repulse some falling teare,
That will against my will some griefe unfold.
And more I owe him for his love to me,
The deepest love that ever yet was seene: [I, 1, 1-58]

　　　.　.　.　.　.　.　.

[Mariam's confusion is intensified by her need to hide her affection for Herod from her
mother, Alexandra, who enters to pronounce a long tirade against Herod.]

[Alex.]   What means these teares? my *Mariam* doth mistake,
           The newes we heard did tell the Tyrants end:
           What weepst thou for thy brothers murthers sake,
           Will ever wight a teare for *Herod* spend?
           My curse pursue his breathles trunke and spirit   [I, 2, 84-88]

　　　.　.　.　.　.　.　.

           Weepst thou because his love to thee was bent?
           And readst thou love in crimson caracters?
           Slew he thy friends to worke thy hearts content?
           No: hate may justly call that action hers.   [108-15]

　　　.　.　.　.　.　.　.

Who knowes if he unconstant wavering Lord,
His love to *Doris* had renew'd againe?
And that he might his bed to her afford,
Perchance he wisht that Mariam might be slaine.   [132-35]

. . . .

[Alexandra claims that Mariam might have attracted Antony's attentions, but Mariam rejects this objective.]

[Mariam]   Not to be Emprise of aspiring Rome,
           Would *Mariam* like to *Cleopatra* live:
           With purest body will I presse my Toome,
           And wish no favours *Anthony* could give.   [205-8]

[To this Alexandra counters a suggestion]

    Alex. Let us retire us, that we may receive
    How now to deale in this reversed state:
    Great are th'affaires that we must now revolve,
    And great affaires must not be taken late.   [209-12]

. . . .

[Mariam's conscious, deliberate chastity is reaffirmed at the entrance of Herod's sister, Salome, who openly declares her dislike for Mariam and her own liberated sexual ideals. The three women who are the central actors of the play are introduced in the first act, and their characters are clearly drawn. Mariam is a high-minded woman unable to accept either an altogether submissive role or a scheming one. Alexandra is unprincipled; like Tourneur's Gratiana, she thinks nothing of misusing her daughter for the sake of bettering herself; she is also a futile and inept schemer who is more of a dreamer than an effecter. Both her later disloyalty to Mariam and her ineffectuality are given a foundation here. Salome has revealed herself as an enemy to Mariam; in the remainder of the first act she fully reveals both her lasciviousness and the scheme for a divorce alluded to earlier. Therefore, she is a schemer like Alexandra, but a more forth-right and forceful one; her later success is believably founded on the insights into her character furnished in Act I, scene 3.]

[Sal.]   More plotting yet? Why? now you have the thing
           For which so oft you spent your supliant breath:
           And *Mariam* hopes to have another King,
           Her eyes doe sparkle joy for *Herods* death.
               Alex. If she desir'd another King to have,
           She might before she came in *Herods* bed
           Have had her wish. More Kings then one did crave,
           For leave to set a Crowne upon her head.

. . . .

Sal. You durst not thus have given your tongue the raine,
If noble *Herod* still remained in life:
Your daughters betters farre I dare maintaine,
Might have rejoyc'd to be my brothers wife.

  Mar. My betters farre, base woman t'is untrue,
You scarce have ever my superiors seene:
For *Mariams* servants were as good as you,
Before she came to be *Judeas* Queene.

  Sal. Now stirs the tongue that is so quickly mov'd
But more then once your collor have I borne:
Your fumish words are sooner sayd then prov'd,
And *Salomes* reply is onely scorne.

  Mar. Scorne those that are for thy companions held,
Though I thy brothers face had never seene,
My birth, thy baser birth so farre exceld,
I had to both of you the Princesse bene.
Thou party Jew, and party Edomite,
Thou Mongrell: issu'd from rejected race,
Thy Ancestors against the Heavens did fight,
And thou like them wilt heavenly birth disgrace.

  Sal. Still twit you me with nothing but my birth,
What ods betwixt your ancestors and mine?
Both borne of *Adam*, both were made of Earth,
And both did come from holy *Abrahams* line.

  Mar. I favour thee when nothing else I say,
With thy blacke acts ile not pollute my breath:
Else to thy charge I might full justly lay
A shamefull life, besides a husbands death.

  Sal. Tis true indeed, I did the plots reveale,
That past betwixt your favorites and you:
I ment not I, a traytor to conceale.
Thus *Salome* your Mynion *Joseph* slue.

  Mar. Heaven, dost thou meane this Infamy to smother?
Let slandred *Mariam* ope thy closed eare:
Selfe-guilt hath ever bene suspitious mother,
And therefore I this speech with patience beare.
No, had not *Salomes* unstedfast heart,
In *Josephus* stead her *Constabarus* plast,
To free her selfe, she had not usde the art,
To slander haplesse *Mariam* for unchast.

  Alex. Come *Mariam*, let us goe: it is no boote
To let the head contend against the foote.   [I, 3, 228-68]

. . . .

Left alone, Salome expresses her hatred for Mariam, her passion for Silleus, and her determination to divorce her husband despite all precedent.]

>   *Sal.* Lives *Salome*, to get so base a stile
> As foote, to the proud *Mariam Herods* spirit:
> In happy time for her endured exile,
> For did he live she should not misse her merit:
> But he is dead: and though he were my Brother,
> His death such store of Cinders cannot cast
> My Coales of love to quench: for though they smother
> The flames a while, yet will they out at last.   [I, 4, 270-77]

>   . . . .

> [Sal.]   Had not my Fate bene too too contrary,
> When I on *Constabarus* first did gaze,
> *Silleus* had beene object to mine eye:
> Whose lookes and personage must allyes amaze.
> But now ill Fated *Salome*, thy tongue
> To *Constabarus* by it selfe is tide:
> And now except I doe the Ebrew wrong
> I cannot be the faire *Arabian* Bride: [283-90]

>   . . . .

> He loves, I love; what then can be the cause,
> Keepes me for being the *Arabians* wife?
> It is the principles of *Moses* lawes,
> For *Constabarus* still remaines in life,
> If he to me did beare as Earnest hate,
> As I to him, for him there were an ease,
> A separating bill might free his fate:
> From such a yoke that did so much displease.
> Why should such priviledge to man be given?
> Or given to them, why bard from women then?
> Are men then we in greater grace with Heaven?
> Or cannot women hate as well as men?
> Ile be the custome-breaker: and beginne
> To shew my Sexe the way to freedomes doore,
> And with an offring will I purge my sinne,
> The lawe was made for none but who are poore.   [303-23]

>   . . . .

[In the next scene, when Constabarus discovers Salome's intentions, he reacts in astonishment.]

> [Con.]   Didst thou but know the worth of honest fame,
> How much a vertuous woman is esteem'd,

Thou wouldest like hell eschew deserved shame,
And seeke to be both chast and chastly deem'd.

.   .   .   .

Are Hebrew women now transform'd to men?
Why do you not as well our battels fight,
And weare our armour? suffer this, and then
Let all the world be topsie turved quite.   [I, 4, 405-38]

.   .   .   .

Salom. Hold on your talke, till it be time to end,
For me I am resolv'd it shall be so:
Though I be first that to this course do bend,
I shall not be the last full well I know.   [447-50]

.   .   .   .

[Constabarus' last thoughts in this scene remind us that Herod is about to return and wreak vengeance, although the actors themselves are unaware of this fact.]

Had he enjoyed his breath, not I alone
Had beene in danger of a deadly fall:
But *Mariam* had the way of perill gone,
Though by the Tyrant most belov'd of all,
The sweet fac'd *Mariam* as free from guilt
As Heaven from spots, yet had her Lord come backe
Her purest blood had beene unjustly spilt.
And *Salome* it was would worke her wracke.
Though all Judea yeeld her innocent,
She often hath bene neere to punishment.   [496-507]

[The choral song concluding this act comments on the value of contentment.]

Chorus.   Those mindes that wholy dote upon delight,
Except they onely joy in inward good:
Still hope at last to hop upon the right,
And so from Sand they leape in loathsome mud.
Fond wretches, seeking what they cannot finde,
For no content attends a wavering minde.

.   .   .   .

. . . *Mariam* wisht she from her Lord were free,
For expectation of varietie:
Yet now she sees her wishes prosperous bee,
She grieves, because her Lord so soone did die.
Who can those vast imaginations feede,
Where in a propertie, contempt doth breede?

Were *Herod* now perchance to live againe,
She would againe as much be grieved at that:

All that she may, she ever doth disdaine,
Her wishes guide her to she knowes not what.
And sad must be their lookes, their honor sower,
That care for nothing being in their power.   [508-43]
. . . .

[In Acts II and III, additional motifs of loyalty, disloyalty, and dependence upon the king are introduced; a general condition of scheming, intrigue, and ineffectuality is made plain. Among these events is the advent in Jerusalem of Doris, Herod's first wife, with their son, Antipater, to attempt to secure recognition for Antipater and his brothers in place of Mariam's children. Doris has accepted the fact that she has lost her hold on Herod; therefore, she attempts to expand herself through her children. She says to Antipater, on their arrival in Jerusalem:]

Dor.   . . . long it is since *Mariams* purer cheeke
            Did rob from mine the glory. And so long
            Since I returned my native Towne to seeke:
            And with me nothing but the sence of wrong.
                        . . . .
            With thee sweet Boy I came, and came to try
            If thou before his bastards might be plac'd
            In *Herods* royall seat and dignitie.
            But *Mariams* infants here are onely grac'd,
            And now for us there doth no hope remaine:
            Yet we will not returne till *Herods* end
            Be more confirmed, perchance he is not slaine.
            So glorious Fortunes may my Boy attend,
            For if he live, hee'll thinke it doth suffice,
            That he to Doris shows such crueltie:
            For as he did my wretched life dispise,
            So do I know I shall despised die.
            Let him but prove as naturall to thee,
            As cruell to thy miserable mother:
            His crueltie shall not upbraided bee
            But in thy fortunes I his faults will smother.   [II, 3, 772-823]
                Antipat. Each mouth within the Citie loudly cries
            That *Herods* death is certaine; therefore wee
            Had best some subtill hidden plot devise,
            That *Mariams* children might subverted bee,
            By poisons drinke, or else by murtherous Knife,
            So we may be advanc'd, it skils not how:
            They are but Bastards, you were *Herods* wife,
            And foule adultery blotteth *Mariams* brow.   [824-31]
                . . . .

[Most important of the motifs in this act is Salome's plot against Mariam.]

Sal. Mariam shall not linger long behinde.
First Jealousie, if that availe not, feare
Shalbe my minister to worke her end:
A common error moves not *Herods* eare,
Which doth so firmly to his *Mariam* bend.
She shall be charged with so horrid crime,
As *Herods* feare shall turne his love to hate:
Ile make some sweare that she desires to clime,
And seekes to poyson him for his estate.
I scorne that she should live my birth t'upbraid,
To call me base and hungry Edomite:
With patient show her choller I betrayd,
And watcht the time to be reveng'd by slite.
Now tongue of mine with scandall load her name,
Turne hers to fountaines, *Herods* eyes to flame: [III, 2, 1080-1095]

. . . .

[Salome's machinations strengthen, by contrast, our sense of Mariam's innocence; this quality emerges from the following dialogue between Mariam and her jailer, when they have learned of Herod's return.]

Sohem. Be not impatient Madam, be but milde,
His [Herod's] love to you againe will soone be bred: [1133-34]
    Mar. I will not to his love be reconcilde,
With solemne vowes I have forsworne his Bed.   [1135-36]
    Sohem. But you must breake those vowes.   [1137]
    Mar. Ile rather breake
The heart of *Mariam.* Cursed is my Fate:
But speake no more to me, in vaine ye speake
To live with him I so profoundly hate.   [1138-41]
Sohem.   *Sohemus* cannot now your will obey:
If your command should me to silence drive,
It were not to obey, but to betray.   [1143-45]
    Mari. And must I to my Prison turne againe?
Oh, now I see I was an hypocrite:
I did this morning for his death complaine,
And yet doe mourne, because he lives ere night.
When I his death beleev'd, compassion wrought,
And was the stickler twixt my heart and him:
But now that Curtaine's drawne from off my thought,
Hate doth appeare againe with visage grim:
And paints the face of *Herod* in my heart,
In horred colours with detested looke:
Then feare would come, but scorne doth play her part
And saith that scorne with feare can never brooke.

I know I could inchaine him with a smile:
And lead him captive with a gentle word,
I scorne my looke should ever man beguile,
Or other speech, then meaning to afford.

. . . .

Oh what a shelter is mine innocence,
To shield me from the pangs of inward griefe:
Gainst all mishaps it is my faire defence,
And to my sorrowes yeelds a large reliefe.
To be commandresse of the triple earth,
And sit in safetie from a fall secure:
To have all nations celebrate my birth,
I would not that my spirit were impure.
Let my distressed state unpittied bee,
Mine innocence is hope enough for mee. *Exit.*   [1166-83]
        Sohem. Poore guiltles Queene. Oh that my wish might place
A little temper now about thy heart:
Unbridled speech is *Mariams* worst disgrace,
And will indanger her without desart.
I am in greater hazard. O're my head,
The fattall axe doth hang unstedily:
My disobedience once discovered,
Will shake it downe: *Sohemus* so shall die.

. . . .

But fare thee well chast Queene, well may I see
The darknes palpable, and rivers part:
The sunne stand still. Nay more retorted bee,
But never woman with so pure a heart.
Thine eyes grave majestie keepes all in awe,
And cuts the winges of every loose desire:
Thy brow is table to the modest lawe,
Yet though we dare not love, we may admire.
And if I die, it shall my soule content,
My breath in *Mariams* service shall be spent.   [1184-1217]

[The chorus, however, belittles Mariam's chastity as insufficient in the dependent wife.]

[Chorus.] Tis not enough for one that is a wife
           To keepe her spotles from an act of ill:
           But from suspition she should free her life,
           And bare her selfe of power as well as will.
                Tis not so glorious for her to be free,
                As by her proper selfe restrain'd to bee.

. . . .

When to their Husbands they themselves doe bind,
Doe they not wholy give themselves away?
Or give they but their body not their mind,
Reserving that though best, for others pray?
No sure, their thoughts no more can be their owne,
And therefore should to none but one be knowne.

Then she usurpes upon anothers right,
That seekes to be by publike language grac't:
And though her thoughts reflect with purest light,
Her mind if not peculiar is not chast.
    For in a wife it is no worse to finde,
    A common body, then a common minde.   [1219-48]

[In the fourth act, all the schemes initiated earlier are completed. Minor courtiers fail in their plots. Herod returns, his mind filled with thoughts of Mariam. But their meeting is jarring.]

[Herod.]   And heere she comes indeed: happily met
    My best, and deerest halfe: what ailes my deare?
    Thou doest the difference certainly forget
    Twixt Duskey habits, and a time so cleare.   [IV, 4, 1348-50]
        Mar. My Lord, I suit my garment to my minde,
    And there no cheerfull colours can I finde.
        Herod. Is this my welcome? have I longd so much
    To see my dearest *Mariam* discontent?
    What ist that is the cause thy heart to touch?
    Oh speake, that I thy sorrow may prevent.
    Art thou not *Juries* Queene, and *Herods* too?
    Be my Commandres, be my Soveraigne guide:
    To be by thee directed I will woo,
    For in thy pleasure lies my highest pride.   [IV, 4, 1349-62]

        Mar. I neither have of power nor riches want,
    I have enough, nor doe I wish for more:
    Your offers to my heart no ease can grant,
    Except they could my brothers life restore.
    No, had you wisht the wretched *Mariam* glad,
    Or had your love to her bene truly tide:
    Nay, you had not desir'd to make her sad,
    My brother nor my Grandsyre had not dide.   [1373-80]

        Herod. I will not speake, unles to be belev'd,
    This froward humor will not doe you good:
    It hath too much already *Herod* griev'd,

To thinke that you on termes of hate have stood.
Yet smile my dearest *Mariam*, doe but smile
And I will all unkind conceits exile.   [1410-15]

    . . . .

[Salome's plot is implemented, and, finally, Salome convinces Herod that Mariam
should be executed.]

   Sal. Tis time to speake: for *Herod* sure forgets
That Mariams very tresses hide deceit.   [IV, 7, 1691-92]

    . . . .

She speaks a beautious language, but within
Her heart is false as powder: and her tongue
Doth but allure the auditors to sinne,
And is the instrument to doe you wrong.   [1701-4]

    . . . .

Your thoughts do rave with doating on the Queen,
Her eyes are ebon hewde, and you'll confesse:
A sable starre hath beene but seldome seene,
Then speake of reason more, of Mariam lesse.   [1725-28]

    . . . .

Then youle no more remember that hath past,
Sohemus love, and hers shall be forgot:
Tis well in truth: that fault may be her last,
And she may mend, though yet she love you not.   [1741-44]

    . . . .

Sure she never more will breake her vow,
Sohemus and *Josephus* both are dead.
   Herod. She shall not live, nor will I see her face,
A long heald wound, a second time doth bleed:
With *Joseph* I remember her disgrace,
A shamefull end ensues a shamefull deed.
Oh that I had not cald to minde anew,
The discontent of *Mariams* wavering hart:
Twas you: you foule mouth'd *Ate*, none but you,
That did the thought hereof to me impart.
Hence from my sight, my blacke tormenter hence,
For hadst not thou made *Herod* unsecure:
I had not doubted *Mariams* innocence,
But still had held her in my heart for pure.   [1775-88]

    . . . .

[Mariam, herself, considers her behavior and decides that she is guilty of disloyalty to
Herod, since she has failed to subordinate her mind to his.]

[Mar.]   Had I but with humilitie bene grac'te,
           As well as faire I might have prov'd me wise:
           But I did thinke because I knew me chaste,
           One vertue for a woman, might suffice.
           That mind for glory of our sexe might stand,
           Wherein humilitie and chastitie
           Doth march with equall paces hand in hand,
           But one if single seene, who setteth by?
           And I had singly one, but tis my joy,
           That I was ever innocent, though sower:
           And therefore can they but my life destroy,
           My Soule is free from adversaries power.   [IV, 8, 1833-44]

           . . . .

[Doris reappears, Queen Margaret-like, to curse Mariam and her children.]

[Dor.]   These thrice three yeares have I with hands held up,
           And bowed knees fast nailed to the ground:
           Besought for thee the dreggs of that same cup:
           That cup of wrath that is for sinners found.
           And now thou art to drinke it: *Doris* curse,
           Upon thyselfe did all this while attend,
           But now it shall pursue thy children worse.   [1871-77]
            Mar. Oh Doris now to thee my knees I bend,
           That hart that never bow'd to thee doth bow:
           Curse not mine infants, let it thee suffice,
           That Heav'n doth punishment to me allow.
           Thy curse is cause that guiltles Mariam dies.   [1878-82]

[Dor.]   Had I ten thousand tongues, and ev'ry tongue
           Inflam'd with poisons power, and steept in gall:
           My curses would not answere for my wrong,
           Though I in cursing thee imployd them all.
           Heare thou that didst mount Gerarim command,
           To be a place whereon with cause to curse:
           Stretch thy revenging arme: thrust forth thy hand,
           And plague the mother much: the children worse.
           Throw flaming fire upon the baseborne heads
           That were begotten in unlawfull beds.
           But let them live till they have sense to know
           What tis to be in miserable state:
           Then be their nearest friends their overthrow,
           Attended be they by suspitious hate.
           And *Mariam*, I doe hope this boy of mine

Shall one day come to be the death of thine. *Exit.*
    Mar. Oh! Heaven forbid. I hope the world shall see,
This curse of thine shall be return'd on thee.   [1883-1902]

[The chorus criticizes Mariam for having resented her wrongs at Herod's hands, and
states that she would not have been renounced had she accepted his behavior.]

[Chorus.]   The fairest action of our humane life,
        Is scorning to revenge an injurie:
        For who forgives without a further strife,
        His adversaries heart to him doth tie.
            And tis a firmer conquest truely sed,
            To winne the heart, then overthrow the head.

                    . . . .

        A noble heart doth teach a vertuous scorne,
        To scorne to owe a dutie over-long:
        To scorne to be for benefits forborne,
        To scorne to lie, to scorne to doe a wrong.
            To scorne to beare an injurie in minde,
            To scorne a free-borne heart slave-like to binde.

                    . . . .

        Had *Mariam* scorn'd to leave a due unpaide,
        Shee would to *Herod* then have paid her love:
        And not have bene by sullen passion swaide
        To fixe her thoughts all injurie above
            Is vertuous pride. Had *Mariam* thus bene prov'd,
            Long famous life to her had bene allowd.   [1903-39]

                    . . . .

[In the last act, Herod, already repentant of his haste in condemning Mariam, learns
that she was, in fact, faithful to him. Alexandra's perfidy, which is reported, is therefore
doubly damned as both untruthful and disloyal. The play ends with a chiding by the
chorus of Herod's impatience and a denunciation of the many changes in this day.]

[Chorus.]   Who ever hath beheld with steadfast eye,
        The strange events of this one onely day:
        How many were deceiv'd? How many die,
        That once to day did grounds of safetie lay?
            It will from them all certaintie bereve,
            Since twice sixe hours so many can deceive.

                    . . . .

        Herod this morning did expect with joy,
        To see his *Mariams* much beloved face:
        And yet ere night he did her life destroy,

And surely thought she did her name disgrace.
  Yet now againe so short do humors last,
  He both repents her death and knowes her chast.
Had he with wisedome now her death delaide,
He at his pleasure might command her death:
But now he hath his power so much betraide,
As all his woes cannot restore her breath.
  Now doth he strangely lunatickly rave,
  Because his *Mariams* life he cannot save.
This daies events were certainly ordainde,
To be the warning to posteritie:
So many changes are therein containde,
So admirablie strange varietie.
  This day alone, our sagest *Hebrewes* shall
  In after times the schoole of wisedome call.   [2202-37]
                          [sigs. A3-I]

CONCLUSION

THE chronological coincidence of Renaissance and Reformation in England, and the overt lack of equality of opportunity for Renaissance Englishwomen, as well as the religious activities of these women, have misled many students of the English Renaissance to a downplaying of the significance of humanism as opposed to religious thought for Renaissance Englishwomen. "Women in sixteenth-century England were disciples of the Reformation rather than of the Renaissance,"[1] states Ruth Willard Hughey. But Joan Kelly-Gadol's demonstration of the underlying, patriarchal bias of humanism[2] suggests that the subordination of women was congenial to the humanist spirit, and that women may have engaged in religious activities not only because they were more deeply influenced by religion, but because of the nature of the opportunities afforded them even through humanism. Certainly the many erudite and secular writings by Renaissance Englishwomen indicate their interest in nonreligious matters. Thus, Kelly-Gadol's theory suggests a need for a reexamination of traditional thinking about Renaissance Englishwomen. Certainly a similarity in the thinking of humanists and reformers would further explain the acceptance by Renaissance women of what would be an all-pervasive sense of their subordinated status.[3]

At the onset of the Renaissance, most Englishwomen were subordinated to men in every area of life—scholastically, socially, religiously, legally, and economically. The exceptions were the powerful and learned abbess, the dowered widow who often was also the feme sole in business, and of course reigning queens who were exceptional (though not invulnerable) throughout history.

What changes took place for Englishwomen during the Renaissance? The answer to this question is complex; in some areas there was considerable change, in others, none. And change was not always progress.

First, Christian humanism encouraged learning in women. By advocating a change in the quality of daily life, and by asserting the spiritual-intellectual-moral equivalency of men and women, Christian humanism laid the foundation for the equal education of men and women. In England, by establishing what Erasmus termed a "Christian academy" in his Chelsea home, Sir Thomas More set an effective example for the tutelage of women. Many noble families followed suit, and such erudite Tudor women as Anna Bacon and Jane Dudley bear witness to this fact.[4]

Because the system of private tutelage was a privileged one, not accessible to the less privileged members of society, it was women of the upper classes who were first affected by the new ideals because they became the recipients of intensified tutoring aimed at promoting Christian life. In the later part of the sixteenth century, Protestant reformers and humanist educators advocated the extension of schooling for all women, primarily so that they could function properly in their religious and family roles. Their suggested program of studies was a less erudite or a more practical one than that of the earlier Tudor women. But it was also characteristic of the emerging values of the ascending and prospering middle class, which became characterized by a great thirst for learning for a variety of reasons.[5] Middle-class Englishwomen like Rachel Speght and Katherine Stubbes assimilated the new ideals for women.

Ruth Kelso, who has explored the mores of the Renaissance with great thoroughness, has postulated an expansivist, Machiavellian ideal for the Renaissance gentleman, but no parallel ideal for the Renaissance lady. She says, "there was no such thing as the lady so far as theory went, no formulated ideal for the lady as such, distinguished either from the gentleman or from any other woman. . . . The lady, shall we venture to say, turns out to be merely the wife."[6] This domestic pattern, which Kelso terms Christian, is indeed postulated for the Renaissance woman, but Kelso fails to note the new significance with which the role of the wife and mother was invested in the English Renaissance. That the gentleman was less limited in his prospects than the lady is agreed upon universally, and regretted rarely, by writers of the Renaissance. One could say that the gentleman was permitted to be expansive in all his activities, while the lady was accorded some expansiveness in the domestic sphere.

Popular continental opinion considered Englishwomen to enjoy great freedom within marriage;[7] indeed, England was termed a "Paradice of Weomen."[8] However exaggerated this opinion may have been, Englishwomen were certainly accorded great scope as "new mothers" during the Renaissance. Richard T. Vann has noted the development of the role or career of the mother in the time of preindustrial capitalism, but he has not noted its first beginnings in the sixteenth century.[9] In fact, the elevation of the state of marriage and the growing emphasis on education for religious purposes, as well as the receptivity of the growing middle class to the new ideas, led to the development of a newly defined role for woman as a "new mother" in the sixteenth century.

The educational programs of Christian humanists and Protestant reformers were also tied to the concepts of pious behavior. The reformers were strongly impelled by their belief in the priesthood of all believers to educate women so that they could be saved and could rear their children to share in eternal life. This positive program provided scope for women's activities as members of a church where, although denied positions of authority, they were allowed and encouraged to voice and offer support to the new faith and criticize short-comings. It provided them with new importance and authority in the home as nurturers of young Christian souls. It also raised the prestige of home life and the state of marriage.

Legally, in the larger society, the position of the Englishwoman remained static or perhaps declined. She remained politically disfranchised. Despite such important factors as the influence of Catherine of Aragon and her humanists, the interest in marriage questions generated both by the marital problems of Henry VIII and the theories of the religious reformers, and the prestige of Elizabeth I, all of which raised popular opinion about women, the Englishwoman remained subordinated to her husband or other male guardian. No provision was made for the full participation of the Renaissance Englishwoman in the professional and intellectual life of her time; she might glitter or scintillate at court, but she was not expected to compete with men.[10]

Economically, it has often been noted that while the medieval woman had frequently worked as a feme sole, and that while this option continued to some extent early in the English Renaissance, large business activity by women was rare by the mid-seventeenth century.[11] And there was similar decline in smaller business affairs. Pearl Hogrefe has stated, "in any industry, . . . the development of capitalism would make it harder for a single woman or a married one working as a feme sole to get a business established."[12] And Hogrefe cites other contributing factors to the known fact that the participation of women in England in economic affairs declined during the Renais-sance.[13] Simultaneously, the option of a religious career as a nun or abbess was closed to women in Protestant countries like England, so that their effective choices for a lifetime vocation were greatly limited. The woman's role in the home became increasingly the only, but at the same time the newly elevated, role for women. Thus, germinal, early feminism in the country that became the seedbed for North American and for much of future European civilization was ambiguous—both an advancement and a limitation for the woman, since it elevated her in her traditional roles and confined her to them. This partial advancement did not constitute a fundamental change in the actual power structure of English society. The institutionalizing of this partial, nonfundamental change in the seventeenth century represented a regression in the history of the liberation of women. For the British experience was trans-mitted around the world by British trade and colonization.

The qualities of the British middle class, fostered by and even common to the Tudor monarchs,[14] were, in Louis B. Wright's words, largely responsible for the development of London as "the economic capital of Europe, a banking center, the seat of merchant princes, a distributing point for foreign and domestic goods. . . the leading city of the world in commerce and industry, the meeting place of traders from the ends of the earth."[15] The development of this important cosmopolitan center and of a vibrant middle class had significance beyond England; in the Renaissance, "England was laying the foundations for Anglo-Saxon dominion in realms of mind and matter."[16] Consequently, the changes in the position of women in England would have an impact beyond the British borders; particularly in areas of the world colonized by the British and in areas with which the British traded.

While Englishwomen were allowed to develop as individuals, wives, and especially as mothers, they could take no enfranchised part in the larger world. Finally, their development as individuals was ambiguous at best, and this ambiguity is obviously still central to Western conceptions of women.

NOTES

Preface To The Morningside Edition

I am deeply indebted to Elizabeth H. Hageman, who took the time to read the revisions to this edition and to comment on them, and to Patrick Cullen, who offered good advice on many occasions concerning the preparation of this edition, and who read, disagreed about, and discussed the preface with me. Neither of these colleagues, of course, is responsible for any mistakes I may have retained.

1. The phrase "doubled vision" is from Joan Kelly, "The Doubled Vision of Feminist Theory," in *Women, History, and Theory: The Essays of Joan Kelly,* Catharine Stimpson, ed. (Chicago: University of Chicago Press, 1984), pp. 51-64. For a trenchant recent analysis of the gendered discourses of the Renaissance, see Margaret W. Ferguson with Maureen Quilligan and Nancy J. Vickers, "Introduction," *Rewriting,* pp. xv-xxxi.

2. Merry E. Wiesner, "Beyond Women and the Family: Towards a Gender Analysis of the Reformation," *SCJ* 18.3 (1987): 311–21; Maryanne Cline Horowitz, "The Woman Question in Renaissance Texts," *History of European Ideas* 8. 4/5 (1987): 587-95; Travitsky, "PIW."

3. See, for example, Elizabeth H. Hageman, "Did Shakespeare Have Any Sisters? Editing Women Writers of the Renaissance," a paper delivered at the Renaissance English Text Society section held at the annual convention of the Modern Language Association, December 28, 1987; Travitsky, "PIW"; for more general insights, see Lillian S. Robinson, "Treason Our Text: Feminist Challenges to the Literary Canon," in *The New Feminist Criticism: Essays on Women, Literature, and Theory* (New York: Pantheon, 1985), pp. 105-21.

4. Rosalie L. Colie, *The Resources of Kind: Genre Theory in the Renaissance,* Barbara K. Lewalski, ed. (Los Angeles: University of California Press, 1973), p. 76.

5. Barbara Herrnstein Smith, "Value," in *Canons,* Robert von Hallberg, ed. (Chicago: University of Chicago Press, 1983), p. 28.

6. See the notes to chapter 2 for references to studies of these private forms.

7. Travitsky, "PIW."

8. The issue of women's participation in the Renaissance was first raised by Kelly-Gadol in her essay, "Did Women?" Among those who have refined her paradigm are Ferguson et al, in their introduction. Also see Travitsky, "PIW."

9. Wilson, "Introduction," *WWRR,* pp. xxviii-xxx. I discuss this subject at greater length in 'PIW."

10. See Cressy; Stock; Gardiner.

11. I take the term from Catherine Belsey, *The Subject of Tragedy: Identity & Difference in Renaissance Drama* (London: Methuen, 1985), passim.

12. Hughey, p. 98. See the Bibliography below, pp. 271-73.

13. On Mary Stuart, see chapter 5; on Cary, Krontiris, cited in the notes to chapters 3 and 6; on the 'feminist' protests, Kahin, Jones, and Woodbridge, cited in the notes to chapter 3; on Wroth, Josephine A. Roberts, "An Unpublished Literary Quarrrel Concerning the Suppression of Mary Wroth's *Urania* (1621)," *N&Q* 222 (1977): 532-35; and on Douglas, Cope, cited in the notes to chapter 3.

14. These include Roberts MW; Bradner; Rowse; Shepherd; Gary F. Waller, *"The Triumph of Death" and other Unpublished and Uncollected Poems by Mary Sidney, Countess of Pembroke* (Salzburg, 1977); J. C. A. Rathmell, *The Psalms of Sir Philip Sidney and the Countess of Pembroke* (New York, 1963); R. Valerie Lucas, *Mariam Faire Queene of Jewry* [by Elizabeth Cary], for Nottingham Drama Texts, forthcoming.

15. Among them, see especially Hageman "16 c"; Hageman "17 c"; Roberts "MS"; Margaret W. Ferguson, Maureen Quilligan, and Nancy J. Vickers, "Selected Bibliography," in *Rewriting*, pp. 393-412; Rosemary Masek, "Women in an Age of Transition, 1485-1714," in *Women of England from Anglo-Saxon Times to the Present*, Barbara Kanner, ed. (Hamden, Conn.: Archon Books, 1979), pp. 138-82; Norma Greco and Ronaele Novotny, "Bibliography of Women in the English Renaissance," *University of Michigan Occasional Papers in Women's Studies* 1 (1974): 29-57; Merry E. Wiesner, *Women in the Sixteenth Century: A Bibliography* (St. Louis: Center for Reformation Research, 1983); individual bibliographies by the contributors to *Ambiguous;* and by the contributors to Wilson *MWW;* and Wilson *WWRR.*

16. These include the following: Crawford; Hull; Ruth Kelso, "Bibliographical List for the Lady," in Kelso, pp. 326-424; Katherine Usher Henderson and Barbara F. McManus, "Selected Bibliography of Pamphlets from the Controversy," in *Humankind*, pp. 381-85; Patricia Gartenberg and Nena Thames Whittemore, "A Checklist of English Women in Print, 1475-1640," *BB* 34 (1977): 1-13; Travitsky, "NM"; and the bibliography at the end of this volume; Elaine V. Beilin, "List of Works by Women, 1521-1624," in Beilin *RE;* and Beilin "CB."

17. Perhaps the most exciting and most ambitious new work in prospect is the NEH-funded project which will soon be underway under Woods' direction. Tentatively titled "Women Writers in English, 1330-1830," this collaborative effort will put together a computer data base of texts of pre-Victorian women's writings in English, tagged for computer retrieval. Hard text copy of some of these source materials is also planned.

18. Inadvertently, earlier versions of Elizabeth's poems were printed in the 1981 edition of *Paradise of Women* in place of Bradner's texts, a mistake which has been corrected in this edition. At the suggestion of Michael Smith, I have indicated that the attribution of "The Dolefull Lay" to Mary Herbert has been questioned, although most scholars agree that the poem is hers. (See Beilin, *RE*, p. 310, n. 19, for a discussion of this question.) I thank Mr. Smith for bringing these points to my attention.

19. I thank Muriel Bradbrook for this observation and for questioning comments (which I have amended) on Dorothy Leigh and the Princess Elizabeth.

20. Beilin "CB."

Preface

1. Burckhardt, p. 3.

2. Despite the ubiquity of the 'good-night' in scaffold literature, and the contrite 'confessions' often included in broadside newspamphlets, there seem to be very few extant writings

unquestionably from the pens of disreputable women. My forthcoming "Child Murder in Renaissance Life and Drama," which will apppear in *MaRDiE* 5 (1989) is part of a longer projected study of criminal and deviant women in Renaissance England that takes account of confessional and admonitory conversations and writings purportedly composed by such women. Related recent studies include Catherine Belsey, "Alice Arden's Crime," *RD* 13 (1982): 83-102; Leonore Lieblein, "The Context of Murder in English Domestic Plays, 1590-1610," *SEL* 23 (1983): 181-96; and Lena Cowen Orlin, "Man's House as His Castle in *Arden of Feversham*," *MaRDiE* 2 (1985): 57-89.

Introduction

1. Two important early studies were written by Hughey and Kohler. Hughey's count of eighty-five books published by English women during the Renaissance is repeated by later pioneers like Carroll Camden (*The Elizabethan Woman* [New York: Elsevier Press, 1952], p. 9). But many other writings have been enumerated since Hughey's work was completed; Hughey mentions only six works by Esther (Inglis) Kello, for example, but Jackson has located thirty-five, and Williams, several more.

Among ambitious recent studies are Woodbridge; Hannay; *Humankind*; Beilin, *RE*; and *REP*; the fine essays in Wilson *WWRR* include careful editions of some texts. Several lengthy bibliographies on women writers of the English Renaissance, enumerated in notes 13 and 14 to the Morningside Preface have also been published; of these the two by Elizabeth H. Hageman are the most comprehensive. The Woods project (Morningside Preface, n. 17) is particularly exciting.

2. For detailed discussions of the varied positions of women in these ancient cultures, see Marylin Arthur, "Liberated Women: The Classical Era," in *Visible*, pp. 60-89; Sarah B. Pomeroy, *Goddesses, Whores, Wives, and Slaves* (New York: Schocken Books, 1975); Phyllis Bird, "Images of Women in the Old Testament," in Ruether, pp. 41-88; and James Bryce, "The Roman Law of Marriage," in *The Family, Past and Present*, Bernhard J. Stern, ed. (New York: D. Appleton-Century Co. Inc., 1938), pp. 93-98. A rapid assessment is given by Stock, pp. 19-22.

3. Henry C. Lea, *An Historical Sketch of Sacredotal Celibacy in the Christen Church* (Philadelphia: J. B. Lippincott Co., 1867); Constance Parvey, "The Theology and Leadership of Women in the New Testament," in Ruether, pp. 117-49 (esp. 123-46); Edith Deen, *All of the Women of the Bible* (New York: Harper and Row, 1955), p. 401; Shahar, pp. 22-26.

4. Rosemary Radford Ruether, "Misogynism and Virginal Feminism in the Fathers of the Church," in Ruether, pp. 150-83. A famous example of this attitude is Tertullian's outburst against women, "You are the devil's gateway. . . . It was you who coaxed your way around him whom the devil had not the force to attack. With what ease you shattered that image of God: man!" Tertullian, *De Cultu Feminarum*, I, 1. This translation is taken from Julia O'Faoline and Lauro Martines, eds., *Not in God's Image* (New York: Harper, 1973).

For further discussion of some consequences of the identification of ordinary women with the body, see Shahar; on the veneration of the celibate woman, see Marina Warner, *Alone of All Her Sex: The Myth and the Cult of the Virgin Mary* (1976); Rpt, New York: Vintage Books, 1983; and on a mediating figure, see Clarissa W. Atkinson, " 'Your Servant, My Mother': The Figure of Saint Monica in the Ideology of Christian Motherhood," in *Immaculate and Powerful: The Female in Sacred Image and Social Reality*, Clarissa W. Atkinson, Constance H. Buchanan, and Margaret R. Miles, eds. (Boston: Beacon Press, 1985).

5. In my discussion of the Middle Ages, I follow primarily Jo Ann McNamara and Suzanne

Wemple, "Sanctity and Power: The Dual Pursuit of Medieval Women," in *Visible*, pp. 92-118. See also Ruether, in Ruether, esp. pp. 156-60; and McLaughlin; Power, *MW*, and "The Position of Women," in *Legacy of the Middle Ages*, C. G. Crump and E. F. Jacob, eds. (Oxford: Clarendon Press, 1926), pp. 401-23, p. 404; Susan Mosher Stuard, "Introduction," in *Women in Medieval Society*, Susan Mosher Stuard, ed. (Philadelphia: University of Pennsylvania Press, 1976), pp. 1-12; Kelly-Gadol; and Shahar.

6. On courtly love literature and medieval women, see Kelly-Gadol; Power, *MW*, pp. 26-28; Joan Ferrante, "Male fantasy and female reality in courtly literature," *Women's Studies* 11 (1984): 67-97; and Stock, esp. pp. 26-28; on "Public and Legal Rights," see Shahar, pp. 11-21. Kelly-Gadol's argument is partially debated, and refined, by Judith Brown in "A Woman's Place Was in the Home: Women's Work in Renaissance Tuscany," in *Rewriting*, pp. 206-24 (esp. 206-8).

7. See Ian Maclean, *The Renaissance Notion of Woman* (Cambridge: Cambridge University Press, 1980), for a survey of scholastic thinking on women; and Hull for a discussion of Renaissance insistence on traditional ideals for women.

8. Phillippe de Navarre, *Les Quatre Ages de l'homme*, M. de Freville, ed. (Paris, 1888). This graceful translation is taken from Power, "Position."

9. See Watson, pp. 3-4, who draws his information from a study by Alice Hentsch, *De la Litterature Didactique du Moyen Age s'addressant specialement aux Femmes* (Cahors, 1903). The seven works Hentsch lists are *de Laudibus Virginitatis* (7th century); *Exhortatio ad Sacras Virgines* (1160); *Ancren Riwle* (ca. 1250); *How the good wiif taughte hir Doughtir* (ca. 1430); *Myroure of our Ladye* (15th century); *Garmont of gud Ladeis* (ca. 1500); "the seventh is anonymous (Anglo-Norman), and is of slight pedagogical interest" (Watson, p. 3). The reader will note that some of these works are addressed to women of the religious orders and not to women in general.

Some educational plans for women in religious orders are discussed by Joan M. Ferrante, "The Education of Women in the Middle Ages in Theory, Fact, and Fantasy," in *Beyond their Sex: Learned Women of the European Past*, Patricia H. Labalme, ed. (New York: New York University Press, 1984), pp. 9-42.

10. However, medieval nuns, and particularly abbesses, did have the opportunity to become highly educated, and some of these nuns, as opposed to laywomen, did write. See Ferrante, "Education of Women"; and Katharina M. Wilson, "Introduction," in Wilson *MWW*, pp. vii-xxix. On the spread of literacy among the lower-classes, see Spufford.

An exceptional laywoman with peripheral interest for England was Christine de Pisan (1364-1430), the noted poet, who concerned herself with feminist issues but took a conventional, submissive view of the position of women *(Cite des Dames; Livre des Trois Vertus)*. Although she was known in Renaissance England (see P. G. C. Campbell, "Christine de Pisan en Angleterre," in *Revue de litterature comparee* [Paris, 1926], pp. 659-70), she is not cited by the English humanists, and therefore may be inferred to have had no influence on their thinking, although her submissive, domesticated point of view is analogous to that developed by the English theorists. (A great deal of recent work has appeared on Christine de Pisan; for a recent study and bibliography, see Charity Cannon Willard, "The Franco-Italian Professional Writer: Christine de Pizan," in Wilson *MWW*, pp. 333-63).

11. Hughey gives some of this information, pp. 1-2. The three works are the following: Margary Kempe's *Boke of Margarie Kempe* (first printed, in part, in 1501 by Wynkyn de Worde); Juliana of Norwich's *Revelations of Divine Love* (first printed in 1670); and Juliana Berner's *Boke of Haukyng and Huntyng, and also of Cootamuris* (printed in 1486; if this is by

a woman, a moot point, it is the first book written by an Englishwoman and printed in England).

12. Juan Luis Vives, author of the tract which Kelso terms the "most influential in shaping opinion in England and on the continent for the greater part of the sixteenth century" (p. 71), makes a highly similar statement: "though the preceptes for men be innumerable: women yet may be enfourmed with few wordes. . . . for a woman hath no charge to se to, but her honestie and chastyte. Wherfore whan she is enfurmed of that, she is sufficiently appoynted" (*ICW,* B1r). Vives' peculiar, but very influential, blend of progressiveness and restrictiveness on the subject of women's education is discussed by Gloria Kaufman, "Juan Luis Vives on the Education of Women," *Signs* 3. 4 (1978): 891-96; and by Wayne.

13. William Wotten, *Reflections upon Ancient and Modern Learning* (London: J. Leake for Peter Buck, 1694), p. 350. See Stock, pp. 49-80; Gardiner, esp. pp. 141-93. For a conservative estimate of the effects of the new educational theories, see Warnicke, esp. pp. 3 and 205-9.

14. On the legal position of Renaissance Englishwomen, see J. H. Baker, *Introduction to English Legal History* (London: Butterworths, 1972); and Hogrefe "LR."

15. For a negative appraisal of the humanist ideals for English women, see Janis Butler Holm, "The Myth of a Feminist Humanism: Thomas Salter's *The Mirrhor of Modestie,*" in *Ambiguous,* 197-218. For a negative evaluation of their effects on Italian women, see Lisa Jardine and Anthony Grafton, *From Humanism to the Humanities . . .* (Cambridge, MA: Harvard University Press, 1986), pp. 29-57.

16. Udall, quoted by Ballard, pp. 127-28. See p. 90, below.

17. Wyntjes, p. 186. For valuable discussions of the evolution and enhancement of the role of the woman in the home during the English Renaissance, see Powell; Hallers; and Wright. Hogrefe argues for the ability of Renaissance Englishwomen to function in wider spheres: "many [Elizabethan women], like Renaissance gentlemen, developed all their powers." But Hogrefe generalizes on the basis of exceptional women, and this basis is illogical (*TW,* p. 3). On the other hand, Kelso does not appear to appreciate the enhancement of woman's private sphere; "the lady," she states, "turns out to be merely the wife" (p. 1).

Clark, who studied seventeenth-century Englishwomen from an economist's perspective, noted early in this century that the importance ascribed to activities at home, particularly child-nurture, inhibited married women from working outside the home, although cottage industries could not compete with large factories. Thus seventeenth-century women ceased to be providers and became consumers. This development extends beyond the Renaissance, although it begins within the period. Building on Clark's work, Cahn argues in her recent study that limitations on woman's public work and the enhancement of her private functions acted to confine her in private roles. See "Familial and Personal Writings," chapter 2.

18. The similarities between the two groups—and between their ideas on the family—are discussed by Davies and Todd. Davis presents an even-handed estimate of the effects on women of the theories of the two groups of reformers.

19. See Pearl Hogrefe, *The Sir Thomas More Circle: A Program of Ideas and their impact on secular drama* (Urbana: University of Illinois Press, 1959), pp. 201-50, for a discussion of some of the planks of the humanist platform. On the effects of the Protestant theories, see Wyntjes; and Nancy L. Roelker, "The Appeal of Calvinism to French Noblewomen in the Sixteenth Century," *JIH* 2 (1972): 391-418. On the noble and court-affiliated Englishwomen affected by the humanist programs, see Warnicke. The new theories were slow in reaching the lower levels of society. See Cressy; and Stock, esp. pp. 59-80.

20. Mary Agnes Cannon, *The Education of Women during the Renaissance* (Washington, D.C.: National Capital Press, 1916), pp. 51-53. Isabella took the time, after ascending the

throne, to acquire a scholarly knowledge of Latin, to establish a school for young noblemen under the tutelage of Peter Martyr, and to found a library of manuscripts, etc. See Watson, pp. 6-7; Stock, p. 51.

21. That the position and treatment of women in the Italian Renaissance was not as progressive as Burckhardt had claimed is by now a commonplace, first voiced by Kelly-Gadol. See Ferguson et al, "Introduction," in *Rewriting;* and Travitsky, "PIW," for a discussion of this subject.

Although England had had a learned, royal patroness of learning in Margaret Beaufort, before Catherine's time, Beaufort gave no particular attention to women's education. See William E. Axon, "The Lady Margaret as a Lover of Literature," *Library* 8 (1907): 34-41, for a discussion of Beaufort's literary activities. For a recent assessment of her influence, particularly at Cambridge, see Malcolm G. Underwood, "The Lady Margaret and her Cambridge Connections," *SCJ* 13.1 (1982): 67-81.

22. Watson, pp. 1-11. Watson terms the years 1523-1538 the "Age of Queen Catherine of Aragon." The seven works, which he edits and excerpts in his text, are the following: Vives' *ICW* (1521; trans. into English by Richard Hyrde by 1529); his *De Ratione Studii Puerilis* and *Satellitium sive Symbola* (1523; trans. into English by Foster Watson in 1912)—both these works were composed for the use of the Princess Mary; and his *OD* (1529; translated into English by Thomas Paynell by 1553); Hyrde (1524; Erasmus' Latin text was issued in 1523— Hyrde's "Letter" is a strong argument for the higher education of women); Sir Thomas More, "Letter to William Gonell" (1518? [see n. 31, below]); and Elyot (1540). A comment by Gardiner seems appropriate here: "The Cinderella of social problems has become a subject of interest, even of personal enthusiasm, to a group of scholars of the first rank; . . . its tutelary spirit is a queen" (p. 158).

On the importance of Catherine to this group of theorists see McConica, esp. p. 7 and pp. 53-58; and Jordan, "FH."

23. Vives, *ICW,* sigs. A2-A3. See also p. 17, below.

24. On the exclusion of women from the total curriculum offered men, see Walter J. Ong, S. J., "Latin Language Study as a Renaissance Puberty Rite," *SP* 56.2 (1959): 103-24. If the prescribed reading programs for men and women are compared with one another, the limitations on women's learning become clearer, with any remotely salacious materials removed from the reading lists for women. Perhaps the key distinction, however, between the programs developed for men and women is the removal of rhetoric, essential to a public role, from the curriculum of even those privileged women who were taught Latin.

25. *ICW,* l3v. In his *OD,* Vives recommends some authors for this purpose: "Plato, Cicero, Seneca and Plutarche. And in this thinge those writers do helpe, that declare the notable examples of vertue, worthy to be ensued & folowed, as Valerius Maximus, Sebellicus, and in like maner the laudable workes of the holy and vertuous men of oure religion, and likewise of those, that have folowed the worldly wisdome. Aristotle and Zenophon do write how men shall governe their house, and family, & of the education & bringing up of children. . . . ," sig. N2. See below, p. 50.

26. Mulcaster, pp. 178, 181. See pp. 91 and 92, below.

27. Powell, in his important work on the genre, describes the complete domestic conduct book as a pedantic, nonliterary tract, heavily glossed with biblical citations, and regarding "four principal subjects; 1) discussion of the marriage state from religious and secular standpoints, 2) the legal elements involved in contracting matrimony, 3) mutual relations of husband and wife, 4) the government of the family, including housekeeping, the upbringing of children, the

management of servants, and general household economics" (pp. 101-2). See also Todd; and Davies.

28. But see Cahn for a negative interpretation of the elevation of the function of the mother.

29. Becon, *NC,* fol. CCCCCxxxviii. See Stock, pp. 59-80, for a lucid discussion of the development of Catholic and Protestant schooling for women. See below, p. 90.

30. Quoted by Watson from an undated letter by Erasmus to John Faber, in Watson, p. 175.

31. "Letter to William Gonell" (1518), in *Saint Thomas More: Selected Letters,* ed. and trans. Elizabeth F. Rogers (New Haven: Yale University Press, 1961), pp. 103-4. All quotations from More's letters are from this edition.

Despite his deep commitment to the education of women, More suggests later in this same letter that women are inherently more resistant to 'cultivation' than men: "But if the soil of a woman be naturally bad, and apter to bear fern than grain, by which saying many keep women from study. I think, on the contrary, that a woman's wit is the more diligently to be cultivated, so that nature's defect may be redressed by industry" (p. 105).

32. Hyrde, sigs. b-b2. For a keen discussion of the translation, see McCutcheon, esp. pp. 460-62. And see below, p. 35.

33. Vives, *OD,* sig. M8. See p. 69, below.

34. Bentley, p. 119. The *Monument* numbers 1,586 pages and comprises both religious works composed and translated by women and works directed to women by men "to the intent that all godlie and devout women readers might have in some measure, wherewith to exercise their faith, to stir up their devotion, and to satisfie their godlie desires: . . . whether they would either by praier aske, by meditation ponder, by precepts learne, or by examples imitate, or avoid to their comfort & edification" (sigs. B1-B2). Bentley divided the work into seven books or "lampes" which, he says, are "readie and replenished and prepared of the wise virgins, with that fragrant oile, pretious perfume, and odoriferous incense of holie invocation, pure praier, divine sacrifice, and heavenlie worship . . . ," (sig. B2). On Bentley's use of iconography, see John N. King, "The Godly Woman in Elizabethan Iconography," *RQ* 38.1 (1985): 41-84, esp. pp. 70-79.

Since women were granted no actual positions within the church hierarchy, and no lasting power, the interest of the reformers can be interpreted as manipulative, or political. See Charmarie Jenkins Blaisdell, "Calvin's Letters to Women: The Courting of Ladies in High Places," *SCJ* 13.3 (1982): 67-84, for an analysis of Calvin's letters that concludes that "his concern for women was more political than spiritual" (84).

35. Heinrich Bullinger, *The golden boke of christen matrimonye . . . ,* trans. Miles Coverdale (London: J. Mayler, 1541), fol. lxxii. See notes 27 and 43 to this Introduction.

36. Lady Jane (Grey) Dudley (1538-1554), the "nine days' queen," was the correspondent of such learned divines as Heinrich Bullinger and the subject of Ascham's famous anecdote on the pleasure of learning Plato; she composed several moving and fervent prayers and letters; Lady Elizabeth (Melville) Colville of Culros (fl. 1603) composed an imaginative, vehemently anti-Catholic poem describing a journey to the Afterworld; Bessie Clerksone (n.d.) made an anguished effort to believe; and Katherine (Emmes) Stubbes (1571?-1590), wife of Philip Stubbes (fl. 1581-93), engaged in a vivid final encounter with Satan just before her final victory over death. Religious poetry and prose by Renaissance Englishwomen are presented in chapter 1.

37. Queen Catherine Parr (1512-1548), *The lamentacion or complaynt of a sinner . . . ,* sig. A1. See excerpt in chapter 1. And see King.

38. On this point, see McLaughlin, in Ruether, p. 223; Shahar, pp. 98-106, 138-45, 183-89,

and 230-36; Travitsky, "NM." See n. 2, chapter 2. (But see n. 28, above, for Cahn's differing assessment.)

39. Desiderius Erasmus, *A ryghte frutefull Epystle . . . in laude and prayse of Matrimony* (London: Robert Redman, n.d.). Erasmus couples this praise with condemnations of promiscuity among the clergy: "what thyng is more honeste then matrimony . . . What is more holy then that which the creatour of all thynges hath ordeyned, copeled, sanctifyed? . . . now such is the state of thynges and tymes, that no where ye may fynd the purenes and perfection of maners les spotted and contaminate, than amonge wedded persons. Let the swarmes of monkes, fryers, chanons, and nunnys avaunce theyr professyon as moch as they wyll . . . suerly the most holy kynd of lyfe is wedlocke puerly and chastly kept. . . . ther is every where so greate a multytude of prestes, of which (alas) how few lyve a chast lyfe?" (C1v-C2r). Erasmus' longest work on Christian marriage, the *Christiani matrimonii institutio* (1526), was dedicated to Catherine of Aragon. See n. 7, chapter 2 for a listing of some other related writings by Erasmus.

40. Thomas Becon *Boke of Matrimony*. In *Worckes of Thomas Becon* (London: John Daye, 1564), fol. CCCCCLXXV.

41. Ibid., fol. DCXVI.

42. Vives, *ICW*, n3r.

43. Gouge, pp. 554-55. Powell notes the strong similarity among the domestic conduct books; ideas similar to Gouge's can be found in such works as Batty; Robert Cleaver, *A godly forme of householde government . . .* (London: Imprinted by T. Creede, for T. Man, 1598); and Mathew Griffeth, *Bethel: or a forme for families . . .* (London: R. Badger for J. Bloome, 1633). See p. 50, below.

44. Elizabeth (Bernye) Grymeston (d. 1603), *Miscelanae, Meditations, Memoratives*, p. 1. See selections in chapter 2.

45. Dorothy (Kemp) Leigh (n.d.) was a pious, middle-class widow who wrote a compendious advice book to her three sons; Elizabeth (Brooke) Joceline (1596-1622) wrote a legacy of advice to her unborn child during her first pregnancy in the event, which did transpire, that she die in childbirth; Elizabeth (Knevet) Clinton, countess of Lincoln (1574?-1630?), published a book enjoining mothers to nurse their own children, a practice advocated by both humanists and reformers. Writings by these women are found in chapter 2.

46. Vives, *OD*, sigs. Q6-Q7. The enthusiasm of the humanists for the new learning often supplied them with surprising historical and legendary models for Renaissance women. Penelope and Andromache, for example, are not commonly celebrated for their erudition. And the historical position of women in Greek and Roman civilization was often far from even the subordinated but respected model posited by Renaissance thinkers. (See Arthur, Pomeroy, and Bryce, cited in n. 2, above.) Gardiner states, "Girlhood at the Renaissance . . . owed a great debt to the education of Greek and Roman women at certain periods of brilliancy; even to the intellectual pursuits of goddess and nymph; *as these things appeared through the medium of a fervent and romantic imagination"* (p. 147; emphasis mine.)

47. Vives, *OD*, sig. O6. See p. 69, below.

48. More. Hythloday states, for example, "The wyfes bee ministers to theyr husbandes, the chyldren to theyr parentes, and, to bee shorte, the yonger to theyr elders" (p. 67).

49. Gentian Hervet, trans., *Treatise of Houshold* (London, 1532). Like the domestic conduct book, the "family treatise," exemplified by Alberti's *Della Famiglia*, was a popular form of domestic instruction.

50. Gouge, pp. 260-61. Citations of biblical models are endemic in the Protestant tracts. Lawrence Stone argues for the greater subordination of Protestant wives who were expected to

render loving submission to their husbands (*Family, Sex and Marriage in England 1500-1800.* [New York: Harper and Row, 1977], p. 202).

51. Kohler, p. 238. See p. 36, below.

52. On the plot against Catherine, see Levin, "QC." On the iconography featuring Henry as Moses, see King, "Godly Woman," pp. 44-45 and 76; and see below, pp. 38 and 170; n. 33, chapter 2; n. 17, chapter 4.

53. For a discussion of the entire episode, see Stenton, p. 126. And see below, p. 92; and n. 9, chapter 3.

54. See Leah S. Marcus, "Shakespeare's Comic Heroines, Elizabeth I, and the Political Uses of Androgyny," in Rose, pp. 135-54; Louis A. Montrose," *A Midsummer Night's Dream* and the Shaping Fantasies of Elizabethan Culture . . ." in *Rewriting,* pp. 50-65; and Jordan, "SP."

55. Elizabeth herself did little to advance other women, perhaps because her own wielding of power depended on setting herself apart from ordinary womanhood. Under her successor, James I, there was a reaction against the new woman. See Stenton, esp. pp. 125-37; Reynolds, pp. 4-23; Woodbridge; Travitsky, "PlW." And see p. 91, below.

56. The disastrous experiences of Elizabeth's stepsister, Mary Tudor, and her cousin, Mary Stuart, demonstrate the loss of a married queen's personal independence and political sovereignty. For a sophisticated recent discussion of the problem, see Constance Jordan, "Woman's Rule in Sixteenth-Century British Political Thought," *RQ* 40 (1987): 421-51. See p. 191, below.

57. Margaret Tyler (fl. 1579), "M.T. to the Reader," in her translation of *The mirrour of princely deeds . . . ,* sigs. A4-A5.

58. See Jones; and Woodbridge. See below, pp. 92-93.

59. Lady Mary Wroth (1586?-1640), niece of Sir Philip Sidney, was the first Englishwoman to write a prose romance in English; Isabella Whitney (fl. 1567-1573) is possibly the first Englishwoman to have declared herself a poet by profession; Jane Anger [pseud.] and Rachel Speght (fl. 1617-1621) are two early English "feminists." Societal and secular writings by Renaissance Englishwomen are found in chapter 3.

60. See chapter 4.

61. See chapter 5.

62. See chapter 6.

Chapter 1

1. Vives, *ICW,* sigs. A2-A3. Similar ideas are expressed by other members of Vives's circle: Elyot; Erasmus in such colloquies as "The New Mother" (1523), "A Marriage in Name Only" (1523), and "The Abbot and the Learned Woman" (1524 [see Erasmus, CE]); Hyrde; More in parts of the *Utopia.*

A critical edition of *ICW* now under preparation by members of the Folger Shakespeare Library Colloquium on Women in the Renaissance will provide a reliable edition of this influential text.

2. Among them are Margaret Roper, trans., *A devout treatise upon the Pater Noster . . .* (1524); her daughter, Mary Basset, trans., "An Exposition of . . . the passion . . . ," in *Workes of Sir Thomas More* (1557); the Princess Elizabeth, trans., *A godly Medytacyon of the christen Sowle . . .* (1548); the Princess Mary, trans., *Paraphrase of the Gospel of St. John* (1548); Anna Bacon, trans., *Apologie or answeare in defence of the Churche of Englande . . .* (1564) and *Certaine Sermons of . . . Master Bernadine Ochine . . .* (1550); Elizabeth Russell, trans., *Way of Reconciliation . . .* (1605); and Mary Herbert, trans., *Discourse of Life and Death . . .* (1592).

On these translators, see Beilin *RE* and "CB"; Warnicke; Hogrefe *WA;* Diane Bornstein, "The Style of the Countess of Pembroke's Translation of Philippe de Mornay's *Discours de la vie et de la mort,"* in Hannay, pp. 126-48; Anne Lake Prescott, "The Pearl of the Valois and Elizabeth I: Marguerite de Navarre's *Miroir* and Tudor England," in Hannay, pp. 61-76; Margaret P. Hannay, " 'Doo What Men May Sing': Mary Sidney and the Tradition of Admonitory Dedication," in Hannay, pp. 149-65; Rita Verbrugge, "Margaret More Roper's Personal Expression in the *Devout Treatise Upon the Pater Noster,"* in Hannay, pp. 30–42; Lamb; and Wayne.

3. The following are some translators of religious poetry: the Princess Elizabeth, trans., Psalm 14, in *Godly Medytacyon* (1548); Mary (Sidney) Herbert, trans., Psalms 44-150 in *Psalmes of David* . . . (first published in London, 1823); Elizabeth Grymeston (d. 1603), trans. several psalms, in *Miscelenea. Meditations. Memoratives.* (1604); Helen Livingston, countess of Linlithgow (fl. 1629), trans. several psalms in *Confession and Conversion* . . . (1629); and Anna Hume (fl. 1644), trans., *Triumphs* . . . (1644).

In addition to the studies named above, see H & H; Roberts, MS; and Bainton.

4. Some of these learned women wrote religious poetry in languages other than English: Anne, Jane, and Margaret Seymour, *Mortum Margaritas Valesiae, Navorrorum Reginae, Hecatadistichon* . . . (Parisius, 1550), also translated into French as *Le Tombeau de Marguerite de Valois* (1551); Mary Stuart, several poems, first collected by Sharman. See Prescott.

5. Gardiner, p. 170. Later writers on women's education in the Renaissance, Stock, for example, do not alter Gardiner's assessment. On the parallel use to which some women put their knowledge of French and Italian, see pp. 143, 159, and 220, below.

6. Bradner, p. 3. Woodstock was a residence in which Elizabeth was held virtually a prisoner.

7. Bradner, p. 5. The superiority of these verses over the rest of Elizabeth's poems is most easily attributed to Elizabeth's strong feelings for Essex, although it is sometimes claimed that her subject was Anjou.

8. Reynolds, p. 21. Agreement with this assessment is attested to by the large and still growing bibliography of studies of Mary Herbert. A good initiation into this material is provided by Roberts, "MS," although, of course, a great deal has been written about Herbert since 1984.

9. Quoted by Luce, p. 11.

10. "Hoby, Sir Thomas (1530-1566)," in *DNB,* IX, 950. See Lamb, pp. 111-12, for speculation on the influence of Hoby on his wife's work.

11. Stenton, p. 134. See Elizabeth Farber, "The Letters of Lady Elizabeth Russell (1540-1609)," Ph.D. dissertation, Columbia University, 1977, for an edition of Lady Russell's correspondence.

12. "Kello, Mrs. Esther or Hesta (1571-1624)," in *DNB,* X, 1234.

13. Jackson, n.p.n. This number has been enlarged by Williams.

14. Hughey, p. 65.

15. Kohler, p. 312. Beilin's estimate is somewhat more tempered (*RE,* pp. 107-10).

16. Kohler, p. 388. See Barbara K. Lewalski, "Of God and Good Women," in Hannay, pp. 203-24, for a valuable discussion of Lanyer's achievements. And see Beilin, *RE,* pp. 177-207.

17. In *Sex and Society in Shakespeare's Age* . . . (New York: Charles Scribner's Sons, 1974), A. L. Rowse claims "that here [in Lanyer] we have the Dark Lady [of Shakespeare's sonnets]" (p. 117). Rowse gives Lanyer's birth date as 1569, and notes, in a reading which is not altogether satisfactory, "the strongly feminist vein" of her poem (p. 105). See also the introduction to his edition of Lanyer's text [Rowse], in which he includes a prose letter by Lanyer, "To the Vertuous Reader," which is not included in the first issue of Lanyer's poem, but which appears in *STC* 15227.5 (First edition, second issue). For a reply to Rowse's

unconvincing arguments on Lanyer's connection with Shakespeare, see S. Schoenbaum, *Shakespeare and Others* (Washington, D.C.: Folger Books, 1985), pp. 54-79.

18. "Howard, Philip . . . (1557-1595)," in *DNB*, X, 53.

19. Kohler, p. 171. H. E. Rollins suggests an alternative ascription of the poem (*Pepys Ballads*, I, 237-41 [1929]).

20. Watson, p. 159.

21. Hyrde, sigs. b-b2. Most writers on the More household have identified the "Frances" of Hyrde's preface as Frances Brandon; more recent studies suggest that she was Frances Staverton, More's niece (e.g., McCutcheon, p. 460).

22. A paper entitled "Religious Writing of Women in the Renaissance," presented by Marilyn J. Thorssen of the University of Pittsburgh at the 1977 MLA convention, summarizes this material succinctly. See Crawford for a valuable checklist coupled with statistical analysis.

23. See McCutcheon; Verbrugge; Beilin, *RE*, esp. pp. 3-28. In addition, recent issues of *Moreana* include several articles on the women of the More household. (See Hageman, "16 c.")

Reference should perhaps be made here to a third, less well-known woman who also, apparently, did not compose original work: Dorcas Martin (d. 1599), possibly the wife of Richard Martin, one time lord mayor of London, and translator of *An Instruction for Christians . . . translated out of French into English . . .*, in Bentley, Lampe 2, pp. 221-31.

Generally, translations are cited in those sections of *Paradise of Women* containing original work by the translator.

24. Hyrde, sig. b.

25. Kohler, p. 238.

26. Mary Bassett, trans., "An Exposition of a parte of the passion . . . ," pp. 1351-404.

27. "Printer's Letter," in "Exposition," p. 1350.

28. Among these writers are the following: Alice Sutcliffe, *Meditacions of Mans Mortality* (1634); Jane Owen, *An Antidote against Purgatory* (1634); and Katherine Chidley (fl. 1641), *Justification of the Independent Churches of Christ* (1641).

29. Juliana of Norwich, *XVI Revelations of Divine Love* (R. F. S. Cressy, 1670); this was the first publication of the manuscript, which is dated 1413.

30. Margary Kempe, *The Boke of Margary Kempe*, ms. 1440-1450; published in part by Wynkyn de Worde, *Shorte Treatyse of Contemplacyon* (London, 1501); no complete editions until 1936.

31. "Bradford, John (1510?–1555)," in *DNB*, II, 1065.

32. "Catherine Parr (1512-1548)," in *DNB*, III, 1217. For valuable assessments of Catherine's influence on contemporary events, see McConica, pp. 200-34; and King.

33. John Foxe recounts this episode, which reaffirms the sense of confinement that must have enveloped even the relatively liberated woman of the Renaissance:

The queen perceiving to what purpose this talk did tend, not being unprovided in what sort to behave herself towards the king, with such answers resolved his questions as the time and opportunity present did require, mildly and with a reverent countenance answering again after this manner.

'Your majesty doth right well know, neither I myself am ignorant, what great imperfection and weakness by our first creation, is alloted unto us women to be ordained and appointed as inferior and subject unto man as our head, from which head all our direction ought to proceed, and that as God made man to his own shape and likeness . . . even so made he woman of man,

of whom and by whom she is to be governed, commanded, and directed . . . so that by his wisdom such things as are lacking in her, ought to be supplied.' Now then, the king's mind was clean altered.
From John Foxe, as quoted in *Writings*, pp. 173-85.

34. Ascham, pp. 35-36. See Levin, "LJG."

35. Foxe also gives the original Latin of these poems. He heads the group of verses, "Certaine pretie verses wrytten by the said Lady Jane with a pynne" (*Actes*, p. 922):

> Non aliena putes homini quae obtingere possunt,
> Sors hodier na mihi, cras erit illa tibi.
>   Jane Dudley
> Deo iuuante, nil nocet liuor malus:
> Et non iuuante, nil iuuat labor gravis.
>   Post tenebras spero lucem.

Chapter 2

1. Powell, pp. 169-76; Wright, pp. 201-4, 226-27, and 506-7; Hallers, 235-72; Jane Dempsey Douglass, "Women and the Continental Reformation," in Ruether, p. 294; Wyntjes, p. 186. See Davis; Todd; and John Bossy, *The English Catholic Community, 1570-1850* (New York: Oxford University Press, 1976). See p. 10 and n. 17, Introduction.

2. McLaughlin, p. 222; Shahar, pp. 98-106, 138-45, 182-89, and 230-36.

3. Watson, p. 4, n. See n. 9, Introduction.

4. With only slight variations in stanza order, the text of *The Northern Mothers Blessing* (Rpt. in *Certaine worthye manuscript poems of great antiquitie . . .* [London: for R. D., 1597]) is identical with that of the work called *How the good wiif taughte hir Doughtir* (Rpt. by Charles Hindley, *The Old Book Collector's Miscellany* [London, 1871], I, 2-17). A sample stanza is the following:

> My doughter gif thou be a wife, wisely thou werke,
> Looke ever thou love God and the holy Kirke,
> Go to Kirke when thou may, and let for no rayne,
> And then shall thou fare the bet, when thou God has sayn

> Full well may they thrive
> That serven God in their live.
> My leve dere child.   [stanza 2]

5. Dusinberre, pp. 206-10. Cahn, pp. 94-118 and 150-55, describes these results negatively.

6. Vives, *ICW*, l3v.

7. See Vives, *OD;* Elyot; and the marriage group of Erasmus' colloquies (CE). The term "new mother" is appropriated from the title of one of these colloquies. Watson gives selections from all the members of the circle.

8. Gouge, pp. 554-55. The reformers differed from the humanists chiefly in limiting their educational program to a more practical level. See also Becon, *NC;* Batty; Richard Braithwaite,

The English Gentlewoman . . . (London, 1631). In his important study of the genre, Powell notes the strong similarity among the religious tracts. *See* nn. 27 and 43, Introduction.

9. Hallers, p. 265.

10. Beilin, *RE*, pp. 266-85; Betty S. Travitsky, "The New Mother of the English Renaissance: Her Writings on Motherhood," *The Lost Tradition: Mothers and Daughters in Literature*, ed. E. M. Broner and Cathy Davidson (New York: Ungar, 1980), pp. 33-43; and "NM." Christine Sizemore, "Early Seventeenth-Century Advice Books: The Female Viewpoint," *SAB* 41.1 (1976): 41-48, discusses three advice tracts. Sara Heller Mendelson notes what she calls "a specific genre . . . the maternal advice-book intended for children whom the mother might not live to educate," and states that it was "inspired" by "[w]omen's fear of death in childbirth" (*The Mental World of Stuart Women* [Amherst: University of Massachusetts Press, 1987], p. 29). Some selections from maternal advice books excerpted in this chapter do not follow this pattern.

Besides the tracts included in this chapter, other materials by Renaissance English mothers are placed in other sections. See especially "Letters and Diaries" and "Prefaces."

11. Kohler, p. 300.

12. Ibid., p. 296. See H & H for a useful study of the work. Portions of the tract are reproduced by B. Y. Fletcher and C. W. Sizemore as "Elizabeth Grymeston's *Miscelenea. Meditations. Memoratives.* Introduction and Selected Text," *LC* 47 (1981): 53-83.

13. Mrs. Leigh states that she chose the princess as the protector of her work because she believed that her "heart was bent to do good to all: wherefore, without feare, and with much faith, I adventured to make your Grace the Protectresse of this my booke, knowing that if you would but suffer your name to be seene in it, wisedome would allow of it, & all the wicked wind in the world could not blow it away" (sig. A4). See Sizemore, "Advice Books"; Beilin, *RE*, pp. 275-80.

14. See especially Erasmus, "The New Mother" (Basel, 1523; rpt. in Erasmus CE). R.V. Schnucker discusses this belief among the Protestants in "The English Puritans and Pregnancy, Delivery and Breast Feeding," *HCQ* 2.1 (1973-74): 637-58.

15. Reynolds, p. 29; see Beilin, *RE*, pp. 271-75; and Sizemore, "Advice Books."

16. "I thought," Mrs. Joceline states, "there was some good office I might doe for my childe more than only to bring it forth" ("Epistle," n. p. n.). There were five editions by 1635.

17. Reynolds, p. 30.

18. In her "Epistle," she makes the following statement to her husband:

I desire her bringing up may bee learning the Bible, as my sisters doe, good housewifery, writing, and good workes: other learning a woman needs not; though I admire it in those whom God hath blest with discretion, yet I desired not much in my owne, having seene that sometimes women have greater portions of learning than wisdome, which is of no better use to them than a main saile to a flye-boate, which runs it under water. But where learning and wisdom meet in a vertuous disposed woman she is the fittest closet for all goodnesse. She is like a well-balanced ship that may beare all her saile. She is, Indeed, I should but shame my self, if I should goe about to praise her more. . . . Yet I leave it to thy will. . . . If thou desirest a learned daughter, I pray God give her a wise and religious heart, that she may use it to his glory, thy comfort, and her owne salvation. [sigs. B4-5]

19. E.g., on p. 13 and p. 19, *FQ* V,v,25; on p. 11, *FQ* II,ix,1. See Beilin, *RE*, pp. 282-85. Crawford believes M. R. to have been a man (p. 278, n. 87).

20. On the letter as a private but literary form, see Virginia Woolf, *The Second Common Reader* (New York: Harcourt, Brace and World, 1932; Rpt., 1960), pp. 50-57; Joanne E. Cooper, "Shaping Meaning: Women's Diaries, Journals, and Letters—The Old and the New," *WSIF* 10.1 (1987): 95-99.

21. Vives, *OD,* sigs, P2-P8.

22. Watson, p. 4. Watson so names the years 1523-1538 in which seven treatises on women's education were published in England. See n. 21, Introduction, for information on the Lady Margaret; also Hogrefe, *WA;* and Linda Simon, *Of Virtue Rare: Margaret Beaufort, Matriarch of the House of Tudor* (Boston: Houghton Mifflin, 1982).

23. See the Bibliography, below.

24. *Ordinances and reformations of apparel for princes and estates* . . . (1493); *Hystorye of Kynge Blanchardyne and Queen Eglantyne, his wyfe* (1493); *Ladder of Perfection* (1494); *Treatise concerning the seven Penetencyal Psalmes* (1509). For more information on these commissioned and recommended works, see Kohler, pp. 49-51.

25. According to Ballard, "She had a fine library, which was well stored with Latin, French, and English books not collected for ornament, or to make a figure (as is frequently the case), but for use" (p. 14).

26. The elegy, composed by Skelton in Latin, is given both in Latin and in English translation by Ballard, who writes that the verses were inscribed "upon a tablet near to the monument" (p. 24). The following lines give the flavor of the rest:

> Queen Tanaquil's exalted mind and birth,
> (Whom Livy's pen extolls 'bove all on earth)
> Fall short of Margaret's' ev'n Penelope
> Was less renowned for chastity than she:
> Prudent as Abigail, King David's wife;
> As Hester bold, in hazarding her life
> To plead her peoples' cause; resembling three
> The noblest Princesses in history.

> Thou great illustrious ruler of the sky
> Who mads't the world and reign'st eternally
> Gracious admit this princess to thy throne
> Renowned for several virtues like thy own.   [pp. 25-27]

27. However, she was able to give forceful direction. See, for example, her letter (1503? to Sir John Paston?) in Gairdner, VI, 158.

28. Anne Boleyn has been credited with two moving poems, "Defiled is my name full sore" and "O Death! rocke me on slepe." These first appear in print, however, in Sir John Hawkins, *A General History of the Science and Practice of Music* (London, 1776), and Boleyn's authorship has been questioned. Her early training in France would give some basis for the polish and sophistication of these verses, if they are indeed hers.

29. "Anne (1507-1536), the second queen of Henry VIII," *DNB,* I, 428. For a fascinating account of her last days, see Margery Stone Schauer and Frederick Schauer, "Law as the Engine of State: The Trial of Anne Boleyn," *William and Mary Law Review* 22 (1980): 49-84.

30. Green [Wood], II, 45.

31. Watson, pp. 1-11. See McConica; Warnicke, pp. 35-6.

32. Mary M. Luke, *Catherine the Queen* (New York: Coward-McCann, Inc., 1967), pp. 296, 417-19, and 434-39; Jordan, "FH."

33. Hester Chapman, *Two Tudor Portraits* (London: Jonathan Cape, 1960), pp. 170-72. See also Beilin, *RE*, pp. 75-80; Levin, "LJG."

34. See Bibliography; different editions contain varying numbers of sermons. See Hogrefe, *WA;* and Lamb.

35. Quoted in "Bacon, Ann, Lady (1528-1610)," *DNB*, I, 796.

36. "Harley, Lady Brilliana (1600?-1643)," *DNB*, VIII, 1276.

37. Kohler, pp. 368-71. The diary, or journal, or occasional memoir has been the subject of intense recent interest as a private form (akin to autobiography and particularly congenial to women), that has been excluded from the traditional canon. Among many studies, see Mary Beth Rose, "Gender, Genre, and History: Seventeenth-Century English Women and the Art of Autobiography," in Rose, pp. 245-78; Estelle C. Jelinek, *The Tradition of Women's Autobiography from Antiquity to Present* (Boston: Twayne Publishers, 1986); Mary G. Mason, "The Other Voice: Autobiographies of Women Writers," in *Autobiography: Essays Theoretical and Critical*, ed. James Olney (1980), pp. 207-35. See Mendelson; and Travitsky "His wife's prayers and meditations: MS Egerton 607," forthcoming in *REP.*

38. "Clifford, Anne, Countess of Dorset, Pembroke, and Montgomery (1590-1676)," *DNB*, IV, 524; Kohler, pp. 372-80; Ballard, pp. 307-15.

Chapter 3

1. Hughey, p. 256.

2. G. M. Trevelyan, *English Social History: A Survey of Six Centuries, Chaucer to Queen Victoria* (New York: David McKay Company, 1965), p. 101.

3. Udall, quoted by Ballard, p. 127.

4. Becon, *NC,* fol. CCCCCxxxviii.

5. Mulcaster, pp. 173-75.

6. Wright, esp. pp. 1-18, 106-7, and 226-27. See Stock's evaluation of educational provisions for Renaissance women, pp. 29-80; Cressy; and Keith Wrightson and David Levine, *Poverty and Piety in an English Village Terling 1525-1700* (New York: Academic Press, 1979), esp. pp. 142-72.

7. Hogrefe notes that the role of women in the economy became more restricted during the Renaissance. (*TW,* 41-58). We may note that while one or two manuals on useful arts were written by Renaissance women, there is a dearth of materials by women on business affairs. See Cahn (esp. pp. 86-125) for a negative assessment of the revaluation of domestic activity for women.

8. T. E., *The Lawes Resolutions of Womens Rights* (London: Assignes of J. More, 1632), sig. B3v. See Hogrefe, "LR."

9. Knox, *The First Blast of the Trumpet against the monstrous Regiment of Women* (Geneva, 1558), p. 52. Knox had intended to blow his trumpet twice more against the Catholic Mary; her death left him in the uncomfortable position of apparently attacking the new Protestant queen to whom he, like other Protestants, had looked for support.

10. Stenton, pp. 126-27; Levin, "QC"; Jordan, "SP."

11. Kohler, p. 301. See Beilin, *RE*, pp. 101-7.

12. Kohler, p. 280. See Kahin; Woodbridge, esp. pp. 63-66; Beilin, *RE,* pp. 250-53; Betty S. Travitsky, " 'The Lady Doth Protest,' " *ELR* 14 (1984): 255-83.

13. Joseph Swetnam, *The Arraignment of Lewd, Idle, Froward, and unconstant women: or the vanitie of them, choose you whether* . . . (London: Edwarde Allde for Thomas Archer, 1615). On the controversy in general, see *Humankind,* esp. pp. 3-46; Hull, pp. 106-26; and Shepherd, pp. 9-23.

14. Kohler, p. 246. See Beilin, *RE,* pp. 253-66; and Jones.

15. Hughey, p. 94.

16. Queen Elizabeth, to whom approximately 250 works were dedicated, was a very popular figure. Lucy Russell, countess of Bedford; Mary Herbert, countess of Pembroke; and Magdalen Herbert, mother of the poet George Herbert and close friend of John Donne, were also figures of importance among patrons of art and learning. Franklin B. Williams, *Index of Dedications and Commendatory Verses in English Books before 1641* (London: Bibliography Society, 1962).

17. Margaret Tyler, "M. T. to the Reader," in *The mirrour of princely deedes and knighthood,* sigs. A4-A5.

18. Lady Joanna Lumley, trans., *Iphigenia at Aulis,* p. v. See Beilin, *RE,* pp. 152-57.

19. Luce, p. 39. Among the works listed by Luce as occasioned or influenced by Lady Herbert's translation are Thomas Kyd's translation of Garnier's *Cornelie* (1594); Samuel Daniel's *Cleopatra* (1594); and *Philotas* (1605); Fulke-Greville's *Alaham* (first printed 1633) and *Mustapha* (1609); and Samuel Brandon's *Tragicomedie of the Vertuous Octavia* (1598). For secondary literature on Mary Herbert see Roberts MS; and Beilin, *RE,* pp. 121-50.

20. Luce, p. 47.

21. Kohler, p. 80. See *Queen Elizabeth's Englishings* . . . , Caroline Pemberton, ed. (Early English Text Society, 1899; rpt. 1973); and Bradner, pp. 13-68.

22. Hughey, pp. 99-100. The manuscripts of these translations are in the British Library.

23. Bradner notes that Bodleian Rawlinson poetical 85, fo. 1, which attributes the poem to Elizabeth, states that the poem was written when she "was suposed to be in love with mounsyre" (p. 75).

24. She is included as Whitney's sister under "Whitney, Geoffrey (1584?-1601?)," in *DNB,* XXI, 142. See Henry Green, *On the Emblems of Geffrey Whitney* . . . (Chester: Minskill and Hughes, 1865); and Betty Travitsky, "The 'Wyll and Testament' of Isabella Whitney (fl. 1567-1573)," *ELR* 10. 1 (1980): 76-94. See R. J. Fehrenbach, "Isabella Whitney, Sir Hugh Plat, Geoffrey Whitney, and 'Sister Eldershae,' " *ELN* 21 (1983): 7-11 for differing conclusions, and his "Isabella Whitney and the Popular Miscellanies of Richard Jones," *CahiersE* 19 (1981): 85-87. Ann Jones discusses Whitney in Chapter 2 of her *Negotiating Eros: Women's Love Lyric in Europe (1550-1620)* (Bloomington: University of Indiana Press, forthcoming 1989). For a differing interpretation of Whitney, see Beilin, *RE,* pp. 88-101.

25. Virginia Woolf, *A Room of One's Own* (New York: Harcourt, Brace, 1929), pp. 71-100. Woolf wrote, for example, "it is a perennial puzzle why no woman wrote a word of that extraordinary literature [under Elizabeth I] when every other man, it seemed, was capable of song or sonnet. . . . [A]ny woman born with a great gift in the sixteenth century would certainly have gone craz'd, shot herself, or ended her days in some lonely cottage, half witch, half wizard, feared and mocked at. . . . [W]hatever she had written would have been twisted and deformed, issuing from a strained and morbid imagination" (pp. 71-87).

26. A recent survey of this tradition is presented by Moers.

27. The countess's translation remained unpublished until 1912, when it was included in a biography by Frances B. Young, *Mary Sidney, Countess of Pembroke* (London, 1912), pp. 207-18. The translation is in the terza rima of the original. Anna Hume's translation, which was

printed as *The Triumphs of love: chastitie: death: translated out of Petrarch by Mris. Anna Hume* (Edinburgh: Evan Tyler, 1644), is in rhyming couplets.

28. E. D. may have been the Elizabeth (Douglas) Coburne, daughter of William Douglas of Whittingehame, who is the subject of a funeral sonnet by Fowler (I, 9), or she may have been the countess of Errol, the third wife of Francis, ninth earl of Errol, and daughter of William, earl of Morton. (See Meikle, vol. III, p. 4, n. to p. 9; vol. III, p. 5, n. to p. 19; and vol. III, p. 28, n. to p. 259.) The poem by E. D. is prefixed to the manuscript, "The Triumphs of the most Famous Poet, Mr. Frances Petrarke," presented to Edinburgh University in 1627 by William Drummond of Hawthorndorn; reprinted by Alexander Dyce, *Specimens of British Poetesses . . .* (London: T. Rodd, 1827), p. 11.

29. There is no evidence that this visit actually took place. The poem is discussed by Beilin, *RE,* pp. 139-42.

30. It also shows the influence of her father. Katherine Duncan-Jones states that "the one author in print who displays unambiguously a knowledge of Robert Sidney's poems is his daughter, Lady Mary Wroth, who in her long romance *Urania* models a substantial number of poems on her father's." "Roses and Lysa: Selections from the Poems of Sir Robert Sidney," *ELR* 9 (Spring, 1979), 243.

A great deal of attention has been accorded Lady Wroth's life and works, much of it summarized in Hageman "17 c." See particularly Roberts, *MW.* An edition of the *Urania,* under Roberts' direction, is to be published by the Renaissance English Text Society. Maureen Quilligan's essay, "Feminine Endings: The Sexual Politics of Sidney's and Spenser's Rhyming," forthcoming in *REP,* discusses Wroth's *Urania* in the context of earlier romances.

31. Kohler, pp. 220-21.

32. William Cecil, "Preface," *The lamentacion . . . of a sinner, . . .* (London: E. Whitchurche, 1548), sigs. A4-A5. *STC* 4828. On the pious works sponsored by Parr and like-minded women, see King; Hogrefe, *WA;* and Bainton, pp. 161-80.

33. Rachel Speght, "To the Reader," prefixed to *Mortalities Memorandum,* n. p. n. For an unusual reading of Speght, see Beilin, *RE,* pp. 110-17 and 253-57.

34. Hughey, p. 48. Similar titles are Henry Denham's *The Footepath to Felicitie . . . A swarme of Bees With their Honie and Honiecombes . . .* (1581) and his *A Plant of Pleasure, bearing fourteen several flowers . . .* (1581); and George Gascoigne's *Hundredth sundrie Flowers . . .* (1573).

35. An interesting study of Lady Russell's correspondence, "The Letters of Lady Elizabeth Russell (1540-1609)," was presented at the MLA conference in December 1977 by Dr. Elizabeth Farber, whose dissertation on Russell's letters is cited above (ch. 1, n. 11).

36. For information on Lady Douglas's writings, see C. J. Hindle, "A Bibliography of the Printed Pamphlets and Broadsides of Lady Eleanor Douglas, the Seventeenth-Century Prophetess," *Papers of the Edinburgh Bibliographical Society* 15 (1935): 35-54. For a recent discussion, see Cope.

37. The information about Alexia Grey is taken from A. L. Ward, Abbess, "Obituary Notices of the nuns of the English Benedictine abbey of Ghent in Flanders, 1627-1811," in *Catholic Record Society Publications* 19 (1917), 25-27. I am indebted to Lawrence H. Hill, O.S.B., at Abbot Vincent Taylor Library of Belmont Abbey College; Benjamin J. Stein, O. S. B., cataloger of the Alcuin Library of St. John's University in Collegeville, Minnesota; and Emilian Muschete, O. S. B., acting librarian of St. Maur Priory in Indianapolis, for their help in securing this information.

38. Long Meg was an Amazonian character in a jest book, *Long Meg of Westminster* (1582),

who was incorporated by Thomas Deloney into his *Gentill Craft, the Second Part* (1639). On Long Meg (and on Moll Cutpurse another unusual figure) see Frederick O. Waage, "Meg and Moll: Two Renaissance London Heroines," *JPC* 20.1 (1986): 105-17.

Chapter 4

1. Foxe, passim. See also *DNB*, II, 748-49 (Joan Bocher); *DNB*, IV, 559 (Margaret Clitherow); and *DNB*, XI, 1069-70 (Joyce Lewis).
2. Wright, pp. 49, 106-7, and 204; Stock, esp. pp. 59-80.
3. Hallers, p. 252; and Davis.
4. Gouge, p. 273. This is not to say that the Protestant writers did not advocate obedience. See R. Valerie Lucas, "Puritan Preaching and the Politics of the Family," in *REP*.
5. Powell, p. 124.
6. Cited by Hogrefe, *TW*, p. 17 (from James Gairdner and Ascham).
7. Anne Askew, *The lattre examinacyon*, p. 15.
8. "Askew, Anne (1521-1546)," *DNB*, I, 662.
9. Maria Lamb Webb, *The Fells of Swarthmoor Hall and their Friends, with an account of their ancestor Anne Askewe, the Martyr. . . .* (London: Alfred W. Bennett, 1865), p. 6. There is a reference here to a son of Anne Askew's named William, but no further details or corroboration. See Beilin, *RE*, pp. 29-47.
10. Wyntjes, p. 173.
11. *Writings*, p. 238.
12. Webb, p. 9.
13. Foxe, p. 680. Foxe's account is drawn from Bale, with whom he enjoyed a close friendship.
14. Kohler, p. 65.
15. Wyntjes, p. 173.
16. Ibid., pp. 184-85.
17. *Writings*, pp. 176-84 and 238; John Bowle, *Henry VIII* (Boston: Little, Brown, 1964), p. 292; Lacey Baldwin Smith, *Henry VIII: The Mask of Royalty* (Boston: Houghton Mifflin Company, 1971), p. 240.
18. Smith, p. 240.
19. Hogrefe, *TW*, pp. 80-81. With the exception of two minor phrases, Leslie P. Fairfield also accepts the fundamental veracity of the accounts ("John Bale and the Development of Protestant Hagiography in England," *Journal of Ecclesiastical History* 24. 2 [1973]: 146-160).
20. Hogrefe, *TW*, pp. 80-81.
21. Anne Askew, *The lattre examinacyon*, p. 45.
22. Anne Askew, *The first examinacyon*, p. 29.
23. Anne Askew, *The lattre examinacyon*, p. 50.
24. Anne Askew, "The voyce of Anne Askewe out of the 54 Psalme of David, called Deus in nomine tuo," in *The first examinacyon* (1546). The translation, which is not included here, is skillfully done in rimed couplets.
25. Jane Williams, *Literary Women of England, including a Biographical Epitome of all the most eminent to the year 1700 and sketches of the poetesses to the year 1850* (London: Saunders, Otley, 1861), pp. 43-44.
26. Anne Askew, "The Balade whych Anne Askewe made and sange when she was in Newgate," in *The lattre examinacyon* (1547). Mention should be made of a folk ballad that

celebrates the staunch faith of Anne Askew. The ballad ("An Askew, Intituled, I am a Woman Poor and Blind") was apparently first printed in *Roxburghe Ballads*, I (London, 1635), p. 8. According to William Chappell, editor of a later edition of these ballads (*Roxburghe Ballads* [London: Printed for the Ballad Society, 1871]), John Bale states that Anne Askew wrote many songs and ballads (*Illustrium Scriptorium Brittanae Summarium*, 1548, fol. 229); Chappell ascribes this second ballad to Anne Askew; however, its tone, style, and sentiments differ markedly from those of her other writings.

Chapter 5

1. Antonia Fraser, *Mary Queen of Scots* (New York: Delacorte Press, 1969), p. 181. Also, the whole of Julian Sharman, *Library of Mary, Queen of Scots with an historical introduction and a rare portrait of the Queen* (London: Eliot Stock, 1889).

2. Apologists ignore the influence of Catherine de Medici and of Diane de Poitiers, the wife and the mistress of Henry II, on the royal nursery, and concentrate on Mary's formal Catholic upbringing and on the intellectual brilliance of the French court.

3. According to Fraser, "Mary was given all-round education; she learnt to draw; she learnt to dance . . . ; she learnt to sing . . . ; she learnt to play the lute . . ." (p. 50).

4. Fraser claims that Mary was in love with Darnley, but not with either of her other husbands; in fact, she claims that Mary had been so hurt by her infatuation with Darnley that she was proof against a second, similar match (pp. 317-18). In contrast, George Malcolm Thomson claims that Mary despised her first two husbands and was passionately in love with Bothwell. *The Crime of Mary Stuart* (London: Hutchinson and Co., 1967), pp. 51-52 and 106.

5. Thomson believes that Mary was guilty of at least foreknowledge of the murder of Darnley; this is tantamount to complicity since she had constant opportunity to warn him of the plot (pp. 78, 103, and 146-47).

6. Fraser claims that Mary was in a state of complete breakdown during the period in which the plot against Darnley was formed and executed and until after her imprisonment following her marriage to Bothwell (pp. 307-33).

7. Fraser describes incidents which show Mary to have been prudish (pp. 188 and 204-6); Thomson recounts anecdotes which show Mary in a far different light (pp. 119-20).

8. The differing accounts of the same incidents in Fraser (pp. 94 and 204) and in Thomson (pp. 18 and 119) show the queen to have been unable to tolerate cruelty or, alternately, to have been altogether unmoved by it.

9. The original manuscripts, taken from a silver casket on the person of George Dalgleish, one of Bothwell's servants, were never produced by the Scottish lords; they sent copies to Elizabeth. These lords, some of whom were Catholic, swore that they had scrutinized the materials. For a clear discussion of the subject, see Conyers Read, *Mr. Secretary Cecil and Queen Elizabeth* (New York: Alfred A. Knopf, 1955), pp. 398-415.

10. Clifford Bax, ed. and trans., *Letters and Poems of Mary, Queen of Scots, supposed author*, p. 8.

11. Mrs. Stewart-MacKenzie-Arbuthnot, ed., *Queen Mary's Book*, pp. 154-55.

12. For a detailed discussion of the differences between Du Bellay and Ronsard and of their reciprocal influences on one another, see Marcel Raymond, "Ronsard et Du Bellay," in his *L'Influence de Ronsard sur la Poésie Française (1550-1585)* (Paris: Librarie Ancienne Honore Champion, 1927), pp. 98-130. Raymond cites Du Bellay's "predilection pour le lyrisme moyen,"

(p. 107) and his use of the Petrarchan sonnet form "pour joindre ensemble quatrains et tercets" (p. 98).

13. Sharman, *Library*, p. 86, notes Mary's possession of Du Bellay's sonnet sequence, *The Olive Augmentit*, the form of which is quite close to that of Mary's own love poems. See also Fraser, p. 181.

14. Moers, p. 169. Moers defines a tradition which ultimately is derived from Ovid's *Heroides*, and which gives "tongue to the heroine of love" (p. 147). Moers does not discuss the sonnets of Mary Stuart, but she describes the qualities of works within the tradition of "loving heroinism"; and these qualities are found in the sonnets of Mary Stuart, poems that are notable for their display of self-knowledge and unconventional morality: "Verse letters of love that a woman writes to a man. . . . I-you poetry, not I-he poetry on the whole: the effect is [of] letters directed by a woman to the specific man she loves, and not about him: women poets do not celebrate *his* eyes . . . ; they mostly write about *Me*. . . . [A] certain realism results. . . . Women poets do not complain of the power of love. . . . on the contrary, they rejoice in love, and boast of the transformation in themselves. . . . [T]hey exult in the revelation love has brought . . . [W]omen poets seem to devote a special ingenuity to imagining the lovers as high/low and, simultaneously, on a plane of equality. . . . [T]here is no avoidance of physicality in women's love poetry; on the contrary, . . . women's love poems thrive on the touch" (pp. 164-69).

15. Sharman, n. p. n.

16. Raymond states,

'Cette mystique' s'exprime, dans les grandes odes, par des figures, des mouvements, un appareil verbal, des procedes de style empruntés à Pindare ou a son émule latin, Horace. Mais les thèmes principaux des odes de 1550 n'exigent pas seulment du lecteur une vague adhesion sentimentale; ils se proposent avec une telle force que l'admiration qu'ils provoquent est tyrannique: c'est un language nouveau qui envahit d'un coup l'esprit des contemporains. Qu'ils soient poètes ou s'imaginent l'être, désormais ils ne pourront dire leurs pensées, feintes ou sincères, qu'en adoptant le vocabulaire et le style des odes pindariques. Nous avons déjà vu que dans les oeuvres de Pontus de Tyard, Des Autels et quel'ques autres, la lyre résonne 'sur le mont au double coupeau,' les traits de louange proprement "empenées" transpercent 'les verteux,' et ou d'une Minerve au casque de Gorgone. Pareilles imaginations, neuf fois sur dix, viennent de Ronsard, et non point de ses modèles anciens. Telle est l'emprise du poète sur ses disciples qu'il ne leur est plus possible de chanter autrement que lui, avec d'autres mots que les siens." [p. 105]

17. Moers, p. 146.

18. John Stuart Mill, "The Subjection of Women," in *On Liberty, the Subjection of Women, Representative Government* (London: Oxford University Press, 1912), p. 493.

19. Fraser, p. 211.

20. Dusinberre, p. 273.

21. Mill, p. 493.

22. Arbuthnot, pp. 85-88; first printed in Brantome's *Vies des Dames Illustres* (1665); the translation is by Agnes Strickland. There is some question, however, of Mary's authorship; a manuscript of the poem has been found among the papers of Brantome.

23. This translation of the sonnets is by Clifford Bax (see n. 10), pp. 48-58. Another version is by Hugh Campbell (in *Love Letters of Mary queen of Scots . . .* , 1824). The French text

given in notes 23-34 is taken from a reprint entitled *Poems of Mary, Queen of Scots, to the Earl of Bothwell*. On the page facing the last of the sonnets, the following comment appears: "These poems are printed from the manuscript in the University Library Cambridge."

The following is the text of the first sonnet:

O dieux ayes de moy compassion
& m'enseignes quelle preuue certane
ie puis donner qui ne luy semble vain
de mon amour et ferme affeĉtion
las n'est il pas ia en possession   [5]
du corps du cueur qui ne refuse peine
ni dishoneur ni la vie incertane
offence de parents ne pire affliĉtion
pour luy tous mes amys i'estime moins que rien
et de mes ennemis ie veulx esperere bien   [10]
i'ay hasarde pour luy au monde renoncer
ie veux pour luy au monde renoncer
ie veux mourire pour luy auancer
que reste il plus pour prouuer ma constance?

24. Entre ses mains et en son plein pouuoir   [15]
le metz mon filz mon honneur et ma vie
mon pais mes subjeĉts, mon ame assubieĉtie
et toute a luy, et nay autre vouloir
pour mon objeĉt que sens le disseuoir
suiure ie veux malgre toute l'envie   [20]
qu'issir en peult car ie nay autre envie
que de ma foy luy faire apparceuoir
que pour tempest ou bonnace qui face
iamais ne veux changer demeure ou place
brief ie fairay de ma foy telle preuue   [25]
quil connoistra sens feinte ma constance
non par mes pleurs ou feinte obeissance
come autres ont fait, mais par diuers espreuue

25. Elle pour son honneur vous doibt obeissance
moy uous obeissant, i'en puys resseuoir blasme   [30]
nestant (a mon regret) come elle est vostre femme
et si n'aura pourtant en ce point preeminence
pour son proffit elle use de constance
car ce n'est peu dhonneur destre de voz biens dame
et moy pour vous aymer i'en puix resseuoir blame   [35]
et ne luy veux ceder en toute l'obseruance
elle de vostre mal n'a lapprehension
moy ie n'ay nul repos tant ie crains l'apparence
par l'aduis des parents elle eut vostre acointance
moy mangre tous les meins vous port affeĉtion   [40]
et toutesfois mon coeur vous doutez ma constance
et de sa loyaute prenes ferme asseurance

26. Par vous (mon coeur) et par vostre alliance
    elle a remis sa maison en honneur
    elle a iouy par vous de la grandeur   [45]
    dont tous les siens n'auoyent nul asseurance
    de vous mon bien elle a eu lacointance
    et a guagne pour vn temps vostre cueur
    par vous elle a eu plaisir et bonheur
    et par vous a receu honneur et reuerence   [50]
    et n'a perdu sinon la iouissance
    d'un fascheux sot qu'elle aymoit cherement
    ie ne la plains d'aymer dont ardemment
    Celuy qui n'a en sens ne en vaillance
    en beaute en bonte ni en constance   [55]
    point de second ie vis en ceste foy.
27. Quant vous l'aymes elle vsoit de froideur
    si vous souffries pour s'amour passion
    qui vient d'aymer de trop d'affection
    son doil monstroit la tristesse de coeur   [60]
    n'ayant plesir de vostre grand'ardeur
    en ses habits monstroit sens fiction
    qu'elle n'auoyt peur qu'imperfection
    peult l'affasser hors de ce loyal coeur
    de vostre mort ie ne vis la peaur   [65]
    que meritoit tel mary et seigneur
    Somme de vous elle a eu tout son bien
    et n'a prise ni iamais estime
    vn si grand heur si non puis qu'il n'est sien
    et maintenant dist l'auoyr tant ayme   [70]
28. Et maintenant elle commence a voire
    qu'elle estoit bien de mauuais iugement
    de n'estimer l'amour d'un tel amant
    et vouldroit bien mon any desseuoir
    par les escripts tout fardes de şcauoir   [75]
    qui pour tant n'est en son esprit croissant
    ayns emprunte de quelque auteur eluissant
    a feint tresbien vn envoy sens l'auoyr
    et toutes fois ses parolles fardez
    ses pleus, ses plaints remplis de fiction   [80]
    et ses hautes cris et lamentations
    ont tant guagne que par vous sont guardes
    ses lettres escripts ausquels vous donnes foy
    et si l'aymes et croyez plus que moy
29. Vous la croyes las trop ie l'apperçoy   [85]
    et vous doutez de ma ferme constance
    o mon seul bien et mon seul esperance
    et ne vous peux asseurer de ma foy
    vous m'estimes legier ie le voy

et si n'auez en moy nul asseurance [90]
et soubçonnes mon coeur sans apparence
vous deffiant a trop grande tort de moy
vous ignores l'amour que ie vous porte
vous soubçonnes qu'autre amour me transport
vous estimes mes parolles du vent [95]
vous depeignes de cire mon las coeur
vous me penses femme sans iugement
et tout cela augment mon ardeur
30. Mon amour croist et plus en plus croistra
tant que ie viuray et tiendra a grandheur [100]
Tant seulement dauoir part en ce coeur
vers qui en fin mon amour paroitra
si tres a cler que iamais n'en doutra
pour luy ie veux faire teste au malheure
pour luy ie veux rechercher la grandeure [105]
et faira tant qu'en vray connoistra
que ie n'ay bien heur ni contentement
qu'a l'obeyr et seruir loyamment
pour luy iattendz tout bon fortune
pour luy ie veux guarder sante et vie [110]
pour luy tout vertue de suiure i'ay enuie
et sens changer me trouuera tout une
31. Pour luy aussi ie iete mainte larme
premier quant il se fit de ce corps possesseur
du quel alors il n'auoyt pas le coeur [115]
puis me donna une autre dure alarme
quand il versa de son sang maint drasme
dont de grief doil me vint ceste dolleur
qui me pensa oster la vie et la frayeur
por perdre las la seule rempar qui m'arme [120]
pour luy depuis i'ay mesprise lhonneur
ce qui nous peut seul prouoir de bonheur
pour luy iay hasarde honneur et conscience
pour luy tous mes parens iay quiste et amys
et tous aultres respects sont a part mis [125]
brief de vous seul ie cherche l'alliance
32. De vous ie dis seul soubtien de ma vie
tant seulement ie cherche m'asseurer
et si ose de moy tant presumer
de vous gaugner mangre toute l'enuie [130]
car c'est le seul desir de votre chere amye
de vous seruir et loyaument aymer
et tous malheurs moins que rien estimer
et votre volunte de la mien suiure
vous conoitres auecques obeissance [135]
de mon loyal deuoir n'obmettant la science

a quoy i'estudiray pour tousiours vous complair
sans aymer rien que vous soubs la subiection
de qui ie veux sens nulle fiction
viure et mourir et a ce i'obtempere   [140]
33. Mon coeur mon sang mon ame et mon soussi
las vous m'aues promis qu'aurois ce plaisir
de deuiser auecques vous a loysir
Toute la nuit ou ie languis icy
ayant le coeur dextreme peaur transie   [145]
pour voir absent le but de mon desir
Crainte doubly vn coup me vient a saissir
et l'autrefois ie crains qui rendursi
soit contre moy vostre amiable coeur
par quelque dit d'un meschant rapporteur   [150]
vn autrefoys ie crains quelque auenture
qui par chemin deturne mon amant
par vn fascheux et nouueau accident
dieu deturne toute malheureax augure
34. Ne vous voyant selon qu'aues promis   [155]
iay mis la main au papier pour escrire
d'un different que ie voulou transcrire
ie ne sçay pas quel sera vostre aduise
mais ie scay bien qui mieux aymer sçaura
vous diries bien qui plus y guagnera   [160]

35. Translated by Arbuthnot, pp. 100-01, who gives as the ultimate source the Cotton ms., Caligula B. V., fol. 316. The poem was published in Malcolm Laing's *History of Scotland* (1800). Arbuthnot draws attention to the use of similar imagery in a poem by Elizabeth Tudor concerning Mary Stuart. That poem, entitled "The Doubt of Future Foes," is included in chapter 3. The French text which follows is from Sharman, *Poems,* pp. 27-28.

Une seul penser qui me profficte et nuit
Amer et doulx, change en mon coeur sans cesse,
Entre le doubte, et l'espoir il m'opresse
Tant que la paix et le repos me fuit.
Donc chere soeur, si ceste carte suit   [5]
L'affeĉtion de vous veoir qui m'opresse,
C'est que je viz en pein et en tristresse,
Si promptement l'effeĉt ne s'ensuit.
J'ay veu la nef relacher par contraincte
En haulte mer, proche d'entrer au port,   [10]
Et le serain se convertir en trouble:
Ainsi je suis en soucy et en craincte,
Non pas de vous, mais quantes fois à tort
Fortune rompt voille et cordage double.

36. Prince Alexander Labanoff, III, 77-78. The countess accused Queen Mary of the murder of her son, Lord Darnley.

37. Translated by Arbuthnot, pp. 106-10. The poem was sent to the bishop of Ross by Queen Mary in 1573 and was included by the bishop in his *Piae Afflicti Animi Consolationes* (1574).

38. Arbuthnot, p. 111; translated by Strickland. Also first printed by the bishop of Ross (1574). The French text that follows is taken from Sharman, *Poems*, pp. 37-38, and titled "Sonnet, Written during her Imprisonment."

L'ire de Dieu par le sang ne s'appaise
   De boêufs ny boucs espandu sur l'autel,
   Ny par encens, ou Sacrifice tel,
Le Souverain ne reçoit aucun aise.

Qui veult, Seigneur, faire oeuure qui te plaise,   [5]
   Il faut qu'il ayt la foy en l'Immortel,
   Avec espoir, charité au mortel,
Et bien faisant que ton loz il ne taise.

L'oblation, qui t'est seul agréable,
   C'est un esprit en oraison constant,
   Humble et devot, en un corps chaste estant.   [10]
O Tout-puissant, sois moy si favorable,
   Que pour tousjours ces graces dans mon coeur
   Puissent rester à tal gloire et honneur.
            Va, tv meriteras.

39. Translated by Arbuthnot, pp. 116-27; she is the first to have published the essay which she located in the State Paper Office, Mary Queen of Scots, vol. xi, 37.

40. Translated by Arbuthnot, pp. 129-30; from Mary Stuart, Arch. F.C.8, No. 22, in the Bodleian Library at Oxford.

41. Translated by Arbuthnot, p. 131; her source is the same ms., Mary Stuart, Arch. F.C.8 No. 22b, in the Bodleian Library. The French text that follows is from Sharman, *Poems*, p. 40.

Ronsart si ton bon cueur de gentille nature
Tement pour le respect d'un peu de nouriture
Quentes plus juenes ans tu as resceu d'un roy,
De ton Rooyalie et de sa mesme loy,
Je diray non couart ni tasche d'avarice,   [5]
Mays digne a mon advis du nom de branc prince;
Elas! ne scrives pas ses fayts ni ses grandeurs,
Mays qu'il a bien voulu empesche de malheurs.

42. Labanoff, VI, 190-94.

43. Arbuthnot, p. 135; translated by Strickland. The original ms. is Mary Queen of Scots, Arch. F. C.8, No. 24, in the Bodleian Library. The French text that follows is from Sharman, *Poems*, p. 39, and titled "Verses written at Fotheringay."

Que suis-je helas? et de quoi sert ma vie
J'en suis fors qu'un corps privé de cueur
Un ombre vayn, un objet de malheur,

Qui n'a plus rien que de mourir en vie.
Plus ne portez, O enemys, danvie.   [5]
Qui n'a plus l'esprit a la grandeur:
J'ai consommé d'excessive douleur,
Voltre ire en bref de voir assouvie,
Et vous amys qui m'avez tenu chere,
Souvenez-vous que sans cueur, et sans santey.   [10]
Je ne scaurois auqun bon oeuvre faire.
Souhaitez donc fin de calamitay
Et que sus bas etant asses punie,
J'aie ma part en la joye infinie.

44. *The Last Letter of Mary Queen of Scotland* . . . , n.p.n. The translator is not named.

45. Arbuthnot, p. 136; translated by Strickland, who accepted the poem as genuine. The earliest source has not been found. The Latin text that follows is from Sharman, p. 12.

O Domine Deus! speravi in Te;
O care mi Jesu! nunc libera me.
In durâ catenâ, in miserâ poenâ, desidero te;
Languendo, gemendo, et genu flectendo,
Adoro, imploro, ut liberes me!   [5]

Chapter 6

1. R.[ichard] S.[impson], ed., *The Lady Falkland, her Life From a ms.* [supposedly written by a daughter] *in the Imperial Archives at Lisle* (London: Catholic Publishing and Bookselling Co., Ltd., 1861), n. p. n. Two other important biographies are Georgianna Fullerton's *Life of Elizabeth, Lady Falkland 1582-1639* (London: Burns and Oates, 1883); and Kenneth B. Murdoch's *Sun at Noon: Three Biographical Sketches* (New York: Macmillan Company, 1939). See also the long account under "Cary, Sir Henry, first Viscount Falkland (d. 1633)," in the *DNB*, III, 1150-51.

2. Murdoch, p. 20.

3. Donald A. Stauffer, "A Deep and Sad Passion," in *The Parrott Presentation Volume*, ed. H. Craig (Princeton: Princeton University Press, 1935), pp. 312-13. Stauffer states that Lucius Cary's "philosophical nature . . . his ability to see two sides of a question . . . his feminine sensitivity and grief at the tragic division of England. . . . [T]hese qualities in the young Lord Falkland are not his father's. . . . His mother . . . possessed all of Lucius Cary's finer traits."

4. Maurice Valency, *Tragedies of Herod and Mariamne* (New York: Columbia University Press, 1940), p. 87. See, above, chapter 3.

5. John Davies, "Dedicatory Sonnet," to *Muses Sacrifice or Divine Meditations* (London: T.S. for George Norton, 1612), p. 5; Rpt., in *Complete Works*, Alexander Grosart, ed. (Edinburgh: Cambridge University Press, 1878).

6. Stauffer, p. 314. Although transcribed in prose, the *History* is in blank verse. Krontiris discusses the play at length.

7. There are also similarities; Stauffer points to the same "uniformity of technique, thoughts circumscribed in two verses, almost invariably end-stopped lines, and lengthy philosophical disquisitions" in both plays (p. 313).

8. Simpson, p. 54.

9. *DNB*, III, 1151.

10. Apparently they are not extant.

11. Prefixed to the *Reply of the Cardinall of Perron to the . . . King of Great Britaine*, Elizabeth Cary, trans. (Douay: M. Bogart, 1630), are several laudatory poems by some of Lady Falkland's admirers (sigs. C2-C3). See Sandra K. Fischer, "Elizabeth Cary and Tyranny, Domestic and Religious," in Hannay, pp. 225-237.

12. William Sheares, "To . . . Lady Elizabeth Carie . . . ," in *Works of Mr. John Marston* (London: William Sheares, 1633), sig. A4.

13. Falkland, p. v.

14. The earlier married Sir George Cary; she was related to Edmund Spenser, the poet, who dedicated his *Muiopotmos* to her and praised her patronage. Nashe dedicated his *Christ's Tears* to her in 1593, and Dowland, the first book of *Songs and Ayres* in 1597. Her daughter, Elizabeth, married Sir Thomas Berkley, and is also remembered as a patroness. She is addressed by Nashe, in *Terrors of the Night*, as "a worthy daughter . . . to so worthy a mother." The dates of the first Lady Cary are uncertain; her daughter's death date is 1635 (*DNB*, III, 973).

15. Dunstan quotes Davies's sonnet to "Elizabeth, Lady Cary (wife of Sir Henry Cary)." Dunstan then shows that prefaced to *Mariam* itself was a dedicatory sonnet to "my worthy sister Mistris Elizabeth Carye" which was signed E. C. The only Lady Elizabeth Cary to have had a sister (in law) of the same name and to have been married to a Sir Henry Cary was Elizabeth, Lady Falkland (Falkland, v-ix).

16. Falkland, pp. xiii-xv.

17. Valency, p. 15.

18. Ibid., p. 88. He differs from Dunstan, who states that *Mariam* is "one of the most if not the most regular of all English classical dramas" (*Examination of Two English Dramas* [Konigsburg, 1908], p. 4). For other studies of the play, see Beilin, *RE*, pp. 157-76; Nancy Cotton Pearse, *Women Playwrights in England, 1363-1750* (1980), pp. 27-54; and Betty S. Travitsky, "The *Feme Covert* in Elizabeth Cary's *Mariam*," in *Ambiguous*, pp. 184-96.

19. Valency, p. 16. Others in the period are Massinger's *Duke of Millaine* and Markham and Sampson's *Herod and Antipater*.

20. Valency, p. 42.

21. Josephus, *Works*, trans. with notes by William Whiston (New York: Mason, 1869), III, 530.

22. Ibid., p. 528.

23. Ibid., pp. 530-31.

24. Valency, p. 90.

25. Ibid., p. 91.

26. Ibid., p. 36 and n., p. 67.

27. Leonora Brodwin, *Elizabethan Love Tragedy 1587-1625* (New York: New York University Press, 1971), p. 18.

28. Kohler, pp. 189-93.

29. Ibid., pp. 183-84: "All things considered, *Mariam* was probably only read aloud to a small circle of intimates or perhaps circulated in manuscript form among those who were interested in classical drama or in the author. . . . *Mariam* is not, of course, at all suitable for acting."

30. Valency, pp. 87-88.

31. The reader's attention is drawn to the fact that Edward's speech is written in almost perfect blank verse, although transcribed in prose.

Conclusion

1. Hughey, p. 256. The title of Bainton's study of sixteenth-century Englishwomen implies the same point of view.

2. Kelly-Gadol, pp. 151–52. As noted above in the Introduction, this point has been well established. See Ferguson's "Introduction," in *Rewriting* for a careful evaluation of Renaissance "discourses of gender."

3. See Todd and Davies who argue for such a similarity.

4. For a contemporary roll call of noble families who provided such education for their daughters, as well as a fairly comprehensive list of learned Tudor women, see William Bercher (Barker), *A Dyssputatacion off the Nobylyte off Wymen . . .* (written, London, 1559; first printed by Charles Brinsley Marley, owner of the ms.), edited by R. Warwick Bond (London: Roxburghe Club, 1904). See Reynolds, pp. 1-45; and, for a less enthusiastic estimate, Warnicke.

5. Wright, p. 17. See Cressy; and Spufford, esp. 410-11; 417; 427; and 434-35.

6. Kelso, p. 1.

7. Wyntjes, p. 186.

8. Quoted by Wright, p. 466. The full proverb is given as the epigraph to this book.

9. Richard T. Vann, "Toward a New Lifestyle: Women in Preindustrial Capitalism," in *Visible,* pp. 208-9. As noted earlier, Cahn, who discusses this development at length, considers the trend to enhance woman's domestic role a negative one.

10. Cardinal Bembo's famous remark is perhaps apropos: "Little girls should learn Latin; it completes their charm." See Kelly-Gadol, pp. 150-51; Ferguson, et al, "Introduction" to *Rewriting;* and Travitsky, "PIW."

11. Hogrefe, *TW,* pp. 41-42; Cahn, passim.

12. Hogrefe, *TW,* p. 54.

13. Ibid., pp. 52-58. For the medieval position, see Power, *MW,* pp. 53-75. With the growth of work centers away from the home as capitalism developed, woman became disadvantaged economically. See Clark, the first scholar to give serious attention to this problem; and see Cahn's recent study which supports much of Clark's pioneering work.

14. Wright, p. 5. "Though the mystical ancestry of the Tudors went back to King Arthur, Queen Elizabeth had a nearer progenitor, a great-grandfather, who was a London merchant."

15. Ibid., p. 11. Lacey Baldwin Smith suggests that the English achievements, as far as Elizabeth's role in them was concerned, may have been largely fortuitous rather than perspicacious (*Elizabeth Tudor Portrait of a Queen* [Boston: Little, Brown, 1975]).

16. Wright, p. 18.

BIBLIOGRAPHY

LISTINGS refer to first editions unless otherwise noted. When applicable, *STC* numbers have been appended as well as the reel numbers of the University of Michigan series, "Early English Books I (1475-1640)." When available, authors' maiden names have been included, and cross-references have been given in some instances. Although the following lists are selective, they are not limited to the works in this anthology.

WORKS CONTAINING WRITINGS BY RENAISSANCE ENGLISHWOMEN

Bentley, Thomas, ed. *Monument of Matrones: conteining seven severall Lamps of Virginitie, or distinct treatises: whereof the first five concerne praier and meditation; the other two last, precepts and examples, as the woorthie works partlie of men, partlie of women; compiled for the necessarie use of both sexes out of the sacred scriptures, and other aprooved authors by Thomas Bentley of Graies Inne Student.* London: H. Denham, 1582 (Parts 1-4 and 5); London: Thomas Dawson, 1582 (Parts 6 and 7). *STC* 1892-94. Reel nos. 174 and 377.

Dyce, Alexander, ed. *Specimens of British Poetesses, selected and chronologically arranged.* London: T. Rodd, 1827.

Ferrar, Edward, ed. *Select Poetry Chiefly Devotional of the Reign of Queen Elizabeth. Collected and Edited for the Parker Society.* 2 vols. Cambridge: University Press, 1845.

Foxe, John. *Actes and monuments of these latter and perillous dayes, touching matters of the church, wherein are comprehended and described the great persecutions. A horrible troubles, that have bene wrought and practised by the Romishe prelates speciallye in this realme of England and Scotland, from the yeare of our Lorde a thousande, unto the tyme nowe present.* London: John Daye, 1563. *STC* 11222. Reel no. 230.

Green [Wood], May Anne Everett, ed. *Letters of Royal and Illustrious Ladies of Great Britain, from the Commencement of the twelfth century to the close of the reign of Queen Mary.* 3 vols. London: Henry Colburn, 1846.

Robinson, Hastings, ed. and trans. *Original Letters Relative to the English Reformation. Written During the Reigns of King Henry VIII, King Edward VI, and Queen Mary: Chiefly from the Archives of Zurich.* Cambridge: University Press, 1847.

Soowthern, John. *Pandora, the Musyque of the beautie of his Mistresse Diana. Composed by John Soowthern Gentleman, and dedicated to the right Honorable, Edward Dever, Earle of Oxenford.* London: Thomas Hackette, 1584. *STC* 22928. Reel no. 354.

ORIGINAL WRITINGS BY
RENAISSANCE ENGLISHWOMEN

Anger, Jane (pseud.). *Jane Anger, her Protection for Women. To defend them against the Scandelous reports of a late Surfeiting Lover, and all other like Venerians, that complaine so to bee overcloyed with womens kindnesse, written by Ja: A Gent.* London: Richard Jones and Thomas Orwin, 1589. *STC* 644. Reel no. 165.

Askew, Anne. *See* Kyme.

Audeley, Eleanor. *See* Douglas.

Cary (née Tansfield), Lady Elizabeth Falkland. *The History of the Life, Reign, and Death of Edward II, King of England, and Lord of Ireland. With the Rise and Fall of his great favourites, Gaveston and the Spencers. Written by E. F. in the year 1627. And Printed verbatim from the Original.* London: J. C. for Charles Harper, Samuel Crouch, and Thomas Fox, 1680.

_____. *The History of the most unfortunate Prince, King Edward the second: with choice Political Observations on him and his unhappy Favourites, Gaveston and Spencer: Containing several rare Passages of those Times, not found in other Historians; found among the Papers of and (supposed to be) writ by the Right Honourable Henry Viscount Faulkland, some time Lord Deputy of Ireland.* In *Harleian Miscellany.* I. London: John White, John Murray, John Harding, 1808.

_____. *The Tragedie of Mariam, Faire Queene of Jewry. Written by that learned, vertuous, and truly noble Ladie, E. C.* London: Thomas Creede for Richard Hawkins, 1613. *STC* 4613. Reel no. 830. Rpt. Malone Society. London: Charles Wittingham and Co. at the Cheswick Press, 1914.

Catherine Parr, Queen of England. *The lamentacion or complaynt of a sinner, made by the most vertuous Ladie, Quene Caterin, bewayling the ignoraunce of her blind life: set forth and put in print at the instaunt desire of the righte gracious ladie Caterin Duchesse of Suffolke, & the earnest requeste of the right honorable Lord, William Parre, Marquesse of North Hampton.* London: E. Whitchurche, 1547. *STC* 4827-4829. Reel no. 29. (Other ed. 1548 and 1563; *see* Bentley).

_____. *Prayers, or Meditations, wherein the mynd is stirred, paciently to suffre all afflictions here, to set at nought the vaine prosperitie of this worlde, and always to longe for the everlasting felicitie: collected out of holy woorkes by the most vertuous and gracious Princess Katherine queene of Englande, Fraunce, and*

Irelande. London: T. Berthelet, 1545. *STC* 4818-4826. Reel no. 61. (Other ed. 1545, 1546, 1546-47, 1547, 1545, 1545, n.p.d., 1556, 1559; *see* Bentley.)

Clerksone, Bessie. *The Conflict in Conscience of a deare Christian, named Bessie Clerksone in the parish of Lanerk, which shee lay under three yeare & an half. With the conference that past betwixt her pastor and her at diverse times.* (Transcribed by the pastor, William Livingstone.) Newly corr. and amended. Edinburgh: John Wreittoun, 1631. *STC* 16611. Reel no. 809.

Clifford, Anne. *See* Herbert, Anne.

Clinton (née Knevet), Elizabeth, Countess of Lincoln. *The Countesse of Lincolnes Nurserie.* Oxford: John Lichfield and James Short, 1622. *STC* 5432. Reel no. 984.

Colville (née Melville), Lady Elizabeth of Culros. *Ane Godlie Dreame, Compyled by El. Melville, Ladie Culros younger, at the request of a friend.* (Appended to this is "A Verie Comfortable Song, To the Tune of, Shall I let her goe.") Edinburgh: Robert Charteris, 1606. *STC* 17811-17814. Reel no. 1247. (Other ed. 1603, 1604?, 1620.)

Douglas (née Touchet), Lady Eleanor. *A Warning to the Dragon and all his angels.* London?, 1625. *STC* 904. Reel no. 869.

    Information on forty-two works by Lady Eleanor can be found in C. J. Hindle, "A Bibliography of the Printed Pamphlets and Broadsides of Lady Eleanor Douglas, the 17th Century Prophetess." Edinburgh: Papers of the Edinburgh Bibliographical Society 1930-1935, 15 (1935), 35-54.

Dowriche, Anne. *See* Trefusis.

Dudley (née Grey), Lady Jane. "A Conference Dialogue-wise between the Lady Jane and M. Feckenham" in *Life, Death, and Actions of the Most Chast, learned, and Religious Lady, the Lady Jane Grey, Daughter to the Duke of Suffolke. Containing Foure Principall Discourses written by her owne hands. The first an Admonition to such as are weake in Faith: the second a Catechisme: the Third an Exhortation to her Sister: and the last her words at Death.* London: G. Eld for I. Wright, 1615. *STC* 7281. Reel no. 955. (*See* Foxe and Bentley.)

Elizabeth Tudor, Queen of England. *Poems of Queen Elizabeth I*, ed. Leicester Bradner. Providence, R.I.: Brown University Press, 1964.

    Bradner provides a modernized, emended text, information on his sources, and, often, variant readings.

Fage, Mary. *Fames Roule: or the names of our dread, Soveraigne Lord King Charles, his Royall Queen Mary, and his most hopefull posterity: Together with The names of the Dukes, Marquesses, Earles, Viscounts, Bishops, Barons, Privie Counsellors, Knyghts of the Garter, and Judges. Of his three renowned Kingdomes, England, Scotland, and Ireland: Anagrammiz'd and espressed by acrosticke line on their names. By Mistris Mary Fage, wife of Robert Fage, the younger Gentleman.* London: Richard Culton, 1637. *STC* 10667. Reel no. 789.

Grey, Jane. *See* Dudley, Jane.

Grymeston (née Bernye) Elizabeth. *Miscelanea, Meditations, Memoratives, By Elizabeth Grymeston.* London: Printed by M. Bradwood for F. Norton, 1604. *STC* 12407-12411. Reel no. 1068. (Other ed. 1606?, 1606?, 1608?, 1610?)

Harley (née Conway), Lady Brilliana. *Letters of the Lady Brilliana Harley, wife of Sir Robert Harley, of Brampton Bryan, Knight of the Bath*. Ed. T. T. Lewis. London: Camden Society, 1854.

Herbert (née Clifford), Anne. *Diary of the Lady Anne Clifford*. Ed. V. Sackville-West. London: William Heinemann, 1923.

Hoby (née Dakins), Margaret. *The Diary of Lady Hoby*. Ed. Dorothy M. Meads. London: G. Routledge and Sons, 1930.

Joceline (née Brooke), Elizabeth. *The Mothers Legacie to her unborn childe*. London: John Haviland, 1624. STC 14624-14625.7 Reel no. 745. (Other ed. 1624, 1625, 1632, 1635.)

Kello (née Inglis), Esther. *Octonaries upon the vanitie and Inconstancie of the World, Writin and Limd be Esther Inglis*. Edinburgh, January 1, 1609.

For information on Kello's other works, see Dorothy Judd Jackson, *Esther Inglis: Calligrapher (1571-1624)*. New York: Privately printed at the Spiral Club, 1937.

Kyme (née Askew), Anne. *The first examinacyon of Anne Askewe, latelye martyred in Smythefelde, by the Romysh popes upholders, with the Elucydacyon of Johan Bale*. Wesel: D. van der Straten, 1546. STC 848-849. Reel no. 21. (Other ed. 1585?)

———. *The lattre examinacyon of Anne Askewe, latelye martyred in Smythfelde, by the wycked Synagoge of Antichrist, with the Elucydacyon of Johan Bale*. Wesel: D. van der Straten, 1547. STC 850-853. Reel no. 21. (Other ed. 1546-47, 1548, 1548-49.)

Lanyer (née Bassano), Aemilia. *Salve Deux Rex Judaeorum. Containing 1. The passion of Christ 2. Eves Apologie in defence of Women 3. The teares of the Daughters of Jerusalem 4. The salutation and Sorrow of the Virgine Marie. With divers other things not unfit to be read. Written by Mistris Aemelia Lanyer, wife to Captain Alfonso Lanyer Servant to the Kings Majestie*. London: Valentine Simmes for Richard Bonian, 1611. STC 15227-15227.5. Reel no. 803. (Another issue, 1611.)

———. *Poems of Shakespeare's Dark Lady*. Ed. A. L. Rowse. New York: Clarksone N. Potter, Inc., 1979.

Leigh, (née Kemp) Dorothy. *The Mothers Blessing: or the godly counsaile of a gentlewoman, not long deceased, left behind her for her children: contayning many good exhortations, and godly admonitions profitable for all parents, to leave as a legacy for their children*. London: for John Budge, 1616. STC 15402-15408. Reel no. 805. (Other ed. 1617, 1618, 1621, 1627, 1629, 1630, 1633, 1634, 1636, 1640.)

Livingston, Helen, Countess of Linlithgow. *The Confession and Conversion of the Right Honourable, Most Illustrious and Elect Lady, My C. of L.* Edinburgh: John Wreitton, 1629. STC 16610. Reel no. 1145.

Mary Stuart, Queen of Scots. *Last Letter of Mary Queen of Scotland Addressed to her brother in law Henry III King of France on the night before her execution at Fotheringay Castle 8th February 1587*. Chelsea: Swan Press, 1927.

———. *Letters and Poems of Mary, Queen of Scots, supposed author*. Ed. and trans. Clifford Bax. New York: Philosophical Library, 1947.

_____. *Poems of Mary Queen of Scots.* Ed. Julian Sharman. London: Basil Montagu Pickering, 1873.

_____. *Poems of Mary Queen of Scots, to the Earl of Bothwell.* Haarlem: J. Enschede en Zonen, 1932.

_____. *Queen Mary's Book, A Collection of Poems and Essays by Mary Queen of Scots.* Ed. Mrs. P. Stewart-Mackenzie-Arbuthnot. London: George Bell and Sons, 1907.

_____. *Recueil des Lettres et Memoires de Marie Stuart.* Ed. Prince Alexander Labanoff. 7 vols. London: Charles Dolman, 1844.

Mildmay (née Sherrington), Lady Grace. "Journal." Manuscript described only as a "thick black volume . . . so neat that it seems to spell refinement" (and partly reprinted by) Rachel Wiegall. "An Elizabethan Gentlewoman." *Q.R.* 215 (1911), 119-138.

Munda, Constantia (pseud.). *The Worming of a madde Dogge: or a Soppe for Cerberus the Jaylor of Hell. No confutation but a sharpe Redargution of the bayter of Women.* By Constantia Munda. London: Printed for Lawrence Hayes, 1617. *STC* 18257. Reel no. 967.

Neville (née Manners), Lady Frances Abergavennie. *Prayers made by the right honorable Lady Frances Abergavennie, and comited at the hour of her death to the right worshipful lady Marie Fane (her only daughter) as a Jewell of health for the soule, and a perfect path to paradise very profitable to be used of every faithful Christian man and woman.* See Bentley.

Owen, Jane. *An Antidote against Purgatory, or Discourse, wherein is shewed that Good-Workes, and Almes-deeds are a chiefe meanes for the preventing, or mitigating the Torments of Purgatory. Written by that Vertuous and Right worthy Gentle-woman (the Honour of her Sexe for Learning in England.) Jane Owen, late of Godstow, in Oxfordshire, deceased, and now published after her death.* St. Omer, 1634. *STC* 18984. Reel no. 1212.

Primrose, Diana. *A Chaine of Pearle, Or a Memoriall of the peerles Graces, and Heroick Vertues of Queene Elizabeth, of Glorious Memory. Composed by the Noble Lady, Diana Primrose.* London: for Thomas Paine, 1630. *STC* 20388. Reel no. 971.

R., M. *The Mothers Counsell, or Live within Compasse, Being the last Will and Testament to her dearest Daughter, which may serve for a worthy Legacie to all the Women in the World, which desire good report from men in this world, and grace from Christ Jesus in the last day.* London: John Wright, 1630?. *STC* 20583. Reel no. 1033. (Entered in Stat. Reg. on 24, Jan, 1623, and may have been companion work to *Keep within compasse, or the worthy legacy of a wise father to his beloved sonne,* according to the *STC.*)

Seymour, Anne, Jane, Margaret. *Mortem Margaritas Valesiae. Navorrum Reginae. Hecatadistichon.* Paris, 1550.

_____. *Le Tombeau de Marguerite de Valois.* Paris, 1551.

Sowernam, Ester (pseud.). *Ester hath hang'd Haman: or an Answere to a lewd Pamphlet, entituled, The Arraignment of Women. With the arraignment of lewd, idle, froward, and unconstant men, and Husbands. Divided into Two Parts. The first proveth the dignity and worthinesse of Women, out of divine*

Testimonies. The second shewing the estimation of the Foe-minine Sexe, in ancient and Pagan times: all which is acknowledged by men themselves in their actions. Written by Ester Sowernam, neither Maide, Wife nor Widdowe, yet really all, and therefore experienced to defend all. London: Printed for Nicholas Bourne, 1617. STC 22974. Reel no. 1188.

Speght, Rachel. *Mortalities Memorandum, with a Dreame Prefixed, imaginarie in manner; reall in matter.* London: Edward Griffin for Jacob Bloome, 1621. STC 23057. Reel no. 1220.

———. *A Mouzell for Melastomus, the Cynical Bayter of, and foule mouthed Barker against Euahs sex. Or an Apologeticall Answere to that Irreligious and Illiterate Pamphlet made by Jo. Sw. and by him Intituled, The Arraignment of Women.* London: Nicholas Okes for Thomas Archer, 1617. STC 23058. Reel no. 939.

Stubbes (née Emmes) Katherine. "A most heavenly confession of the Christian faith." In Philip Stubbes, *Christal Glas for Christian Women.* London, 1592. STC 23381-23395a. Reel no. 861. (Other ed. 1591, 1600, 1603, 1606, 1610, 1612, 1618, 1620, 1621, 1623, 1624, 1626, 1627, 1629, 1630, 1631, 1633, 1634, 1635, 1637, 1665.)

Sutcliffe, Alice. *Meditacions of Mans Mortality or a way to true Blessednesse. Written by Mrs. Alice Sutcliffe, wife of John Sutcliffe, Esquire, Groome to his Majesties most Honourable Privie Chamber.* London: B. A. and T. F. for Henry Seyle, 1634. STC 23447. Reel no. 1010.

Tattlewell, Mary (pseud.) and Joane hit him-home (pseud.). *The womens sharpe revenge. Or an answer to Sir Seldome Sober that writ those railing Pamphlets called the Juniper and the Crab-tree Lectures, etc. Being a sound Reply and a full confutation of those Bookes: with an Apology in this case for the defence of us women. Performed by Mary Tattle-well, and Joane hit-him-home, Spinsters.* London: J. Oakes for Ja. Becket, 1640. STC 23706. Reel no. 1010.

Trefusis (née Edgcumbe), Anne. *The French Historie: that is, a lamentable Discourse of three of the chiefe and most famous bloodie broiles that have happened in France for the Gospell of Jesus Christ Namelie: 1-The outrage called the winning of S. James his Streete 1557. 2-The Constant Martirdome of Annas Burgaus one of the K. Councell 1559. 3-The bloodie Marriage of Margaret sister to Charles the 9. Anno 1572.* London: T. Orwin for T. Man, 1589. STC 7159. Reel no. 289.

Tyrwhit, Lady Elizabeth. *Morning and Evening praiers, with-divers Psalmes, Hymnes, and Meditations, made and set forth by the Ladie Elizabeth Tyrwhit.* See Bentley.

W., Ez. *The Answere of a Mother Unto her seduced sonnes letter.* Amsterdam, 1627. STC 24903-24903.5 Reel no. 641. (Other ed., *A mothers teares over hir seduced sonne: or a dissuasive from idolatry.* London, 1627.)

Wheathill, Anne. *A handfull of holesome though homely hearbes, gathered out of the goodly garden of Gods most holy word, dedicated to all religious ladies, gentlewomen and others, by Anne Wheathill.* London: Henry Denham, 1584. STC 25329. Reel no. 719.

Whitney, Isabella. *The Copy of a Letter, lately written in meeter, by a Yonge Gentilwoman: to her unconstant Lover. With an admonition to al yong Gentilwomen, and to all other mayds in general to beware of mennes flattery. By Is. W. Newly*

joyned to a Loveletter sent by a Bacheler (a most faithfull Lover) to an unconstant and faithles mayden. London: Richarde Jhones, 1567. STC 25439. Reel
no. 1016.

―――. A sweet Nosegay, or pleasant Posye, contayninge a hundred and ten Phylos-
ophicall Flowers. London: 1573. STC 25440. Reel no. 1048.

Wroth (née Sidney), Lady Mary. The Countesse of Mountgomeries Urania. London:
John Marriott and John Grismond, 1621. STC 26051. Reel no. 980.

WORKS TRANSLATED BY
RENAISSANCE ENGLISHWOMEN

Bacon (née Cooke), Lady Anna, trans. An Apologie or answeare in defence of the
Churche of England concerning the state of religion used in the same. Newly
set forth in Latine, and nowe translated into Englishe. London: Reginald Wolfe,
1564. STC 14591. Reel no. 420.

―――, trans. Certayne Sermons of the ryghte famous and excellente clerk Master
Bernardine Ochine, borne within the famous universitie of Siena in Italy, now
also an exyle in thys lyfe, for the faithful testimony of Jesus Christe. Faithfully
translated into Englyshe. London: Jhon Daye, 1550. STC 18764-18768. Reel
no. 121. (Other ed. 1548, 1551?, 1570.)

Basset (née Roper), Mary, trans. An Exposition of a part of the passion made in Latine
by Sir Thomas More, knight (while he was prisoner in the tower of London)
and translated into englyshe by Maystres Mary Basset. In Workes of Sir Thomas
More. London: John Cawood, 1557 (pp. 1351-1404). STC 18076. Reel no.
438.

Cary (née Tanfield), Lady Elizabeth Falkland, trans. Reply of the Cardinall of Perron
to the Answeare of the King of Great Britaine. Douay: M. Bogart, 1630. STC
6385. Reel no. 985.

du Vegerre, Suzanne, trans. Admirable Events, selected out of four bookes, written in
French by John Peter Camus. Together with Morall Relations and translated
into English by S. Du Verger. London: T. Harper for W. Brooks, 1639. STC
4549. Reel no. 1166.

Elizabeth Tudor, trans. The godly Medytacyon of the christen Sowle Concerning a
love towarde God and hys Christe, compyled in frenche by lady Margarete
quene of Naver, and aptely translated into Englysh by the ryght vertuous lady
Elizabeth doughter to our late Soverayne Kynge Henry the VIII. Wesel: D. Van
der Straten, 1548. STC 17320. Reel no. 56.

Herbert (née Sidney), Lady Mary, Countess of Pembroke, trans. A Discourse of Life
and Death. Written in French by Ph. Mornay. Antonius, a Tragedie written also
in French by Ro. Garnier. Both done in English by the Countess of Pembroke.
London: J. Windet for William Ponsonby, 1592. STC 18138. Reel no. 440.

―――. Phillipe de Mornay. Six Excellent Treatises of Life and death (His Discourse of
life and death, done into English by the Countess of Pembroke.) London: H.
Lownes for M. Lownes, 1607. STC 18155. Reel no. 1029.

―――, trans. The Tragedie of Antonie Doone into English by the Countesse of Pembroke. London: for William Ponsonby, 1595. STC 11623. Reel no. 243.

(Other ed. 1592.) Rpt. "Countess of Pembroke's *Antonie.*" Ed. Alice Luce. In *Litterarhistorische Forschungen.* III. Weimar: Verlag von Emil Felber, 1897.

———, trans. *The Psalmes of David; translated into divers and sundry kindes of verse, more rare and excellent for the method and varietie than ever yet hath bene don in English: begun by the noble and learned gentleman Sir Philip Sidney, Knt., and finished by the Right Honorable the Countess of Pembroke his sister, now first printed from a copy of the original manuscript, transcribed by John Davies of Hereford, in the reign of James the First.* London: Chiswick Press by C. Whittingham for Robert Triphook, 1823.

———, trans. *Psalms of Sir Philip Sidney and the Countess of Pembroke.* Ed. J. C. A. Rathmell. New York: Anchor Books, 1963.

———, trans. *The Triumphe of death.* (Ms. 538.43.1, ff. 286-289. Library of the Inner Temple, London.) Rpt. "*The Triumph of Death* Translated out of Italian by the Countess of Pembroke." Ed. Frances Young. *PMLA,* 27 (1912), 47-75.

Lumley (née Fitzalan), Lady Joanna, trans. *Iphigenia at Aulis.* (Br. Mus. MS. Reg. 15. A. ix.) Printed by Malone Society. London: Charles Whittington and Co. at the Chiswick Press, 1909.

Martin (née Eglestone), Dorcas, trans. *An Instruction for Christians conteining a fruitfull and godlie exercise, as well in wholsome and fruitfull praiers, as in reverend discerning of Gods holie Commandements and Sacraments: translated out of French into English by a right vertuous and godlie Matrone and Gentlewoman named Mistresse Dorcas Martin.* See Bentley.

Mary Tudor, trans. *Paraphrase of the Gospel of St. John.* In *The first tome or volume of the paraphrase of Erasmus upon the newe testamente.* Ed. Nicholas Udall. London: Edward Whitechurche, last daie of January, 1548. *STC* 2134. Reel no. 302.

Prowse (née Vaughan), Anne, trans. *Of the markes of the children of God, and their comforts in afflictions. To the faithfull of the Low Countrie. By John Taffin. Overseen againe and augmented by the Author; and translated out of the French by Anne Prowse.* London: Thomas Orwin for Thomas Man, 1590. *STC* 23652. Reel no. 358.

———, trans. *Sermons of John Calvin, upon the songe that Ezechias made after he had bene sicke, and afflicted by the hand of God, conteyned in the 38. Chapiter of Esay. Translated out of Frenche into Englishe.* London: by John Day, 1560. *STC* 11478.

Roper (née More), Margaret, trans. *A devout treatise upon the Pater Noster made fyrst in latyn by the moost famous doctour mayster Erasmus Roterdamus and tourned into englisshe by a yong vertuous and well lerned gentylewoman of xix yere of age.* London: T. Berthelet, 1624. *STC* 10477. Reel no. 37.

Russell (née Cooke), Lady Elizabeth, trans. (John Poynet,) *Way of Reconciliation of a Good and Learned Man, Touching the Trueth, Nature, and Substance of the Body and Blood of Christ in the Sacrament. Translated out of Latin into English by the Right Honourable Lady Elizabeth Russell, Dowager to the Right Honourable the Lord John Russell, Baron, and sonne and heire to Francis Earle of Bedford.* London: R. B., 1605. *STC* 21456. Reel no. 974.

Stanley (née Beaufort), Margaret, Countess of Richmond, trans. "Here begineth the forthe boke of the folowynge Jesu cryst of the contêpnĩge of the world. In

prynted at the comaûdêmet of the most excellent princes Margarete: moder
unto our sovereine lorde: kinge Henrye the vii. Countes of Rychemoût &
Derby. And by the same prynces it was trâslated out of freĉhe into Englysshe in
fourme & maner ensuynge. The yere of our lorde God MDiiii." In *The full
devoute and gostely treatyse of the Imytacyon and folowynge of the blessed
lyfe of our moste mercyfull Sauyour cryste:* . . . London: Richard Pynson,
1517. *STC* 23957. Reel no. 449.

———, trans. *The mirroure of golde for the Synfull soule.* London: Wynkyn de
Worde, 1522. *STC* 6895. Reel no. 34.

Tyler, Margaret, trans. *The mirrour of princely deedes and knighthood.* London: T.
East, 1578. *STC* 18859-18861. Reel no. 1029. (Other ed. 1580?, 1599?)

INDEX

The names of authors whose works are included in *Paradise of Women* are in CAPITALS. Names of works that are included are in *italics*. Entries listed in the table of abbreviations are starred (*). The first lines of poems and other entries are in roman type.